本研究得到中南民族大学校学术团队：
英汉语言对比及研究基金、
中南民族大学中央高校基金"中西民俗对比研究"
的赞助，特此感谢

张立玉　陈珞瑜　著

中西民俗对比研究

A Comparative Study Between Chinese and Western Folklore

▼
▼
▼

中国社会科学出版社

图书在版编目（CIP）数据

中西民俗对比研究／张立玉，陈珞瑜著. —北京：中国社会科学
出版社，2016.3
ISBN 978 - 7 - 5161 - 7802 - 7

Ⅰ.①中…　Ⅱ.①张…②陈…　Ⅲ.①风俗习惯—对比研究—中国、
西方国家　Ⅳ.①K891

中国版本图书馆 CIP 数据核字（2016）第 051384 号

出 版 人　赵剑英
责任编辑　张　林
特约编辑　文一鸥
责任校对　张立玉
责任印制　戴　宽

出　　　版　中国社会科学出版社
社　　　址　北京鼓楼西大街甲 158 号
邮　　　编　100720
网　　　址　http://www.csspw.cn
发 行 部　010 - 84083685
门 市 部　010 - 84029450
经　　　销　新华书店及其他书店

印刷装订　三河市君旺印务有限公司
版　　次　2016 年 3 月第 1 版
印　　次　2016 年 3 月第 1 次印刷

开　　本　710×1000　1/16
印　　张　25.25
插　　页　2
字　　数　415 千字
定　　价　92.00 元

前　言

进入新纪元，世界的发展在全球化的背景下进入多元化。为促进相互了解并将本土文化发扬光大，世界各国愈发注重弘扬其文化传统，同时吸收学习其他国家的文化精华。

中西方民俗是人类文明中的两颗璀璨明珠，前者是主要基于儒家、佛教及道教的伦理文化，视人与自然的和谐关系为其传统文化之根基，追求真、善、美，提倡乐善好施，总之，中华民俗博大精深。而西方传统民俗，以古希腊文化、古罗马文化为根源，深受基督教文化的影响，其特点是契约文化，注重人与自然的对抗，积极向上，征服自然。在公正与法制的前提下，注重人与人的平等、自尊、自信，有宗教意识，又提倡科学精神。

文化是国家的根基，本书试图用比较的方式来展现传统的中西方民俗，国内相关的著作颇丰，但用英语撰写的专著则较少。一方面，国内读者可以从各方面深入了解西方民俗，同时，在中国与其他国家交流日益频繁的前提下，本书能够使西方读者更好地理解中国传统民俗，从而为中西方文化的交流提供便利。

《中西民俗对比研究》全书用英文撰写，共有十二章，第一章对民俗从定义、分类、特点、功能等方面做了简介，并简要回顾了中西方民俗的历史及其发展。第二至第十二章则分别对中西方的饮食、服饰、住宅、出生、结婚、丧葬、节日、信仰与禁忌、社交礼仪、民间艺术、民间娱乐等各方面进行了详细的介绍与比较。需特别说明的是，中国少数民族众多，在比较时，篇幅所限，未能一一列出。同理，相对于中国而言，"西方"是一个非常宽泛的概念，本书中的"西方"主要以欧美等发达国家为代表。

由于选题之故，本书涉及内容颇为庞杂，在成书过程中，作者查阅较多出版物，但可供参考的关于中国民俗的英文著作极为缺乏；作者也借鉴了众多网络资源，在书中已纠正其错误不实之处，其来源一并列在参考书目中。书中涉及中国历史朝代之处甚多，方便起见，并未在文中一一列出年代，而是在书后附录了中国历史朝代表，供读者查阅。即便如此，能力有限，错误不可避免，欢迎读者批评指正。此外，书中的图片均来自互联网，作者不详，出处未能列出，见谅。

张立玉，陈珞瑜

2015 年 5 月

目　　录

Contents

Chapter One

Introduction to Folklore

Folk customs are popular habits and conventions that the common people of a nation create and practice in their production and life, and pass on from one generation to another. In fact, folk customs are an assembly of various mass cultures which may include proprieties, festivals, civilizations, artisanship, and beliefs in the folks. Folk customs possess features of instructiveness, inheritance, expandability and variability. Generated from social practice, folk customs exhibit a lot of social codes of common manners and behaviors which are then used to guide, normalize, regulate and serve people's productive and living activities, thus satisfy people's needs for a diversified social life.

1. Definition of Folklore

Folklore is the conventional art, knowledge, and practicewide spread primarily through oral and behavioral communication. Every community with a sense of its own identity shares, as a central part of that identity, folk traditions-something that people traditionally believe (planting practices, family traditions, and other elements of world philosophy), do (dance, music, making clothing), know (the way to build an irrigation dam, how to deal with an ailment, how to prepare barbecue), make (craft, architecture, art,), and say (personal experience stories, song lyrics, riddles). As these examples illustrate, in most instances there is no such hard-and-fast separation of these categories, no matter in everyday life or in folklorists' work.

The word "folklore" contains an enormous and comprehensive dimension of culture. Considering how large and complicated this subject is, it is no wonder that folklorists define and describe folklore so differently. But one thing in common among these definitions is that they challenge the notion of folklore as something characteristic of being "old-fashioned," "exotic," "rural," "uneducated," "unreal," or "dying out. " Though folklore connects people to their past, it is a key part of life in the present, and is at the heart of the global culture.

The following are some typical definitions:

Folklore is many things, and it's almost impossible to define simply. It's both what folklorists study and the name of the discipline they work within. Folklore is folk songs and legends. It's also quilts, Boy Scout badges, high school marching band initiations, jokes, nicknames, holiday food… and many other things you might or might not expect. Folklore exists in cities, suburbs and rural villages, in families, work groups and dormitories. Folklore is present in many kinds of informal communication, whether verbal (oral and written texts), customary (behaviors, rituals) or material (physical objects) . It involves values, traditions, ways of thinking and behaving. It's about art. It's about people and the way people learn. It helps us learn who we are and how to make meaning in the world around us. [1]

Folklore is a meta-cultural category used to mark certain genres and practices within modern societies as being not modern. By extension, the word refers to the study of such materials. More specific definitions place folklore on the far side of the various epistemological, aesthetic and technological binary oppositions that distinguish the modern from its presumptive contraries. Folklore therefore typically evokes both repudiation and nostalgia. [2]

Folklore has four basic meanings. First, it denotes oral narration, rituals, crafts, and other forms of vernacular expressive culture. Second, folklore, or

---

① Martha C. Sims and Martine Stephens. Living Folklore: An Introduction to the Study of People and their. Tradifions. Cogan: Utah State University Press, 2005.

② Dorothy Noyes. Folklore. In The Social Science Encyclopedia. 3rd edition. Eds. Adam Kuper and Jessica Kuper, New York: Routledge, 2004.

'folkloristics', names an academic discipline devoted to the study of such phenomena. Third, in everyday usage, folklore sometimes describes colorful 'folkloric' phenomena linked to the music, tourist, and fashion industries. Fourth, like myth, folklore can mean falsehood. ①

After all, Folklore is the totality of convention-based creations of a community with the same culture, which is expressed collectively or individually and recognized as mirroring the expectations of a community since they reflect its cultural and social identity. Its values and standards are verbally transmitted by means of imitation, its forms being, among others, language, literature, games, music, dance, mythology, customs, rituals, handicrafts, architecture and other arts.

As a result, folklore culture always possesses obvious features of region and folk. Closely connected with one place, it is both a limitation and a feature deep-rooted in people's mind.

2. Classifications of Folklore

Folklore is a complexity, ranging from society-based economic activities and corresponding relations to the various systems and ideologies of the superstructure, all of which involve certain folk phenomena and related mental activity. Therefore, it is generally divided into the following four categories:

(1) Material Folklore

It refers to the repetitive and stereotyped activities that people conduct in the process of creating and consuming material wealth, which basically concerns aspects such as production, trade, food, costumes, residence, transportation and health etc.

---

① Barbro Klein. Folklore. In International Encyclopedia of the Social and Behavioral Sciences. Volume 8. New York: Elsevier, 2001.

(2) Social Folklore

Social folklore, also known as social structural and institutional folklore, is the social-related routine formed under certain conditions. It is also a collective behavioral mode that people apply and pass on from generation to generation in daily interaction from the level of individual, family, community, nationality and internationality. The tradition primarily consists of social structural folklore (blood relations, geographical relations and occupational relations), social institutional folklore (customary law, life rituals), festival folklore and entertaining folklore.

(3) Spiritual Folklore

It is the ideological convention formed on the basis of material culture and institutional culture. Being the mental experience that human generated from the process of realizing and transforming nature and society, it becomes spiritual folklore once becoming collective mental habits and given behaviors inherited from ancestors. This type of folklore usually comprises folk beliefs, magic, philosophy, ethics and art etc.

(4) Verbal Folklore

Verbal folklore refers to the information exchange system established through oral convention and collective heritage, which consists of two parts: the folk language and folk literature. Language is a cultural carrier, with every region and nation owning its specific tongue, thus those national languages and dialects are broad folk languages. Correspondingly, narrow folk languages are the recurring formula adopted in certain regions or nations with specific meanings, such as folk sayings, proverbs, riddles, twisters, street buzzwords, cants, drinking games and so on. As to folklore literature, it is the collectively created and popular oral literature, namely myths, folk tales, folk songs and other forms.

Social life is an integrity, accordingly, folklore is systematic as well. Therefore, there exist mutual restricted or beneficial connections among the above mentioned four categories which influence each other and constantly change with the development of the times.

3. The Features of Folklore

The characteristics of folklore can be of variety. The features of different regions, nationalities and nations can be both common and unique. The comprehensive portray of the shared traits can be understandably difficult. However, some of the similar aspects are listed in the following:

(1) Collectivism

This is one of the basic but essential features embodied in the production and circulation of folklore. The fundamental human attribute is its sociality. Consequently, the emergence of folklore is evidently a result of collective activities.

In the progress of the society, with the appearance of maternal or paternal human society to tribes and nationalities, colorful folklore has been created and improved, which is definitely a fruit of group wisdom. Once it has been formed, it turns out to be the collective behavioral habits, and mobilizes in the immense scope of time and space. The liquidity is not the mechanic repetition, but the continuous enrichment of the folklore itself. In other words, when folklore initially came into being, its pattern and content were relatively simple; however, in the chronic historical development, the folklore tends to be more complex, the outcome of collective recreation.

Collectivism manifests the integral consciousness of folklore as a whole, which determines its value orientation and that is where the vitality of folklore culture lies.

(2) Hereditability and Transmissibility

The former refers to the developing continuity in time, namely diachronic vertical continuity; meanwhile it is a transmission mode of folk culture. The letter indicates the spatial cultural spread, but also known as the horizontal diffusion of folklore. The combination of the two makes folk cultural heritage a space-time continuum.

Hereditability is determined by its function, demonstrating the responsibility of enlightenment, with inheritance being one form and means. In the traditional and the modern society, each person's growth is inseparable from the edification of folk culture. From childhood to adulthood, people have obtained a range of knowledge, skills and ethics, even the ancestral concept from folk culture. This is a potential ability of human beings, with all the education implemented unknowingly, enabling people to acquire knowledge and skills unconsciously during the process of cultural inheritance. Meanwhile, folklore inheritance is implemented purposefully due to its active feature since the elders in the family always bear responsibility to the younger at home and village, community and numerous non-governmental organizations also are responsible for the inheritance to the involved members. Thus, folklore is passed on from generation to generation unceasingly.

On the other hand, transmissibility refers to the spatial expansion of folk culture. The combination of vertical and horizontal stretch induces a diversified folk culture formed through mutual impact and incorporation. Being a mental, linguistic and behavioral pattern, it is not static but dynamic. Different from top-to-bottom hereditability, transmissibility is spatial movement. When a new folklore takes shape in a region or a nation, its function and value can be fully revealed after gradual improvement. It is not only accepted regionally as the continuation of traditional culture, but also begins to penetrate to other ethnic areas.

However, such spread is selective. Judging from its own regularity, folklore with long history and extensive social functions possess more comprehensive transmissibility compared with those unripe and uncommon ones. Furthermore, the study of transmissibility used to focus on the similarities of regional folklore to seek their homology, whereas it is undeniable that the geographical, ethnic and cultural differences can't afford to be discounted in folkloristics, a proof that the transmissibility is subjected to various conditions.

Individual and collective transmission of folklore can both lead to the various types of spread to other areas. But generally speaking, the mode can be of two kinds, namely normal and abnormal. The former is naturally conducted in peaceful environment, a result of mutual national communication. A complete process is usually realized in the following steps: Firstly, people make value judgment to the new folk culture, comparing it with its traditional ones. Secondly, the decision of acceptance or dropping is made after the comparison. Finally, even if the decision is positively made, transformation is also necessary to new folklore in its form, meaning and function to suit it in the original convention. The abnormal transmission is carried out under certain circumstances such as wars, famines and plagues. Because of such unexpected events, massive migration produces the shift of folk culture. Some integrate with local folklore while others are preserved and come down through the years.

The research on the hereditability and transmissibility is of great significance to the birth, advance, evolution, spread and geographical distribution of the folklore.

(3) Stability and Variability

Folklore is the cultural phenomenon created, inherited and enjoyed by common people in long-term social practice. The same as the mainstream upper-class culture, the lower-class folklore is stable as well, especially in the underdeveloped ages. However, this culture may transform, deteriorate, even go extinct in the process of social development.

Once produced, folklore will become a part of people's daily life accompanied by their fixed productive and living mode. In other words, as long as the society remains stable, the folk culture tends to be more unchanged. Folklore is formed on the basis of given politics, economy, society and culture, so, provided that the economic foundation doesn't alter, folklore still possesses consistency even if great changes have taken place in society. In addition, the inheritance of folk culture is often restricted by conventional ideas, thus it won't lose ideological basis if social transformation is not blended with ideal changes. Take China for example, being a civilization with a long history, it has experienced many sovereign and social reforms, therefore, some of the folk custom naturally died out with the progress of historical advance and social production. Yet some folklores have been preserved till now after being supplemented and improved.

The stability of the folk culture is relative, always containing variables, which is where the variability lies. Variability is characteristic of folk culture, with the spontaneous and gradual changes arising in the process of folklore inheritance and expansion. Folk heritage is dependent of language and behavior, implying that folklore is bound to change constantly to adapt to the surroundings diachronically and synchronically. Therefore, variation is actually a self-adjustment of folklore organism, also the root of its vitality, which is indispensable for folk culture. The majority of folk custom of the modern society are the fruits of ancient folk mutation. In this sense, variation is the inner motive of folklore preservation and development.

Folklore variation is more complex compared with stability, with cases such as part or whole; forms or contents; quantitative or qualitative; but all the changes are spontaneous and gradual. For instance, mythology, an often discussed subject in folk culture, is basically no longer generated with the maturity of human civilization, but it does not equal to its thinking and psychological extinction. In some remote nationalities, particularly the regions where agricultural technology is still primitive, myth remains to circulate with the existence of soil for its conservation and variation.

Folklore changes also constantly adapt to the need of social progress. Apart from some naturally perished custom, some also mutate in social transformation. For instance, feet binding, a custom of ancient Chinese women, approximately formed in the five dynasties period and became the essential conventions of most Han female nationalities after three dynasties of Song, Yuan, and Ming. In the early years of the Qing dynasty, the emperor issued imperial edicts banning feet-binding, but the convention still existed. The foundation of the people's republic of China saw the entire discard of this undesirable custom, indicating the abolishment of such custom is not easy. Anyway, changes are usually the positive participants of social development.

(4) Formulation

Formulation of folklore is the commonly-observed standard of its manifestation pattern, which can be a stereotyped thinking habit, or a conventional behavior, a concept different from the individuality and originality of upper-class culture. Unlike folklore, the personality of artists is determined by temporal, national and regional traits, in which character is of great value. However, folk culture is collective creation, plus constant spread and variation, making it hard to form characteristic symbolic system, which accounts for the reason why folk transmission is not unique but typological. Take folk literature for example, the authors are mostly anonymous, and the works can be revised by different people. Therefore, the original simple plot snowballed into more colorful stories through different ages. What's more, variation appears when the same work circulates in various nationalities and areas, forming different types of folk literature.

The types of folklore refer to the similar ones in form and content. Chinese famous four tales such as *the Cowherd and the Weaving Maid*, *Legend of White Snake*, *Lady Meng Jiang's Bitter Weeping* and *The Butterfly Lovers* are closely related with Chinese social development and people's aspirations. Moreover, literature types of Two Brothers, artful women, silly son-in-laws, swan virgins are no exception, that is, the general plot are alike and repetitive despite different story-tellers from different places. If we take the folk performance and story narration as a folk cultural heritage, it definitely reflects group aesthetic ideas and value orientation.

As to folk literature, especially the study of story types, it has become world knowledge. With the stories being regarded as plot narrations, experts make parallelism of "motif (plot unit)" by slight changes of similar plots, inducing certain types. Can other categories of folk custom being classified as folk stories? There is much room for exploration. For instance, resident folk custom can be architecturally sorted as tents, caves, piles etc. Certainly, regional and national diversity exists even among the same type. Despite the complexity of folklore classification, it is feasible to make structural attempts needing careful analysis on the basis of field work.

In sum, formulation study not only reveals inner folklore structure, but also helps people learn the interrelation and influence of regional and national folk culture, gaining further knowledge about its inheriting and spreading laws.

(5) Normalization and Serviceability

In essence, folklore is the lingual and behavioral pattern people create in chronic productive and social practice, or the code that common people invent and observe, the mode and rule adapt immensely to natural and social surroundings. Being characteristic of reflecting collective mental and survival needs, folk culture possess considerable stability. It is not unusual to see the unwritten laws executed in folk society since they pose great constraints on folks, forcing them to conduct by certain specification to obtain the psychological and environmental balance.

The formation of folk standardization is a historical process. Human beings primitive natural worship, totem worship, witchery and divination, etc. are mostly everybody's concern in the clans and tribes. Totem norm, namely the concept and behavior regulation, is very rigid. In a sense, totem is the social structure of the clan society through which people's behavior is restrained. For instance, totem is sacrosanct forbidden from any blasphemy. In case the totem is accidentally offended, a series of ceremony must be performed to make redemption. Marriage is absolutely prohibited among clan members. All the taboos become conscious behavior of each member.

People entering class society, folk norm changes significantly due to the emergence of private ownership and it gradually complicates after the appearance of countries. Politics starts to impose intervention on the standardization, primarily absorbing the self-beneficial part and promoting it to official etiquette for implementation among upper ruling classes. Such practice of upgrading folk habits into laws is not rare. In a word, all aspects of social life are not free from normalization. Activities such as marriages and funerals must undergo certain procedures and specifications; so do dietary structure and eating manners. It is apparent that to coordinate the life, people are always adjusting their own ideas and behavior with standardized folk principles.

Folklore contains rich cultural connotation and reflects the collective wisdom and creation. Being inexhaustible cultural treasure, traditional folk culture is an enormous knowledge system comprising beliefs, religion, morality, law, literature and art. Folks create abundant folk culture with uniform will and behavior, and this is where the serviceability lies.

First, the existence of the folklore is to serve the society, since folk norms are inevitably social norms, which is determined by its collectivism. For example, the custom of respecting the old and care for the child is not only applied within families, but also among the society. And the hospitality culture embodies the similar concept of respect for the seniors. Living a life abiding by such norms is a typical case of their service for the society.

Second, the accumulation of generations of folk culture has formed its own knowledge system, which in turn serves their production and life. For instance, the combination of astronomical observation and agricultural production results in the agricultural production custom. The division of Chinese annual 24 solar terms is mainly in the service of farming activities; and the integration of beliefs, farming and folk arts generates festival culture. It is the perfect reflection of serviceability as people enjoy immensely the joy brought by the holidays.

Third, folk culture coordinates public psychology to meet their aesthetic need. Human beings both live in the physical and mental environment, with the folklore being the product. In mental life, national belief matters significantly whereas the materialization of beliefs is various in forms. Sometimes it is rituals while sometimes it is artistic production. The former, such as the widespread custom of God or Buddha worshipping, being somewhat superstitious, belongs to public faith. In the view of atheists, all religious practice is absurd; but for theists, gods not only exist in fantasy but also dominate world fortune. Thus, they pray piously for spiritual blessing. Rituals are performed to meet some desire and seek psychological balance. The prevailing praying activities in agricultural society are also conducted in the hope for good weather and fine harvest. In the era of advanced technology, the beliefs are likely to shift or vanish but the folk art that they spark is still common. For example, the series of mascot provide people with aesthetic beauty, reflecting people's aesthetic consciousness and the creation of wisdom.

All in all, the above mentioned five aspects are not the entire traits of all folklore. However, they are relatively universal and representative.

4. The Functions of Folklore

The existence and development of every subject depends on the role it plays in social life. Therefore, it is necessary to have the comprehensive knowledge of the social function of folk custom.

The function of folklore, a component of the organic system consisting of social life and relative culture, is its position in the social cultural system and the relationship between it and other cultural factors.

In general, folklore has the following four social functions:

(1) Education

Educational function refers to the enlightening and molding role that folklore plays in socializing process of individuals. Folks need to master the living patterns and standards passed from generations in which shape the experience and behavior ever since they are born. Then they become the participants and creators of their own culture as they grow up. Yet it is undeniable that they are always constraint in the culture.

All in all, human beings are the product of culture. Therefore, being a cultural phenomenon, folklore possesses significant status in individual socialization process. People are encompassed by folk norms all his life: he might be greeted with birth ritual the day he was born; then language is obtained when he imitates people who surround; interpersonal relationship is understood through protocols of appellation and communication; he marries according to the certain marriage customs; and specific funeral ritual held for him after his death. Folklore is to human beings what water is to fish.

(2) Normalization

Normative function is the binding effect that folklore has to individual behavior.

There exist many choices to fulfill human social needs. For example, people can eat by knives and forks or chopsticks even hands. The role of folk custom is to affirm and reinforce a given way according to specific conditions, making it a kind of collective standardized mode to ensure the regular advance of social life.

Social norms take on a variety of forms with rough divisions into four levels: law, discipline, morality and folklore among which the fourth is the earliest and comprehensive one.

Folklore is the social norm with the longest history. Engels once pointed out that in the primitive stage of social development, it was required to generalize the repetitive behavior of product manufacture, distribution and exchange with common rules, which first characterized by habit, later became law. The habit mentioned here is the original folk custom.

Folklore is the most constrained behavioral norm. It is admitted that the conduct code established by law is just a minor part that people must observe; however, folk custom is the invisible hand that virtually dominates people's behavior. And they unconsciously comply with the folk custom from the basic necessities such as food, clothing, shelter and transportation to common rituals of weddings and funerals, from social interaction to spiritual beliefs.

It is hard to realize the impact of folk custom specification in daily life, which hardly rouses folks' resistance. Therefore, the control of folklore is a "soft control", the most formidably intensive one.

(3) Maintenance

Maintaining function refers to the unification of collective thought and behavior. The constant social change requires the continuous cultural adjustment made on the basis of internal and external variation. Folk customs, as a cultural inheritance, is bound to undergo continual offspring replication to keep the social continuity. Even in the large-scale sudden social reform, changes are always local and gradient compared with the whole system, a means that effectively prevent cultural rupture to maintain the relative stability of social life.

For one thing, folk customs unify the behavior of social members, for another, they sustain the group or nationality's cultural psychology. Every nation or social groups, living in the specific natural conditions and social environment, has its own unique historical path, forming the particular collective psychology. Folk custom is the label for people to achieve group identity. For instance, overseas Chinese scatter in every corner of the globe, but they speak Chinese, eat Chinese food and celebrate Chinese traditional festival to maintain their own national identity.

(4) Relief

Relieving function means the entertaining, venting and compensative effect of folklore, enabling people to be relieved from stressful social life and psychology.

The apparent entertaining function of folklore provides opportunities for people to enjoy the culture they produce. To gain refreshment from heavy workload, folks need to be involved in proper recreations to repose themselves, enjoying lives by participating social activities. No nation in the world has no holidays, games, folk literature, art and sports, which are the desirable supplement of human life.

Folklore is also an outlet for people venting emotions. In social life, the individual biological instinct inevitably suffers from certain degree of physical or mental depression, which can be immensely destructive. Some folklore appears accordingly. For instance, ancient Romans drink and revel during Bacchanalia without everyday taboos. And this wild carnival festival is not rare in history, such as the Chinese Water-splashing Festival of the Dai Nationality, Nadan Festival of the Mongols etc. Other folk games, such as Rooster Fighting, Bull Fighting, Cricket Fighting etc. all can be relaxing. Besides, Chinese customs of teasing the newlyweds in the wedding or wails in the funeral are both ways unleashing mental energy to serve as emotional catharsis.

Finally, folklore can be compensative for people who are incapable of fulfilling their dreams in the harsh reality. Engels once mentioned that a farmer gain comfort and joy from German folk tales after daily exhausting work, discounting fatigue and imagining his humble house to be a fragrant garden. Such is a case of spiritual compensation. Similarly, people long for affection from folk love songs; folks forget sufferings from religious ceremony. And a variety of folk craft and art furnish people with beauty and hope which are the compensation people obtain from everyday life.

The above four are just the primary functions of the folklore. And it is necessary to note that folk culture varies and the study of its social function deserves further exploration.

5. The History and Study of Chinese Folklore

Chinese folklore possesses a long history, with its evolution being roughly divided into three stages: the prehistoric, ancient and modern times.

(1) Prehistoric Folklore

It refers to the custom established before the 21st century B. C. of Xia dynasty, namely the folklore of the primitive society.

Chinese culture is the native and systematic culture of its own cultivated in the vast soils in which the ancestors labor, live and breed. Archaeological findings show that from the apes to homo erectus, early homo sapiens, late homo sapiens there is no absence of link in Chinese human evolution sequence; and the cultural progressive thread is relatively complete from the paleolithic to the neolithic era.

The emergence of prehistoric folk custom accompanies the appearance of the Chinese. Originally, like other animals, humans live collectively outdoors by simple food collection and hunting. They eat raw and wear no clothes, fighting against nature with bare hands. Later, they learn to have the food cooked since their employment of stone and fire, a basic distinction from lower animals. Then, the introduction of agriculture and the invention of pottery marks the establishment of the elementary food structure lasting thousands of years. Beijing cavemen have been sewn with spicules to make fur clothing, and worn animal teeth and shells for decorations since then, which follows the custom of clothes-making with wild plant fiber and silks. The dwelling of the northern primitives develops from caves to semi caves and finally to permanent housing while the southerners' residence shifts from nest to stilt style architecture. Tools such as bows, arrows, vehicles and ships have been invented and widely used till the end of the primitive society. Gradually the folk custom of material production and consumption system takes shape, consisting of the dry land farming region centered the Yellow River; the rice farming area centered the Yangtze River and the fishing and hunting area mainly in northeast, northwest China and inner Mongolia.

The spirit culture of the primitives develops along with the progress of material culture, forming the corresponding folklore. The primitives begin to create myths and songs since the appearance of languages. The emergence of ancient folk art such as pottery paintings, images, sculptures, bone carvings, wood carvings and cliff paintings reflects the growth of the primitive aesthetic consciousness. Excavations of unearthed bone whistles and wooden drums etc, as well as the dancing images on ceramics and paintings represent the noisy scene. Calendars and folk festivals might have appeared since the agriculture and animal husbandry are both dependent on seasonal changes. The ideas and rituals of natural, totem, soul and ancestor worship are prevailing with the prosperity of primitive religions. The concept of soul has come into being with proofs that hematite found on cavemen's corpses which are buried with simple productive tools (stones) . The heads of the bodies found in many tombs face to the same direction, reflecting the wish to return to the shore of the world. Witchcraft is popular with further division of specialized flamen and wizards.

Primitive community starts to transit to the matriarchal clan which conducts exogamy. Women enjoy high status within the group with children raised by the mother. Bloodline calculation and property inheritance are also implemented maternally. Many female ancestors exist in myth, like Jianjing and Jiangyuan who give birth to children and raise them single-handedly. Ethnology material also provides living proof to the status of the matriarchal clan. For example, Naxi nationality, living gregariously now by the Lugu Lake in Yongning, Yunnan province, still maintains a residual of the matrilineal system. The matriarchal clan commune reaches it prime in about sixty-seven thousand years ago when some clans of the Yellow River and the Yangtze river basin turn into patriarchal clan commune one or twelve thousand years later. Females live with the husband tribes after marriage with children's blood confirmed to be the natural heirs of fathers' property. Women are gradually confined to housework and family care, even reduced to the tool of family reproduction.

The late primitive society sees the emergence of private ownership and the frequency of tribal wars. War and productivity (especially the flood control) expansion prompts the amplification of tribal alliances, ultimately leading to the birth of the first slavery system: Xia dynasty, a new era in Chinese history.

There is no state power imposed on clan members in prehistoric times, everything being conducted by established conventions. Therefore, the folk custom is the sole norm of primitive society, a distinct character of prehistoric folklore.

(2) Ancient Folklore

The word ancient refers to the times from Xia dynasty to the Opium War, which can be divided into two stages: the former is the history before Han dynasty, the formative phase of Han nationality (the Chinese main ethnic group) and Chinese ancient folk system while the latter witnesses the development and prosperity of Chinese feudal social folklore.

Chinese folklore is in its budding status in Xia, Shang and Zhou dynasty. A number of unearthed oracles of Shang reveal the intense influence of primitive custom concerning frequently adopted divination and a mass of funerary objects. The official protocols forms in Zhou dynasty forms, demonstrated from works such as Rites of the Zhou and the Book of Rites. Some folk customs, like the six stages of marriage is the main mode followed in feudal society.

The ages from the Spring and Autumn Period to Qin and Han dynasty is one of the greatest nationality blending periods in history. With the establishment of the feudal social system and the unified realm, Han ethnic group, the pillar of the Chinese, takes dominating shape during the assimilation with other tribes and nationalities. Shi Huang, the first emperor of Qin, attaches importance to the unity of the folk custom as well. For example, he unifies costumes with civilians wearing black shawls to symbolize common people. He also orders to implement simple funerary manner. The advance of Chinese feudal society reaches its peak in Western and Eastern Han dynasties which lasts approximately four hundred years, a period for the principal formation of Chinese folklore.

Chinese feudal folklore achieves highest prosperity till Sui and Tang dynasty, during which Han and other nationalities mix immensely due to long-lasting ethnic wars and large scale national movement. Minor nationalities like Xiongnu, Xianbei, Qiang, Man and Yue etc. all are greatly influenced by Han's culture and custom. Meanwhile, their folklore also spread to the Han people. In Tang dynasty, rulers initiatively introduce minority folklore and the combination of Tang music and Kuchean music enormously enriches Chinese folk music. The rise of Buddhism and Taoism has increasingly huge impact on the folk custom from Han to Tang dynasty. Beliefs such as karma, heaven and hell are greatly popular among people, with a large number of mystery novels and legends prevailing at that moment. After the Han dynasty, festival culture is gradually systematic because most of the traditional holidays observed nowadays like the Spring Festival, the tomb-sweeping day, dragon-boat festival, the double ninth festival have already found its way in people life from then on.

The festival custom is more complete till Song dynasty and folklore becomes increasingly diverse which has been portrayed in *Dongjing Dream*. Chinese folk witch crafts such as fortune-telling and *Fengshui* are also wide spread in Song dynasty. Even though the governors of Liao, Jin and Yuan are minorities, their folks are gradually assimilated by the Han people to observe Han folks. Ming and Qing dynasty see the recession of Chinese feudality, but the conventional folklore including holidays, recreations, beliefs and religions has generally fixed until then. Even though the decree of hair-wearing has been imposed on the Han people, it receives strong resistance. All in all, besides changes of a handful of folk customs, people inherit major folks of Han ethnic groups in Qing dynasty.

The ancient folklore possesses some notable features compared with prehistoric ones:

①The scale of nationality merging is unprecedentedly wide, leading to the continuous exchanges and assimilation of folklore;

②Despite the great changes, it always remains the elementary structure centered on Han nationality, reflecting the tenacious continuity of folk activities;

③Due to the emergence of state power, the ruling class itself also develops a set of official etiquette corresponding to the concept of folk custom, influencing and transforming mutually which contributes to the complexity of the interrelationship.

(3) Modern Folklore

It means the folklore passes on till now since the Opium War in 1840, during which Chinese politics, economy and class relations undergo radical changes under the stimulus of western civilization. China experiences historical events such as the 1911 Revolution, New-Democratic Revolution, Socialist Revolution and Construction in less than two hundred years, striding towards a modern and civilized nationality. Accordingly, the folklore transits significantly with some outdated ones like foot-binding, long gowns and mandarin jackets perishing. Meanwhile, some western folk custom are introduced into China, integrating with Chinese existing ones to meet the needs of new society. People continuously create some new folklore that suit the development of modern life.

In the modern history, every big revolution sparks oscillation of the traditional folk custom. Liang Qichao advocates "custom revolution" in the Hundred Day's Reform. The 1911 Revolution not only overthrows the Qing dynasty but also brings about the liberation of women's feet and the elimination of men's braids. The republic of China adopts the Gregorian calendar, promoting new-style weddings and funerals, changing robes to Chinese tunic suits and western suits. Civilian literature and free marriages are promoted with the introduction of folk science, and folk dialects, beliefs, arts start to gain concern in May

Fourth Movement. During the revolutionary civil war, under the leadership of the communist party, new marriage law is issued and the folk recreational activities such as Yangko advances to a new stage. After the establishment of the People's Republic of China, the government does substantial work in transforming social traditions. Especially in recent years, due to the reform and opening-up policy, people's economic life has been greatly improved with their life and values transforming constantly, which results in great changes of traditional folk custom. On the one hand, western customs such as jeans, dance halls, karaoke, Santa Claus come into China successively; on the other hand, due to the stimulation of the economic and cultural needs, traditional activities revive and flourish to promote Chinese traditional culture. The Chinese folklore system takes on a new look, its own traditions being the principal and western ones being the supplements.

As to the study of folklore in China, *The Book of Songs* (*Shi Jing*) was the earliest known Chinese collection of poetry, comprising 160 folk songs as well as courtly songs and hymns. One tradition believes that Confucius himself collected these songs, while another claims that an emperor compiled them as a means to manipulate the mood of the people and the effectiveness of his rule.

It is believed that the followers of Confucius were encouraged to study the songs contained in *Shi Jing*, a mean helps to secure *Shi Jing's* place among the Five Classics. After Confucian ideas became further established in Chinese culture, Confucius' endorsement prompted many scholars to study the lyrics of *Shi Jing* and presented them as political allegories and commentaries.

With the commencement of the campaign to formally employ Vernacular Chinese as the education and literature language, Chinese folklore started to gain popularity as an area of study around the 1910s, attracting scholars to pay attention to the impacts that Vernacular Chinese folklore had had on classical literature since Vernacular Chinese was the language in which most folklore was produced. Hu Shi, the strong advocate of the adoption of Vernacular Chinese, stated that Chinese literature went through a renaissance when massive Chinese writers gained inspiration from folk traditions such as traditional tales and songs; and they are inclined to lose touch with the common people if they overlook these sources. A revival of the folklore study would undoubtedly bring in a new renaissance of Chinese literature.

Meanwhile, an increasing sense of national identity partially contributes to the regained interest in conventional folklore. The first issue of the "Folk-Song Weekly", a publication issued by the Folk-Song Research Society, stated that "Based on the folksongs, on the real feeling of the nation, a kind of new national poetry may be produced. "

Some folklore enthusiasts also believed it essential to comprehend the ideas, values and customs of the people in order to help better their condition and hoped to further social reforms with the help of the their work.

Since 1949, Chinese scholars have collected many folk songs and stories and they reinvented and reinterpreted these folk songs and stories with an attempt to emphasize such themes as the virtue of the working class and the evil of aristocracy. Stories that expressed praise for the emperor were frequently left out of the collections. Some folk tales and folk plays emphasize particular social morals.

For ages, Chinese folklore has always nourished Chinese writers and poets. For instance, folk songs, the form that were basically accompanied with dance and other styles of performing arts, provided inspiration for courtly poetry. Classical fiction was modeled after spoken traditions and began in the Han dynasty, while Mongol and Ming dramatic plays were influenced by folk plays.

Contemporary versions of Chinese folk stories can be globally found as well as in Chinese literature. Maxine Hong Kingston's *Chinaman*, Laurence Yep's and Walt Disney Pictures' *Mulan* are all traced into Chinese folklore traditions.

6. The History and Study of Western Folklore

Western folklore or European folklore refers to the folklore of the western world, particularly when discussed comparatively. In other words, no single European culture, but nevertheless the common history of Christendom during the Middle Ages and the Early Modern Period has produced a number of traditions shared in many European regional and ethnic cultures.

(1) Europe

This particularly involves average traditions derived from Christian mythology, i. e. certain commonalities in the celebration of Christmas, such as the various Christmas gift-bringers, or customs associated with All Souls' Day. In addition, there are certain apotropaic practices or gestures adopted in large parts of Europe, say the fingers crossed gesture or the knocking on wood.

The culture of folk heritage, including mythology, Hellenistic religion and cultic or magical practice was greatly influential on the formative phase of Christianity, and serves as the foundation in the traditions of all territories formerly ruled by the Roman Empire, and by extension in those areas reached by Christianization during the Middle Ages, encompassing all of Europe, and much of the Middle East and North Africa. Though inherited from Roman folk beliefs, these conventions were combined with local traditions, especially Slavic, Germanic and Celtic. Many folk traditions also originated by contact with the Islamic world, especially in the Balkans and in the Iberian peninsula, which were ruled by Islamic empires before being re-conquered (in the case of the Balkans, partially) by Christian forces, giving rise to visible result of cultural contact. For example, the typical England Morris Dance is actually an adaptation of the "moorish" dances of the late medieval period. Meanwhile, the results were related but regionally distinct as folk traditions existed in Europe on the eve of the Early Modern period. In modern times, and particularly since the 19th century, there has been a lot of cross-pollination between these traditions, often by the detour of American folklore. ①

(2) America

Folk conventions that have developed on the North American continent contribute to American folklore since the arrival of Europeans in the 16th century. While it contains largely in the way of Native American tradition, it should not be confused with the tribal beliefs of any community of native people.

---

① http: //en. wikipedia. org/wiki/European_ folklore

Native American culture is abundant in myths and legends that were adopted in the explanation of mysterious natural phenomena, the most common myths being the creation myths which tell stories to explain the formation of the earth. Others include interpretations about the constellations, sun, moon, seasons, animals and weather. This is the root of their culture, one of the ways that many tribes kept their cultures alive; it was not merely a collection of stories, but of their beliefs, their ways, and their lives. The kinds of the stories are many. Some are called "hero stories", stories of immortalized great men who lived at one time and revered by common people. Some are "trickster stories" concerning the different trickster figures of the tribes. There are tales that are merely warnings to warn people against doing something that may bring harm in some way. Many of these tales have morals or some form of belief that is being passed down from generations since this is how the things were remembered.

Besides, legends and tall tales are told in the founding of the United States. Many stories have evolved since the founding long ago to become a part of America's folklore and cultural awareness, and non-native American folklore especially includes any narrative which makes great contribution to the shaping of American values and belief systems. The veracity of the narratives does not really matter therefore these stories may be true or may be false.

Christopher Columbus, an important figure in the pantheon of American myth, was viewed as symbolic hero in terms of Native American folk, with his status being representative of the self-perception of the American society, being chosen as hero instead of his own accomplishments. But all in all, being separated from Britain and its cultural icons, America Folklore was left without history or heroes and it was often based on a shared sense of their social selves. ①

---

① http://en.wikipedia.org/wiki/Folklore_of_the_United_States

Chapter Two

Customs of Cuisine

1. General Introduction

Cuisine customs refers to people's way of food choice and process as well as their eating habits. Food, the basic necessities of human beings, plays an indispensable role in everyday life, which not only satisfies people's physical needs, but also meets their spiritual requirement. Cuisine customs are bound to be colorful with rich cultural connotations.

(1) Formation

Cuisine customs of different regions and ethnic groups are various, the major factors being the following five aspects:

①Natural Conditions

Folks' diet customs are inevitably influenced by natural environment especially in early stages of human life since food materials all come from nature. People living by the water must favor fish and shrimps; mountain and forest residents tend to like meat and fungus. Northerners enjoy cold drinks while southerners love hot soups. For those who never see asparagus, it would be impossible for them to fancy the food. Therefore, natural conditions are of significance to the evolution of diet customs.

②Economic Production

Production is the foundation of human diet. Diverse material productions give birth to correspondent eating structure and habits. Southern Chinese eat rice since it is grown there whereas those coming from central plains consume noodles

with wheat planted in the areas; and in the vast prairie where depends on gra-
ziery, people basically feed on beef, mutton and kinds of diary food.

③Psychological Concept

The eating habit is directly related to psychological concept. For instance,
in northern Chinese, people rarely eat mice and snakes out of disgust. However,
in southern China, mice and snakes can be regarded as classic food. Thus, different food cognition passed from generations result in distinct diet habits.

④Religious Belief

Particular nationalities possess different food customs out of individual religions. For examples, Chinese Hui, Uyghur nationalities and Kazakhstans, influenced by Islam, see pigs, dogs and donkeys as unclean and inedible and
Buddhists are not allowed to eat meat for the creed of ahimsa.

⑤Foreign Influence

Like other cultural phenomena, diet habits are changing under the influence of foreign customs. For Chinese, the alien food customs such as milk,
beer and hamburger consumption are now comprehensively adopted among Chinese.

(2) Development

The discovery and control of fire is the most important factor in the early
development of cooking. Chances are that men found this means accidentally. Probably a piece of raw meat fell into a fire, and people thought it more delicious and easier to chew, thus became the unique creature to cook his meal.

The first method of cooking was believed to be broiling. People placed an
animal on the end of a stick, holding it over a fire until it was well done. Later
it was found that food tasted better when the removal of furs or feathers is completed and the insides of the food were taken out and replaced with a stuffing of
herbs or grains before cooking. Further discovery was that a metal rod conducted
heat to the inside, enabling the food to be cooked more quickly. Therefore,
roasting is still adopted in outdoor barbecues.

Human being started to be interested in controlling his food sources with the
development of different cooking methods. All food was originally provided natu-

rally, including wild animals, fish, birds, fruit, vegetables and nuts. 8000 B. C witnessed the domestication of wild animals when man tried to tame sheep, goats, cattle and other animals. Meanwhile, grain and other crops started to be cultivated, proving that man was capable of exerting certain influence over his food supply.

With the progress of sciences such as physics and chemistry, man began to apply new knowledge to prepare and preserve food. Later on, people replaced the open fireplace with cast-iron range, which was viewed as one of the biggest changes in the middle of 19th century. The acquisition and preservation of a wide variety of foods was made possible when means of transportation, refrigeration, freezing, and canning advanced more rapidly. Electricity has proved useful not only in kitchen stoves, but also in appliances such as mixers, blenders, frying pans, and coffee makers.

(3) Functions

①Physiological Functions

There is not a single moment in life when the body is completely at rest and does not require energy. Energy is also required to carry out professional, household and recreational activities which are supplied from foods like carbohydrates and fats. Besides, food protects the body against diseases since elements such as vitamins and minerals are needed for maintaining the general health of the body.

②Psychological Functions

People find that the consumption of food can provide satisfaction to their certain emotional needs and they view it as a source of psychological safety. So, a baby is secure when his mother feeds him. On the contrary, when a child learns the shortage of food in his home and he always needs to face hunger, he will gain no confidence and the sense of belonging.

What's more, food can serve as the emotional outlet. As a relief from tension, one may tend to not eat or over-eat. For some people, continuous nibbling at food can magically reduce their loneliness and boredom.

③Socio-cultural Function

The socio-cultural function of foods has always existed since ancient times when it is regarded as a symbol to express friendship among people. We present food or drink to a guest to show our hospitality. People use food as an instrument to establish social bonds in social gatherings.

To sum up, food serves as not only a substance supplying nutrients for people's physical health, but also represents their culture, emotional outlet, pleasure, satisfaction, status and a relief from intense pressure. Besides being a means of personal interaction, it offers people a sense of security, all of which interwoven in the fabric of life and unconsciously expressed in food likes and dislikes.

2. Chinese Cuisine Customs

Laotse, the famous Chinese philosopher, once said: "Governing a great nation is much like cooking a small fish", which clearly illustrates the importance of food in Chinese culture.

(1) Staple Food (Fan) and Prepared Dishes (Cai)

China, a vast land with abundant resources, produces different regional staple food. Generally speaking, the staple food in the North includes wheat, rice, corn, soybeans, millet, beans and peas. And people in the South traditionally take dry cooked rice or rice porridge as their staple food since rice mainly grows in the south. One type of rice called glutinous rice is usually used to make traditional Chinese rice-pudding, eight treasures congee and various types of desserts.

Wheat flour and rice were generally regarded as food for the upper classes since ancient times while coarse cereals or side crops are consumed by common people. Gradually wheat flour and rice were considered as "refined grains" and maize, sorghum and millet as "coarse grains". The latter being their daily staple food, ordinary families eat rice food or meat dumplings on the rare occasion such as festivals.

China implemented the planned economy after the foundation of People's Republic of China. The food coupons and ration booklets were distributed to urban household in 1955. A grain ration book was monthly issued by 50 percent in wheat flour, 20 percent in rice, and the rest for buying kitchen goods such as bowls or noodles in restaurants. In rural areas, for example, in northwestern China, farmers usually had more wheat-flour-made food after a summer wheat harvest. In the second half of a year the other types of autumn grains like maize and soybeans are more consumed in place of wheat.

Such a situation lasted until earlier 1990s after China started carrying out the policies of the domestic reform and market economy, which led to the abundant supply of "refined grains" and "coarse grains" in food markets, supermarkets, and department stores across the country. At present, people either in cities or rural areas have a diverse choice of staple food according to their daily menu. ①

Along with *fan*, staple food, *cai*, prepared dishes of supplementary meat or vegetable is also consumed. But all in all, *fan* is more fundamental since Chinese are more accustomed to the habit of eating more of this food and less of non-staple dishes. A person's caloric intake mostly comes from grains consumption and a grown-up usually has two small bowls of rice or a large bowl of noodles. Individuals have their own bowl of *fan* at the daily dining table; but if a lot of *cai* dishes are served, some may refer not to eat any additional *fan*.

When preparing *cai*, people use multiple ingredients and several flavors. These dishes are usually placed at the center of the table to be shared by all, an occasion conductive to family unity and togetherness. In restaurants, "public" chopsticks or spoons are used to take food from the dishes for the sake of hygiene.

(2) Classification

Various standards lead to different outcome of classification.

①Regions

This refers to a class of dishes with very strong local flavors that came into

---

① http://studyinchina. universiablogs. net/2013/08/23/what-are-the-features-of-traditional-chinese-staple-food/

existence in line with history, cooking features, geography, climate, resources and life styles. Roughly it falls into northern and southern styles. In general, the former is oily without being cloying and the flavors of vinegar and garlic tend to be stronger.

Food made from wheat is an indispensable part in northern cooking, with noodles, ravioli-like dumplings, steamed stuffed buns, fried meat dumplings, and steamed buns being the most common flour-based foods. However, representative southern cooking styles include rice products such as rice noodles, rice cakes, and rice congee. Among all the regions, the most influential and typical cuisine are Shandong, Guangdong, Sichuan and Yangzhou.

● Shandong

Shandong cuisine, *Lu Cai* for short, possesses a long history and exerts strong influence as a significant part of Chinese culinary arts. Shandong cuisine can find its origin in the Spring and Autumn Period. Quickly developed in the South and North dynasty, it was recognized as an important style of cooking in the Qing dynasty. Its techniques have been widely applied in northeast China, thus Shandong cuisine is undoubtedly a representative of northern China's cooking.

Shandong cuisine gradually spread to Beijing, Tianjin, Northeast China, and strongly influenced the imperial food. It is regarded as one of the most influential part of Chinese cuisine since most of the culinary styles in China having evolved from it. Also, the typical dishes in most North China households' meals are simplified version of Shandong methods.

With the Yellow River meandering through the center, Shandong is a large peninsula surrounded by the sea. Therefore, seafood constitutes a major component of the cuisine, including scallops, prawns, clams, sea cucumbers and squids, all of which are well-known in Shandong as local ingredients of exemplary quality. The most famous and truly authentic dish is the sweet and sour carp coming from the Yellow River. In addition, typical courses in the cuisine include braised abalone with shells, fried sea cucumber with chinese onion, fragrant calamus in milk soup, quick-fried double fats (a very traditional dish consisting of pork tripe and chicken gizzards). Dezhou stewed chicken is known nationwide as well. The chicken is so well cooked that the meat easily separates from the bone while the chicken shape is perfectly preserved.

Apart from the seafood, Shandong is somewhat special for its wide use of corn, a local cash crop that is not commonly planted elsewhere. With a grassy aroma, Shandong corn is chewy and starchy, unlike the sweet corn of North America. It can be served simply as boiled or steamed cobs, or lightly fried without cobs.

Another distinct feature of Shandong cuisine lies in its wide use of a variety of small grains. Millet, wheat, oat and barley can be found in the local diet, often eaten as porridge, or milled and cooked into one of the many varieties of steamed, baked and fried breads or buns, pancakes, crisp cakes, and big cakes stuffed with minced meats.

Despite its rich agricultural output, a variety of vegetables which are often seen in many southern Chinese cooking are traditionally used in Shandong cuisine. Potatoes, tomatoes, cabbages, mushrooms, onions, garlic and eggplants make up the major vegetables in the Shandong diet. Grassy greens, sea grasses, and bell peppers are also not uncommon. The large, sweet cabbages grown in central Shandong are renowned for their delicate flavor and hardiness. As has been the case for generations, these cabbages are a staple of the winter diet throughout much of the province, and are featured in a great number of dishes. [1]

● Guangdong

Being a historical key port for Chinese international trade, Guangzhou witnesses the development of food culture and Cantonese takes pride in their dishes originated in Lingnan. Guangdong cooking was developed unceasingly without sacrificing its own feature. What's amazing to a gourmet is that any creature flying in the sky, swimming in water, crawling on the around can find a way on to menu to become an unforgettable dish.

Generally, Guangdong dishes use less spicy sauces to keep the original delicious flavors, so Guangdong food tastes crisp, light and fresh with the use of

---

[1]   http: //english. eastday. com/e/cy/u1a4035663. html

different seasonings. Usually fresh and light in summer but a bit heavy in winter and spring, the dish is well-known for its five tastes (fragrant, soft, crisp, rich and thick) .

Chaozhou dishes are local in Chaozhou and Shantou. Chaoshan flavors are like those from south Fujian, but influenced by Guangzhou. Chaozhou cooking is notable for seafood, soup in particular, elaborately done in many ways to preserves stewing, frying, steaming, deep-frying, and roasting. After cooking and seasoning with local condiments, a dish is delicious, a soup thick, but not heavy. Smashed taro and five-fruit soup are best deserts.

Also called Hakka style, Dongjiang food refers to the local flavor along the Dongjiang River. It features the main ingredient, a strong flavor and primitive shape. Most dishes are the combination of meat and vegetables. A bit heavier than other styles, and a bit salty, its stews are well known. Other famous dishes are pickled chicken, bean curd, pork with plum, and duck seasoned with eight treasures. ①

● Sichuan

The Sichuan cuisine is marked by its rich traditional flavors, which stems from a culture of hundreds of years and are in part shaped by the natural forces of climate. Arising from a culturally distinct area in Sichuan, a province in central China, Sichuan is often hot and humid, which is conducive to faster food spoilage, resulting in foods preparation in ways that differ greatly from other regions of China. Therefore, Sichuan cuisine enjoys the reputation of being hot and spicy since the fresh food supply was not as reliable as in places that traditionally used a lighter hand in their use of spices. This feature, particularly in the past, requires necessary food preservation techniques such as salting, pickling, drying, and smoking. Thus, spices served to mask the less than fresh foods flavors or not to reveal their natural flavors by methods of food preservation. In addition, the prevailing use of hot spices, such as chili peppers, tends to be more common to hot climates, as they possess the function to produce more sweat to cool the body.

---

① http: //english. eastday. com/e/cy/u1 a4035705. html

A variety of spices and ingredients are used in Sichuan cuisine to achieve the desired taste sensations. These include a variety of chili peppers, different peppercorns and Sichuan peppers, a type of fruit rather than real peppers, can produce a numbing but warm flavor. Sichuan peppers, also named flower pepper and mountain pepper, are a traditional element of the Chinese five-spice powder, and the use of which is regarded as the most authentic versions of Sichuan cuisine.

There are other commonly used ingredients in Sichuan cuisine to create the five fundamental taste sensations. Salt is important, and the area produces uniquely flavored salts that makes the authentic Sichuan cuisine different from the other Chinese regional cuisines. The sour comes from pickled vegetables and different varieties of vinegar. A special bitter melon is added to many dishes to offer bitterness that supplements other flavors. Sugars are many, such as cane sugar and beetroot sugar as well as local fruits for sweetness. Other spices and flavors include garlic, ginger, dried orange peel, sesames oil and bean paste. After all, Authentic Sichuan cuisine offers a unique dining experience made up of adventurous and creative taste sensations[1].

- Huaiyang

Huaiyang cuisine encompasses the styles of Yangzhou, Nanjing, Suzhou and Zhenjiang dishes, is one of the major branches of Chinese cuisines, which is especially popular in the lower reach of the Yangtze River.

Renowned as "a land of fish and rice" in China, Jiangsu Province has an abundant variety of components available for cooking. With the typical raw materials being fresh and live aquatic products, Jiangsu cuisine is characteristics of strictly chosen ingredients, elegant appearance, exquisite workmanship, and rich cultural connotation. It attaches great importance to the freshness of ingredients. Other cooking ingredients include high quality tealeaves, bamboo shoots, pears, mushrooms, and dates. Delicate carving techniques are appealing, especially the melon carving technique. Due to the methods of stewing, braising,

---

① http: //www. articles3k. com/article/318/12289/Regional_ Cuisine_ Of_ China_ Sichuan_ Style/

quick-frying, warming-up, stir-frying, wine sauce pickling and adding some sugar as condiments, Jiangsu dishes taste fresh, mild and light.

In addition, the different kinds of vegetables available in the region enable them to be widely used in many dishes. To ensure the vegetables and meat to absorb more sauces during cooking, it always takes relatively long time to prepare Huaiyang cuisine. The seasonings tend to be sweeter with more sugar and dark soy applied in its production[1].

②Origins

The system of origins involves the dishes of the imperials, officials, common people, mountain, ethnic minorities and foreign nations, basing on the rigid ranking of China's feudal society. This kind of food classification can be found in the *Unofficial Annals* of the States in the Spring and Autumn Period as follows: "The emperor ate ox, sheep; officials ate pig; scholars ate fish; and the common people ate vegetables. "

To be relevant of folks, two of the above mentioned kinds: family and ethnic minorities' dishes need to be discussed here.

• Family Dishes

In Chinese cooking, color, aroma, and flavor are of equal importance in the preparation of each dish, in satisfying the gustatory, olfactory, and visual senses. Any entrée is a combination of three to five colors. Usually, a meat and vegetable dish is used as one main ingredient and two to three secondary ingredient to add contrasting colors. Then cook it appropriately with seasonings and sauces to make the dish aesthetically attractive. The basic methods of preparation include stir-frying, stewing, steaming, deep-frying, flash-frying, and pan-frying.

Besides, fragrant aroma of the dish is highly valued in Chinese cooking. Some ingredients such as scallions, fresh ginger root, garlic, chili peppers, wine, star anise, cinnamon stick, pepper, sesame oil, and dried black Chinese mushroom contribute to a mouth-watering aroma to stimulate the appetite or help to preserve the fresh, natural flavor of the ingredients and to re-

---

[1]　http: //www. chinaculture. org/gb/en_ chinaway/2003 - 09/24/content_ 29399. htm

move any unpleasant fish or game odors. In Western cooking, lemon is often used to remove smells of fish; however, in Chinese cooking, scallions and ginger serve the function similarly. What's more, vinegar, soy sauce, sugar and other seasonings add richness to a dish without depriving the natural flavor of the ingredients. All in all, seasoning helps to create various tastes in Chinese food: salty, sweet, sour, pungent, fragrant, bitter and so on. The proper use of seasonings will produce a variety of dishes to cater to a variety of appetites such as *mala* (numbing spicy sauce), *guaiwei* (strange salty, spicy, and sesame sauce), yuxiang (taste fish-flavored sauce) and so on.

However, compared with color, aroma, and flavor, nutrition is what really matters in Chinese household cooking. A statement of the "harmonization of foods" can be traced back to Yi Yin, a famous scholar in Shang dynasty. He created the theory that the five flavors of sweet, bitter, piquant, sour and salty can be related to the nutritional needs of the five major human organ systems (the heart, spleen, lungs, liver, and kidney), stressing their role to facilitate good physical health. In fact, many of the frequently-used plants in Chinese cooking such as scallions, fresh ginger root, garlic, dried lily, and tree fungus have functions of preventing and relieving various illnesses. It is traditionally advocated in China that food and medicine share the same origin and therefore food possesses a medicinal value. Following this theory, people find that an appropriate proportion of meat to vegetable ingredients should be balanced to ensure the greatest nutritional value[1].

• Ethnic Cuisine

Besides the various Han cuisines, the other 55 ethnic groups each have their own. With their peculiar religions and geographical zones, their diets differ respectively. Ethnic food serves as a marker of ethnicity in ethnic theme parks, as in Xishuang Banna, in southern Yunnan. Certain food, such as the sour moss of the Banna Tai (Dai), is known as the prototypical food of various groups. It is impossible to cite every ethnic food here, therefore, some typical cuisines are presented in the following.

––––––––––––––––

[1] http: //www. seeraa. com/china-culture/china-cuisine-culture. html

—Southern China Minority Food

In southern China, no regions like Yunnan Province, Guizhou province and Guangxi Zhuang Autonomous Region have the largest concentration of ethnic minorities anywhere in China, among which, the Zhuang, Miao, Yi, Yao, Bai, Dai, Dong, Hani, Naxi, and Shui are some of the notable and dominating groupings.

Rice food is popular among those minorities: one is called rice cake (baba), which is made by oil tea, home-brewed rice wine, and sticky rice; and another is glutinous rice wrap (zongzi). Besides, they often produce their own home-smoked meats.

Typical Zhuang foods include oil tea, sticky rice cakes, and pork-stuffed snail shells. Multicolored sticky rice is eaten on festivals such as Tomb Sweeping Day and the Zhuang Song Festival. The Yao are most famous for their oil tea, a broth of fried tea leaves, and their foods include sweet potato noodles, mugwort rice cakes (aiyeba), stuffed green peppers, and stuffed bitter cucumber.

In Miao culture a chicken or duck is usually killed to entertain a guest on important occasions and sticky rice cakes are exchanged as symbols of love. Yi meals are based on buckwheat, corn and potatoes, and meats are often cooked in large joints.

The Baiare fond of making a lot of pickles and pork dishes. Dai cuisine is greatly influenced by Thai food. Sour and spicy food, wild vegetables, and blood cakes are popular among the Hani of Southwest Yunnan. Mushrooms stuffed with pork and butter tea are Naxi specialties. The Shui have a simpler cuisine, including glutinous rice, pork and beef bone hotpots, and steamed fish, with chilies, tomatoes, and pickles[1].

—Chinese Islamic Cuisine

Chinese Islamic cuisine is the cuisine of the Hui and other Muslims living in China.

With a large number of Muslim residing in western China, many Chinese restaurants cater to, or are run by, Muslims. Originally, Northern Chinese Is-

---

[1] http: //www. chinahighlights. com/travelguide/chinese-food/southern-minority-food. htm

lamic cuisine is greatly influenced by Beijing cuisine, with nearly all cooking methods similar, and differs only in material out of religious restrictions. During the Yuan dynasty, Genghis Khan banned Halal methods of animal slaughtering and food preparation, forcing them to follow the Mongol method, and then the restriction remains till today.

Despite that mutton and lamb are both utilized in Islamic food, there exists a traditional distinction between northern and southern Chinese Islamic cuisine. The former feeds heavily on beef, but rarely ducks, geese, shrimp or other seafood, while the latter is the reverse. The difference lies in the availability of the cooking materials. On one hand, oxen have long been used for farming in northern China, then beef is consumed as major food for Muslim of the minority-dominated regions; on the other hand, ducks, geese, and shrimp are rare in comparison to southern China due to the arid climate of northern China.

Having the majority of Muslim in China, the Hui nationality cuisine represents Chinese Muslim food with the core value embodying their living habit: hygiene. Pork, the meat of non-ruminating animals, fierce animals and their blood are forbidden in their diet. But those meats that are allowed and which have been prepared under the auspices of an imam can be made into delicious dishes.

For Muslims, they are not allowed to smoke or drink wines, but they are encouraged to enjoy tea. When guests come to visit, hospitable hosts will present tea together with fruits and fried cakes. Coupled with tea are highly nutritious ingredients, such as sugar, Chinese wolfberry, red Chinese date, longan, sesame, and raisins. Besides, sweeteners play an important role in the meals, these people tend to add honey or sugar to their dishes. As to staple food, Hui people prefer food made of flour to rice with many varieties. They have also adjusted and adapted aspects of Han cuisine-for example dumplings in a sour soup is one of their favorites.

Lamian (stretched noodles) is a typical Hui dish of hand-made noodles, which involves taking a lump of dough and continuously stretching it to produce a single extremely long noodle. It is usually served in a beef or mutton-flavored soup, but sometimes stir-fried and served with a tomato-based sauce. Beef noodle soup is a noodle soup dish consists of stewed beef, beef broth, vegetables and wheat noodles, a traditional food created by the Hui people since the Tang dynasty[①].

In addition to Hui cuisine, Uyghur food is also representative Islamic food which is characterized by mutton, beef, camel, chicken, goose, carrots, tomatoes, onions, peppers, eggplant, celery, various dairy foods, and fruits.

Uyghur-style breakfast is tea with home-baked bread, hardened yogurt, olives, honey, raisins, and almonds. Welcoming Uyghurs like to treat guests with tea, naan and fruit before the main dishes are ready.

Snacks are various: Sangza are crispy fried wheat flour dough twists consumed as a holiday specialty. Youtazi is steamed multi-layer bread. Samsa (baked buns) are lamb pies baked with a special brick oven. Göshnan are pan-grilled lamb pies. Pamirdin are baked pies with lamb, carrots, and onion inside.

Polo (pilaf) is another typical Uyghur dish throughout Central Asia. Carrot and mutton (or chicken) are first fried in oil with onion, then rice and water are added and the whole dish steamed probably with raisins and dried apricots.

Other dishes include soups made of lamb or chicken, and kawaplar (kebabs) of lamb or beef, seasoned with chili powder, salt, black pepper, and cumin. When eating it, one may put the skewer parallel to the mouth, holding the kebab closest to the end and biting it off with one's teeth. Another popular Xinjiang dish is *Dapanji* (big plate chicken), a spicy hot chicken stew served on a big plate, and after the chicken has been eaten, wide flat hand-pulled noodles are added to the gravy.

Naan (náng) is the baked flatbread using sesame seeds, butter, milk, vegetable oil, salt, and sugar. Typical beverages include Chinese black tea and kvass, a non-alcoholic drink made with honey[②].

—Tibetan Cuisine

Having a population of over 5 million, Tibetan ethnic group mainly lives in

①　http://en.wikipedia.org/wiki/Chinese_Islamic_cuisine

②　http://en.wikipedia.org/wiki/Xinjiang_cuisine

Tibet Autonomous Region in southeast China, plus neighboring provinces of Qinghai, Gansu, Sichuan and Yunnan. Tibetan people have their own oral and written language belonging to Cambodian branch, Sino-Tibetan language system.

Tibetan cuisine features *Zanba* (roasted highland qingke barley flour), meat, and milk products. The products demonstrate the differences between the various pastoral and farming areas. The generally favored foods are vegetables like cabbages and wine made from *qingke* barley and corn.

Tibetan cuisine can be generally classified into four typical flavors: Ngari's Qiang Cuisine, Nyingchi's Rong cuisine, Lhasa's Lhasa cuisine and the Court Cuisine of former aristocrats of Tibet. Roughly there are over 200 recipes. Qiang cuisine caters for those living in the high altitude pastoral area. Cheese, acidulous milk, butter and stock made from boiled cattle hoofs can produce energy to help them cope with extremely cold climate. Rong Cuisine is popular in southeast Tibet with a relatively lower altitude. Wild fungi and mushrooms are readily available and used to supplement food. Lhasa cuisine applies a variety of ingredients and is cooked diversely. Radish carbonade, boiled mutton, beef catsup are all common dishes. Court cuisine is an elaborate art using the prime traditions of Tibetan dietary skills and cooking methods to produce attractive and flavorsome dishes.

Other specialties are yoghurt made from yak milk, the material also used to make superb cheeses, and a particularly excellent recipe for stewed chicken with mushrooms in Nyingchi, and so on[1].

(3) Food Therapy

The Chinese believed that mixing tonics with food adds flavor to the food and is good for health. Famed medicinal dishes include "lily decoction with chicken" and "porridge with lotus seeds and lily."

Chinese medicine cuisine has a long history which can be traced back to Han dynasty, and now it has evolved into a practical nutritious science with the

---

[1] http: //english. visitbeijing. com. cn/play/culture/n214880745. shtml

continuous improvement during the succeeding dynasties. Not being a mere mixture of food and conventional medicine, it is a characteristic cuisine made from food and medicinal ingredients according to Chinese medicine theory. Generally there are approximately 600 kinds of resources ranging from fruits, vegetables, cereals, marine products and herbal medicines which are appealing in appearance and effective to promote health. Besides, other commonly used items such as almonds, mandarin orange or peanuts can all be utilized in the cooking process.

Medicinal cuisine is roughly categorized into four types according to its respective functions:

①Health-protection Dishes

The dishes aim to keep the organic health through reinforcement of required nutritious food. For instance, a pumpkin and almond soup is believed to help lose weight; soup of angelica and carp can promote beauty; and ginseng congee can offer the consumer more strength.

②Prevention Dishes

Chinese people tend to believe that certain dishes possess the function to resist against potential sufferings. For example, "Mung bean soup" is considered beneficial to add resistance to heat stroke in summer. Lotus seeds, lily, yam, chestnuts, and pears can assist in the precaution of dryness in fall and a reinforcement of resistance to chill in winter.

③Healing Dishes

The dishes are the medicinal food for rehabilitation after severe illness. "Broiled sheep's heart with rose" or "Braised mutton with angelica" help to rebuild healthy constitution.

④Therapeutic Dishes

Specific pathology is expected to be achieved with the application of therapeutic dishes. "Fried potatoes with vinegar" can recuperate the organ and relieve hypertension; "carp soup with Tuckahoe" may amplify the strength of blood plasma albumen to reduce swelling[1].

---

① http://www.travelchinaguide.com/intro/cuisine_ drink/cuisine/medicine.htm

3. Western Cuisine Customs

Western cuisine, or alternatively European cuisine is a generalized expression referring collectively to the cuisines of the Western countries which is rarely used in the West except in the context of contrasting with Asian styles of cooking. To illustrate typical western cuisine, we just name some representative countries.

(1) French Cuisine

French cuisine is literally the cooking originated from France, a production of centuries social and political transformation. For instance, in the Middle Ages, the upper class favor extravagant banquets with ornate and strongly seasoned food; however, the era of the French Revolution witnessed a shift toward fewer spices and more liberal usage of herbs and polished techniques.

French cuisine is primarily associated with some celebrated chefs such as François Pierre La Varenne, Napoleon Bonaparte and Marie-Antoine Carême who are highly respected due to their contribution to the diet culture. The national cuisine evolved firstly in the city of Paris with the chefs to French royalty, but gradually it extended throughout the country and was even exported overseas.

French cuisine varies seasonally. Salads and fruit dishes are prevailing in summer since they are refreshing and abundant. At the end of summer, mushrooms are plentiful and are frequently applied in stews. The hunting season begins in September and runs through February. Game of various kinds is eaten, often cooked elaborately in the celebration of the hunting success. Shellfish are at their peak as winter turns to spring, with oysters appearing in restaurants in immense quantities.

With the advance of air-conditioning and freezing technique, those seasonal features are less remarkable as they used to be, but they are somewhat observed under certain conditions. For example, crayfish has a very rather limited season so it's forbidden to take them outside that time. In addition, they do not survive freezing very well.

Meals of common people follow regular routines. Le petit déjeuner (breakfast) is often a quick meal of crossiants, butter and jam, eggs or ham along with coffee, hot chocolate or tea. Breakfast is always served at home or in cafés early in the day.

Le déjeuner (lunch) of common folk often consists of meat and vegetables, fruits and cakes which used to be a mid-day meal lasting two hour but is currently shortened to an one hour lunch break. Maybe the former is still customary in some smaller towns. Sunday lunches are often longer and are taken with the whole family. Restaurants usually open for lunch at 12: 00 p. m. and close at 2: 30 p. m. Many restaurants close on Saturday and Monday during lunch.

In big cities, most working people and students have their lunch at a corporate or school cafeteria, which normally serve complete meals as described above; students usually do not need to bring their own lunch food. As to white-collars, they are given lunch vouchers as a kind of employee benefits which can be used in most restaurants, supermarkets and traiteurs. Sometimes, people skip lunch due to price and time considerations.

Le dîner (dinner) often comprises three courses: hors d'oeuvre or entrée (introductory course often soup), plat principal (main course), and a cheese course or dessert, sometimes with a salad offered before the cheese or dessert, which can be replaced by yogurt as well, but a normal everyday dessert would be fresh fruit.

Besides, the meal is often served along with bread, wine and mineral water. Wine consumption has been declining recently among young people. Fruit juice consumption has jumped from 25. 6% in 1996 to 31. 6% in 2002. Main meat courses are often served accompanied with vegetables, rice or pasta. Restaurants are often at service at 7: 30 p. m. for dinner and stop accepting orders between the hours around 10: 00 p. m. or 11: 00 p. m.

Generally speaking, French cuisine owns a substantial history, and like many other native cuisines, French cuisine develops thanks to great chefs as well as the some influential impacts from neighbors. Like many cultures, the French spend many years to improve their cuisine, with each generation placing something new to the mix.

(2) English Cuisine

Multiple factors such as history, mild weather plus island geography determine the features of English cuisine. In addition, it is enriched by the interactions with other European countries and the introduction of ingredients and cooking concepts from regions such as North America, China and India as the product of British Empire extension and post-war immigration.

Accordingly, in addition to conventional British food like bread and cheese, roasted and stewed meats, meat pies, and freshwater and saltwater fish, spices and curries from India and Bangladesh, potatoes, tomatoes and chillies from the Americas, and stir-fries based on Chinese and Thai cooking are also welcomed among the British people. French and Italian cuisine, once thought to be alien, are also now favored and borrowed. Britain was also quick to learn to consume fast food from the United States, and keep on absorbing culinary ideas from all other nations.

For instance, spaghetti Bolognese, a typical British family meal since 1960s, is a perfect exemplification of the above mentioned mixture trend. The dish is influenced by Indian sub-continent but modified to please British taste. Furthermore, the British curry, used to be a leftover from the ages of the British ruling, and then transformed by immigrants, tastes spicier than the old North Indian counterparts.

Another notable food of English cuisine is Sunday roast dinner which comprises a roasted joint of meat like roast beef, lamb or chicken with potatoes and other vegetables, coupled with a gravy. Yorkshire pudding and gravy, the food which used to be treated as a "filler" is now always served with the main course.

What's more, fish and chips are specialties of the island with a large number of restaurants and take-away shops catering to them. It is probably the symbol of English dish, accompanied with a side order of mushy peas with salt and vinegar as condiments. A deep fried breaded prawn dish named Scampi, is also on offered as well as fishcakes or a number of other combinations.

In the United Kingdom and some other Commonwealth Realms, traditional tea time is still popular, which is believed to be related with Charles the II, who grew up in exile at The Hague and thus was exposed to the custom of drinking tea. He married Catharine of Braganza, a Portuguese also enjoying tea since she had grown up drinking tea, the preferred beverage of the time, in Portugal. Later on she became known as the tea-drinking queen of Britain.

Though fashionable tea drinking is attributed to Catharine of Braganza, it didn't gain popularity and evolved into a new social event until the late 1830's and early 1840's. Jane Austen mentioned afternoon tea as early as 1804 in an unfinished novel. Story has it that the afternoon tea custom was introduced by Anne, Duchess of Bedford. She demanded that light sandwiches be offered to her in the late afternoon because she had an unbearable feeling because of the long gap between meals. Later on she began to invite others to join her and thus it turned out to be a tradition.

There are various Tea Times in Britain such as:

● Cream Tea—A simple tea consisting of scones, clotted cream, marmalade or lemon curd and tea.

● Low Tea/Afternoon Tea—An afternoon meal including sandwiches, scones, clotted cream, curd, 2 – 3 sweets and tea. It is known as "low tea" because guests were seated in low armchairs with low side-tables on which to place their cups and saucers.

● Elevensies—Morning coffee hour inEngland

● Royale Tea—A social tea served with champagne at the beginning or sherry at the end of the tea.

● High Tea—High teaconnotes an idea of elegancy when in fact it was an evening meal most often enjoyed around 6 pm as laborers and miners returned home. High tea consists of meat and potatoes as well as other foods and tea. It was not exclusively a working class meal but was adopted by all social groups. Families with servants often took high tea on Sundays in order to allow the maids and butlers time to go to church and not worry about cooking an evening meal for the family.

Etiquette to follow when attending a tea party:

- Greeting/handshake

- After sitting down—put purse on lap or behind you against chair back

- Napkin placement—unfold napkin on your lap, if you must leave temporarily place napkin on chair.

- Sugar/lemon—sugar is placed in cup first, then thinly sliced lemon and never milk and lemon together. Milk goes in after tea—much debate over it, but according to Washington School of Protocol, milk goes in last. The habit of putting milk in tea came from the French. "To put milk in your tea before sugar is to cross the path of love, perhaps never to marry." (Tea superstition)

- The correct order when eating on a tea tray is to eat savories first, scones next and sweets last. We have changed our order somewhat. We like guests to eat the scones first while they are hot, then move to savories, then sweets.

- Scones—split horizontally with knife, curd and cream is placed on plate. Use the knife to put cream/curd on each bite. Eat with fingers neatly.

- Proper placement of spoon—the spoon always goes behind cup, also don't leave the spoon in the cup.

- Proper holding of cup—do not put your pinky "up", this is not correct. A guest should look into the teacup when drinking—never over it. [1]

An educated person ate with three fingers while a common person ate with five. Therefore, the use of the raised pinkie is viewed as a symbol of being elite. The former is still applicable when picking up food with the fingers and handling various pieces of flatware.

As to tea cups, they did not have handles at first under the influence of Chinese tea bowls since they were originally made in the conventional Chinese style. In the mid 1750's, a handle was added to prevent the ladies from burning their fingers, an improvement following a posset cup used for hot beverages.

Originally tea was placed into small china bowls that held approximately two to three tablespoons of tea. The idea of the saucer developed in the 17th century when the daughter of a Chinese military official found it awkward to deal

---

[1] http://www.afternoontoremember.com/learn/etiquette

with the hot bowls of tea she brewed and asked a local potter to design a little plate on which to put the bowl. In Victorian days, tea drinkers poured their tea into saucers for it to cool before being sipped, which was once a small dish for sauce.

Unlike people in U. S., Canada, Australia, and Ireland, who call the sweet "dessert", citizens in the UK and other Commonwealth countries refer the sweet to puddings or afters, a reflection of the upper-class/upper-middle-class usage.

(3) American Cuisine

The cuisine of the United States is a cooking style originated from the United States. The cuisine is traced back before the colonial times when the Native Americans had a variety of cooking ways for an equally large amount of ingredients. With the progress of time, especially European colonization, the cooking style changed immensely, with countless ingredients imported from Europe, coupled with cooking styles and modern cookbooks. Despite that, the Native American food would be specifically highlighted in the following:

Native Americans distributed chiefly in five parts of the nation before Europeans settled down in the North America: the Northeast, the Great Plains, the Pacific Coast, the South, and the deserts of the Southwest. Ancient artifacts prove that native peoples fished off the coast of New England as long ago as 3000 B. C Some Native American tribes were collectors since they eat the fruits and vegetables native to their lands. Other tribes who practiced agriculture adopted farming methods to grow crops on the same soil for many years. Native Americans knew how to plant almost 100 different kinds of crops which were used as medicines and dyes, as well as food before the first white settlers arrived.

Apart from gathering and farming, most Native Americans hunted for meat. The Spanish brought horses to America in the 1500s, helping the Indians of the Great Plains to hunt buffalo. Later, however, the accumulation of more Europeans made it increasingly difficult for Native Americans to hunt for food. The white settlers destroyed many forests where once were the homes of wild animals. They also slaughter the animals by hunting, both for meat and for sport or to sell furs and feathers. Anyhow, some Native Americans went on hunting buffalo for food as recently as the end of the 1800s.

Native Americans living in the Northeast and Pacific regions take various seafood, particularly fish, as an indispensable part of their meals. Comparatively, Indians of the Midwestern plains always view meat as the key dietary ingredient, where large buffalo herds roamed. Deer and rabbits were also hunted. What's more, Native tribes of the Northeast hunted elk, moose, and bears.

For native Americans, corn is traditionally treated as being sacred, with different tribes having different names for corn, but all of them relates with the concept of "life." Corn was the most significant dietary staple which can be served at almost every meal. Ears of corn were boiled or roasted over a fire or the corn was pounded into flour to be cooked as cereal (mush) or baked in bread. According to legend, native Americans were also the first people to cook popcorn when an American Indian named Quadequina brought a bowl of popcorn to a Thanksgiving dinner in 1621.

Native Americans celebrated the corn harvest with feasts of several days. Large amounts of food and drink were consumed. In many tribes, the Green Corn Festival, a special event, was even held as soon as the corn began to ripe. For the Creek Indians, this festival was attached great importance that it was regarded as the beginning of the new year. Other occasions are celebrated such as the raspberry harvest or the killing of the first buffalo of the hunting season.

In addition to the above mentioned food, beans were also consumed as a major food. No matter they are fresh or dried, beans can be made differently, cooked in soups and stew, mashed into cakes, or ground into flour. Other popular Native American foods included squash, pumpkins, sunflower seeds, many types of nuts and wild berries, peanuts (first brought to America by the Spanish), and wild rice. Indians of the Northeast tapped maple trees for sap to make maple syrup and maple candy. Chili peppers were also eaten by Indians in the deserts of the Southwest, where the fruit of cactus plants was used to make syrup and jam.

Native Americans possess many spiritual rituals associated with food. The

Comanches used to express their gratitude to the Creator for their food. Holding a piece of food towards the sky, they would burn it as an offering. Cherokee medicine men particularly apologized to the Corn Spirit after their people cut down the ripened corn stalks. In the Southwest, hunters tried to breathe the last breath of the preys so as to ensure that the spirit of the animals would be kept alive.

A couple of food taboos are observed among natives. For example, the Comanches would never take in fish or poultry. In addition, many Native Americans dislike food that came in pairs because twins were thought to be signs of bad luck.

Potlatch is the special occasion for some native tribes to celebrate their day, exhausting as much wealth of the host as possible. Guests stayed for several days in a row and were distributed lavish gifts. Then it would be their turn to host a potlatch the next time.

It was the tradition for Native Americans to be thrifty and they seldom wasted any food. Every part of the buffalo was used in cooking when it is hunted, with the heart left behind, which was believed to help the herd to revive.

Usually, Native Americans ate simple one-course meals without any appetizers or desserts. Cherokee Indians had two main meals a day: cornmeal mush, or cereal was the breakfast and in the evening, they had meat and vegetable stew or broiled meat or fish. Corn was an important snack between meals.

Modern Native Americans have almost the same food as other Americans such as hot dogs, potato chips, hamburgers and ice cream. But fry-bread is still the most popular dish of the Natives, which is served with meals or eaten as a snack or dessert[1].

4. Comparisons

Chinese and Western people vary immensely on diet concerning the follow-

---

[1]   http: //www. foodbycountry. com/Spain-to-Zimbabwe-Cumulative-Index/United-States-Native-Americans. html

ing aspects:

(1) Staple Food

Chinese folks feed on rice and cooked wheaten food for thousands of years as the result of Chinese traditional agricultural-based economy, the supplements being cereals like maize, Kaoliang, grain and tuber crops. However, bread and potatoes are the major staple food for westerners. In addition, Chinese like eating vegetables whereas westerners favor meat very much.

(2) Food Temperature

To facilitate food absorption and digestion, Chinese pay particular attention to temperature while cooking. The eight delicacies of *Ritual of Zhou* call for stewing, braising or simmering over a slow, small fire for a long time. Raw food should be cooked over a small fire as it is cut in large pieces. But westerners tend to eat food cold, undercooked or even raw.

(3) Utensils

The application of chopsticks as the chief tableware can be traced back as early as the Shang and Zhou periods, although hands were probably used more often than chopsticks. Chinese view food not as the prey suffering of the human beings' power and chopsticks are regarded as the gentle medium between man and food, reflecting the harmonious relationship between man and nature. Compared with chopsticks, westerners' knife and fork represent their concept toward food: they are conquerors over nature.

(4) Dining Etiquette

Normally, Chinese would like style of "sharing" when they have a dinner together. The typical Chinese dining table is round or square. The dishes are laid in the center, with each participant being equipped with a bowl of "fan", a pair of chopsticks, a saucer, and a spoon. All at a table take from the dishes as they proceed with the meal. When the dinner starts, the host usually shows a menu to guests asking them to order before making the final decision. When a dinner comes to an end, participants always strive to pay the bill unless some-one has claimed it in advance. The "truth of sharing" reflects a core traditional Chinese value: collectivism. On the other hand, western food culture is characterized by the "separated" style because of the great influence of the individualistic orientation. Westerners do not take the dishes from public plate, but have separate individual plates and the way of "going Dutch" is widely taken when the bill is to be paid.

Chapter Three

Customs of Costumes

1. General Introduction

The term costume, in a broad sense, refers to wardrobe and dress in general, or to the distinctive style of dress of a particular people, class, or period. And it may be used interchangeably with the word *clothing*, or *clothes* in this chapter.

Clothing wearing is the unique feature of human beings which differs ourselves from other animals. Meanwhile, it represents human social attribute. It is believed that man first employ animal skins and vegetation as coverings to protect ourselves from the awful climate such as cold, heat, rain and snow; alternatively, covering may have been produced first for other purposes, such as decoration, cult, or prestige, and later found its practicality as well. The progress of clothing is highly valued as a reflection of the materials availability to a civilization as well as the technologies that it has mastered. The social significance of the finished product absolutely reflects their culture.

(1) Origin

The exact time of man's first wearing clothes is still uncertain, roughly around 100, 000 to 500, 000 years ago, according to anthropologists. The first clothes came naturally: animal furs and skin, leaves and grasses, and bones and shells, which were simply draped or tied. Then 30, 000 years ago, needle work made out of animal bone present evidence of sewn leather and fur garments. Later on, the cloth making which was drawn on basketry techniques appeared as one of human's distinctive technologies when settled neolithic cultures discovered the advantages of woven fibers over animal hides.

Later ages saw development on fabrics and textiles: flax fibers about 8, 000 B. C. , with cotton following approximately 5, 000 – 4, 000 B. C. and wool around 3, 000 B. C. Meanwhile, other fibers such as reed, palm and papyrus were applied together with flax (linen) to make ropes and other textiles since 6, 000 B. C. Silk also was introduced as a fabric around 4, 000 B. C. in China. The Silk Route, which started in 114 B. C. during the Han dynasty, is viewed as one of the most important contributors to the development of the Chinese great civilizations. Together with Egypt, Mesopotamia, Persia, the Indian subcontinent and Rome, it helped to lay the solid foundations for the modern world.

(2) Forms

Costumes encompass four aspects, namely textiles, styles, colors and decorations. Traditional and characteristic costumes exist as the choice and combination of the four to people from different nationalities. The determining factors are as the following:

①Regions

This is the primitive and directive factor. For northerners from cold areas, furs and boots are their first choice while for folks from tropics, their clothes are characteristic of flax, silk, cotton which are usually short and pleasant to wear.

②Productive Methods

Distinct productive methods of the people lead to different clothing traditions. Simple clothes with furs are favored by nomads but elaborate and decorated cotton clothes may be preferred by people engaged in farming.

③Ethnic Psychology

Various tastes and aesthetical standards affect clothing traditions. For instance, white is always appreciated by Koreans whereas Han nationality favors red. Braid was once prevailing among ancient Khitans, Mongolians and Manchus while ancient Han nationality is unwilling to have hair cut for they believe their bodies, including hair, are precious heritage from parents.

④Religions

Religions exert impact on people's life, traditional clothes being no exception. Islam requires both men and women to be modest not only in behavior but in dress. Some Muslim women wear modest dress, or hijab, that covers most of the head and body. Buddhist nuns and monks wear robes in a variety of colors, from gray to orange, depending on their region and their tradition. In many cases, both nuns and monks in the Buddhist tradition shave their heads.

⑤Politics

Politics influences costumes substantially, sometimes even compulsorily. For instance, in ancient China, every dynasty transition involves changes of clothes, ranging from color to styles. Also the official clothing is ranked by distinctive color and patterns.

⑥Time Progress

The social development will definitely witness the progress of costumes. Take China for instance, costumes of Han nationality are once labelled as loose and large robes, Mandarin jackets to Chinese tunic suits. But nowadays the styles and patterns tend to be various and colorful.

⑦Alien Influence

Every nationality is inevitably influenced by foreign clothing customs while retaining its own characteristics. Suits, ties and evening gowns, which are exclusively worn by westerners now find their place in modern Chinese wardrobes.

(3) Functions

①Self-Protection

The protectional function of dress serves as practical and protective dress for individuals. The body needs to be kept at a moderate temperature to ensure blood circulation and comfort. People wear clothes with concerns such as durability, comfort, or ease of care in mind.

②Decoration

Decoration is a way individuals can express his or her own private style of cultural background. Decoration allows us to improve our physical charm, assert our creativity, single membership or ranking within a group or culture.

③Group Membership

People dress alike in order to prove that they belong to a specific organization or group. Clothing can be worn to identify with whom we affiliate. Uniform clothing can help in recognizing an individual's profession, religious affiliation, social standing or lifestyle.

④Ceremony

Ceremonial dress is that clothing has the functional method for people to take part in a specific type of ceremony or special event. A perfect example of ceremonial is a wedding or a graduation cap and gown.

2. Chinese Costume Customs

(1) Ancient Costume Features of Han Nationality

The costumes of ancient China were emblems of Chinese tradition which possess not only an external elegance, but also an internal symbolism, a perfect exemplification being the pair of fighting pheasant feathers in head wear of warriors in the Warring States Period, symbolizing a bold and warlike spirit.

As early as 18, 000 years ago, ornaments and sewing existed in ancient Chinese civilization, with archaeological proofs being artifacts like bone sewing needles, stone beads and shells with holes bored in them. In the era of the Yellow Emperor and the Emperors Yao and Shun, diversity in clothing was generally shaped. The complication and elaboration of clothing was further manifested in the remains of woven silk, hemp articles and antique ceramic objects in the Shang dynasty.

Accordingly, seemingly distinct design and Chinese traditional clothing framework produce various ornamentations such as embroidered edgings, draped cloth or silks, patterns on the shoulders, decorated bands, and sashes. Every dynasty in China had its own notable features.

Qin Dynasty

The dressing style Qin dynasties were impressive. The Emperor Qin held the belief that the Qin dynasty would conquer the Zhou dynasty like water extinguishes fire. Consequently, because the Zhou dynasty admires the golden and red color as the symbol of fire; Qin Shi Huang preferred black, the color related with water. As a result, black was the dominating color within the whole Qin dynasty to symbolize the energy of water, with clothing and adornments all being black.

Han Dynasty

The Han dynasty was divided into two parts: western Han dynasty, and eastern Han dynasty. Guangwu emperor adored red, regarding it as the most respectful color which embodied the virtue of fire. Until the second year of Yongping period, a white layer was added to match the red socks and shoes during ritual performances.

Following the theory of Five Elements, the ceremonial dress colors of government officials were seasonally changing, respectively being gray-green, red, yellow and black from spring to winter.

The dress of an average man, no matter he was a farmer, a worker, a businessman or a scholar, was always the same: a short jacket and trousers in the style of calf's nose, plus a short cloth skirt; with the style of his crown identifying his rank and status. However, a common woman usually wore a short jacket and a long skirt with an adorning belt hung down to the knee. Decorations such as golden earrings, silver rings and bracelets are exquisite.

Tang Dynasty

The Tang dynasty was the most thriving period of ancient Chinese culture.

The distinctive Tang costume was natural, beautiful and elegant. The style of female attire was various which comprised a shirt with short sleeves plus a long skirt; or a loose-sleeved shirt, long skirt and a scarf, or low-cut gowns with a high waistband. Hair was coiled high in a bun, the most popular being the "cloud bun" which covered the temples and framed the face.

Another distinct feature of Tang dynasty was "the rule of the wide belt", applying the quality and number of decorations on the belt to identify the rank of government officials. For example, officials lower than the first rank wore a sword or knife, officials and generals higher than the third rank wore jade belts, officials of the fourth and fifth rank wore gold belts, and the six-and seventh-ranking officials wore silver belts. In contrast, common people could only wear a small bronze or iron knife.

Song Dynasty

Song dynasty women had separate clothes for official, formal and casual occasions. The first type was for empresses and other nobility up to 7 Pin (level). Formal clothes were worn at great events like weddings or to funerals, and the third was casual for daily use. Generally speaking, the clothing designed for government officials was splendid, and common people dressed decently, the fabrics being superb, and the hair styles being special, braided and hung down on the shoulder, People who could not afford fancy jewelry used paper decorations in their hair, fragrance on the body, and wore shoes with embroidered flowers.

Yuan Dynasty

Yuan dynasty (Mongol dynasty), was first established by Genghis Khan in 1206, a dynasty established in China by Mongol nomads which proceeded to copy a Chinese-style administration. Within the Yuan dynasty, "Zhi Sun dresses" were prevailing worn by all classes of individuals which could be produced from materials of varying weight and quality. Aristocratic women had their own styles of dress of leather coats and hats as their national attire, marten and sheepskin clothing was popular as well. Gowns were long and loose with wide sleeves and narrow cuffs.

Ming Dynasty

One of the significant features of Ming clothing was the use of buttons on the forepart, replacing the band knots of thousand years, a breakthrough representing the development of the era.

Compared with Tang attire, the proportion of the upper outer garment to lower skirt was greatly reversed, and the collar was modified from the symmetrical type to the main circular type. Light color was preferred and skirt pleats became in fashion.

In addition, short embroidered capes named "Rosy Cloud Cape" worn over a woman's shoulder were popular in the Ming Dynasty, making the women to be more graceful.

Male attire typically adopted the form of chuddar and circular collar. They featured broad sleeves, inlaid black brims and cyan circular collar. Men wore black silk ribbon, soft chuddar and drooping strap.

Qing Dynasty

Qing attires, or Manchurian-style clothing, featured saddle-shaped collar and short narrow sleeves, and the former had the function of cheek covering and face protection. The whole garment was cut straight from top to bottom without a waist. The box-like look of Qing dynasty clothing indicated a solemn but slightly arrogant image that commanded reverence, which was fairly exclusive.

The Qi robe (Chinese cheongsam dress) and the short clothes resembled the shape of a pi pa (a Chinese musical instrument) front. The sides of the garment, as well as the collar and sleeves, were decorated with inlays and embroidery. The matching skirts and pants were highly decorated with dye printing and embroidery. [1]

(2) Typical Costumes of Han Nationality
①*Hanfu*

The ancient Chinese garment is characteristic of robes, with *Hanfu* being the representative. The record showed that the fundamentals of *Hanfu* was established in Shang dynasty, which consisted of *yi*, a knee-length tunic tied with a sash and narrow cuffs, and *shang*, a narrow and ankle-length skirt, with a length of fabric that reached the knees. The outfit was unisex worn by males and females alike. Due to limited technology, only primary colors were used at that time: blue, red and yellow. Despite the similar choice of clothing colors, the upper classes have more elaborate work and patterns.

In the following Western Zhou dynasty, the authority implemented a clothing reform to complicate the outfits. The higher the social rank, more ornate the garment is. Later on, the *Hanfu* became looser, with sleeves being wider. *Yi* was tightened with a sash decorated with jade ornaments. An interesting fact about *yi* was that it was wrapped from the right side over the left since left-handedness was despised traditionally.

---

① http: //polaris. gseis. ucla. edu/yanglu/ECC_ CULTURE_ CLOTHING. HTM

Roughly speaking, *Hanfu* had two variations: namely *pien-fu* and *shen-yi*, both having wide and long sleeves with loose fittings.

● The *Pien-fu*

A pien is a cylindrical ceremonial cap. The *pien-fu* is actually more of a ceremonial costume of two pieces, with a tunic-like top. It goes to nearly the knees, and the rest of the outfit is a second piece like a skirt for women or a pant for men which goes to the ankles.

Figure 3 – 1　The Pien-fu

● *The Shen-yi*

The skirt or trousers and tunicwere stitched together to make it a one-piece dress, the most widely worn costume of the ancient time.

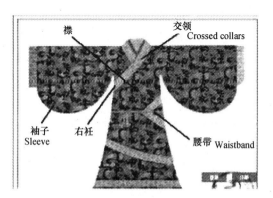

Figure 3 – 2　The Shen-yi

In the ancient Chinese clothing, most of the traditional designs were unisex uncomplicatedly cut. However, with the time progressed, gender distinction e-merged in the *Shen-yi*. The men typically wore pants and women, skirts. Each dynasty had their own styles of *Hanfu* as they developed. [1]

②*Chang-pao*/Long Robe

Chang-pao is a one-piece cloth, broadening from the shoulders to the heels to cover the entire body, with the most notable type being Chinese Cheongsam, or *Qipao*.

Figure 3 – 3   The Cheongsam

The cheongsam, or *Qipao* in Chinese, is the variation of a kind of ancient clothing of Manchu ethnic minority. In ancient times, it generally referred to long gowns worn by the people of Manchuria, Mongolia and the Eight-Banner.

In the early years of the Qing dynasty, long gowns featured collarless, narrow cuff in the shape of a horse's hoof, buttons down the left front, four slits and a fitting waist. Wearers usually coiled up their cuff for convenience, and put it down when hunting or battling to protect hands. In winter, the cuff has the function to prevent them from bitter cold. The gown had four slits, with one on the left, right, front and back, reaching the knees. It was fitted to the body and rather warm. Fastened with a waistband, the long gown could hold solid food and utensils when people went out hunting. Men's long gowns were mostly blue, gray or green; and women's white.

Another characteristic of Manchu cheongsam was that people generally wore

---

① http://traditions. cultural-china. com/en/215Traditions9827. html

it with a waistcoat that was either with buttons down a twisted front, or a lute-shaped front etc.

When the early Manchu rulers came to China proper, they immigrated their capital to Beijing, thus cheongsam began to spread in the Central Plains. The unified Chinese costume was the product of the Qing's unifying China. At that time, men wore a long gown and a mandarin jacket over the gown, while women wore cheongsam. Although the 1911 Revolution overturned the rule of the Qing (Manchu) dynasty, the female dress survived the political chaos and has become the traditional dress for Chinese women with further modification.

Manchu men or women all wore loose-fitting and straight-bottomed broad-sleeved long gowns with a wide front till the 1930s, The lower hem of women's cheongsam reached the calves with embroidered flower patterns on it, while that of men's cheongsam reached the ankles without any fancy decorations.

From the 1930s, cheongsam became prevailing among women just like uniforms.

Folk women, students, workers and upper-class women all dressed themselves in cheongsam, especially on formal occasions such as social intercourses or diplomatic activities. Gradually, cheongsam spread to foreign countries and was immensely favored by foreign females.

Under the influence of new fashion home and abroad after the 1940s, Manchu men's cheongsam was phased out, while women's cheongsam underwent further changes such as narrow sleeve, waist-fitting, loose hip part and lower hem reached the ankles. Then there emerge various forms of cheongsams we see today that emphasize color decoration and set off the beauty of the female shape.

The chief reason why the cheongsam gained such popularity is that it perfectly fits female figures, having simple lines with elegance. The cheongsam can either be long or short, unlined or interlined, woolen or made of silk floss. Therefore, with different materials, the cheongsam presents diverse styles. Cheongsams made of silk with flower patterns, plain lattices or thin lines reflect feminine charm; and those made of brocade are eye-catching, the costumes suitable for important occasions like guest greetings or banquets.

In sum, Cheongsam exemplifies beauty of Chinese traditional costume with intense national flavor. It is more of a Chinese female costume, but a symbol of the oriental tradition. [1]

③Chinese Tunic Suit

Known in China as the Zhongshan Suit (named after Sun Yat-Sen), but in the West as Mao Suit (named after Mao Zedong), the modern Chinese Tunic Suit is a typical male attire. Shortly after the establishment of the Republic of China, Sun Yat-sen popularized the style as a national dress despite its distinctly political and later governmental implication.

As mentioned above, Chinese typical dress before the Republic was founded was primarily Manchu dress, the result of social control of the Qing Dynasty, but actually the older dressing forms had already been on decline.

The Chinese Tunic Suit was intended to satisfy modern dressing sensibility, but not under the influence of western styles. Dr. Sun Yat-sen participated in the design with his overseas experience in Japan and adopted the Japanese uniform as the basis of Zhongshan Suit, plus some minor alteration: rather than the three invisible pockets in Western suits, the Zhongshan suit had four outside pockets following Chinese philosophy of symmetry and harmony. Gradually, the suit underwent some slight modification such as the number of the buttons is decreased from seven to five.

Figure 3 – 4   Chinese Tunic Suit

---

① http: //www1. chinaculture. org/library/2008 – 01/28/content_ 43933. htm

(3) Contemporary Costumes of Han Nationality

The Chinese clothing changed significantly after the 1911 Revolution, with the official cap being removed and hair plaits being cut off. But Chi-pao remained, meanwhile, the blue short gown of teenage girls was dominating and gaining popularity.

Male and female dresses were specifies in the first year of the Republic of China. men attire consisted of dress suits and routine suits. The former were all made of black cloth, pants and cravats. The latter include western and Chinese style, such as long gown and mandarin jacket. Women attires were collared and reaching knees; skirts were decorated with cartouches, pleats and knots.

With the progress of time, foreign culture exerted great influence on China, and western living styles invaded socially. Urban females started to be involved in social activities from 1930s, leading to transformation on social morals. Modern women were affected by Europe and Japan or even Hollywood, wearing one-piece dress, short skirts, underwear with accessories such as glasses and watches.

In the modern society, Chinese wear the clothing with a combination of traditional and new elements which incorporate age-old motifs such as dragons, phoenixes, lion, clouds and masks of Chinese opera characters.

(4) The Costumes of Chinese Ethnic Minorities

Minority costumes differ greatly on many aspects, such as textiles, fashions, decoration, and technology, reflecting distinctive locality respectively. For instance, the ethnic groups who chiefly rely on stockbreeding such as Tibetans, Uygurs, and Mongolians, make the clothes mainly out of animal skins and hair; however, farming minorities like Buyi, Dai, Bai etc. prefer the locally produced cotton or hemp thread to produce clothes.

①Zhuang Nationality

Having the largest population (almost 18 million) among all the 55 Chinese ethnic groups, the majority of Zhuang people live in Guangxi Zhuang Autonomous Region and Yunnan Province. In Guangdong, Hunan, Guizhou and

Sichuan provinces of South China, there exist some distribution of Zhuang People as well.

Figure 3 – 5　Traditional Costume of Zhuang Nationality

They always wear traditional costumes on special occasions. For instance, hand-woven fabrics are used to make different clothes. Usually girls wear a blue-and-black collarless jacket with bright furbelow, baggy trousers or Batik skirt, and a delicately embroidered apron is fastened on the waist. Boys are dressed in black front-opening coat with cloth-wrapped buttons, wearing a belt on the waist. Besides, Zhuang people favor silver accessories immensely.

②Miao Nationality

Miao people reside majorly in southern China like provinces of Guizhou, Yunnan, Guangxi, Sichuan, Hunan, Hubei, and Hainan and surrounding South East Asian countries like Thailand and Vietnam. The majority of the Miao people living in China are located in Guizhou province.

The Miao attire is full of variety and colors, ranging from region to region. In northeast Yunnan and northwest Guizhou, male Miao clothing features linen jackets with colorful designs, and drape woolen blankets with geometric patterns over their shoulders. However, in other areas, men wear short jackets buttoned down the front or to the left, long trousers with wide belts and long black scarves. Extra cloth leggings are added as puttees in winters. Women's clothing differs even more greatly. In west Hunan and northeast Guizhou, women wear jackets buttoned on the right and trousers, with decorations embroidered on collars, sleeves and trouser legs. In other areas, women wear high-collared short jackets and full or half-length pleated skirts. They also wear various kinds of silver jewelry on festive occasions.

Figure 3 – 6   Traditional Costume of Miao Nationality

③Uygur

In China, the major Uygur population live in Xinjiang Uygur Autonomous Region, Henan and Hunan provinces, with the total reaching up to 9.9 million.

The Uygur dress features uniquely. All of them favor the Russian boot and tetragon cap embroidered with black and white or colored silk threads in traditional Uygur designs. Male garment is always an unbuttoned robe outside their shirt with square webbing tied around their waist. Females favor brightly colored attire, their favorite accessories being earrings, bracelets and necklaces. Young girls like to wear dozen pigtails for their additional feminine beauty. But after marriage, women usually wear two pigtails with loose ends, decorated on the head with a crescent shaped comb.

④Mongolian

Having a population of approximately 5.81 million, most Mongolians live in the Inner Mongolia Autonomous Region in North China, and the rest reside in provinces of Jilin, Heilongjiang, Liaoning, Xinjiang, Hebei, and Qinghai and so on.

Figure 3 – 7   Traditional Costume of Uygur

Figure 3 – 8   Traditional Costume of Mongolians

The caftan, hat, sash and boots are the essential part of the Mongolian clothing. With materials ranging from leather to drapery, the caftan possess various functions such as a blanket, a makeshift tent, or a screen, whereas its long and wide sleeves can be rolled down to protect the wearer from the sun, wind or rain. Men's sash is long, folded into a broad band and is tightly fastened around the waist, which may serve to stash the Mongolian knife and attach pouches. Comparatively women's sash is shorter and narrower than men's. In some places, married women wear an embroidered silk vest instead of a sash.

The hat is regarded as a characteristic part of a Mongolian's attire, which is typically decorated with whatever trinkets the owner favored, or with pearls or even precious stones, coupled with long, colorful tassels streaming down. Hats are worn on occasions such as meeting or greeting non-family members, entering a ger (though one may be invited to remove the hat once inside), or when in the street. It is considered indecent to go bareheaded without the hats.

3. Western Costume Customs

Western costume refers to the routine expression about regional scope, a concept contrary to the Orient. The core being Europe, western clothes can be traced back to Mesopotamia and Egypt, which differs sharply from Eastern clothes and represents an important part in human clothes.

(1) Ancient Western Costume Features

①Ancient Greece

Ancient Greek Culture was regarded as the birthplace of Western civilization about 4000 years ago, producing many magnificent achievements in areas of government, science, philosophy and the arts that still influence our lives. Clothing is in no exception.

Greek clothing usually consisted of long, flowing garments, head wreaths, and sandals, which derived from three significant civilizations:

● Minoan Clothing

The Minoan culture originated on the Greek island of Crete in about 3000 B. C. Minoans established a flourishing society around royal palaces and lasted for several hundred years. Professionals have excavated sites in Crete to find pottery, frescoes on the walls of palace remains, and statues, which present a vivid picture of Minoan culture, especially that of the wealthy citizens.

Minoan remains demonstrate that Minoan clothing suit the body contours and required profound knowledge of sewing techniques. Men wore a variety of waist coverings and hardly covered their upper bodies. Women wore tiered, bell-shaped skirts and fitted short-sleeved tops that revealed the breasts. Minoans seemed to favor tiny waists, and both males and females wore tightly fitted belts, or girdles to fasten their waists down to a fashionably small size.

● Mycenaean Clothing

When the Minoan culture declined in about 1600 B. C. , for mysterious yet unknown reasons, the Mycenaean culture began to thrive on mainland Greece and impacted Crete, where they encountered the Minoans. The remains of Minoan culture influenced the Mycenaeans who continued many of their clothing styles. Women's clothing is particularly difficult to distinguish from Minoan clothing. Women wore the same long skirts and short-sleeved tops; however, paintings imply that Mycenaean women did occasionally cover their breasts with a bib or blouse. Likewise, Mycenaean men seem to have worn loin coverings similar to the Minoans, but more frequently they are likely to wear short-sleeved tunics with a belted waist. It was the armor that genuinely characterizes Mycenaeans attire. Evidence reveals that Mycenaeans were warlike peoples. For battle Mycenaean soldiers wore protective clothing that mantled the body from neck to thigh in bronze plates, bronze leg guards, and helmets made of boar's tusks.

● Greek Clothing

With the Mycenaean culture suffering from famines and other environmental disasters in about 1200 B. C, another culture began to prosper. The Dorians, ancient Greeks, dominated and conquered the miserable Mycenaeans. Although no evidence about what Greeks wore has been excavated for life between the twelfth and the eighth centuries B. C, we can judge from examples of Greek art to learn that the ancient Greeks had a great taste for the beauty of the naked body. Early Greek society did not inhibit male public nakedness. Therefore, men always went naked when exercising or competing in athletic games, and both men and women bathed separately naked in public baths. Women were required to keep their bodies covered when they were with men.

By the seventh century B. C. , Greek society was governed by a wealthy class who wore extravagant woven clothes and adorned jewelry. Greeks developed several distinct garment styles from this time until its defeat by the Romans in 146 B. C. , In general, Greeks did not have the clothes cut or sewed until the fourth century B. C. Instead they draped finely woven cloth all over their bodies to create typical styles of dress and protection.

The Greek attire features class division. The wealthiest Greeks wear expensive wool and finely woven linen, an almost transparent and soft cloth. Common people used cloth woven from the flax plant soaked in olive oil, and peasants used textiles made of coarse wool. Chiton, or tunic is the most distinctive Greek clothes. There were two different styles: the Ionic chiton and the Doric chiton, using variations such as length to separate styles for males and females. Crinkles and pleats were adopted to reinforce the fullness of the drape. Over the chiton, Greeks wear various wraps such as himation, chlamys, chlaina, and diplax to gain warmth. By the fourth century B. C. , sewn tunics with a U or V neckline began to be popular despite the continued fashion of drapes, with proofs being a set of tunic styles uncovered in a temple in Attica, a state of Greece that used to be the Greek cultural center.

With the marble sculptures being the sources of our major knowledge about Greek fashion, people took it for granted that white color was the only choices of most Greeks. On the contrary, experts currently learn that even the pale marble of the statues was once coated with bright paint that faded over the centuries. Actually Greeks loved color and many dyed their clothes. For instance, noble aristocrats wore purple clothes dyed from a species of shellfish or pure white linen robes. Women favored yellow clothes particularly. Black clothes were worn by those in memory of the death of a loved one. Peasants dyed their clothing with various colors: a variety of greens, browns, and grays. Soldiers wore dark red clothes to psychologically avoid the appearance of blood on the battlefield.

Besides dyeing, adorning designs were also painted, embroidered, or woven onto attire colorfully. Garments were also decorated with patterns of geometric shapes or dressed up with colorful border designs[1].

---

[1]   http: //www. fashionencyclopedia. com/fashion _ costume _ culture/The-Ancient-World-Greece/Greek-Clothing. html

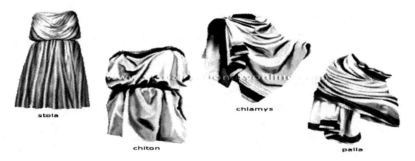

Figure 3 – 9   Ancient Greek Clothing

②Ancient Rome

Roman clothing owed much to that of ancient Greece, but it had distinct forms of its own.

● Clothing and Status

Dress for a Roman often is an indication of rank, status, or authority. The hierarchic and symbolic use of dress as a uniform or costume is undoubtedly an important part of Rome's legacy to Western civilization. Therefore, Much of Roman clothing was designed to expose the wearer's social status, particularly for free men. In typical Roman fashion, the higher social status the wearer had, the more distinctively marked his dress was, whereas the dress of the lowest classes was often without any mark.

Figure 3 – 10   citizen, matron, curule magistrate,
emperor, general, workman, slave

In the above picture, for instance, we can make the judgment that the first man on the left is a Roman citizen (because he wears a toga) but is not an equestrian or senator (because he has no stripes on his tunic) . The next woman is married because she wears a stola. Colored shoes and the broad stripes on his tunic identify the next man as a senator, while the border on his toga indicates that he has held at least one curule office. The laurel wreath on the head of the next man and his special robes indicate that he is an emperor, while the uniform and cloak of the following man identify him as a general. It is more difficult to determine the exact social status of the two men on the right; their hitched-up tunics indicate that they are lower-class working men, but the two lowest social classes in Rome (freed people and slaves) did not have distinctive clothing that clearly indicated their status. These men could both be freed people (or citizens at work, for that matter) ; however, the man in the brown tunic is carrying tools and the other man is lighting his way, so we can deduce that the man in the white tunic may be a slave of the other man.

• Common Styles

Figure 3 – 11   Toga   Stola and Palla   Priest's Toga   Stola and Palla

—The Tunic

The mostcommon clothes in Roman clothing was the tunic (tunica) , the standard dress of Rome. For most of Romans and slaves, the tunic would be the

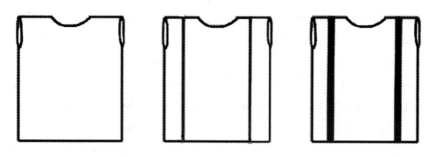

Figure 3 – 12　basic tunic　　　　equestrian tunic　　　　senatorial tunic

sole clothing they wear before going outdoors.

The male tunic would have the length of reaching knees while women's tunics would generally be longer, some even reaching to the ground. Female tunics often had long sleeves. However, it took a long time for men to find long sleeves acceptable. Before that it was perceived as highly lack of masculinity to wear one. In cold winter Romans would wear two or three tunics to keep warm.

A purple stripe worn over the tunic was called a clavus, symbolizing membership to a particular institution. So an equestrian could wear a tunic with two vertical narrow purple stripes on either side of the tunic, and a senator could wear a tunic having a vertical broad purple stripe down the center.

Under many circumstances, the richest form of the long-sleeved tunic, the dalmatica, took the place of the toga entirely in the later years of empire. At the same time, since the Germanic soldiers controlled the army ranks, long, close-fitting trousers were widely worn due to their influence.

—The Toga

The toga was the Roman national garment, which was made of a large woolen cloth with both straight and rounded edges in the early years of Rome. Designed for both males and females, it was not sewn or pinned but rather draped carefully over the body on top of the tunic.

An average toga extended between 2 and 3 meters long, and up to 2 meters wide. Togas were costly, heavy, and ponderous to wear; the wearer looked dignified and stately but would have found it hard to do anything very active. Despite that it was awkward to wear, citizens were supposed to wear togas for all public occasions.

The color of the toga matters significantly to discriminate differences in age and status: white for the common and purple for the officials and emperors.

By the middle of the Republican era, change had it that common prostitute were the only kind of women to wear togas. Unlike men, therefore, toga was used to symbolize the lack of respectability for women. It was strange that while the toga was a mark of honor for a man, it was a symbol of disgrace for a woman. Prostitutes of the lowest class, the street-walker variety, were compelled to wear a plain toga made of coarse wool to claim their identity, and there is some evidence that women convicted of adultery might have been obliged to wear "the prostitute's toga" as a punishment of shame.

—Stola and Palla

Compared with men's dress, fewer restrictions were imposed on women's dress by laws and conventions, and feminine attire can be of almost any color.

Stola was the most common female clothes worn over a long tunic. To display the layers of garment as well as to show off one's fortune and status, stola was shorter than the under tunic. Other ways of wealth exhibition was to add a wide ornamental border on the lower edge of either the under tunic or the stola.

Palla was a draped cloak that was just like a small version of toga, therefore less uncomfortable to wear. Palla features no particular size or shape, which can range from a large coat draped over the body to a piece of cloth no bigger than a scarf.

• Textiles and Dyes

Roman garments were typically made of wool. Women spun the fleece into thread and wove the cloth at home since the early Republic, and women from underprivileged classes continued the practice afterwards. However, by the late Republic, women from wealthy families stop spinning and weaving themselves, with slaves doing the household work or cloth bought in the market. Besides wool, rich Romans could afford to buy cloth made of linen, cotton, or silk.

In addition to spinning and weaving, many businesses were associated with textiles such as dyeing, processing, and cleaning. Clothes were cleaned by fullers using chemicals such as sulfur or even human urine. Status undoubtedly matters significantly in Rome, with Tyrian purple dye being one of the most expensive commodities available in the ancient world.

• Footwear

There were hardly any differences between men and women concerning Roman footwear. Sandals tied round the ankle with thin strips of leather were especially favored.

The calcei were the standard outdoor footwear for a Roman, coupled with toga as the national dress. It was a soft leather shoe, generally symbolizing a cross between a shoe and a sandal.

Sandals with open toes were appropriate for wearing indoors. There were many different designs, from the practical to elegant. When visiting, upper-class Romans took off their shoes at the door and slipped on the sandals that had been carried by their slaves.

There were definitely other types of footwear. The pero was a simple piece of leather wrapped around the foot; the caliga was the hob-nailed military boot/sandal and the sculponea was a wooden clog, worn only by poor peasants and slaves. ①

③Byzantine Empire

The Byzantine costume convention followed the route of the Roman Empire (27 B. C. - 476 A. D.), with its color and decorative tradition deriving from the Orient and the Middle East. The Roman roots were understandable. After all, the Byzantine Empire began in the fourth century.

The Byzantines obtained their basic clothing forms from the Romans: the tunic and toga for males, and the stola, a type of long dress, for females, as well as their shoes and hairstyles. These basic attire evolved into more ornate and luxurious style late in the Roman Empire; yet it was not long after the fall of the Roman Empire in 476 A. D. that the Byzantines start to make adjustment to the Roman costume tradition, thus forming something unique of their own.

By the end of the Roman Empire, the toga lost its dominance and was worn only on great events such as ceremonies since the Byzantines favored simple

---

①   http: //www. vroma. org/ ~ bmcmanus/clothing. html

flowing clothes more than draping of the toga. Men wore the dalmatica, a long and flowing tunic, or shirt with wide sleeves and hem; women preferred stola.

Unlike the Romans, the Byzantines tended to be very conservative about any flesh exposure. They wear the clothes tight to the neck, with sleeves extended all the way to the wrist; and the bottom edge of their exterior garments reached all the way to the ground.

The Byzantine Empire witnessed the significant trade with the Middle East and the Orient. Byzantines were greatly appealed by the exotic fabrics and patterns, adopting those new elements into their costume tradition, finally leading to the multiple colors and ornamentations of the Byzantine garments. Deep reds, blues, greens, and yellows became common on the clothes of the well-to-do people, but purple, was still reserved for royalty. On foreign visiting occasions, Byzantine emperors costumed themselves in rich purple robes, shimmering with gold embroidery and jewels sewn onto the fabric.

Silk was particularly favored by the Byzantines among all the textiles. Silk was believed to be originated in China. However, two Persian monks, from what is modern-day Iran, smuggled silkworms out of China and began to produce silk within the Byzantine Empire in 552 A. D. Since then the Byzantines wove their silk into a strong fabric called samite, which sometimes had gold thread woven into the material. Immensely valuing the silk, wealthy Byzantines employed it to make a variety of garments as well as for embroidery.

Figure 3 – 13   Byzantine Costume

In Rome Empire, strict laws imposed restrictions on different social classes concerning the clothes that they must wear. However, the Byzantines were free to choose the clothes they want to wear as long as they could afford it. But still, silk, jewels, and embroidery that distinguished Byzantine clothing could only be acceptable by the wealthiest due to their extremely high price. Most Byzantines wore much simpler versions of the common garments. Unfortunately, it was impossible to gain an insight of the clothes worn by the lowest class of citizens since they were unable to survive the passage of time, a phenomenon quite common in many ancient cultures. The remaining remnants of Byzantine culture—tile mosaics, statues, and paintings—merely reflect the costumes of the very rich or members of the church. ①

④Middle Ages

The Middle Ages (500 A. D. – 1500 A. D.) was, as its name implies, a great transitional period lasting one thousand years. The European earliest civilization provider, Roman Empire, perished in 476, and the vast land of western Europe was controlled by the bands of nomad—Goths, Huns, Vandals, Franks, and others—who were viewed by the Romans as barbarians. These new Europeans retained the Catholic Church and the Latin language, yet most every other area of culture changed, with one of the most remarkable modifications being the area of clothing. The fine linen and silk togas and draped robes of the Romans were replaced by crude wool leggings and fur-lined tunics, or shirts. Meanwhile, the emerging kingdoms of Europe began to develop more elaborate costume traditions particularly in about the eleventh century. With the development of trade, travel, and wealth, clothing became more exquisite. By the end of the Middle Ages, Europe had formed distinctive and refined costume traditions of its own.

Unlike the Romans, nomad tribes used to live in a harsh environment of coldness. Cool weather and sheep herding customs led to the choice of wool as their primary fabric. The basic garment for both males and females throughout

---

① http: //www. fashionencyclopedia. com/fashion_ costume_ culture/Early-Cultures-The-Byzantine-Empire/Clothing-of-the-Byzantine-Empire. html

this period was the tunic: a thin under-tunic and a heavier over-tunic. The gender difference only lied in length, with women's tunics falling to the ground while men's tunics gradually shortened, a design similar to a modern shirt. Both sexes wore a belt around their tunics. Men typically wore leg coverings, in the forms of simple trousers early in the period with a hose and breeches, or short pants, later in the period. In winter, people, no matter the poor or the rich, wore a fur tunic to keep warm; yet the wealthy people were able to afford better and softer furs such as ermine, or weasels, and mink.

But still little is known about clothing in the early Middle Ages since early Europeans just buried their body underground, where their burial clothes quickly went ruined rather than preserving the bodies and clothing items in the protected tombs. Another reason was that Early Europeans seldom used paintings to record daily life realistically, most of their art revolving around religious subjects. Luckily, records for the period increased from about the eleventh century, a turning point in medieval fashion, with one key aspect being the distinction between male and female attire. Women continued to wear long robes made in separate pieces of fabric with a snug-fitting top or bodice matched to a flowing and bountiful skirt. Men's tunics, which used to reach the ankle, got much shorter, until by the 14th and 15th centuries they ended at the waist. Men also wore tight-fitting hose to reveal the shape of their legs.

The basic cause of this fashion breakthrough was the appearance of the professional tailor. In the past, people had made their own clothes or, rich people wore clothes made by the servants. Therefore, most clothes were rather simple. Later on, skilled craftsmen began to form the trade of tailoring, making, repairing, and altering clothes who developed their skills and soon made tailoring a job for men instead of women. By 1300 roughly seven hundred tailors worked in Paris, France and they cultivated new cutting and sewing methods that allowed for more fitting and intricate clothing.

All in all, the Middle Ages was perhaps the last period in European history when clothing was principally a simple living necessity rather than luxurious, ever-changing fashion①.

⑤The Baroque Period

The Baroque period lasted from the early 1600s to the mid – 1700s. It was a time of indulgence and impracticality mirrored by extreme ornaments, a trend started from France then impacted the entire European continent.

Baroque fashion featured flamboyance, with typical large, ruffled collars and oversized, balloon-like sleeves. Costly fabrics such as velvet, silk, and brocade were frequently applied. Vivid colors, ribbons, and beaded embroidery were typical of baroque fashion. Overall, looser clothing were prevailing for the purpose of free movement, with the corsets worn by women being the exception, which exhibited the beauty of female figure by creating a narrow waistline with the decoration of embroidery, ribbons, and bows. Corsets were uncomfortable to wear since no flexible fabrics were available at that time. Meanwhile, collars on women's clothing were smaller than men's collars since female necklines were lowered to highlight the bustline.

Baroque fashion differed greatly from current fashion in its emphasis on male dress: First, women covered their legs even their ankles with long dress, whereas men showed theirs off by wearing tight breeches ending at the knee and silk stockings decorated with embroidery to arouse attention to their legs.

Second, Men's styles were generally more eye-catching than women's with the employment of plumed hats, laced cuffs, and brighter colors. Wigs were applied to demonstrate their wealth and social position. Besides, men wore high-heeled shoes decorated with bows. Their hairstyles generally reached their shoulders and sometimes flowing down past the waist. Goatees and mustaches were both popular.

Cotton, an import, was rejected during this time for the unity of the European textile market. Therefore, upper-class turned to linen as the material for undergarments, although it was not considered fine enough for outerwear.

The colors and patterns of the clothes worn by different classes were dis-

---

① http：//www. fashionencyclopedia. com/fashion ＿ costume ＿ culture/Early-Cultures-Europe-in-the-Middle-Ages/Clothing-of-the-Middle-Ages. html

tinct. The upper class wore pastels and bright colors. In the early Baroque period, they preferred large floral patterns, but later, small scrolling floral patterns and stripes were more favored. Comparatively, the middle class viewed dark colors as a means of displaying their wealth since dying these colors was more demanding and thus more expensive. The poor wore light, dingy shades because dyes of pure colors were barely affordable to them[1].

⑥The Rococo Period

The Rococo was the last period (1715 – 1789) in which courtly fashion gained the dominance which was characterized by a visible improvement in living standard. The Demand for rich fabrics and precious jewelry explodes. Thus, wealth was not the only aspect mattered concerning the choice of clothes, education and aesthetics worded as well.

Compared with men's clothing, women's underwent considerable change in the 18th Century. The stiff pomp that once prevailed at the court was gradually eliminated. The negligee, a "morning robe" was not only worn at home, producing a trend of simple upper garments.

After the tall, narrow look of the 1680s and 1690s, the European fashion in the following fifty years was characterized by a unisex widening, full-skirted silhouette. White wigs remained essential for men of substance; natural hair was powdered to achieve the fashionable look.

Separation was made in this period between full dress worn at Court and for formal occasions, and undress or daytime clothes. With the advance of times, increasingly fewer occasions called for full dress which had all but receded by the end of the century.

(2) Contemporary Western Costume Features

①19th Century

• Men's Dress

The early 19th century witnessed an utter change in men's fashions. The coat was cut higher in front, with the waist-length square-cut waistcoat showing

---

① http://www. wisegeek. com/what-is-baroque-fashion. htm

under it. In the early 19th century some dandies wore boned corsets to give them a small waist.

Gradually long trousers replaced knee breeches, and the former became increasingly fashionable in the first quarter of the 19th century. During the second half of the 19th century men retained the white waistcoat and black tail-coat and trousers of the early 19th century for evening wear. For day wear they wore a frock coat with straight trousers, a short waistcoat and a shirt with a high stiff collar. The single-or double-breasted frock coat fitted quite closely to the torso and had a waist seam. The skirts were straight and finished at mid-thigh or below. The front of the coat was square cut. Hair was still styled but by the late 19th century it was short and cut close to the head. Many men wore beards and moustaches.

● Women's Dress

The 19th century witnessed more changes on women's garments, the basic one being more revealing in the figure of the body. In the 1820s and 1830s the waistline was deepened, returning to its natural position. Lightly boned and quilted corsets were remained. Some petticoats of the 1840s were feather-quilted. Later examples of the 1850s and 1860s were made of 'crin' and steel hoops.

Bonnets and hats were worn until the 1860s when small, elegant styles appeared, just perching on top of the head and smaller ones appeared a couple of years later with hairstyles becoming popular in the form of elaborate chignons. Later, small hats decorated with birds and feathers and artificial flowers were in fashion.

By the 1880s, the upper class women began to adopt artistic dress, a simpler and easier style, which was cut far more loosely than traditional attire and did not require restrictive corsetry to be worn.

During the late 19th century, women's hair usually were arranged on the top of the head in a bun and puffed out around the face. A large-brimmed hat would be fastened on with hat pins except for smaller hats on informal occasions. The skirt was floor length with a slight train with the waist remaining small. In the 1890s, the top of the sleeves were sometimes puffed into an enormous leg of mutton' shape which required lightweight stiffening or padding. Women shifted to a simple and rather masculine-looking shirt, jacket and skirt for day wear.

Towards the end of the 19th century, it was evident that the pace of fashion change quickened. Meanwhile, the growing publicity of women's fashion periodicals facilitated home dress-making during the second half of the 19th century[1].

②20th Century

With the development of the fashion and media industry, the people's garment experienced even greater changes by the 20th century.

• Men's Dress

People's attire became simpler in the early 20th century. Men's suits became more casual, featuring a larger torso with enlarged shoulder pads and double-breasted buttoning. Plaid patterning caught on during this period, as well as other textures such as herringbone and houndstooth. Besides, blazers also become popular summer daytime attire under the influences of university and sporting colors and markings.

The post-war fashion witnessed young men as the leader to guide trend, with the older men being the followers. The colored, casual button-down shirt was first introduced as beachwear, and was quickly seen on men globally. Suits were still popular, but the post war culture demanded a revolt from the identical look of matching pants and jackets. Ties of different patterns add to the variety of a man's attire, sparking a revolution in the way men would think about clothing in the coming decade.

In the 1950s, males favor bright shirts and casual narrow pants. Short sleeved shirts were also popular. Meanwhile, streetwear takes the dominance with denim jeans being the representative.

A decade later, men's suits tended to be modern, slim and feminine as well with the styles being tighter, coupled with more color and patterns. Velvet was widely used as a major fabric and men's shoes were even pointier. Sportswear emerged in the 1970s since sneakers and T-shirts were popular a-

---

① http: //www. vam. ac. uk/content/articles/i/introduction-to – 19th-century-fashion/

mong young men. The 1980s saw the first emergence of couture culture for men especially in business wear.

The late 1990s saw many revivals from previous year, the mode of the 1960s, the 1970s color and later, the khaki period, which saw men of all ages take tips from golfing and other sporting fashion with Dockers and cargo-style pants[1].

　● Women's Dress

Female clothes featured the mature and full-figured body, with dress styles being low busted and hips curved. Skirts used to be long, similar to wedding gowns. But gradually it grew shorter, revealing the ankle. The overall silhouette of dresses also changed slightly, moving toward a narrower, straighter line.

From 1910, bustles and trains were removed from dresses to reveal new areas of skin. However, flapper styles of short skirts, low waistlines, and bobbed hair characterized women's attire in the late 1920s. During this time, women were liberated from constricting clothes and favored trousers and short skirts.

The styles of the flapper era lasted from the 1920s to the early 1930s before the Great Depression of more conservation. Later on, skirts became longer and highlighted the natural waistline of dresses since a more conventional feminine look was highly valued.

The 1930s witnessed the first distinction between day and evening clothes. Simple skirts and pared-down outfits allowed for ease of mobility in the daytime, while new fabrics such as metallic lamé became popular for more luxurious evening wear. The rayon, newly improved and synthetic fabric, became important during the 1930s, coupled with cotton and silk remaining to be the primary fabric of most dresses.

During the Second World War, due to the lack of materials, all types of cloth were needed for wartime purposes. Therefore, women wore shorter skirts and blocky jackets. Buttons were reduced to three for every clothing item. Nylon stockings were scarcity, and women were used to wear ankle socks and bare legs.

---

　① http://www.nzs.com/new-zealand-articles/lifestyle/mens-fashion-clothing.html

By the 1940s and 1950s, women were tired of the utilitarian, minimalist clothing of the wartime era, chasing elegance and luxury that had been discarded during the wartime. During this period, the clothes featured rounded shoulders, full skirts, and narrow waists with luxurious and expensive fabrics, coupled with ornaments.

During the 1960s and 1970s, bell bottoms, increasingly short miniskirts, hot pants and blue jeans became popular. Power and money dominated the styles of the 1980s, with women favoring expensive business suits and dresses during the day and extravagant gowns in the evening. But by the 1990s, women started to choose more comfortable and casual clothing such as Flannel shirts and ripped jeans under the influence of the grunge movement in rock and roll while the rising hip-hop movement brought baggy pants into fashion. Anyhow, comfort remained the major factor in clothing choice for most women in the 1990s and 2000s. Even standards for work relaxed somewhat, and casual dresses and pants became popular workplace attire[1].

4. Comparisons

(1) Clothing Concepts

Obvious differences exist between Chinese and Western people. Influenced by Confucian value and ethics, Chinese people have always maintained a conservative style, believing that body is to be concealed. To some extent, Chinese clothing culture is a kind of "cover" culture. People should not "reveal" body shape and even skin, which kept clothing relative unchangeable on form, but to develop more decoration, patterns, colors and material textures. In contrast, in western culture, except for a period when people are influenced by the Christianity that denied the existence of human and human body's performance, Western clothing was used to present body shape in a very realistic and even exaggerated way, reflected both in ancient "loose clothing" culture and "close-fitting clothing" culture since the Renaissance. Clothing has been used to

---

① http://www.randomhistory.com/1-50/003clothing.html

"stand out" and even "intensify" different sex characteristics between male and female, and skin were more and more exposed (especially for women's clothing). They have also found some methods to "further expose" skin. This brought many profile changes and man-made structure to Western clothing.

(2) Function Awareness

Chinese people have attached significance to social ethics function of clothing since ancient times. They defined the function not only concerning warm and decorative features, but more concerning social status. From the Xia, Shang to Zhou dynasty, this concept has never been given up in the improvement of ceremonial costume. Every ruler in every dynasty has attached great importance to unify people's thought by means of clothing. However, although the Romans pay attention to identity function of clothing, and have introduced a variety of apparel ban in feudal times, very few cultures have such social function development of clothing as in China still. Most of them focused mainly on wealth and aesthetic functions of clothing.

(3) Textiles

Human beings in different environment have created their own material culture since the end of Primitive society. From long time ago, Chinese people have begun to use plant fiber, such as linen, ramie, etc., and animal fibers, such as wool to weave, and they have begun to weave silk sericulture. Silk is a great contribution to human life from Chinese people. Different from silk culture in China, flax culture prevails in ancient Egypt, wool in the Mesopotamia and cotton in India. Ancient Greece and Ancient Rome have no pioneering work in materials, and they imports flax and wool cultures from Mediterranean coasts and Upper Paleozoic civilizations. As for silk, although ancient Rome has touched silk from Far East through Silk Road, they were never able to understand the mysteries of this beautiful fabric. Lately, they known the secrets of silk from two missionaries send to China by the Byzantine Empire. Then one century later, the first silk is produced in Byzantine Empire, but Europeans produced first silk until the Italian Renaissance in 13th – 14th century.

(4) Dressing Ways

Chinese clothing is featured of upper and lower part separated, with opening in front and using ties to fix clothing for the convenience to wear off; and Western clothing developed from put-on style to cast-over style, and then to front-open style in various forms and complex dressing skill, in which, pins or buttons are often used to fix clothing. It is hard to see cast-over clothing method in China. However, this style is very sophisticated in Western countries from Tunic in ancient Egypt to Tunica in ancient Rome. Cast-over style is often found in one-piece clothing, a very sophisticated women's clothing in nowadays, or in other words, the most formal clothing is still in cast-over style. Although "long gown" has shown in the Spring and Autumn Period, it is front-open style from the start, and all kinds of gowns, shirts later on are still in this style. The Western shirts in front-open style nowadays are also developed from cast-over style in the past. Front-open shirts emerged only since mid – 19th century.

In addition, put-on style clothing are every popular in Western countries, but it is only introduced to China with Buddhism from India far later, and it only can be seen on monk's robes even in nowadays. The clothing going with a piece of cloth, focuses on fold down effect when put on. This is also a style different from traditional Chinese costumes and dressing way. The words "loose clothing" has totally different forms, content, concept and effect in Chinese culture and Western culture.

(5) Colors

The representative color of clothing is also different. we all know that red is known as the Chinese element, which represents happiness, so when holding wedding ceremony , everyone is supposed to wear red clothes. And yellow is considered as a kind of special color, only used by emperors. In the West, however, people prefer white since it is on behalf of purity, integrity; or people prefer black, a color representing nobility and mystery.

Chapter Four

Customs of Residence

1. General Introduction

Architectural works, in the material form of buildings, are often regarded as cultural symbols or even works of art. Meanwhile, great historical civilizations are often identified with their surviving architectural achievements.

Vernacular architecture is a category of architecture which was built according to regional needs and construction materials available, a reflection of local traditions which evolve over time concerning aspects such as the environmental, cultural, technological, and historical context in which it exists.

(1) Definition

Vernacular architecture is a broad, grassroots concept which encompasses fields including aboriginal, indigenous, ancestral, rural, and ethnic architecture. Ronald Brunskill has defined the ultimate in vernacular architecture as:

> ... a building designed by an amateur without any training in design; the individual will have been guided by a series of conventions built up in his locality, paying little attention to what may be fashionable. The function of the building would be the dominant factor, aesthetic considerations, though present to some small degree, being quite minimal. Local materials would be used as a matter of course, other materials being chosen and imported quite exceptionally. [1]

---

[1] Ronald W. Brunskil, Traditional Buildings of Britain : An Introduction to Vernacular Architecture, London: Victor Gollancz Ltd. 1981.

The Encyclopedia of Vernacular Architecture of the World defines vernacular architecture as:

> ... comprising the dwellings and all other buildings of the people. Related to their environmental contexts and available resources they are customarily owner-or community-built, utilizing traditional technologies. All forms of vernacular architecture are built to meet specific needs, accommodating the values, economies and ways of life of the cultures that produce them. [1]

(2) Formation and Development

Throughout the human history, the formation of dwelling custom experiences a substantially long progress which is determined by the production capacity and specific productive mode of the social community. Roughly speaking, it is divided into three phases:

①Budding Stage

The earliest human living modes involve the employment of natural space such as caves and hollow trees in which demonstrates the common primitive features:

• Gregariousness

All the people live under the same roof to protect themselves from external attack.

• Separation

Separation between the living and the dead. For instance, in the Peking Man Site of Zhoukoudian, the upper cave is for the living while the lower is the cemetery of the body.

• Instability

The characteristic life of fishing and hunting result in the frequent migration of the primitives, contributing to their regular residence shifts.

②Transitional Stage

---

① Paul Oliver, Encyclopedia of Vernacular Architecture of the World . Cambridge: Cambridge University Press, 1998.

Wind fences, one of the most ancient buildings in the history, are easily constructed and simply structured. With trunks inserted into the soils, a slope of wall is formed which is covered by barks, branches and thatches to shelter people, the famous case being the pattern of Moso People in Sichuan, China. Comparatively, tent is similar but more advanced, with its varieties such as Immortal Column and Pinch of Luozi of Chinese Hezhe, Elunchun and Ewenke nationalities as well as Sky Curtains of Indian Americans. The two serve as the transitional means of human residence. On one hand, they are easily built to meet the needs of movement; on the other hand, they imply the tendency of domicile.

③Improvement Stage

With the social development, especially the emergence of agricultural production, people gradually changed the migrating life and settled. Due to the diverse global natural environment and cultural advance, various and distinct folk residence arise: woods or bricks; caves or bungalows; roofs or free of roofs. The residence features of this stage are rather apparent:

- Rich Cultural Connotation
- Diversity
- Stability
- Practicality

(3) Influences on the Vernacular Buildings

Many variations determine the styles of vernacular architecture, the major ones being the following three:

①Climate

One of the key influences on vernacular architecture is the climate of the area in which the building is constructed. For instance, buildings in cold climates inevitably possess high thermal mass or significant amounts of insulation, greatly sealed to prevent heat loss. Meanwhile, the rooms usually have small windows or even without windows. On the contrary, houses in warm climates are often constructed of lighter materials, allowing great cross-ventilation through various openings.

What's more, buildings for a continental climate need to be capable of coping with different variations in temperature, and may even be adjusted seasonally by their residents.

Buildings take on various forms depending on local precipitation levels. Therefore, regions threatened by frequent rains and floods tend to build houses on stilts and flat roofs are rarely built in areas with high levels of precipitation. Likewise, buildings in areas with high winds will be reinforced structurally and they will be oriented to present minimal area to the direction of prevailing winds.

Climatic influences on vernacular architecture are considerable and can be of extreme complication. Architecture with a courtyard plus a fountain or pond are frequently seen in Mediterranean areas well as the Middle East; in this case, air cooled by water mist and evaporations drawn through the building by the natural ventilation. Such specializations are not professionally designed, but learnt by trial and error over generations of building construction, often existing long before the scientific theories to present reasonable explanations.

②Environment and Materials

The local environment and the construction materials it can provide have great influence on vernacular architecture. It is highly possible that areas abundant in trees will construct a wooden vernacular, whereas areas without much wood may turn to mud or stone. Bamboos are common building materials in the Far East since it is both plentiful and versatile. Vernacular is bound to be sustainable and will not exhaust the local resources. If it is not sustainable, it is not suitable for its local context, and cannot be called vernacular.

③Culture

The third factor influencing the layout and size of the vernacular buildings is culture, namely the way the locals live their lives, the way they use their shelters, the size of the family units, how food is prepared and consumed, how people deal with each other, as well as many other cultural elements.

For instance, in some East African ethnic communities, the extended family live together, surrounded by marked boundaries, in which separate single-roomed dwellings are built to house different members of the family. The built structural division controls the social interaction between family members and provides privacy for them.

Culture also exerts a great influence on the exterior and interior of vernacular buildings since people often decorate buildings following local customs and ideas.

For example, many cultures around the world live nomadic life and they have all developed vernacular shelter solutions such as simple construction of huts and transportable facilities of tents.

Meanwhile, some shelters are made to suit the local climate. The Mongolian gers (yurts), for example, are able to be cool in hot continental summers and warm in the sub-zero temperatures of Mongolian winters, even include a closeable ventilation hole at the center and a chimney for a stove. Usually, a ger is not often relocated, therefore, it is sturdy and secure, composing of wooden front door and several layers of coverings. A berber tent, however, is much lighter and quicker to erect and dismantle due to the possible relocation.

When people settle somewhere permanently, the materials used in architecture construction will become heavier with more solidity and durability. They may also become more complicated and more expensive to build since the capital and labor devoted to construction is a one-time cost[1].

2. Chinese Residential Customs

China, a land with vast territory, varied topography and diversified climate, possesses a rich variety of settlements and traditional vernacular dwellings owing to its different kinds of nationalities and cultures.

(1) Basic Elements of Chinese Housing

Homes all over China in pre-modern times share some common features among the rich and poor, both in earlier and later times.

①*Fengshui*

Fengshui is a Chinese traditional discipline studying the way human beings

---

① http://en. wikipedia. org/wiki/Vernacular_ architecture

co-exist harmoniously with nature. *Feng* means wind and *Shui* means water. Another key concept is Qi, a mystical natural drive greatly influencing people's daily life, which has been valued as the natural rules by Chinese ancestors during their long labor. They originally used the rules of Qi simply to choose the locations of their houses and graves, believing that well-being would knock befall as long as they follow the law.

There are mainly three principles of *Fengshui*: The unity of human beings with nature; the balance between *Yin* and *Yang*, and the attraction and repulsion of five elements-metal, wood, water, fire and earth. The combination of the three helps people to seek good fortune and avoid disaster, thus bettering their life.

As to how and where to build houses, *Fengshui* offers people many suggestions. For example, houses are believed to have their backs to the north and fronts to the south so as to ensure they easily absorb sunshine and avoid cold north winds in winter, a tradition highly beneficial to people's health that has been passed to the present, particularly in rural areas. Meanwhile, the size of a house must be moderate, neither too large nor too small in accord with the Chinese conventional doctrine of the Mean.

Since ancient times, *Fengshui* has rigid requirements on the proper positioning of the central axis in cities construction. To be more specific, the central axis should run from north to south, with its north end pointing directly to a mountain running from east to west which is viewed as the guardian of the city. Besides, a winding river around the city adds prosperity to the city. The Forbidden City is a perfect example that was built in accordance with these rules.

Currently, *Fengshui* still finds its way in people's accommodation and is widely applied in house decorations. For instance, beds shouldn't be placed too close to windows because strong beams of light would directly affect the sleep quality. Mirrors should not be hung on walls opposite to beds to ensure a sound sleep. And beds should not face directly to doors, otherwise the sleepers may feel unsafe.

To sum up, *Fengshui* is a great treasure of Chinese traditional culture, which embodies a simple recognition of nature by Chinese ancestors①.

②Foundation and Roofs

Besides the resident location, the appropriate building materials were believed to bring energy for the inhabitants. The most common building materials for Chinese house construction are earth and wood, both of which bring about positive associations.

The pounded earth is usually applied as the foundation of a house, and it is used as a replacement of wood in the construction of walls when the latter is not easily available, pounded into shape or made into bricks.

The materials for roofs can vary depending on the construction budget, among which clay is the most common choice. In some underdeveloped regions, thatch and bamboo can be also proper choices.

③Wood Framing

The wood framework systems for Chinese homes and other buildings, the support provided for the roof, were standardized since the Ming dynasty and were quite different from wooden frameworks used in other parts of the world. Ordinary people could do much of the construction, but often experts were needed for framing.

The basic building block of Chinese architecture is the bay or "the space between," which are significant in house construction because they determine the size of the house. Chinese houses almost always consist of an odd number of bays since an even number is considered unlucky. Therefore, three-or five-bay houses are common.

④Courtyards

As mentioned above, the three-bay house is viewed as the basic unit of Chinese homes, one common extension of which was the creation of a courtyard dwelling. Traditionally, one family would share a courtyard space.

In Beijing, the courtyard residence has become characteristic vernacular since the Yuan dynasty, epitomizing conventional Chinese architecture.

The architecture is completely enclosed by buildings and walls which typi-

---

① http://english.visitbeijing.com.cn/play/culture/n214960582.shtml

cally features the courtyard. The front gate is the only opening to the outside with no windows on the exterior walls.

Courtyards help to protect privacy since it is hard to see the detailed arrangement of the complex just through the front gate. When one looks through the first doorway, he sees only a brick screen.

Due to the wealth, size and the taste of the family, the size of courtyard houses differ greatly. However, it is typical for the building to have an inner courtyard, and the house needs to be designed on a north-south axis, with the door of the main rooms facing south.

(2) Characteristic Dwellings of Han Nationality

The most representative civilian residences of Han in China are the *Siheyuan* of Beijing, Cave Dwellings of the Loess Plateau, northwest China, the Earthen Tower of Kejia (or Hakka) people in Fujian and Guangdong *provinces*.

①*Siheyuan*

Siheyuan, a conventional structure with 2, 000 years of histories, was typical residence in the northern China, particularly in Beijing. It is a courtyard surrounded by four buildings which are normally positioned along the north-south and east-west axes. Situated in the north of the compound and faces south, the building usually contains inner and outer yards. The seniors and the head of the family live in the main house, the one faces south which is viewed as the living room and bedroom while the younger live in the wing-rooms in each side of the east and west. The north-facing houses are generally for servants or serve as store rooms. The entrance gate, usually painted vermilion and with copper door knockers on it, is usually at the southeastern corner of the compound. All of the rooms around the courtyard are equipped with large windows facing onto the yard and small windows high up on the back wall facing out onto the street. The layout of *Siheyuan* embodies the character of legitimacy and preciseness of Chinese northerners.

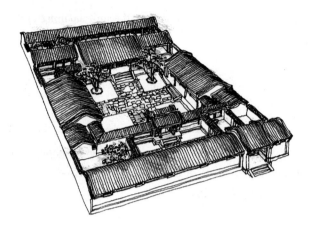

Figure 4 – 1   Siheyuan

②Cave Dwellings

Figure 4 – 2   Cave Dwellings

The central and west provinces such as Henan, Shanxi and Shaanxi are characteristic of Cave dwellings where the loess is abundant and of great depth. Possessing little seepage and a strong vertical nature, the loess conveniently becomes the perfect material for the construction of the cave dwellings, which is cool in summer and warm in winter. It is a harmonious combination of natural environment and human activities. Traditional cave dwellings are round, revealing the notion of round heaven and the square earth. Meanwhile, the window high on the circular arch brings brightness into the cave. Generally there are three categories of cave dwellings, including earth kiln, stone kiln and brick kiln cave dwellings.

③The Earthen Tower

Figure 4 – 3   The Earthen Tower

Kejia people, the Han people who moved to the south from the middle and lower reaches of the Yellow River over 1900 years ago, now distribute in Fujian and Guangdong provinces and they live in the residence of the Earthen Tower for the purpose of family protection originally. One such accommodation is capable of containing a large family of a whole clan with a total of up to hundreds people. The towers are usually round or square in shape, the former being more representative which is made up of two or three circles of houses. The outer circle could be over ten meters high, with 100 to 200 rooms. The ground floor is used as kitchens and dining rooms while the second floor is for the function of storage. The third and fourth floors are the living quarters and bedrooms. The second circle has two stories with 30 to 50 rooms which are chiefly reserved for guests. In the middle there stands an ancestral hall that can hold several hundred people where pubic activities are conducted. Within an earthen tower, there are bathrooms, toilets and a well. The immense size and the characteristic design of the earthen tower are highly praised and appreciated by many architects all globally①.

(3) Characteristic Dwellings of the Minorities

①Yurts of Mongolians

The Mongolian Yurt, is a domed pealed tent which was also named "a vaulted tent" or "felt tent" in ancient times. The yurt frame is supported by a ring of two-meter-long slim wooden poles which are fastened with leather thongs and studs to form a fence-like structure called "Hana." The frame is covered with a thick piece of felt, fastened from the outside of the yurt with ropes. The felt strip is usually white with the decoration of red, blue, yellow or another color cloth, plus an opening on top to provide both light and ventilation. Typically, a yurt is 3 to 5 meters high, with the wooden door usually facing south or southeast. Mostly every yurt is equipped with a bare stick called "Jiebang" which was believed to belong to Suwu, an envoy of the Han dynasty who was honored by people for his high morality. The Jiebang is the symbol of power and morality in ancient China, which is worshipped by Mongolians and strangers are not allowed to get close to it.

Mongolian yurt is the product of their nomadic lifestyle because they need to move about for new water sources and pastures. The yurt is practical for its portability and disassembly. Besides, it is free from snow or water accumulation due to its domed pattern, and the structure can also withstand storms. All in all, the thick felt can be adjusted according to the temperature, and the bottom of the felt can be rolled up for ventilation②.

②*Diaofang*/Stone Chamber of Tibetans

Stone chambers are the most common residence of Tibetans, which existed before 111 A. D. according to the historical record. The structure is constructed with stone and earth to the height of two to three storeys, giving its name of *Diaofang* for it truly resembles *diaolou*, a blockhouse. The origin of its name can

---

① http://www. foreignercn. com/index. php? option = com_ content&view = article&id = 5128：chinese-civilian-residence&catid = 1：history-and-culture&Itemid = 114

② http://www. chinaculture. org/gb/en_ curiosity/2003 – 09/24/content_ 29639. htm

Figure 4 – 4   Yurts of Mongolians

be dated to 1736 in Emperor *Qianlong's* reign of the Qing dynasty.

The stone chambers are built compactly with multiple storeys due to the mountainous environmental limitation of the Qinghai-Tibet Plateau. The houses are also equipped with skylights and ventilation outlets, with the interior being elaborately decorated and the exterior being grand and powerful.

The first floor is reserved for livestock and poultry, the second served as bedrooms, living rooms, kitchen etc. If there is a third floor, it is usually used as family sutra hall or the balcony.

The stone house features the integration of wood and stonewalls, adding prominence to artistic beauty. In addition, the building is substantially solid to combat earthquakes and prevent heat outflow[1].

Figure 4 – 5   Stone Chamber of Tibetans

[1]　http: //www1. chinaculture. org/library/2008 – 01/16/content_ 38974. htm

③Bamboo Buildings of Dai Ethnics

The bamboo house of Dai people is of stilt style, with bamboo used as the major material as its name reveals. The people living in the house is a branch of Dai ethnic minority named *shuidai* (Water Dai people), who chiefly distributed in Xishuangbanna, and Ruili of Dehong Prefecture. They mostly live in the river valleys featuring low terrain and substantial rainfall. The stilt style building is capable of avoiding insects, snakes and beasts; meanwhile, they are damp-proof and well ventilated. As a result, the bamboo building that is built by taking the local materials becomes the main form of folk houses of the Water Dai people.

Bamboo, the local handy material, is largely applied in the building construction, taken as the purlin, rafter, floor, wall, ladder, handrail and so on. Wood is used as the framework, and the roof is laid with grass or tile. Unlike the closed courtyard of the Han nationality, which is characterized by symmetry and compact form; the bamboo building is spacious with flexible layout. Generally, the house consists of a hall, individual rooms, the front corridor and terrace in the upstairs and staircase as well as the stilt layer in the downstairs. In the hall, there is a fireplace which is regarded as the center of the building. Having been passed down from the ancestors, the fire is supposed to be on unceasingly. Besides the spiritual function, the fireplace is used for cooking or drying clothes. People always surround by the side to enjoy the family time together. The roof is cap-shaped, named after Kongming, a historical legendary strategist in the period of Three Kingdoms since it was him to instruct the locals to build the house. Every building contains a small yard with tropical plants cultivated inside. In the hot days, the main house is extended with a circle of exterior columns to prevent extreme heat. Windows are also opened for the air circulation.

The bamboo building is commonly single building for small family since it is their custom of youngest son inheritance system, with the older sons and daughters living separately with their parents. Structurally the number of wooden pillars in the floor of the building is a reflection of the scale and size of the building, and the big ones can have up to seventy to eighty pillars.

The Water Dai villages are usually located in the hilly countryside. The locals believe in Buddhism, so many Buddhist temples are built in the area. But according to the custom, folk houses cannot be constructed in the neighborhood, particularly not opposite to the temples. Besides, the height of the house should not surpass the plane of seat stand of Buddha statue. To sum up, the construction of the bamboo building is profoundly affected by Buddhist culture. [①].

Figure 4 – 6   Bamboo Buildings of Dai Ethnics

④Mushroom House of Hani Nationality

Hani Nationality traditionally resides on the mountainside facing to the sun and forms their villages along the mountain. Usually approximately 30 to 40 households live in a village, several hundred households at most. The houses of the Hani Nationality are scattered along the sloping area, disorderly with various heights, forming a simple and pure picture.

Hani people used to live in the cave with substantial inconvenience. Later on, they moved to Reluo, a place full of huge mushrooms, which not only resist wind and rain, but also offer shelter for ants and other insects. The people

①   http: //traditions. cultural-china. com/en/124Traditions260. html

Figure 4 – 7   Mushroom House of Hani Nationality

got the inspiration and started to build mushroom house, with the Malizai in Yuanyang County, Honghe State being the largest village of Hani Nationality.

The mushroom house of the Hani Nationality consists of soil foundation wall, bamboo and wood frame and couch grass roof. The house is composed of several layers with four slopes of roof: the lowest layer is to feed cattle and to store agricultural tools; the middle layer of wood board usually contains three rooms. In the middle there is a square fire pond with fire all the year around; the top layer is covered with fire-proofing soil for articles storage.

Soils and stones are the main materials of the mushroom house, the roof being two types: the flat one for Tuzhang house and double-side-slope or four-side-slope roof for couch grass house. The former is more common since it is fire-proofing and convenient for grain drying[①].

⑤Stilt Houses of Tujia, Miao, Yao and Dong Nationalities

Many ethnic groups such as Tujia, Miao, Yao and Dong etc live in the west part of Hunan Province, China, which is characterized by the chain of mountains, weaving rivers and thick forests. The special geography give rises to the characteristic Xiangxi (the west area of Hunan Province) stilt house.

---

① http: //traditions. cultural-china. com/en/124Traditions2097. html

Figure 4 – 8   Stilt Houses of Tujia, Miao, Yao and Dong Nationalities

The stilt house (Diaojiao House) is typically built along the river or in steep mountain areas, which is usually classified into two sections: the front and the rear part. The former is a storied building built on the ground, resembling the fence-style building; while the latter is a bungalow. Wood balusters corridor of one meter high is built in front of the house, with suspended windows equipped in the house for rest and cool. The space of the stilt house is arranged facilely in various shapes. The stilt house takes advantage of hillside or river, which was primarily inconvenient for house construction, with other positive functions such as good ventilation, moisture-proof, and wild animal defense.

Furthermore, different ethnic group culture bestows the stilt house with diverse cultural connotations. For instance, the stilt house of Tujia ethnic minority emphasizes the coexistence of human and God whereas the Dong people prefer an elaborate environment, carving the chapiters into bamboo shape and adding flower patterns on the banisters of the corridor[1].

① http://traditions. cultural-china. com/en/124Traditions111. html

3. Western Residential Customs

As previously mentioned, dwelling is one of the fundamental living modes of human beings, its custom representing the combination of material and spiritual culture. Therefore, western vernacular architectures own their distinct characteristics.

(1) Mediterranean Style

A Mediterranean style house refers to the house styles of countries that border the Mediterranean sea, particularly Italy and Greece and Spain. A couple of typical features help to represent the type, with landscaping and interior decoration being added to the overall style.

A Mediterranean style house is characterized by large windows, columns and high archways, usually no higher than two stories. The declining eaves of the roof line made an overhang, providing shade in hot days. Inviting the outdoors inside is a part of the design structure. Interior courtyards, verandas and balconies are common and practical since Mediterranean climate is mostly mild and warm. As far as artwork is concerned, many houses favor frescoes or large wall murals of natural scenes. Considering the characteristic weather, the interiors always prefer cool colors, such as blue, green, grey, and white, etc.

As to Landscaping, there are a wide variety of choices. Everything from formal Italian gardens with hedges and fountains to Moorish-influenced Spanish gardens can be used to add beauty to this type of design. In addition, tropical landscaping, coupled with palm trees, large ferns, and exotic flowers, gain particular popularity in is a modern Mediterranean house[1].

(2) Tuscan Style

Tuscan design represents the romance and aesthetics of Tuscany, Italy. No matter in the terms of a rustic farm house or a grand villa, a Tuscan style house

---

[1] http://www. wisegeek. com/what-is-a-mediterranean-style-house. htm

usually is unique in the following aspects, namely architecture, building materials, interior design, and landscaping.

A Tuscan style house is typically covered with white, gray, or tan stucco, together with gently sloping roofs of terracotta tiles. Elongated arches feature the house as well, making the style of the house easily recognizable.

For materials, they are utilized locally, such as natural stone and wood. Marble, travertine, and terracotta are various tiles to build floors and roofs. As to colors, the Tuscan style is characteristic of earth tones such as gold, tan, rust, and sage green. Furniture range from house to house, with some people preferring pieces that feature Italian Renaissance design, while others like weathered, simple ones to create a farmhouse-style aesthetic. Besides, wrought iron, an essential part, is often applied in the use of dividing screens, fireplace accoutrements, lamps or even metalwork dining sets.

Artwork complements Tuscan style as well. Works by famous Italian painters such as Michelangelo or Leonardo da Vinci make elaborate and tonally appropriate displays. Murals and trompe l'oeil paintings are also quite common in Tuscan design.

Typical gardens make the style even recognizable, complete with fountains, flagstaff paths, and statuary, embodying the peace and passion of Italy. Plants like herbs, climbing roses, and Mediterranean plants of all kinds. are commonly seen. Besides, Terracotta planters, benches, plus wishing wells can be incorporated into the garden①.

(3) French Style

French architecture appeals to people with its distinctive characteristics, which consists of asymmetrical exteriors with the integration of ornamental attributes. The typical features are: Stucco and brick exterior; steep roof pitches or curved roof pitches at varying heights. These houses usually have two stories with high rooflines with large chimneys, sloped at the base. Meanwhile, its varia-

---

① http: //www. wisegeek. com/what-is-a-tuscan-style-house. htm

tions can be symmetrical style with steep hipped roofs, applying siding, shakes or other materials as the exteriors.

Finding its root in the rural French countryside, the French Country style can be both modest farmhouse designs and estate-like chateaus, representing a rustic warmth and comfort with the elements of curved arches, soft lines and stonework. The common interiors are wood beams, plaster walls and stone floors.

The French Country style is the combination of old world elegance and comfortable interiors. Old and new, formal and informal elements are mixed in houses ranging from humble cottages and farmhouses to grand chateaus since each province has its own characteristics, reflecting a wealth of diversity.

All in all, typical elements comprise tall and thin windows, often with slat-board shutters, steep roofs, various gables, and multiple arches (windows, shutters garage openings and entries). Stucco and stone are usually employed, trimmed with painted timbers, windows boxes, wrought iron railings and brick highlights surrounding windows and doors[1].

(4) British Style

The diversity of Britain building types can be defined geologically, with the splendor of the Cotswolds being the most significant, for this region is set almost entirely on durable limestone, which, due to impurities in the rock, comes in many colors, with mellow yellow being particularly representative of the Cotswolds.

Located in Southern Central England, the Cotswolds are branded as the English idyll. Large areas of waving countryside are dotted with picturesque villages to form the extraordinary natural beauty, with manor houses, churches, cottages and barns, all being alike in style.

The Cotswold architecture is believed to be inspired by Tudor ideals, a legacy from the 16th century when the British economy was overwhelmed with

---

① http://www. aventerraestates. com/idea/modules/Topic/Topicitem. aspx? DocID = 483&Page ID = 328 the wool industry. As a reflection of its former influence and wealth, the land-scape of the Cotswolds was perfectly constructed by such enterprise and those who made their fortune, gaining recognition throughout the world and enjoying a long-established reputation for its well-built stone buildings.

Characterized by stone roofs, coupled with dormer windows, steep gables and a brick or stone chimney, the Cotswolds house tends to possess irregularly shaped rooms and sloping walls on their upper floors, other remarkable features being the heavy mullioned windows, drip moldings, low doors and the detailed carvings.

Stone roofs are seen in abundance, even on the most modest of properties, with the possible history of over 200 years if kept in good condition. A wooden peg fixes the thick tiles to the roof, which is driven through a hole at the top of each slate, with the weight being supported by oak beams in the roof.

Meanwhile, brick-built buildings are the indispensable part of Britain's landscape. From rows of tiny terraced houses to larger more buildings, brick has been widely used across the centuries. It is said that the earliest bricks were made by the Celts. Then the Romans arrived, providing considerable expertise to produce a brick of higher quality, but unfortunately this knowledge vanished with their departure in the fifth century. Thanks to the close trading contacts be-tween towns in Eastern England and the Continent, the Britons saw techniques of brick making and laying revived in the 13th century, which was brought from Holland, Northern Germany and Flanders.

Statue Bricks, a smaller kind that conveniently fit a man's hand was then introduced by Flemish immigrant craftsmen. The color of the brick is determined by the local clay: a clay with little iron but plenty of lime resulted in the white bricks of Sussex and East Anglia, while a clay with a high iron content pro-duced the red color found in Lancashire and Staffordshire.

Besides geography, fashion was crucial as well to determining the color of the brick, which changed from time to time. For instance, during the Tudor years, red brick was favored, however by the Georgian period the preference had altered towards a brown or pinkish grey stock. This was, in turn, replaced at the end of the Georgian era, by London stocks (a yellow marl or malm).

But with the arrival of the Victorians, the trend for red brickwork returned.

On one hand, bricklayers were increasingly appearing as crafts; on the other hand, after the Great Fire of London in 1666, King Charles II's ordered the walls of all new buildings be constructed of brick or stone, leading to the greater popularity of brick. Indeed, it wasn't rare for timber-framed houses to be encompassed in a skin of brickwork[①].

(5) German Style

Conventional German homes feature a steeply pitched roof above a light-colored wall which turns to half by its exposed dark-timber frame. Timber framing was typically put into building practice during the 13th century, with Gothic architecture rising to prominence. One of the long-history half-timbered houses is built in Quedlinburg, which was in the vertical beam style, an implication of a beam runs all the way from the threshold up to the roof. Half-timber architecture remained common for household in towns from the end of the Middle Ages and into the Renaissance while, in the country, half-timbered construction continued into the 20th century.

Gaining popularity into the 19th century, the Hallenhaus (Hall House) is still widely seen in northern Germany, gaining its name from the wide central hallway which possesses the function to divide one side of the home from the other. Characterized as a type of Einhaus and known by several other names, it is primarily an all-in-one house. This usual home of farmers contained living quarters for both the family and the animals, along with hay stored in the home, which is a combination of a home and a barn. Meanwhile, the hallway can function as a threshing floor, and its doors were large enough for a wagon. As was representative of German homes, the walls were timber-framed, with bricks or wattle and daub, which was thatched and supported by wooden posts inside the house.

---

① http: //www. google. co. jp/url? url = http: //www. dhow. co. uk/eva. pdf&rct = j&frm = 1&q = &esrc = s&sa = U&ei = woZdVeKFEeHtmQWWmoHgAg&ved = 0CBoQFjAB&usg = AFQjCNFPg8m RomukPXYZ-SdL1upS_ xT6Tg

Besides, Middle German house is common in central Germany, in which farm families and their animals live together. Likewise, the living area is separated from the work area by a hall containing the cooking area with one of the two fireplaces, the other being in the main living area. The major difference between the Middle German house and the Low lies in the supported roof, the former being held up by the outer walls. The earliest Middle German homes used to have only one story, but two-story homes became popular around the 15th century. Two centuries later, exterior features became increasingly decorative and larger farms were improved by adding outbuildings around a mutual farmyard to achieve the function of separating people's living quarters from animals'.

Entering the modern society, the nation witnessed the construction of considerable Wohnsilos, the tall and usually Spartan-looking apartment towers, to provide housing to citizens since it is a comparatively densely-populated European country. Unlike the charm of traditional European architecture, these living units most often resemble the ordinary condos and apartments all over Europe and the world. Built to tackle the problem of a chronic shortage of housing, these towers are usually constructed in what are called "satellite towns" in the suburb[①].

4. Comparisons

The fundamental differences between Chinese and western vernacular architecture is culturally determined, which reflects the contrast in natural environment, social structure, psychological mode and aesthetic value.

(1) Building Materials

The first distinction should be on the building materials. In ancient times, Chinese architects used wood as the main building materials while Westerners prefer stones. Several reasons contribute to the difference:

The primitive economy in the west is characteristic of hunting, generating

---

① http: //german. answers. com/architecture/architecture-of-traditional-german-homes

westerns' emphasis on the " objects " . With affirmation to stones, westerners tend to seek rational spirit of truth, believing that human beings are the masters of the world to conquer the nature with intelligence and wisdom. However, the primitive agriculture has taken dominant places in ancient China, producing a population who value collection and storage. Therefore, the consequent Chinese traditional philosophy advocates the unity of man and nature, a belief that viewing nature and people as an integrity. Chinese prefer timber as the constructing material because it is representative of life compared with cold stones.

The origins of western civilization are two: ancient Greek civilization and the Christianity civilization in the Middle East. The former gives birth to a bunch of gods with different desires, particularly, God of wine named Dionysus, the symbol of hedonism and individualism. The spirits is tightly associated with harvest and abundance, breeding a parade of people who are joyous and optimistic. Furthermore, democracy and science which are derived from ancient Greece, coupled with the govern of law constitute the foundation of modern society. On the other hand, the Christianity civilization features in culture of original sin and contract, adjusting the relationship between man and society which rectifies the indulgence spirit to a certain degree. To sum up, western culture admires the stone-like characters of being blunt, plain, tough and grand.

Contrarily, Confucianism possesses substantial influence on Chinese, the philosophy stresses modesty, forgiveness and loyalty. With importance attached to self-discipline, the idea highlights inner regulation between the society and individuality. Accordingly, Chinese are well-known for being tolerant and tenacious. What's more, with Buddhism and Taoism serving as supplements to Confucianism, Chinese ideology appreciates the timber-like characters of delicacy and perseverance.

(2) Layout Design

Spatially speaking, Chinese residence tends to be closed, spreading to the ground, the representative being "Siheyuan". With different rooms assigned hierarchically, patriarchal clan system and moral codes are highly valued in China. In contrast, western residence is open, extending towards high altitude. Besides, colonnades, doors and windows are widely used in buildings of city-states in ancient Greece and ancient Rome to enhance the transparency. Therefore, Chinese enclosure culture is enclosed and reserved while western's is spacious and bright.

The difference in layout mirrors the discrepancy of institution and core value between the west and east. For the former, the extroversion and scientific democracy of Ancient Greek not only affected the ancient Rome, but also affected the entire western world. However, the supremacy of imperial power and the ethical order of the feudal society exerted huge impact on Chinese. As to the latter, the western civilization originated from Greece is the adventurous maritime civilization which is full of commercialism, the typical marine adventurers being Odysseus and Jason. Besides, the recorded continuous migration of Jaws in Egypt and Babylon in Bible and Medieval Knight Guerrilla both influenced the western civilization. Later on, the exploration of Magellan and Columbus changed the whole world history. The superpower in the west, The United States, was founded by a group of European adventurers. All in all, western civilization is expansionary.

However, Chinese civilization equals to the loess civilization, the agricultural civilization. Chinese are attached to their native land and unwilling to leave their homeland, the provider of food, clothing, and the ancestral clan. Clinging to sayings such as "When your parents are alive, do not travel far" and "Return to the hometown when one gets old", therefore, Chinese civilization is highly convergent.

(3) Aesthetic Standards

The geomantic culture and the theory of the five natural elements—earth, water, fire, metal, and wood are very popular in Chinese traditional architecture while Western architects care much about aesthetic geometry in their architecture. To put it another way, Chinese traditional architecture seeks the beauty of nature, while Western architecture prefers to advocate artificial beauty. The main reasons for such kind of distinction are the different aesthetic standards and value concepts between Chinese people and Western people. Traditional Chinese people believe in the idea of nature-human integration. In Chinese culture, a harmonious relationship between men and nature is advocated. As for Western people, they prefer individualism which cares much about the individual. Thus the Western buildings tend to be detached patterns while most Chinese traditional buildings are aggregate patterns.

Chapter Five

Customs of Birth

1. General Introduction

Cultural traditions related to new born vary globally. From the prepregnancy period to the birth of the new child all rituals differ from culture to culture with deep meanings hidden behind. A new child brings lots of hope and joy not only to the parents, but also to the family and society So different culture welcomes their new born differently.

Usually the birth custom consists of two sections: pregnancy and birth of children.

(1) Pregnancy

Two of the most significant event in people's life are marriage and child birth, particularly in ancient times. Two reasons account for people's attachment for families. Firstly, without adequate medicare or pension plan, people have no choice but to rely on their adult children to tender them when they age. In Ancient Egyptian, the euphemism for an eldest son is the staff of old age. With no son to take care of them, the seniors were in great trouble. The second reason was more important, which is the need for population increase in the pre-industrial societies since more children, especially sons, stand for more labor. Therefore, the large number of offspring increases the chance of more wealth and prosperity for the whole family, resulting in people's preference for children production.

①Ancient Tests of Getting Pregnant

Ancient Egyptians, due to the lack of the knowledge in anatomy and physiology, failed to explain why some women could get pregnant but some others could not. But generally it was believed that females with wide hips and big, firm breasts would be easy to get pregnant than those who are unluckily less endowed with the features. Besides, they adopted a certain test to measure a woman's ability to be in pregnancy by placing a clove of garlic or an onion in her vagina. If the strong smell could be detected on her breath the following morning, the woman would be considered fertile since it was believed, at that time, that the three channels of a healthy person, namely the alimentary canal, the anal canal and the uterus all were linked together and opened into the belly. If the case was opposite, that the odor did not pass from the vagina to the mouth, there must be a blockage and pregnancy would be out of the question. Interestingly, the ancient Greeks believed the same thing and share the similar practice.

Another test was to apply new oil to a woman's breasts and shoulders when she lay down. If her blood vessels were "fresh and good, none being collapsed" in the following morning, then she will be capable of children production, following the logic that "if she looks healthy then she can deliver."

In addition to knowing whether a woman is capable of conceiving, it was even more significant to know if a person was pregnant or not.

Compared with knowing if a woman could conceive, it was even more important to know if she was pregnant, the common test being keeping emmer wheat and barley seeds moistened with a woman's urine. Seeds sprout is the indication of pregnancy, which has been proved to be fairly accurate. If the barley sprouts first, the child was believed to be male; otherwise the female. But chances that it worked was only 50%.

Another test was to give a woman some crushed melon together with the milk of a mother who had a baby boy. If she got sick after consuming the concoction, then she was pregnant. But this test had been proved to be unreliable.

Placing a date in the vagina was regarded as a cure for sterility. Rubbing the belly and thighs with menstrual blood was believed to be workable as well, which was viewed as a particularly potent force and was applied in various situations. Besides, the long-leafed cos or romaine lettuce with its milky, white juice reminiscent of semen was helpful to improve potency in both males and females[1].

②Strange Pregnancy Traditions

Numerous traditions arise concerning women's pregnancy since the family all wish the birth of a healthy baby which have nothing to do with medicine but turn out to be prejudices and finally became part of local culture.

Japanese consider that a pregnant woman should avoid spicy or salty food. Raw fish is not allowed in the diet. The people in Japan also think it a taboo for pregnant women to look at fire to avoid the birthmarks on baby's body.

In Mongolia, it is interesting that when two pregnant women meet, they are forbidden to touch each other; otherwise the baby's sex can be changed that way. People avoid mentioning the baby's sex straightly until the child is three months or in some cases even over one year old for the belief that people will confuse evil spirits by doing so.

In Akamba, Kenya, a pregnant woman should never see a deceased body since spirit of the dead can impose a threat to pregnancy.

In Jamaica, it is said that plentiful milk consumption of a pregnant women will result in the lighter complexion of the baby. Another popular belief concerns oranges. It is said that failing to meet the desire of eating oranges may generate the orange-shaped birth mark on babies. Interestingly Mexicans share the similar belief but it involves strawberries.

In Mexico an ancient belief of Aztec origin also prevails. An eclipse will threaten a pregnant mother whose baby might suffer a cleft lip. It is necessary for her to carry a key or safety pin to protect her baby[2].

(2) Birth of Children
①Birth Celebration

The birth of a new baby is one of the greatest excitement around the world.

---

① http：//www. womenintheancientworld. com/pregnancy%20and%20childbirth. htm

② http：//traditionscustoms. com/lifestyle/strange-pregnancy-traditions

And it is the occasion when families and communities come together to honor the new angel. The naming of the new born is a serious matter. For instance, Tibetans do not name their baby until after all the birth rituals. Only a few people have the naming privilege, such as a living Buddha, the parents or the most prestigious senior of the community. In Jewish tradition, the female child is named on the first Sabbath from the day she is born, and baby boy is named after the 8th day of the birth. Most unusual one is that of Germany where parents have no choice but to follow the list of government-approved names, for the purpose of avoiding any mockery or hardship deriving from an uncommon name.

Other rituals that mark a child's survival are various as well. For instance, in the United States, baptism and male circumcision are popular baby traditions. Generally, for parents birth rituals and ceremonies not only provide an immediate sense of connection but also create a bond between the child and the tribe or community.

In Indonesia, a 90 minute massage is a routine to a child and mother for at least a month. While in Japan, the families have the tradition to reserve the umbilical cord of the baby in a wooden box for a life time to represent mother and child's relationship. In most of the African countries, it is conventional to bury the placenta under a tree, which is regarded as a dead twin of the living child and people practice respectfully all death rites.

In Ireland, the top tier of the wedding whiskey cake is reserved till the christening ritual of their first child. On the day, the couples apply the cake crumbs to the head of the baby to mark the circle of human life. Another tradition is that Irish bride carries a handkerchief on her wedding day and later it is changed into a bonnet for the new baby on the eve of christening.

A custom in Balinese is that the baby's feet are not allowed to touch the floor for the first six months to ensure good health and prospects for the new born. Therefore, during this period, mother and other family members keep close attention to the child just to see to it that the baby does not contact the ground even by accident.

In addition, in many cultures cutting off the baby's hair is a common practice, especially in Hinduism and Islam ceremonies. In Islam it is conducted as a ritual called Aqeeqah in which the hair is shaved, and an equal amount of either gold or silver is collected to someone needy, a manner to show gratitude to Allah for blessing the parents with a child. Generally the ceremony is practiced after seven days of the child's birth. Then a big get-together is held, with the sacrifice of an animal like goat or buffalo after the charity[1].

②Birthday Celebration

Celebrating birthdays is an important tradition all over the world.

In Vietnam, people celebrate their birthdays on new year's day, or *Tet*. A baby turns one year old on *Tet* no matter when he/she was born that year. On the first morning of the festival, adults congratulate children on becoming a year older by giving them red envelopes, or "Lucky Money".

In Brazil, children like to eat fruit-shaped or vegetable-shaped candies to celebrate birthdays. The houses are particularly decorated for the occasion with banners and paper flowers with multiple colors. The earlobes of the birthday boys or girls will be pulled to mark this special day.

In Israel, to celebrate the occasion, the birthday person wears a crown of leaves or flowers and sits in a chair decorated in streamers. Guests dance and sing around the chair, with the parents lifting the chair while the child sits in it with joy.

In India children are supposed to wear new clothes on their birthday. After getting up, the child gets dressed in new clothes before kneels and touches the feet of their parents to demonstrate his or her respect. Then they all visit a shrine to pray and have the child blessed. In the afternoon a meal is served including a spicy vegetable stew called curry and chutney. Afterwards a dessert known as *dudh pakh*, a rice pudding is presented. It might also be added with pistachios, almonds, raisins, and a spice called cardamom. It is a taboo to offer a birthday present wrapped in black and white which symbols bad luck[2].

---

① http://listdose.com/top-10-rituals-performed-worldwide-newborn/

② https://www.listplanit.com/2011/07/list-of-birthday-traditions-from-around-the-world/

2. Chinese Birth Customs

For the Chinese, the family is regarded as the primary unit of society. A birth within the family therefore holds special significance for the community and is associated with a number of birth rituals, all directing at praying blessing for a new born baby and driving evil spirits away from the mother.

(1) Birth Customs of Han Nationality

①Pre-natal Birth Rituals

As an agricultural country, Chinese families have long favored sons over daughters, therefore, rituals of praying for a son has been prevailing among people. Firstly, people would offer sacrifice to Gods who are in charge of child-bearing, the most popular being Guan Yin, praying for the birth of a son. Further more, the expecting mothers would consume food considered to foster pregnancy such as red painted eggs, lettuce and taro. Finally, people have the custom to pray for a son by giving out items such as lantern, clay doll and kylin basin, the symbols standing for omen for the arrival of a son.

Then, once the pregnancy confirmation is made, pre-natal birth observances are followed concerning both rituals of avoidance and protection, which are based on the belief that the foetus should be nurtured with care and protected from evil impacts to ensure its future well-being.

● Rituals of Avoidance

Many rituals of avoidance are connected with the concept that the position of the foetus should not be disturbed in any way and that any ignorance might bring in dangers such as a difficult birth, miscarriage or injury to the child. Expectant mothers are therefore totally discouraged from actions such as furniture movement or house renovation. Furthermore, they are supposed to avoid activities like digging, slaughtering, hammering and they should keep themselves away from unsightly images. Finally, expectant mothers are not allowed to utter words that are viewed as taboo or disrespectful to the deities and spirits.

Other practices involving the rituals of avoidance include the exclusion of certain types of food that are considered to pose a threat to baby's health. Pregnant Cantonese women should not take in mutton as the Cantonese pronunciation for the meat is the same as the word for epilepsy. Hokkien mothers avoid eating crabs, which they believe may produce a naughty and restless child just like the crab with many "hands". Cooling foods are seldom touched since they have the negative physical effect, particularly weakening the womb.

Actually, there are many ancient food taboos during pregnancy. It's believed that if a pregnant woman usually takes in food cut or mashed randomly, her child will be careless in the future. Or if she prefers light colored foods, chances are that the baby will be fair-skinned. It is also believed that no construction work should be conducted in the house of a pregnant woman, which could lead to severe effect such as an abortion or fetal deformities. Plus, pregnant women are not allowed to attend funerals to avoid the attention of the evil spirits. And to scare away the dirty and filthy evils, Chinese women may sleep with knives under their bed. In some places, a piece of paper cut scissors is hung from bed curtains and tiger skins are hung over the bed.

• Rituals of Protection

Fetus protection is performed to ensure the safety of mother and fetus during the pregnancy. Therefore, diet is placed as the priority for an expectant woman in the prenatal education. Nutritious food such as meat soup, glutinous oil rice, vegetables and fruit are mostly favored. To secure good effect of prenatal education, pregnant woman should keep herself in good attitude and mood, and stay in peace and harmony.

Another ritual of protection commonly practiced by Chinese families is the offering of sacrifice to the Chinese goddesses Bodhisattva Guan Yin (Goddess of Mercy) and Jin Hua Fu Ren (Lady Golden Flower) to pray for the well-being of both mother and child.

Many consider it impropriate to throw a shower for a baby in advance. In China, the parties come after the little one is born. The pregnant mother's own mother is supposed to buy the child's entire layette. Just a month before the baby's birth, the maternal grandmother sends a package of baby's clothing, including a white cloth to wrap the child, for her expectant daughter to hasten the delivery, or called *tsue sheng*. After the baby's birth, the maternal grandmother should not visit immediately but to wait for three days.

②Birth Rituals

The birth of alife is usually followed by the following customary rituals:

• Three Mornings

"Three mornings" is the birth ceremony held on the third morning after a baby is born. Parents send red eggs to close family and friends—an even number for a girl, odd for a boy. Or they may send out boxes of fruit. Return gifts might include two kinds of cake, brown sugar, millet, eggs, and walnut meats. Later, a ceremony of baby bath is performed, and the baby bathed in warm water with herbal medicine, a blessing to drive off evil spirits.

• Birthday Horoscopes

According to Chinese custom, the birth time of the child is born matters greatly. The hour, day, month and year the baby is born is associated with the baby's Eight Characters, which are believed to be important to dominate the child's life. They foretell whether a newly-born will be successful, wealthy, or blessed with good fortune when he grows up. Parents may also hire fortune tellers to read their baby's fortune. The Chinese traditionally believe that each person is composed of some of the five elements-metal, wood, water, fire, and earth. Once a fortune teller diagnoses a child is lacking an element according to its birthday, the missing element is needed to be incorporated in her name-for instance, if a baby lacks metal, then the words contain metal literarily or formally are preferred in the name to supplement the shortcoming. But if water or fire is absent, the parents are free of worry since that is considered a good omen. If a child is born with excessive fire, he could be harmed by fire in his life; likewise, a child with too much water needs to be carefully watched, for she might suffer drowning.

• Choice of Names

Usually, the Chinese wouldn't think of naming a baby before its birth. Instead, false names or milk names are given to trick the evil spirits. According to ancient tradition, parents refer to their children as a humble animal or as something ugly to deceive the spirits into believing the baby is unworthy of a kidnapping. When the child grows older, he is officially named. Besides, the Chinese often value family bonds by adopting generational names.

● First Month Confinement

Chinese women have the tradition to "sit the month." after delivery since the first month is regarded as of primary importance for new mother. She is freed from household burdens and simply lies in bed to rest and feed the infant, which is beneficial to her recuperation. Certain foods, in particular boiled pig's trotters, are encouraged to be consumed which are believed to help the mother regain her strength, regulate her body and dispel air from the womb, contributing thoroughly to her quick recovery. Furthermore, she is forbidden to take a bath as the Chinese believe that this causes "wind" to enter the body, resulting in lifelong harm to the mother's physical health.

Customarily, Chinese mothers may perform some ancient practice for the future physical development of the children. For instance, baby's pillow is filled with rice or beans to ensure the proper shape of the baby's head. And to facilitate a firm step, Chinese mothers once tied their child's ankles loosely with a ribbon for the purpose of keeping the feet in upright positions. It was believed that infants are pure enough to see the evil spirits unseen by the adults. Particularly, if they were nervous and restless, they might be frightened by the evils. To protect these children, Chinese mothers placed small amounts of vermilion in red pouches and pinned them to the child's clothing. Or parents chose to tie golden bells on the child's wrists and ankles to keep away the bad spirits. For a rich, healthy life, the Chinese would also tie coins together with a red strings for their children to wear, implying the longevity of 100 years old. When a baby is born weak, which might be the symbol of spirits' company, the parents may ask friends for bits of cloth to sew into a patchwork coat, disguising the child as a poor beggar so as to trick the sprits. During times that epidemic or contagious illness prevailed, mothers protected their children by stitching red cloth in their clothing. And since tigers are viewed as the protector against demons, many Chinese children will have embroidered tigers on their shoes.

● First Month Celebrations

The Chinese consider the completion of the full 30 days since birth a milestone for the child. While the time scale of celebration may be different, most families would prefer to celebrate the 30th day of the baby's birth.

The Chinese word *Manyue* or "a complete month" celebrations suggest the official commencement of the child's social life and therefore his future well-being and success are the top concerns of the celebrations. The core belief is that these goals are reachable only if the proper words are uttered, the right behavior conducted and the necessary ritual symbols applied.

For the mother, the celebration of the baby's first month is also significant, which means she is allowed to take bath and wash hair. Usually the baby's hair is shaved as a routine ritual. In addition, the baby would be dressed up in new clothes, particularly in red, decorated with gold accessories for the celebration of this occasion.

For families worshipping Buddha and Tao, incense is burned and food offerings are made, a ritual to inform the ancestors of the new family member, and appealing to the spirits for child protection.

Gifts distributed during the *Manyue* celebrations vary regionally but red eggs are essential as a symbol of fertility and the life renewal cycle whose shape is traditionally related with harmony and unity. In old agricultural society in China, the egg was regarded a delicacy, merely to be consumed on grand occasions such as festivals.

Other typical food include cakes, chicken, savory glutinous rice and pig trotters. The food recipients in turn are supposed to present gifts to the newborn baby, which are in the form of gold bangles, chains and usually money in red packets. Gold jewelry is a popular gift among grandparents which is viewed as the most highly prized metal for the Chinese.

Modern *Manyue* celebrations always are performed in restaurants in the form of a dinner. In Guangdong, the restaurants prepare the red eggs and pickled ginger to guests when they arrive. Pickled ginger is preferable because the Cantonese word for sour bears the similar pronunciation as the word for grandson, with families hoping for the arrival of more grandsons[1].

● First Birthday Celebrations

A child's first birthday is a huge event which be celebrated on either the lunar calendar or the solar calendar. Usually, the parents will put on a big banquet for family and friends.

Zhuazhou or "Drawing lots" is the most interesting and important traditional custom, which can be dated back to the Three Kingdoms period. On a child's first birthday anniversary in China, it is a ritual in which the child future is expected to be foretold. During the ceremony, parents place a bunch of items in front of their child, who choose randomly from the articles. What the child has chosen is said to reveal its future characteristic and career preference.

The traditional items for the baby to choose from possess different symbolic meanings: a Chinese brush pen, ink, paper, an ink stone all stands for a future scholar, an abacus means a future businessman, coins signify a future blessed with fortune. With the progress of times, an abacus is replaced by a calculator, and coins by cash money or credit cards.

Decent gifts for this occasion again include cash in a red envelop as symbols for good luck; toys or clothing featuring tigers which are believed to be guardians of safety in Chinese culture; and eggs which are also dyed red for more good blessings.

To summarize, parents and relatives place substantial hope on the future of their children, with the custom of *Zhuazhou* being a way of expressing their good wishes.

● Other Birthday Celebrations

Traditionally, Chinese view only a few birthdays as important, namely 1st, 10th, 60th, 70th and 80th birthday. The reason why the seniors and the babies receive particular consideration is that in Chinese culture, the elderly are honored with great respect and it's a family's responsibility to preserve the bloodline and ensure the inheritance of the following generations.

In particular, a 60th birthday is the occasion when the astrological cycle of

---

① http: //www. wunrn. com/news/2006/04_ 09_ 06/041506_ china_ ancient. htm

12 animals and the five elements of wood, fire, earth, metal and water come together, making it a significant celebration in Chinese culture. Gifts for Chinese elders are usually articles that symbol longevity, including old miniature trees, wine, packages of long noodles and homemade peaches (which aren't really peaches, but steamed wheat shaped like peaches) and money in red envelopes. These gift items are usually given even numbers. Never present a clock as a birthday gift to a Chinese person, especially the seniors, since its pronunciation resembles the pronunciation of word *death* in Chinese.

In addition to the above mentioned occasions, annual solar or lunar birthdays are supposed to be enjoyed by eating long noodles which indicate long life, and they must be consumed without being cut and with every effort made not to bite them short. However, under the influence of western culture, not many Chinese celebrate birthdays in the traditional way, especially among the youngsters. Instead, they observe annual birthday by arranging a gathering and sharing a birthday cake with the participants.

(2) Birth Customs of Chinese Ethnic Minorities
①Birth Customs of the Lisu Nationality

With a population of more than six hundred thousand residents, the Lisu ethnic minority mainly live in the Nujiang Lisu Autonomous Prefecture in Yunnan Province, with a few in other cities within Yunnan and Sichuan, who possesses close ties with the Yi and Naxi ethnic minorities. Generally speaking, the Lisu women are not traditionally obliged to give up given foods during pregnancy and they deal with their household duties as usual before giving birth to children. When the birth is approaching, the husband calls to his ancestors by their spirit name, sacrificing them with salt, poultry and wine while pleading for their blessing in the safe and sound delivery of the child. Meanwhile, the older women gather at the house, applying a hempen string to tie the cord. When the child is born, it is washed and the news is reported to the ancestors by the attendant priest.

On the third morning after birth, the child gets its "Buried" or Spirit name, a name may be used by the parents for a few occasions during childhood, but which is never spoken as the child grows up. Otherwise, it might cause great offence or even bloodshed from the mouth of a stranger. As the name is given by its parents, the father speaks out the buried name to the ancestors, and it is then rarely used until death when the priests use it to summon the departing spirit, quickening it to its ancestral home.

Both mother and child are bathed on the tenth, twentieth and thirtieth day but neither are allowed to leave home until the last bathing is finished, preventing them from suffering disease. Certain food such as peppers, sour bamboo sprouts, strong liquor or sweets are forbidden to be tasted during this period, and the mother is attended by family members, free from any household chores. When the month is due, a fowl is sacrificed to the ancestral ghost and mother and child enjoy the freedom to enter the village. During the confinement, the birth-bed should not be moved, even the father avoids it; and at the end of the period bed and bedding are either cleansed and purified or are burned and destroyed by fire①.

②Birth Customs of the Hani Nationality

Hani Nationality owns a population of 1, 425, 000 in Yunnan, the offspring of ancient Di-Qiang ethnic group in northwest China. Hani people now mostly inhabit in Ailao Mountain along the Red River, South Yunnan and is a characteristic ethnic group on Yunnan-Guizhou Plateau specializing in growing terraced-field rice. The birth customs of Hani Nationality is interesting. When the child is born, the delivery helper will not hold it in the arm until it has cried three times: the first for a long life span, the second for becoming the member of the whole village and the third as a demand of help. The helper must name it temporarily once she picks it up, otherwise evil spirits will name the child and rob it away, or it will be unlucky to live a short life time, according to a legend that a tiger takes off unnamed babies. After the placenta is delivered, it will be buried in a hole inside the home since many Hani think that they must live in the house where their placenta is buried.

Three days later, a ritual is officially conducted to name the baby in which

---

① http: //traditions. cultural-china. com/en/216Traditions9964. html

the family offers a chicken as the sacrifice to the ancestors. Then the respected elders in the community will give their advice to the child's name. Only one syllable is needed to be chosen since the first syllable will be the second syllable of the father's name. Once the name is settled, the oldest senior holds a cup of liquor to bring immediate blessing to the new born:

"Grow up big. Grow up happily. Be healthy… May you have many domestic animals? May your crops be good…? May the great ancestor Taoqpaoq protect you?"

After two months of isolation, consuming substantial eggs, the mother will recover to her normal life. But still she needs to avoid cold water and must wear the full Hani outfit turban for self-protection①.

③Birth Customs of the Jingpo Nationality

The Jingpo nationality mainly distributes in the Dehong, Dai-Jingpo Autonomous Prefectures with some in the Nujiang Lisu Autonomous Prefecture, as well as in Myanmar. As to its birth tradition, an old woman always helps when a pregnant woman is giving birth. After its first cry, the baby would be held by the woman who cuts the umbilical cordon with a bamboo knife sterilized over the fire. Later on, the cordon and placenta will be wrapped in a bamboo leave and be buried beside one of the posts of the house, ensuring a strong bond between the child and his home. In the following days, ceremonies will be held with seniors taking their important responsibilities. For example, an old man will be invited to bind his wrist with cotton strings: a red string for a boy in his right wrist, and the same color for a girl in her left wrist. This done, an old man will give name to the newborn, an implication that the baby is already a member of the human world, protecting it from the disturbance of evil spirits. Following name giving, a ritual is conducted with the old man carrying dry meat, dry dish, fresh ginger and some fragrant vegetables and uttering the blessings for the newborn.

---

① http://traditions.cultural-china.com/en/216Traditions8972.html

Hka prupru ceremony is the most significant birth ritual celebrated on the seventh day, with an old woman carrying the newborn at her back, coupled with his father's sword. The other woman carries his harpoon. The new mother will get out of the house, washing something together with the two women, an indication of the resumption of her domestic labors. Later on, the family will invite the villagers, with a chicken killed for the feast and wine generously offered. In particular, banana leaves will be used to wrap the food in small portions which are presented to the guests as an announcement of good news. [1].

④Birth Customs of the Tibetans

The child birth is valued significantly in Southwest China's Tibet Autonomous Region as well.

On the third day after a Tibetan boy (the fourth day for a girl) is born, a gathering is held among relatives and friends, with *chang* (highland barley wine), butter tea, and clothes for the newborn as gifts to express congratulations. Upon entering the house, they present *hada* scarves to the baby's parents and then the baby. Then they offer toasts, present gifts, and look at the baby while offering good wishes. Some families throw in a pancake feast to entertain the guests. Most Tibetans favor a large family which symbols vitality.

At the same time, the *Pangse* ceremony is held. *Pang* means "fouls" *and se* is "getting rid of". Tibetans believe newborn babies come to the world with fouls, therefore a ceremony should be conducted to wipe them off for babies' healthy growth and mothers' immediate recovery. Possessing over 1500 years history, such rituals can be originated from a Bon religious god-worshipping ritual.

In the morning, the people pick some white small stones (when the baby is a girl, the choice of the stones can be random) and pile them in front of the family to suggest the birth of a baby. Meanwhile, the people burn pine branches. The guests, to show congratulations, sprinkle tsampa (roasted flour usually mixed with tea) on the stone before entering the host house.

A ritual is held when the baby is one month old on an auspicious day. On

---

① http: //traditions. cultural-china. com/en/216Traditions8975. html

this occasion, both the mother and her child will be newly dressed and go out with the company of their relatives. First, it is a routine for them to go to the temple, praying to the Buddha for longevity for the baby. Sometimes they visit some local lucky family from whom they gain blessing for the baby. When the baby is out for the first time, the people often take some soot from the bottom of a pot and put it on the baby's nose, preventing the devils from detecting the baby.

The newborn baby is not named until the end of the birth rituals. Generally, only a Living Buddha or a prestigious senior villager has the privilege to give a name, chosen from the Buddhism scriptures including some words suggesting happiness or luck. In some cases, however, parents name the baby as well. No matter who does the job, the naming is completed according to the hope of the baby's parents for auspiciousness[1].

3. Western Birth Customs

The ancient people never celebrate birthdays when they are ignorant of the method to mark time. Only when they began paying attention to the moon's cycle and the changing seasons did they begin to be conscious of changing times, which is the origin of birthday celebration.

Eventually, the first calendars were established in order to symbolize time changes and other special occasions. From then on, people began to celebrate birthdays and other significant anniversaries the same day each year. Due to the influence of different factors, birth customs vary from country to country in the west, but still they perform some common activities to mark the occasion of birthday.

(1) A History of Baby Showers

"Baby shower", as the ritual concerning childbirth, has been existed for thousands of years in the west.

---

[1] http: //www. chinaculture. org/gb/en_ focus/2005 − 10/27/content_ 75199. htm

As women throughout history confront the dichotomies (e. g. , life/death, sacred/profane, and biological/social birth) that seem to come into tension particularly during pregnancy and childbirth, they have held rituals and ceremonies that allow them to explore forms of "possible selves," an essential element in rites of passages[1]. Indeed, it is believed that women take the rituals concerning pregnancy and birth as the opportunity to fulfill her dual responsibilities: a mother at home and a woman in the society. In this case, different forms of baby showers in different periods help to build up her new image in the community and for the baby as well.

①Ancient Egypt

Similar to many cultures, both ancient and modern, Egyptian childbirth celebrations was held after the birth. Soon after the infant's arrival, the mother and child in the Old Kingdom were separated often for 14 days. There is also evidence that certain domestic rituals took place after 40 days[2].

Though the nature of these rituals remains uncertain, it was most likely that they would visit temples or local shrines, coupled with the ritualized disposal of the after-birth, such as the umbilical cord and the placenta. Archaeological evidence from the site of the New Kingdom village of Deir el-Medina involves "the festival of so-and-so's" daughter, which may concern a gathering or celebration after the birth during which the baby was given a name to symbolize its identity and relative rights and privileges[3]. These rituals highlighted broader identities and membership in the larger community.

②Ancient Greece

Like the Egyptians, ancient Greeks celebrated the occasion after the child birth. Just soon after the child was born, the mothers and attendants shouted "oloyge" to announce the success of labor and arrival of peace. Having got the umbilical cord cut, the baby, as well as mother, was bathed, though they

---

[1]   Van Gennep, Arnold. The Rites of Passage. Chicago: The University of Chicago Press. 1960.

[2]   Johnston, Sarah Illes. *Religions of the Ancient World: A Guide.* Cambridge: Harvard University of Press. 2004.

[3]   Johnston, Sarah Illes. *Religions of the Ancient World: A Guide.* Cambridge: Harvard University of Press. 2004.

would remain unbathed for another 10 days and their helpers for five days[1].

On the fifth or seventh day after birth, a ceremony named Amphidromia (Running Round) would be held to welcome the newborn. The father would walk around the hearth a couple of times to indicate that the infant had become a member of the family. In a ritual named Dekate (Tenth Day), the mother would return to social normal life by having a meal with her close relatives and friends. Mothers would worship the main birth-goddess Eileithyia, presenting gifts such as girdles, dresses, and other birth related objects[2]. For many women in the ancient times, child birth was the only way for them to guarantee their status in a male-dominated world.

③Middle Ages and Baptism Ceremony

During the Middle Ages, childbirth suffers both physical and spiritual danger. As a matter of fact, a woman would be visited by a priest in the process of delivery so she could confess her sins in case she would die during childbirth. If the misfortune really happens, the midwife got the authorization to cut her open and take out the baby for baptism because, according to Augustine of Hippo, unbaptized infants would go straight to hell[3]. What's more, the pains related with pregnancy and childbirth were unfairly regarded as justifiable due to Pope Innocent III's statement that children were produced in sin and that women were rightfully being punished for Eve's sin.

The baby's baptism ceremony was the only occasion comparable to a baby shower in the Middle Ages on the exact day it was born. The mother was confined for 40 days after the birth and, therefore, was not able to attend the baptism unless it was delayed. The godparents played a significant role as spiritual

---

① Gelis, Jacques. History of Childbirth: Fertility, Pregnancy, and Birth in Early Modern Europe. Trans. Rosemary Morris. Boston: Northeastern University Press. 1991.

② Johnston, Sarah Illes. *Religions of the Ancient World: A Guide.* Cambridge: Harvard University of Press. 2004.

③ Gelis, Jacques. History of Childbirth: Fertility, Pregnancy, and Birth in Early Modern Europe. Trans. Rosemary Morris. Boston: Northeastern University Press. 1991.

tutor and he would give gifts to the child, in particular, a pair of silver spoons[1]. There was some temptation that a child may have many godparents so as to receive many gifts. Therefore, the Church stepped in and set a limitation on the number of godparents a child could have.

④Renaissance

Childbirth was almost a mystery during the Renaissance, but fortunately through private inventories, diaries, and letters we learn that pregnancy and birth were celebrated with a variety of birth objects such as wooden trays, bowls, and majolica wares, painting, sculptures, clothing, linens, and food. Particularly, painted childbirth trays were prevailing and were inscribed with wishes for smooth childbirth[2]. Being presents for mother-to-be, they can be used as both food containers and decorations to be hung on the wall. Such gifts embody people's value for the family and procreation, encouraging women to undertake a maternal role.

⑤Victorian Era

The custom to modern-day baby showers began to be in shape during this era. A Victorian woman would not reveal her pregnancy to other people as long as possible and would not attend public activities which were viewed as improper behavior. Even the words " pregnant " or " pregnancy " were almost a taboo. After her giving birth, however, other women would hold tea parties for the new mother, during which women play games of pregnancy prediction. For example, if two teaspoons were accidentally put together on a saucer, it would be possible that a woman might be expecting. In the early 1900s, the post-birth tea parties turned into showers. Gifts were typically handmade, except, as in the Middle Ages, the grandmother would bestow silver. A woman who had a second baby might be thrown a " sprinkling. "

---

① Johnston, Sarah Illes. *Religions of the Ancient World: A Guide.* Cambridge: Harvard University of Press. 2004.

② Musacchio, Jacqueline Marie. The Art and Ritual of Childbirth in Renaissance Italy. New Haven: Yale University Press. 1999.

⑥Modern Era

After the Second World War, the baby boom era, the modern baby shower took shape and developed with the consumer ideology of 1950s and 1960s. In other words, baby shower in the mid-twentieth century was not only the product of economic stimulation which helps to relieve the financial burden of infant consumption, but also emerged as the signal indicating women's role of expecting mothers since the objects concerning pregnancy and birth contribute to the identity construction of the fetus as a social being. Rituals of the modern baby shower consist of different activities, such as "showering" the expectant mother with presents, making shopping trips organized around the baby-to-be, creating a playful atmosphere at the shower, and inviting the mother-to-be to sit on a chair as she uncovers her gifts with happiness and passes them among her guests for appreciation①. The modern baby shower indicates the woman's transition to a more dependent, but pure state. Meanwhile, it enhances the interpersonal relationships among the community②.

⑦Twenty-First Century

Although baby showers continue to exist in the 21 ty century much as they did fifty years ago, several changes do occur, the most obvious one being the involvement of technology. For instance, there might be a game for baby shower participants to identify baby's body parts on an ultrasound, or the traditional activity is even replaced by virtual baby showers. In addition, while conventional baby showers features exclusively female guests at home, 21 ty century baby showers can be divided as workplace and home; mixed sex and female showers.

From ancient Egyptian post-birth rituals to 21 ty century consumeristic baby showers, we can tell that the traditional ways a culture adopted to welcome a newborn child into its community associates with the most fundamental social values. The emerging forms of baby showers seem to relieve the women from the

---

① Clarke, Alison J. "Maternity and Materiality: Becoming a Mother in Consumer Culture." In Consuming Motherhood. Eds. Janelle S. Taylor, Linda L. Layne, Danielle F. Wozniak. Brunswick, New Jersey: Rutgers University Press. 2004.

② Crouch, Mira and Lenore Manderson. *New Motherhood: Cultural and Personal Transitions in the 1980s.* New York: Gordon and Breach Science Publishers. 1993.

anxieties and uncertainties they face in their role transition to motherhood. Actually, it is not merely the transformation from a simple wife to a caring mother, but the combination of the two. Despite that baby showers take in different forms, the core value behind it is the sincere and pure wish to bring the blessing for the mother and children.

(2) Western Birthday Traditions

Generally speaking, there are a number of varied customs associating with the western birthday celebration.

①Birthday Cakes and Candles

The history of cakes and candles was originated to Ancient Greece, when round cakes were made to honor Artemis, the lunar goddess, with a couple of candles lit to symbolize the glow of the moon. Overtime, other cultures began to follow the customs. And instead of being merely taken as sacrifice, the cake was also ate and thus became a common food.

It is believed that the first birthday cake was made in Germany in the middle ages, during which a celebration named Kinderfest was conducted among Germans who celebrate young children's birthday with the cakes. Compared with previous cakes, changes were made to appeal to more people. For instance, alternate ingredients were applied to sweeten the cake than the usual coarse, bread-like cake, turning it into a delicacy. In addition, the cakes became more elaborate with more icing, layers, and decorations. However, these cakes were costly and only affordable by the upper class because of high prices in ingredients. Then in the 18th century, food and cooking utensils were more accessible to common household and the price of cakes descended sharply while the quantity of bakery rose significantly.

Even though, as previously mentioned, some experts attribute the tradition of placing candles on cakes to the Greeks who held the belief that the smoke of lit candles brought their prayers to their Gods in heaven. However, some scholars claim the origin from Germany, where a candle is believed to stand for "the light of life". No matter where did the origin derive from, it still persists in many cultures. Usually, the number of candles represents the age of the birthday person. The prevailing superstition is that to realize the birthday wish, one is supposed to make a silent wish and blow out all the candles with one breath. If the wish is revealed to anyone else, it will never come true①.

②Birthday Cards

The exchange of greeting cards has been existed in every culture since earliest times.

The oldest known card was believed to be created in England in the 1400s, but the birthday cards tradition only become common until the mid – 1800s. Before that, birthday celebration was the luxury for wealthy families. By the middle of the century, though, with the stamps being used, delivery of personal greetings turned easier, and printing processes were less costly, making the cards affordable to common families and their popularity caught on, both in Europe and America.

As an indispensable element of the culture, birthday cards deepen people's connection on their birthday, the opportunity to express a heartfelt message. Meanwhile, the advance of color printing processes contributes to considerable growth in the relative industry during the 1930's. Twenty years late, humor became a theme of birthday cards and is still used in most of cards today.

Due to technological progress, birthday cards have been added with great variety. One change is the application of music, namely "audio cards", which often contain parts of popular songs, or even classic lines from movies or television shows. Another improvement is the use of voice recording technology, adding a personalized voice message for the birthday card recipient. One more current form of birthday cards is the e-card, a supplement, rather than replacement of a physical card.

③Birthday Parties

In ancient times, many superstitious beliefs were related to one's birthday. For instance, both the Greek and Roman cultures held that every person owned a protective spirit who protected him in life, particularly on birthday.

---

① http: //www. laroccacafe. com/#!　Why-We-Eat-Cake-And-Blow-Out-Candles-On-Birthdays/ c1ix4/0F15A3F1 – 8505 – 484B-B752 – 4316298F1E22

Another belief was that birthdays were the occasions where individuals were more vulnerable to be harmed by evil spirits. On this day, to keep the bad spirits away, the celebrant would be surrounded by friends and family with gifts and well-wishing. Noise was deliberately made as an additional way to scare off the bad spirits. Birthday greets was like working a spell for protection, saving people from evil spirits. Been surrounded by personal spirits, the recipient have more exposure to the magic of the spell.

In spite of the belief among historians that people have celebrated their birthdays for a long time, few records did exist of such celebrations, with the celebrant all being important figures such as the kings and high-ranking nobility. No evidence ever proved that common people, particularly children, ever celebrated their birth when the idea came about. Explanation has it that the nobility were the only people rich enough to afford such observations, therefore, the only ones to have been written about, which accounts for the fact that why birthday person is in the custom of wearing birthday "crowns".

With the passage of time, the recognition of one's birthday started to be prevailing. In England, people began making cakes for the birthday person, with coins, rings and thimbles hidden inside. And the concept of children's birthday celebrations was thought to have first started in Germany as previously mentioned.

With the passage of times, birthdays have developed from simple celebration with typical presents and good wishes to a significant annual event in people's everyday lives. Most people now prefer to hold a birthday party-especially for children or on the important occasion such as transition from childhood to adulthood. Examples of such parties include the North American sweet sixteen party and the Latin American quinceañera.

Western birthday parties usually consists of some common rituals. The guests always bring gifts for the birthday person. The surroundings are often decorated with colorful ornaments, such as balloons and banners. A birthday cake is usually presented with lit candles, with guests singing the song of "Happy Birthday to You". After making a wish and blowing out the candles, the person being honored will cut the cake and have it distributed among the guests.

At parties for children, in particular, there is time reserved for the "gift opening" when the birthday kid unpacks each of the gifts respectively in the face of all the guests. On this occasion, it is also common for the host to give parting gifts to the attendees which are called "goodie bags".

④Birthday Songs

According to *The Guinness Book of World Records*, the "Happy Birthday to You" song is the most popular song ever in the western world, and it is also sung with the English lyrics in non-English speaking countries.

The creator of the song is Mildred J. Hill (born 1859) and Patty Smith Hill (born 1868), two sisters. The melody was composed by Mildred and the lyrics were written by Patty, which was primarily for classroom greetings and entitled "Good Morning to All." The song was part of the book *Song Stories for the Kindergarten*, a publication of the sisters in 1893.

Later on, the lyrics were somehow changed from its original form to "Good Morning to You" and then to "Happy Birthday to You." It remains unknown who did the changes, but the new song was first published in 1924. From then on, the song kept on gaining popularity and in 1934, Jessica Hill, another Hill sister, filed a lawsuit for the unauthorized use of the "Happy Birthday to You" melody resembling the song of the sisters. One year later, Jessica copyrighted and published "Happy Birthday."[①]

Traditionally, at a western birthday party, it is the guests to sing the song "Happy Birthday to You" to the birthday person. The guests sometimes announce wishes of "And many more" to symbolize the wish of longevity when the song is sung. Then the birthday person will make a silent wish before blowing out the candles in a breath. With that, people may applaud and share the cake.

In some countries like Australia, the United Kingdom and New Zealand, following the completion of "Happy Birthday" song, it is custom for one of the guests to cheerfully lead with "Hip hip..." and then the rest to join in and utter the exclamation "...hooray!" for three times, a tradition dates back to

---

① http: //musiced. about. com/od/historyofmusic/a/happybirthday. htm

ancient songs in Dutch, German and Swedish.

(3) Some Characteristic Western Birth Customs in Certain Countries

Many factors, namely family history, economic status and culture, all influence the way a person celebrate his birthday, one of the most significant elements being geographic location. Therefore, some characteristic western birth customs in given nations are presented in the below:

①Holland

The Dutch pay special attention to birthdays such as 5, 10, 15, 20, and 21, which are called "crown" years and the birthday person are usually given particular gifts on the occasion, with rooms being decorated with seasonal flowers, paper streamers, and balloons. Typical foods are pancakes sprinkled with powdered sugar and tarties served with lemonade or hot chocolate. Birthday gifts with black and white package are believed to be symbols of misfortune.

②Denmark

In Denmark, a flag flown outside the house can be an indication of birthday celebration. Presents are usually placed around the child's bed so that they will see them immediately and feel the happiness upon awakening.

③England

The Britons had the tradition to mix the small items such as coins and thimbles into the birthday cake since medieval times. It is believed that the person who got the coin would gain a considerable fortune while the finder of the thimble may unluckily never marry. Today, the custom still remains but the items are replaced by fake coins or small candies. Of course, guests are warned in advance so as not to hurt their teeth or swallow a tiny treasure.

Besides, the friends give the birthday person the "bumps", lifting him/her in the air by the hands and feet and raise up and down to the floor, one for each year, then two for luck and three for the old man's coconut! Squash, an orange or lemon flavored Kool-Aid-type drink made from syrup will always be served.

④Germany

A special wooden birthday wreath will always be placed on a kitchen table. The wreath contains small holes for candles and a holder in the center for the life-candle which is taller and beautifully decorated. This candle is lit annually at child's birthday until they are twelve. On the day of the child's birthday, a family member rises early to light the candles on the birthday cake which lasts all day long. For men reaching the age of 30 and who remains single, they have to sweep the stairs of the city hall. All their friends will throw rubble on the stairs and even when it is finished, they'll throw some more rubble to arouse the female's attention to the men in this way.

⑤Russia

Russians prefer to eat a pie rather than a cake on their birthday, with a birthday greeting carved into the crust. School teachers often give a present to the student who is having a birthday. Besides, children usually play a game with a clothesline by which to hang prizes and each guest gets a prize and takes it home.

⑥Norway

In Norway, when children have their birthday, they stand out in front of their class, choosing a friend to dance with them while the other classmates sing a happy birthday song. They eat chocolate cake with chocolate frosting and dishes of red gelatin covered with vanilla sauce at most birthday parties. In addition, guests may go fishing, but not for the purpose of gaining fish. Instead, they play a game named "Fishing for Ice Cream", and everyone pulls up a frozen treat attached to a piece of string.

⑦Canada

In Canada, the birthday person is ambushed with his/her nose greased by butter or margarine. It is believed that the slippery and greased nose protect the person from being caught by evil spirits, which finds its origin from Scottish culture. In some areas like Quebec, the birthday child receives the punches equal to the number of their ages plus one for good luck. As to the birthday cake, a coin might be hidden between the layers of the birthday cake and the finder of which will have good luck.

⑧America

The Native American tribes usually put significant emphasis on milestones in a child's development rather than his/her actual birthday. But in certain places, people do celebrate it. For instance, the Winnebago Indians have a big birthday that anyone can attend, since people find out information about birthday parties through word of mouth. These parties can last all evening till midnight. The cake is taken around and presented to the guests and it is considered an honor to be invited to split the cake.

After the meal the children usually play a hand game, with an adult holding a bone or stone in one of his or her hands and the children have fun to guess where it is.

⑨Australia

Many Australian would like to hold barbeques for their birthday parties as the weather is usually agreeable in this country. The children eat a dish called "Fairy Bread" as a very popular snack.

⑩New Zealand

With the birthday cake being lit, people sing the birthday song merrily and loudly, after which the birthday person receives a clap for each year they have been alive and one for good luck①.

4. Comparisons

(1) Birth Philosophy

Generally speaking, Chinese philosophy towards life is distinct from the westerners'. The former regard life as a responsibility: the responsibility for the parents to look after the baby attentively and the responsibility for the young to take care of the parents when they grow up. Therefore, children are regarded as the center of both the nuclear and extended families that all the family members revolve around them.

However, westerners hold the value of equality and individuality, believing that all the lives are equal, even between parents and children. Thus, the core value of a new life is supposed to be independent. During the process of

---

① http://www.kidsparties.com/TraditionsInDifferentCountries.htm

their growth, they are entitled to the human right to live as an individual, learning to make their own decisions despite their age.

What's more, families being the basic unit of the Chinese society, the bond between the extended families is tighter compared with the westerners. And the patriarchal social structure is formed on the basis of the agricultural economic mode, among which the patriarchal lineage blood system is placed as the core, producing generations with close continuity. However, western nuclear family is the production of geopolitics-based culture, and the value of individuality result in westerners' self-independence, with family relationships being comparatively more unstable and temporary.

(2) Birth Choice

Chinese traditional ideas advocate the birth of more children, the proves being the proverbs such as " A person will have more fortune with more children. ", "There are three ways to be unfilial, the worst is not to produce off-springs. " Therefore, the significance of giving birth to a new life is to maintain the continuity of the clan. The factor contributing to this conception is the long-term enclosed environment of Chinese natural economy, which produces such common beliefs in the process of struggle between human and nature. Furthermore, father-son relationship matters significantly in Chinese conventional society, which was the highlight of traditional birth concept for thousands of years and is still prevailing in modern society.

On the contrary, influenced by the strong individualism, westerners are not bounded to the ideas of producing new members for the family continuity since it is their freedom to make the choice. Giving birth to new lives is by no means placed the number one obligation in the family. Instead, the pursuit of freedom is the priority of the couple and those who believe children might be the burden of their lives are not a few.

To sum up, Chinese shoulder more pressure as to the choice of birth compared with their western counterparts.

Chapter Six

Customs of Marriage

1. General Introduction

Marriage is a socially or ritually recognized union or legal contract between spouses that establishes rights and obligations between them, between them and their children, and between them and their in-laws. The definition of marriage varies according to different cultures, but it is principally an institution in which interpersonal relationships, usually intimate and sexual, are acknowledged. When defined broadly, marriage is considered a cultural universal, an element, pattern, trait, or institution that is common to all human cultures worldwide. [1]

(1) Historical Development

The history of marriage is no shorter than the history of human beings, which can be viewed as a mirror to the development of human civilization since the practice of constructing a family through marriage dates to ancient times. Frankly speaking, the history of marriage is a commentary on the political, social, and economic status rather than the custom ever derived from romance.

①Primitive Group Marriage

People live in groups without any fixed spouses in the primitive society, having sexual relationships randomly with one another. Due to their weak gender

---

[1] http: //en. wikipedia. org/wiki/Marriage

consciousness, they didn't feel ashamed and weren't restricted by customs and etiquettes.

②Consanguineous Marriage

During the middle Neolithic Age, consanguineous marriage arose which forbad a parent-offspring marriage but allowed the marriage within siblings. Consanguineous marriage is viewed as the earliest form of marriage of human beings.

③Exogamous Marriage

Exogamous marriage emerged in the middle and late Neolithic Age, a form that firmly banned the marriage between blood brothers and sisters, and only the marriage among different social groups is allowed.

In this stage, it was a common practice for the brothers of the same family to marry a wife from the other community, and she naturally would be the wife of all the brothers in the family, and vice versa.

④Antithetic Marriage

The antithetic marriage, or paired marriage is a transitional stage between the exogamous marriage and the monogamous marriage, which was also an unstable marriage between males and females during the late Neolithic Age. It retained some vestiges of group marriage, showing tolerance to a husband's or wife's extramarital relationships.

⑤Monogamy Marriage

The ancient monogamy marriage built its foundation on the private ownership of property, with the patriarchal social system replacing the matriarchal social system. In which the husband claimed ownership to everything in the family, including his wife, children and property. The major task of women was to raise children for the purpose of carrying on the paternal lineages[1].

(2) Wedding Customs

A wedding is the ritual in which two people are bonded in marriage. Wedding conventions and customs vary significantly between cultures,

---

① http://www.chinahighlights.com/travelguide/culture/ancient-chinese-marriage-customs.htm

ethnic communities, religions, nations, and social classes. Common wedding ceremonies includes an exchange of wedding vows between the couple, presentation of a gift (offering, ring (s), symbolic item, flowers, money), and a public announcement of marriage by respectful figures or seniors. Special wedding dresses are often worn in the ceremony which is usually followed by a wedding reception. Music, poetry, prayers or readings from Scripture or literature also may be the ingredients of the ceremony.

In India, for instance, weddings persist for a couple of days. Owing to the difference of Indian culture, the wedding styles and rituals may vary sharply amongst various states, regions, religions and communities. On one hand, the Christians of India usually follow a Western wedding ceremony; on the other hand, the Indian Hindus, Muslims, Jains and Sikhs follow traditions quite different from the West.

There are several traditional wedding ceremonies, one is called "tilak" in which the groom is anointed on his forehead and the bride's hand and feet are decorated with henna, coupled with Ladies' Sangeet (music and dance), and many other pre-wedding activities. Another popular ceremony is the "Haldi" where the bride and the groom are anointed with turmeric paste by all the close relatives. On the day (i. e. late evening) of the wedding, there will be a procession called baraat where the bridegroom and his friends and relatives come singing and dancing to the wedding site, followed by religious rituals to solemnize the wedding. No matter the groom wear traditional Sherwani or dhoti or Western suit, his face is usually veiled with a mini-curtain of flowers called sehra. The Hindu or Muslim bride always prefers red clothes, unlike the western white garments since white represents widowhood in Indian culture. In Southern and Eastern states, the bride usually wears a red Sari, but in northern and central states the popular garment is a decorated skirt-blouse and veil called lehenga. After the marriage ceremony, the bride departs with her husband, which is usually a very sad occasion for the bride's relatives for the reason that she is supposed to "cut-off" her relations with her blood relatives to join her husband's family, not temporarily but permanently. There might be a reception held by the groom's parents at the groom's place afterwards. Although gifts and money to the couple are usually given, the traditional dowry from the bride's parents is now officially banned legally.

On the other hand, Muslim weddings in the Arab countries are conducted following Muslim traditions with a Sheikh and Al-kitaab (book) for the bride and groom. A wedding is not Islamically valid without both bride and groom's willingness, and the groom is often encouraged to visit her before the wedding. However, these visits must be accompanied to ensure purity of action between the future couple. Males and females are separated in wedding ceremonies and receptions respectively.

In France, civil weddings are exclusively recognized in law which are performed in the town hall by the mayor or another civil servant instead. At least one of the spouses must reside in the town where the ceremony takes place. Besides, many couples prefer to have an additional religious wedding, which often takes place following the civil one. Town halls often offer an optional but a more elaborate ceremony for couples who do not favor a religious wedding.

If the two ceremonies take place separately, the civil one will usually include close family and witnesses. Once the civil ceremony is complete, the couple will receive a *livret de famille*, a booklet where a copy of the marriage certificate is recorded as an official document. If the couple should have children, each child's birth certificate will be recorded in the *livret de famille* too.

In smaller French towns, the groom may meet his fiancé at her home on the day of the wedding and escort her to the chapel where the ceremony is being held. As the couple proceeds to the chapel, children will stretch long white ribbons across the road which the bride will cut as she passes.

At the reception, the couple customarily uses a toasting cup called a *Coupe de Mariage*. The origin of giving this toast derived in France, with a small piece of toast literally dropped into the couple's wine for a healthy life.

Some couples would like to serve a *croquembouche* instead of a wedding cake, a dessert of a pyramid of cream-filled pastry puffs, drizzled with a caramel glaze.

At a more joyous wedding, the celebration may proceed till very late at night. After the reception, those invited to the wedding will gather outside the newlyweds' window and bang pots and pans; an activity called a *shivaree*. They are then invited into the house for some more drinks in the couple's honor, after which the couple is finally allowed to be alone for their first night together as a couple.

Despite form, marriage is sacred while the weddings are diversified within the globe. Folks are just conducting different rituals to declare and welcome the establishment of new families to their intimate friends and relatives[1].

2. Chinese Marriage Customs

(1) Ancient Chinese Marriage Custom

According to Confucianism, a marriage symbolizes the beginning of ethics, with a wedding ceremony representing the essence of etiquettes, which definitely exerts a significant impact on social stability. Only those marriages with formal wedding ceremonies are socially recognized. Generally speaking, the fundamental principles of an ancient marriage mainly concern the following:

①Matched Social Status

In ancient China, the marriageable age for men was 20 and 16 for women, and an ideal marriage standard was socially and economically well-matched for the two families. In the Western Zhou dynasty, it was totally against the law to conduct the intermarriage between noblemen and commoners. The implementation of the nine-rank system in the Wei, Jin, Southern and Northern dynasties, generated a rigid feudal hierarchy system, apparently making the marriage between a noble and a common civilian infeasible. Although it was substituted by the civil-service examination system in the Sui dynasty, it was still a convention for the two parties to get matched in accordance with their social and economic status, which was followed by the Tang dynasty to the Qing dynasty.

②Dictates of Parents and Advice of Matchmakers

Marriage freedom was completely banned in ancient China and was generally unacceptable as an offence to public decency following the traditional Confu-

---

① http://en. wikipedia. org/wiki/Wedding_ customs_ by_ country

cian ethic codes, therefore it was the responsibility of parents to arrange marriage for their children to maintain order of the traditional patriarchal society. It was not only politically supported and reinforced legally in ancient China, but was also advocated by the whole society.

As a result, the boys and girls were supposed to observe the dictates of their parents, following the advice of the matchmaker on the arranged marriage pattern. Having never seen each other before their wedding day, the marriage is doomed to be unequal and loveless.

③Forbidden Marriage between People Bearing the Same Surname

The policy banning marriage between folks with the same surname was implemented in the Western Zhou Dynasty to ensure a certain feudal patriarchal hierarchy and order of inheritance. People sharing the same surname or coming from the same clan were officially not allowed to get married in the Tang Dynasty, especially among royal members. Later on, the law forbad the intermarriage between people of the same clan in the Ming and the Qing dynasties; but people with the same surname were allowed to get married if they belonged to different clans.

④Tolerance toward Polygamy

Roughly speaking, feudalistic monogamy is taken as a traditional national policy in ancient China. However, polygamy of a man with multi women was commonly applied among the upper and middle class who could afford to raise more wives and children with his abundant fortune. In other words, it was tolerable for a man to take concubines other than his original wife.

⑤Rituals of Traditional Chinese Marriage Customs

The conventional marriage rituals, as reflections of the traditional Chinese culture, vary greatly from region to region over the time. However, despite the shift of dynasties, six rituals of the traditional Chinese marriage customs basically remained, known as "Three Letters and Six Etiquettes".

● Three Letters

The Three Letters refer to the betrothal letter, the gift letter and the wedding letter, each of which is used in a different ritual of the marriage.

—Betrothal Letter: an official contract of a marriage between the two families.

—Gift Letter: a letter with a list clearly defining the kinds and quantities of the attached gifts.

—Wedding Letter: an official letter welcoming the bride to the bridegroom's home.

• Six Etiquettes

The six etiquettes have been adopted in the traditional Chinese marriage customs since the Western Zhou Dynasty, representing the significance that Chinese attached to marriage which is somehow viewed as superstition from the modern perspective.

—Proposing Marriage (*Nali*): the boy's parents asked a go-between to propose to a potential girl at the girl's home.

—Matching Birthdates (*Wenming*): After a smooth proposal, the match-maker would inquire about the four pillars of birth time (referring to the year, month, day and hour of birth respectively, known as *Bazi* in Chinese astrology) of the couple-to-be and presented it to a fortune-teller to see whether the couple would match in the future. Only if the result is positive can the marriage ritual continue.

—Submitting Betrothal Gifts (*Naji*): Once the birthdates of the couple-to-be was proved to be matchable, the boy's parents would arrange and submit betrothal gifts to the girl's family, including the betrothal letter. Among the gifts, a wild migratory goose was the most common one in the Western Zhou (1046 BC – 771 BC) and the Han dynasties (206 BC – 220) since it is representative of loyalty and love.

—Presenting Wedding Gifts (*Nazheng*): Should the betrothal gifts be accepted, the boy's parents would send wedding gifts to the girl's family, the grandest one of the six etiquettes. The wedding gifts usually included money (silver), jewelry, cakes and sacrificial articles.

—Selecting a Wedding Date (*Qingqi*): The boy's parents chose a wedding date according to the divination and solicited agreement of the girl's parents. Once the date is fixed, the girl's party would present the bride's dowry to the bridegroom's house before the wedding day.

The traditional dowry comprised jewelry, scissors (symbol of the insepara-ble future), a ruler (symbol of rich property), sugar (symbol of the happy marriage), a silver purse (symbol of fortune), a vase (symbol of wealth and honor), quilts, pillows, and clothes (symbol of many offsprings).

—Holding a Wedding Ceremony (*Yingqin*)

It was customary for the bridegroom to welcome the bride at her home and carry her to his home in a bride's sedan since the Western Zhou Dynasty. The wedding ceremony would be held at the boy's house, after which he would take her as his wife.

In the morning of the wedding, the bride would be helped by a respectable old woman to tie up her hair with colorful cotton threads. Red skirts were pre-ferred as the color was the indication of fortune. When the bridegroom arrived, the bride, covered by a red head-kerchief, must cry in the face of her family members, showing her reluctance to leave home. Then, her elder brother would lead her to the sedan. Usually the groom would encounter a series of difficulties intentionally set in his path before he successfully handled it and was allowed to see his future wife.

Upon the arrival of the sedan at the boy's residence, there would be music and firecrackers to create a merry atmosphere. The couple would be led along the red carpet and kowtow three times to worship the heaven, parents and spouse. Then the new couple would go to their bridal chamber and guests would be treated to a feast. On the night of the wedding day, a custom in some places was that the relatives or friends were supposed to banter the newlyweds to bring noisiness to scare off the evil spirits deliberately.

On the third day of the marriage, the new couple would return to the bride's home to see the girl's parents before having a dinner with all the rela-tives.

Admittedly, marriage conventions differed from region to region, but some major etiquettes have been maintained for thousands of years. However, people have tended to abandon some of them to advocate simplified procedures and wedding ceremonies after the founding of modern China①.

(2) Contemporary Chinese Marriage Customs

China has undergone dramatic social, economic and cultural changes in the past century, with the rituals of wedding ceremony being no exception. Accordingly, the contemporary Chinese pay more attention to the outcome of relationship-seeking rather than the process of seeking it. Therefore, the procedure of negotiation, and engagement to wedding rituals are dwarfed by the wedding banquet, which is viewed as the core of the whole ceremony.

①Marriage Certificate

The Law of Marriage was the first law since the foundation of the People's Republic of China in 1950, which abolished the feudal elements in traditional marriage and specified the principles for freedom and monogamy of marriage

When the two in love decides to marry, they are expected to register at the local government agencies concerned, applying for the marriage certificate so as to become a legitimate couple.

Though the wedding certificate represents legal status for the marriage, the young couple is publicly regarded as married only after the completion of their wedding ceremony even in contemporary China.

②Wedding Photos

The practice of wedding photos developed from taking a group photo on the occasion of marriage since the 1920s when it became a fashion for the young couples to have pictures taken in wedding garments. In the 1960s, the traditional mandarin cheongsam and western wedding gown were replaced by casual clothes in people's wedding photos. Since 1990s, wedding photos taken by professional photographers and studios have become quite popular, which become a must for young couples.

The newlyweds usually hang up their enlarged wedding photos in the bedroom with most people admitting that the wedding photos remind them of those happy and moments that deserve to be shared with the others.

---

① http: //www. chinahighlights. com/travelguide/culture/ancient-chinese-marriage-customs. htm

③Door-knocking Red Envelops

The door-knocking red envelops custom dated back to ancient times when the family gate of the bride is firmly sealed at first as the groom arrived to pick her up. Only when the groom squeeze in red envelops of lucky money underneath the door would it be opened. With the passage of times, this convention has undergone some interesting changes.

In modern China, when the groom arrives at the bride's home to take her to the wedding, her bedroom will be guarded by her intimate female friends who deliberately block the doorway for red envelops. As a result, the groom and his mates have to struggle through some extremely tough negotiations and hand in the satisfactory amount of lucky money so that the girls finally let them in, accompanying the bride to the wedding ceremony. This activity was primarily intended to reflect the demure manner of females as well as to alert the groom to the hard-won marriage. But the contemporary joking manner of teasing and bargaining is believed to add happy atmosphere to a delightful wedding day.

④Bridal Cars

Coupled with the red envelops, bridal cars are important elements of the wedding. Since the 1930s, the bridal sedan was gradually replaced by automobile which are decorated with bunches of fresh flowers to maintain some elements of tradition. And usually, the more luxurious the cars are, the more face the couple have as a mirror of the groom's wealth.

⑤Ceremonial Reverence

The most significant characteristic of a Chinese wedding is the moment when young couple make ceremonial obeisance.

Originally there were three steps for the procedure. Firstly, the couple needs to take a bow to thank the bride's parents before they leave. Secondly, the two will bow to the groom's parents and ancestors as they arrive at the new home. Finally, in the bridal chamber, the groom stands at the eastern side and the bride at western side, the bride takes a bow to her husband first and the groom answers back with a bow as well. As time passes, the three "obeisance" have turned into one successive ritual performed at the wedding ceremony, including obeisance to heaven and earth, to the parents and to each other, which constitutes the climax of the wedding ceremony.

⑥Wedding Banquet

In modern China, the wedding banquet is still one of the major events of a wedding. The traditional marriage banquet is extremely substantial with over 12 courses. Guests are seated at round tables following the carefully arranged seating chart to ensure that guests are seated with acquaintances who usually present the couple with monetary gift.

Before the feast, guests may take pictures with the bride and groom. During the meal, the bride and groom will go from table to table to toast the guests with the companion of the best man and maid of honor. The guests will also toast the bride and groom. Meanwhile, the friends will often play pranks on the newly-weds, with the intention of creating a merry atmosphere, making the groom publicly express his love and care for the bride. The bride will change into several different gowns over the course of the wedding day.

In the end, the newlyweds and their relatives will stand at the door and thank the guests as they leave.

⑦Wedding Candies

Wedding candies are distributed to friends and relatives during the wedding dinner, a way to demonstrate appreciation to guests' arrival at the dinner. Wedding candies is indispensable to such event, adding to the festive elements with the representation of sweetness between newlyweds and blessings from family members. Today, the wedding candies are usually sweets or chocolates, with the packages becoming increasingly elaborate.

⑧Bridal Chamber

After the wedding banquet, the bride and groom are expected to enter the bridal chamber.

There are a wealth of specific requirements on the settings of the bridal chamber. The room is decorated with the red paper-cut Chinese characters: double-happiness, which is not frequently used in daily written Chinese, but just adopted for wedding occasions. "喜喜 Double-Happiness" is formed by piling up two Chinese characters "喜 Happiness" together, symbolizing a couple. Moreover, items in the room should be prepared in pairs, serving as an indication that the newly-married will become a couple from the day on.

In the ancient times, a pair of candles with dragon and phoenix patterns were an indispensable decoration of the chamber called "flowery candles" which can stay aflame all night through. Consequently, the Chinese would label the first night of the new couple as the "night of the flowery candles". In some areas of contemporary China, a lamp in the bridal chamber is turned on throughout the whole night to symbolize bright and pleasant life in the future-a modern resemblance to the old dragon and phoenix candle. Interestingly, trend of renaissance of traditional culture sweep China in recent years. Therefore, the dragon and phoenix candle reappeared in the wedding ceremony.

⑨Bridal Bed

In the old times, a bowl full of jujube, chestnut, peanut and coins would be thrown onto the bridal bed, accompanied with blessing songs.

Today, the ritual is seldom seen, but still it is the common practice to put dates, peanuts, chestnuts and eggs tinted in red on the bed, under the mattress or inside the quilt and pillows, which are regarded as symbols of many children due to their similar pronunciation to "having a baby soon", and "blessed with both a son and a daughter".

The Chinese attach extreme significance to the male offspring in the family, therefore, a bunch of customs in the groom's part relate with the birth of a child, especially a boy. Particularly, on the eve of the wedding day, a baby boy would be placed on the bridal bed, intending to bless the new couple with a son soon after the marriage, namely "weighing the bed" in Chinese.

⑩Returning Home

"Returning Home" means the bride return to her parents' house for the first time after the wedding.

The date of returning home varies. The earliest can be the 3rd day after the wedding ceremony. In most cases the bride will come back home with her husband a month later. The son-in-law should offer some gifts to parents-in-law. The bride's family will prepare for the daughter some rice cakes made from glutinous rice or bun made of wheat flour in peach shape in return to her husband's family.

For the bride's family, this visit is considered the first time to accept the groom a member of the family clan which is held in his honor. The son-in-law enjoys a high status in his wife's family and he is often called the "master of the girl". In colloquial, he calls the parents of his wife papa and mama, or to show respect, "Father of Mountain (father-in-law)" and "mother of Mountain (mother-in-law)".

(3) The Marriage Rituals of Chinese Ethnic Minorities

Marriage doesn't always come easy. Marriage conventions of different nationalities are diversified. The following wedding customs from five ethnic minorities demonstrate its difficulty and rich ethnic implications.

①Weeping Marriage of Tujia Ethnic Minority

The marriage ritual for girls of Tujia Ethnic Minority is characteristic of crying. According to custom, the new bride should begin to cry half a month or even one month before the wedding ceremony. In a sense, the girl's capability of crying over her marriage reflects her virtue.

For the sake of being regarded as a good wife, the girl starts to learn how to cry for marriage since twelve years old. Some will invite an experienced person to instruct them. When 15 years old, crying competition will be held among girls and the winner can be a good teacher to other participants, with girls discussing methods of crying after the match.

The Tujia girls are famous for capable of singing weeping song for marriage, with the content involving parents, sister, brothers, the matchmaker and ancestors. The emotions are fully expressed through the mournful tones even to move a hardhearted listener. In fact, for girls, the weeping songs were primarily sung before marriage to protest the arranged marriage system under the feudalism, expressing sentimental affection to their parents and other relatives.

The weeping songs can be sung solely or dually. When one girl sings, she will usually cry for her destiny; while two girls weep together, it is called "sister crying". The bride cries and sings first, and then the other one will sing together with the bride to comfort her.

As mentioned above, the weeping marriage custom derived from the unreasonable marriage system in ancient times. Girls sang and cried denouncing the marriage system and dreaming of struggling for free themselves from restrictions of the system. Now, although Tujia girls can enjoy the marriage freedom, they still cry following the tradition[①].

②Marriage Rituals of Yugur

The ancestors of Yugur people were the Huihu people, the nomads around the E'erhun River during the Tang Dynasty. Currently this ethnic group owns a population of about 15, 000, with 90 percent of them living in the Su'nan Yugur Autonomous County, and the Huangnibao Yugur Township of the city Jiuquan, in Northwest China's Gansu Province. In Chinese, "Yugur" is representative of "wealth and stability".

Yugur people traditionally hold grand wedding ceremonies, which commonly last two days for ordinary people and several days for the wealthy. One typical but somewhat unique custom is for the bridegroom to shoot three arrows free of arrowheads to his bride and then breaks the arrows and the bow during the wedding ceremony, a symbol of forever love between the couple. It is highly prohibited for the people of the same surname or kin to marry and monogamy is conducted.

During the common Yugur two-day wedding ceremony, the activities of the first day is held in the bride's house and second day is much more ceremoniously in the groom's. On the first day, relatives from the bride side will come to express their congratulations to the bride's family, presenting the gift of hada.

The most sacred and pleasant moment in a Yugur girl's life is the ceremony of "putting on the headdress", a ritual symbolizes a girl's turning to a bride. On the wedding day, the bride's mother does the hairdressing for her daughter by helping her to put on the headdress which is made of silver, jade, coral, agate, and seashell. At the same time, she sings the traditional "wearing headdress song".

Despite her reluctance to leave the family, the bride rides on a white horse which resembles the heavenly white elephant in Yugur legends, heading for her

---

① http: //www. chinaculture. org/chineseway/2011 – 08/31/content_ 422722. htm

future-husband's house with the companion of her brother. Before they start off, the bride's parents are expected to toast the party escorting her.

Having arrived at the groom's house, some experienced riders from among the bride's relatives ride a horse or a camel with the pretended intention to "destroy" the bridal chamber that has been established by the groom's family. Meanwhile, it is the responsibility of the groom's relatives to protect the bridal chamber from being damaged. This "fight" ends with those riders from the bride side riding around the bridal chamber three times. The implied culture behind this activity is to display the groom's strong protection to his wife.

The groom's family welcomes the bride's arrival with as much warmth hospitality as possible. After the "off-the-horse" toasts have been presented to the guests, people from both sides enter a big tent to attend a solemn ceremony. With the wedding hats on, the groom steps on the design made by scattering rice on the ground, which represents a never-ending happy marriage to the couple. Afterwards, one of the bride's uncles begins to address the audience concerning the creation of the world, the origin of marriage, the obligation of the newlyweds to take care of their parents, coupled with their mutual life-long faithfulness. The uncle chanting the blessings of a happy life for the young couple, the groom's forehead is applied with ghee and the bride's girdle is tied with a leg of lamb. Finally, the bridegroom shoots three arrows (arrows without arrowheads that won't hurt anyone) to his bride before breaking the arrows and the bow①.

③Walking Marriages of Mosuo

Mosuo culture features the unique marriage practice: walking marriage (*zou hun* in Chinese) . For males and females, there is no role of husbands or wives in their traditional marriage. Instead, sexual partners can be changeable and they do not live permanently under the same roof. Children of such relationships are raised by their mothers and the maternal families.

The Mosuo people favor large extended families, with several generations live together in communal quarters. All on-going sexual relationships in Mosuo

---

① http: //traditions. cultural-china. com/en/115Traditions4116. html

culture are called "walking marriages." literarily which means flexible relationship based on mutual affection. When a Mosuo woman or man is attracted to a potential partner, it is the woman who permits the man to visit her at night secretly. When dawn arrives, the man returns to his own home. Mosuo women and men can engage in sexual relations with as many partners as they like.

Though a love relationship may be long-term, the man never lives with the woman's family, or vice versa. Mosuo couples continue to live with and be responsible to their respective families. Property is not shared and the father rarely shoulders responsibility for his children who are taken care of by the women's brothers. A male never becomes a member of the lover's family. Whether or not the father is involved, children are raised in the mother's home and assume her family name.

This type of relationship yield many positive outcomes. First, it gives the couples equal marital freedom which can be initiated and ended without legal restrictions. If a matriarch disapproves of a female "visitor," she can order the female to terminate the relationship, but this seldom happens in reality. In other Asian cultures, marriage involves a collective decision rather than that of a couple. Particularly in China, families ties are focused on rather than the individuals and the two people connect by marriage work to serve the economic and political interests of these larger parties. Walking marriages, however, relieve people from these social pressures and allow more independence.

Another important result of this custom is the free of male children preference which is a commonly adopted attitude among people in other regions of China, particularly in rural areas.

However, among the Mosuo, since neither the male nor female children ever leave the household after marriage, therefore, no particular preference for one gender over the other exists when women give birth to children, resulting in roughly the same proportion of males to females within a household.

The large majority of women identify exactly who are their children's fathers. But, unlike many cultures which censure mothers and children without clear paternity, Mosuo children incur no such contempt. When a child is born, the father, and sisters come to celebrate, presenting gifts. On New Year's Day, a child visits the father to show respect to him and his household. A father also participates in the coming-of-age ceremony, an indication of his indispensable role during the process of the child's growth①.

④Marriage Rituals of Yi Nationality

The wedding ceremony of Yi people is solemn but interesting. If a male and female decide to get married, the parents of the young man, would invite the Bimo, a respectable person in the ethnic group, to choose a lucky day for the wedding ceremony, with the permission of the girl's parents. A couple of days before the wedding, the young woman is supposed to consume less or even forbidden to take in food to get prepared for the wedding day.

To welcome all the guests attending the wedding, the groom's family would establish a shed decorated with colored festoons in the center of the yard. In addition, there is a shrine for the Goddess of Luck in the middle of the shed. The wedding is joyous with singers singing unceasingly for celebration.

When the bridegroom arrives at the bride's home with the escort procession, they would be greeted with water-sprinkling which symbolizes fortune and blessing. With sprinkling water, the bride would be free of the trouble of drought and have substantial food and water. Upon entering the house, the escort party is expected to burn incense and kowtow in front of the altar before presenting the gifts, so would the bride's family exhibit the trousseaux. And then the singer commences to sing wedding songs according to which the Betrothal gifts are demonstrated. If the groom fails to show the gifts in accordance with the song, the singer would hit three strokes to the head of the escort men with a dustpan to add to the joy of the atmosphere.

After the betrothal gifts exhibition, the bride's family would treat the bridegroom's escort with drink-tea first and then sweet water, symbolizing bitterness prior to sweetness. Then the uncle of the bride will be invited to address the audience with blessings to their future marriage. Following the speech, a red box will be opened from which two pieces of silk strips will be taken out to be put on the groom's shoulder. When all the ritual is complete, banquet will be ar-

---

① http: //en. wikipedia. org/wiki/Mosuo

ranged to entertain the bridegroom's relatives and friends. During the dinner, the bridegroom bows and toasts at each table. After the banquet, the bride will leave with the groom to his house.

While all the above activities are holding sequentially, the bride will not present but stay upstairs, dressing and putting on make up. Before departure, the bridegroom would be led by the bride's uncle to the memorial tablets of the bride's ancestors to bid farewell, while the bride would be shouldered by her brother downstairs to join the bridegroom, heading towards his house with the company of the guests. Traditionally, the escort team should walk their way to the groom's family despite the long distance. In recent years, however, some couples would prefer taking vehicles.

Upon their arrival at the bridegroom's house, firecrackers would be set off and honorable Bimo would be invited to chant Wedding Scripture. Accompanied by two girls holding two torches, the bride would walk across the gate, entering the bridal chamber and sitting on the bed. Then the couple would drink the "cross-cupped wine". Conventionally, the bride should not have supper made by the bridegroom's family, but rather to eat the meal brought from the bride's family together with the bridegroom. Then a banquet would be held to entertain all guests, with everyone singing and dancing around the bonfires.

At dawn, the bride would carry two buckets of water to the kitchen, firing the kitchen stove as an indication of her participation in the bridegroom's family and the commencement of her marriage life. On that day, the bridegroom's family would invite all guests of the same family clan to dinner. Two days later, the bride would back to her parents' home commonly referred to as "*huimen*" (returning home).

In certain Yi areas in Yunnan Province, there remains an ancient wedding custom called "bride kidnapping", which is acted dramatically just for fun. The groom's family, on the one hand, will send betrothal gifts to the bride's family, but on the other hand, another group of people are sent to the bride's house to take the bride by force and carry her home on horseback. The bride is expected to cry for help, with her family members pretending to chase after the kidnappers and fight against them with water, cudgels and stove ashes, trying to regain the bride. When the kidnappers take the bride to the groom's house with black ashes on their faces, everybody talks joking about the seemingly fierce but actually happy scene[1].

⑤Marriage Rituals of Dai Nationality

Quite contrary to common Chinese marriage ritual, men are married to women and become a member of the women's family. Dai boys and girls usually fall in love during adolescence with a characteristic of the puppy love. And men are traditionally considered civilized and educated only after becoming monks for several years in the temples who are not forbidden to fall in love with girls.

Dai people prefer to express their love by singing in antiphony through asking questions and answering with shyness and elegance. The songs are euphemistically and beautifully full of wisdom with simple beats. When night falls, the girls would carry the spinning wheel to spin but actually they are waiting the young man to come. At this moment, the young man of neighboring village approach to their favored girls' bamboo houses, playing their instruments and singing love songs. If the girl also takes fancy to the man, she will respond with the sound of spinning wheel, or even confess the affections to him.

If a couple decides to get married, the conventionally simple wedding will be held in the bride's home among which the thread-fastening rite is the most significant section. In the Dai language, thread-fastening rite is called "*Shu-huan*" which is to tie the bride's and the bridegroom's spirits together. On the wedding, the toastmaster will respectively tie white thread on the bride's and bridegroom's wrists and wish them happy marriage in harmony. Meanwhile, the old people present also tie some white thread on the couple's wrists with blessing. What follows the ceremony is an ample banquet to cater to the guests. The bride and groom propose toast to guests, answering questions raised by the guests to create a joyous air. The atmosphere is brimmed with warmth and excitement by the accompaniment of the Kazakhstan (the Dai singer) .

---

① http: //traditions. cultural-china. com/en/115Traditions5080. html

3. Western Marriage Customs

(1) A Brief History of Marriage

Like most other social institutions, marriage is the product of social development, which has increased in complexity as the society have turned increasingly sophisticated and civilized. Deeply rooted in custom and convention, religion and civil law, many marriage practices have disappeared and been replaced by new ones.

Generally speaking, marriage has evolved through three stages: marriage by force or capture, marriage by purchase or contract, and marriage by mutual love.

①Marriage by Force or Capture

In primitive society, wars between tribal groups were common and women of the opponent tribes were captured and conquered as the trophy. The custom of having a "best man" to accompany the bridegroom at the wedding can be dated back to the days in which the grooms' best man served as a fellow-warrior. When a man aimed to grab a woman from another tribe, he would often bring along his "best" man to assist him to carry away the bride-to-be. In better times when tribes were on good terms, women could be exchanged easily; otherwise they were simply abducted and raped. The maid of honor and bride's maids were the women who originally helped the bride get away from her protective family and from other pursuers so that she could be captured by the man she wanted. When such eccentric way of getting the bride and groom together lost its popularity and died away, the honor rules remained.

In addition, the honeymoon is a remnant of those days. Generally, the tribe from which a bride was plundered would come seeking for her, forcing the warrior and his new wife to hide in a secret place. The honeymoon of modern society, therefore, evolved to symbolize the couple's seclusion period. According to an old French custom, when the moon went through all its phases, the couple drank metheglin, a wine made with honey; hence the honeymoon. Contemporarily, many couples still prefer to keep their honeymoon plans a secret, not being afraid of being located by relatives, but for reasons of romance.

②Marriage by Purchase or Contract

This stage is an evolvement from marriage by force. Being tired of the endless fights caused by stolen brides, men started to offer compensation to her family or tribe to avoid the revenge. The custom of purchasing a wife was gaining popularity for the bridegroom to comfort enraged parents as well as to evade tribal warfare. Instead of paying a price, an exchange for the bride can be made, with the form being his own sister, his livestock, or his land etc. Therefore, he is not only able to save his own life, but also to regain his freedom and new wife.

Generally speaking, marriage comprised two transactions. First, the bridegroom and the bride's father or guardian reached an agreement, with each binding himself to his part of the marriage agreement—the establishment of the contract. Second, it was the delivery of the bride in return for the price agreed upon, or payment of part of the price and security that the remainder would be paid to the widow in case of the husband's untimely death. Besides, the custom of the dower dated back to this time which can be viewed as a provision for widowhood. Rather than paying the agreed money to the father or guardian of the bride, the husband gave the fee to the bride herself as a sort of "life insurance". On the other hand, the dowry could find its origination in the bride's family as well. The bride's father supplied a wealth of goods, land, or money for his daughter to attract a suitable husband. The groom still present a gift, but he also received more than just a bride. The dowry was in part a bride's insurance against divorce or her husband's death. But the husband was in charge of the dowry as long as the marriage existed. Roughly speaking, it was a gift from father to son-in-law to add to the bride's status in the family.

To sum up, the purchase/contract marriage took on various forms, such as exchange, outright sale, service, child betrothal or gift giving. Except for the gift giving and the dowry, these customs have almost melted from western culture. Marriage by contract or purchase lasted in England as late as the middle of the sixteenth century. In France, it was customary up until the marriage of Louis XVI to pay thirteen deniers upon the conclusion of the marriage contract. What's more, the practice of "giving the bride away" in the modern ceremony dated back to the time when the bride was really sold. It was her parents to arrange her marriage and she was literally given to the groom. Today, a woman is commonly considered under her father's care until she is married. Therefore, the father walks to the altar with his daughter to signify his approval and blessing to his daughter's marriage.

③Marriage by Mutual Love

It was not until the 9th or 10th century that women enenjoyed the freedom to choose their husbands. Even though stories, legends, and myths reveal that love has always been an indispensable ingredient of marriage, civilization has to advance beyond the primitive stages before marriage by love became the common practice. As a matter of fact, the position of the woman is a reflection of the degree of social civilization since marriage by capture constitutes the lowest stages of barbarism while marriage through mutual love is the mark of a civilized society.

Elopement is one of the unexpected product of marriage by mutual love which was nearly impossible in primitive times when women were guarded closely. Parents and guardians arranged marriage to suit their own greedy ends, completely ignoring the desires or the ultimate happiness of the bride-to-be. With the passage of times, elopement gradually emerged as the sole feasible alternative to marriage by capture or by purchase, firstly a rarity but then turned more common. To avoid the marriage with a man she disliked but who was able to pay the price her parent's demanded, a young woman would decide to elope with the man of her choice. Meanwhile, in order to avoid having to accumulate property until he could pay the bride-price, or to escape from a service contract, a young man would try every means to induce the girl he loved to elope with him.

Marriage has been developed under religious and civil control. Today marriage is governed by civil law as well as ecclesiastical canon law, particularly the latter. Most couples celebrate their wedding in the presence of a priest, rabbi, or minister, yet their marriage would be of no valid if they fail to register with the State. For instance, in New York, it is illegal for a marriage officiant to perform a wedding without first being presented a valid marriage license.

During the Roman Republic, marriage ceremony used to be a solemn religious ritual. But later, religion was greeted with contempt and marriage became virtually a civil contract. Then gradually, Christianity recovered its religious character in marriage with couples pairing off together to ask for the blessings of their priests. By the Middle Ages, the religious significance of marriage had reached its peak. The custom of religious marriage, whether performed in the church or by a clergyman at home, gained more popularity during the Middle Ages and persists till modern life.

It was not until 1563 that it was obligatory for a marriage to be performed by a priest in the presence of two or three witnesses the Catholic church. Subsequently, marriage continued to be viewed as a divine institution until the French Revolution, when the new Constitution made civil marriage mandatory in 1791.

Thanks to the impact of Christianity, the modern marriage has a more solemn and religious tone. Despite this religious character, however, segments of the old customs remain in the average memory. Outmoded traditions reemerge as symbols with the combination of the old with the new, making modern marriages vital and romantic[1].

(2) Contemporary Western Marriage Customs

Courtship and marriage are socially significant and all sorts of customs and rituals have arisen related with these events.

①Engagement

An engagement refers to a promise of marriage between two people. It also refers to period of time spent between the proposal and the marriage,

---

① http: //www. limarriages. com/customs. html

during which the parents would make arrangement for the marriage of their children, usually several years under the matrimonial age. Nowadays, it is the common practice for the couple themselves to arrange the engagement.

The concept of having an engagement period between the proposal and the marriage ceremony can be dated back to 1215. At the Fourth Lateran Council, Pope Innocent III declared that marriages should be announced in public by the church priests for a predetermined amount of time in case there were any impediments or illegitimacies.

In Western culture, engagement rings are apparently associated with marriage, particularly worn by the woman to make a silent declaration of her betrothal.

The original adoption of jewelry as an indication of a strong relationship or bond with another person was through chains and bracelets. The concept of using the ring is closely related with its shape. In Ancient Egypt, the ring also symbolizes the sacred moon and sun gods, with the circular shape representing an eternal bond. Meanwhile, the hole in the center of the ring implies a doorway into the unknown world.

It is widely believed that the Holy Roman Emperor: Maximilian I was the earliest one to use an engagement ring. In 1477 he presented his fiancée with a diamond ring. Nowadays, some wedding rings are designed in two halves. The woman wears one half as an engagement ring and then the other half after she gets married.

The engagement ring is worn on the fourth finger of the left hand in the United States, the United Kingdom, Ireland, Canada, and Australia. Continental Europe and some other countries wear it on the other hand instead.

The reason why the fourth finger is the ring finger concerns the *vena amoris*, Latin for the "vein of love", which supposedly runs in a direct line from the ring finger to the heart. [1]

②Weddings

The wedding is one of life's primeval and indispensable rites of pas-

---

[1] http：//zh. scribd. com/doc/202329521/R-E-Report

sage. Nearly all of the customs we observe today are the heritage of the past. Everything from the veil and the flowers, to the bridesmaids and processionals bore its specific meaning. Today, despite the subsidence of the original feature, we maintain the major customs in our weddings because they are conventional and ritualistic.

Usually, the activities such as bachelor party and bridal showers will be held before the wedding of the couple.

● Bachelor Party

Bachelor party, the celebration in the groom's honor used to be called the bachelor dinner, or stag party, is the marriage custom that has stood the test of time. Firstly appeared in the fifth century in Sparta, the activity was the occasion for military soldiers to feast and toast on the eve of a friend's wedding. In the contemporary time, a bachelor party usually takes place closely prior to the actual wedding date, as the time for the groom to have the last taste of freedom. Although may be viewed as raucous, bachelor parties are originally conducted to allow the groom and his wedding attendants to relieve themselves from the great nervousness before the big day.

● Bridal Showers

The origin of bridal showers comes from Holland. If a bride's father did not favor the husband-to-be, he would show his disagreement by not providing her with the necessary dowry. Therefore, the bride's friends would support her by "showering" her with gifts so she would raise enough dowries to marry the man of her choice. While the customs of dowries are long gone today, the practice of presenting gifts to the bride-to-be survives.

● White Weddings

The custom of wearing white could be attributed to Queen Victoria who broke convention and wore a white wedding dress on the royal wedding. Before that, white was not considered suitable for a royal wedding but Victoria's dress popularized white wedding gowns and the color caught on ever since. New brides used to wear the best clothes they had on the wedding. After Victoria's wedding, gold dresses or gold threaded dresses gained popularity among the royals while other brides would wear white or pastel dresses, a way that reflected their social status.

Up to the mid-twentieth century, many brides in the United Kingdom would rather wear a special dress such as an evening dress than to wear a traditional or gown-type wedding dress. In America, it was the same case that practical brides preferred a formal dress that could be dressed on other occasions.

A western white wedding will typically conducted in a church, particularly the beautiful and special one. Some churches require that the couples should join parish or pledge to do so after marriage. The White weddings in the United States can also be held at home, a private club or somewhere like a garden, etc.

- The Wedding Ceremony

It was regarded good luck if a bride saw a chimney sweep on the way to church since story had it that once King George III's carriage horses bolted and the only person who was brave enough to stop them was a small, sooty man. Even though there are not so many sweeps in the days of smokeless fuel, those who make a living with the chimney brush are usually happy to add to the joyous atmosphere at a wedding.

It is a long-lasting tradition that a peal of bells in the middle of a Saturday afternoon announces a couple's union in sacred matrimony. According to medieval myth, bells were sounded to frighten the evil spirits lurking close by.

In the west, there is a popular bridal attire rhyme dating back to the Victorian times, which is "something old, something new, something borrowed, something blue and a silver sixpence in your shoe".

Something old represents the connection with the bride's family and the past as symbols of continuity. Usually, the bride wears a piece of family jewelry or maybe her mother's or even grandmother's wedding dress. Other common choices include a handkerchief, a scarf or a piece of lace.

Something new implies good fortune and the brides' hopes for a bright future in her new life. The wedding gown is often new or anything bought new for the wedding such as the wedding flowers or the wedding rings.

Something borrowed indicates that friends and family will be there for her on the special occasion as well as in the future when help is needed. Wearing something borrowed, particularly the one from a happily married woman, lending the bride some of her own marital happiness.

Wearing something blue dates back to biblical times when the color blue was believed to be the symbol of faithfulness, purity and loyalty. With the passage of time, it has evolved from wearing blue clothing to wearing a blue band around the bottom of the bride's dress or a blue or blue trimmed garter. Today some brides even get a blue tattoo, wear blue nail polish or wear blue shoes.

A silver sixpence in the bride's shoe symbolizes wealth, not only financially but also a wealth of happiness and joy throughout her married life.

When guests arrive at the church they are greeted by the ushers, with guests from the bride family and the groom family sitting separately. The front rows are usually reserved for family and close friends. In many ceremonies the bridal party will stand at the alter, but if not they will be seated in the very front rows.

The bride will arrive at the church in elegant cars, limos, or sometimes carriages for special effect. The bridal companion typically comprises the bride and her father, the bridesmaids, the maids of honor and the flower girls etc.

When the ceremony begins, the groom and his groomsmen stand with the minister, facing the audience. Music signals the entrance of the bride, accompanied by her father, who gives his daughter's hand to the lucky groom. Then the young couple utter their vows, promising to love each other "for better, for worse, for richer, for poorer, in sickness and in health." But from time to time the couple would compose their own words. They exchange rings to symbolize their marriage commitment. Finally the minister announces the most important moment: "I now pronounce you man and wife. You may kiss the bride!"

After the ceremony, the bride and groom will go to a side room with the priest and two witnesses to sign the state-issued marriage license in the

United States. In the United Kingdom, however, wedding register is signed.

The bouquet is an indispensable element of the wedding as well, which was originally worn by both the bride and groom to symbolize happiness. Traditional Celtic bouquets consist of ivy, thistle and heather. Another type of popular wreath used herbs rather than flowers because people used to believe that herbs—especially garlic—had the power to drive away evil spirits. In addition, sage (the herb of wisdom) stood for wisdom while dill meant lust. Flower girls commonly carried sheaves of wheat, a symbol of growth, fertility, and renewal. Later on, flowers took the place of herbs without losing all the meanings. For instance, orange blossoms mean happiness and fertility. Ivy means fidelity and lilies mean purity.

The guests will then throw flower petals, rice, birdseed or confetti over the newlyweds when they leave the church and enter the cars for the reception. Such traditions originated from the ancient Pagan ritual since grain and the seed represent fruit and fertility.

Some gifts are distributed to the guests attending the wedding, a custom originated in Italy which is called *Bomboniere*. The Italians use elaborate tulles and fine boxes to contain five delicious sugared almonds as the symbols of health, wealth, happiness, long life and fertility. They do become lovely souvenirs of the marriage which is designed to match the flowers or the bridesmaids' dresses[1].

● Wedding Reception

At the wedding reception, the bride and groom are appreciative to their guests and they cut the wedding cake and everyone shares a bite. Guests interact with each other while enjoying cake, punch and other treats. An interesting activity is for the bride to throw her bouquet to a group of single girls, with the lucky girl catching the bouquet being the next to marry. During the reception, playful friends "decorate" the couple's car with tissue paper, tin cans or a "Just Married" sign. Once the reception is over, the newlyweds run to their car and speed off. Many couples prefer to

---

① http: //services. eveningnews24. co. uk/norfolk/weddings/WeddingGuide/Traditions. aspx

take a honeymoon, a one to two week vacation trip, to celebrate the new stage in their life.

4. Comparisons

With the historical advance, marriage, as a symbol of the progress of human civilization, is getting increasing attention and gradually develops into a stable social ritual. Many factors, such as history, religion, geography, democracy, etc, lead to a wealth of wedding customs with their unique features.

(1) Marriage Values
①Religious Influences

British marital customs is one of the long-lasting traditions in the Great Britain. Due to different beliefs, there are three kinds of weddings: Church Weddings, Catholic Weddings and Civil Weddings. British wedding registration is a conventional church marriage one, which usually needs to be reserved six months in advance. Besides, the new marriage is to be announced publicly for a month before the wedding. However, in China, the land of courtesy, traditional marriage is complicated and solemn under the influence of patriarchal clan system. The whole process is arranged by mutual parents, a result of parental respect deeply rooted in Confucianism.

Monogamy has always been the sacred marital system of Christianity. A sentence of "Yes, I do" means significantly to most westerners. It is a vow that people make in wedding ceremonies in the presence of all the relatives and friends, which is like a contract with God. Besides, westerners attach great importance to wedding anniversaries, with almost every year sending each other gifts to honor the day. On the other hand, marriage is far from being sacred in ancient China since the greatest purpose of marriage is to perpetuate the families as the old saying goes that "There are many forms of unfilial conduct of which the worst is to have no descendants."

②Philosophies

The marriage value between westerners and Chinese differ greatly. First of all, the most apparent one is the standards of a lifelong partner. Generally speaking, if a westerner wants to choose a companion, they prefer the one with similar values. They take more about hobby, personality, interest into consideration rather than height, appearance, age and social status. They even discount how many kids the partner has or his/her marriage history. Independent, capable, mature ladies are more popular than young ladies in marriage market while in China pretty young girls are the favors and targets of men. When comes to partner choosing, girls are told to get a better education and accomplishment even a perfect figure in order to marry an excellent husband with a successful career. It is very common, in China, for parents to disagree their daughter marry a guy without an apartment or a car even any accounts. In traditional China, sharing the same social background is the primary thing of love and marriage. If love in American can be described as mental and romantic one, the Chinese love is somewhat more substantial.

What's more, westerners regard marriage as their own private business not involves morality and no one can interfere. Everyone was given right to live a happy life with beloved one. They can definitely choose partner again, of course, when they discover the present marriage a huge mistake especially there is no love left. In contrast, in China a marriage without love continues to exist because there are a lot of reasons to maintain it such as family ties, responsibilities, moralities, concept of clan, children and so on. As a result, they avoid or put off marriage and refuse to build or hold an unhappy marriage. While in China, traditional culture paid attention to the stability of family. Chinese would utilize all means to mortify the family life which is full of breaches when crisis lie in the marriage.

③Consuming Attitudes

The weddings of Americans can be luxurious or simple, depending on the economic realities of the families. According to recent survey, the average wedding consumption of Americans is 22, 000 dollars. The major reason is that most of them are Puritans who advocate frugality, with restrictions on pleasure pursuit. However, most Chinese value marriage as one of the most significant events in life, believing that it is an occasion worth displaying their wealth. In other words, people tend to go in for pomp and unrealistic comparison with others when holding the wedding ceremonies.

(2) Weddings

①Colors

The main color in western wedding ceremony is white, the symbol of virginity and purity so that everything appears on the wedding should be white. Besides, they take white as in the Catholic tradition, the white color represents happiness, holiness and fidelity, so the bride's flowers and the decoration of surrounding environment are also in white, but in china white means death, sorrow, sadness and loss. On the other hand, the main color in Chinese traditional wedding is red, the so-called "Chinese Red", a color representing a festival atmosphere, happiness and good luck, Then Chinese will adorn everything red on a wedding ceremony. To the contrary, red in western countries usually means bleeding, fire, revenge and death.

• Presents

Sending a present to the newly-weds is the custom that prevails in the western countries. First, the present has no need to be too expensive. Second, it should be valuable in material sense or spiritual sense. Usually the couple might make a gift list for the friends and relatives to refer to. Whereas in China, people won't bother to buy the wedding gift but give the couple a red envelop with cash inside to signify their best wishes.

• Atmosphere

In the traditional wedding in China, the drums and firecrackers are essential. The bridal chamber after banquet shows the bustling atmosphere even more. The western wedding is romantic, with usually the wedding being held in a church hosted by a priest. The bride usually wears a long beautiful white wedding gown, her face being covered by a white veil, making the wedding solemn and serious. In a word, western wedding is purely romantic but Chinese wedding is happy and lively.

Each marriage custom has its own cultural sources. Due to different aesthetics, religious and cultural origins, Chinese and western marriage customs vary obviously.

Chapter Seven

Customs of Death

1. General Introduction

Death refers to the logical end of physical existence of a person when all biological symptoms of a human being cease to operate. Death and its spiritual ramifications are debated in every manner all over the world. Most civilizations dispose of their dead with rituals developed through spiritual traditions.

Men buried their dead with ritual and ceremony as early as 60, 000 B. C. , Researchers have even found proof that Neanderthals buried their dead with flowers, which bore much resemblance to what we do today.

(1) History of Burial Rituals

The history of funeral service is definitely a history of mankind since funeral customs are as old as civilization itself.

①Early Funeral Rites

Every culture and civilization pays attention to the appropriate care of their dead. Generally speaking, there are three things in common concerning death and the disposition of the dead:

- Funeral rituals and ceremonies
- A sacred and holy place for the dead
- Memorialization of the dead

As mentioned above, burial grounds of Neanderthal man dating to 60, 000 B. C. are discovered with animal antlers on the body and flower fragments next to the corpse as an indication of some primitive forms of ritual and gifts for remembrance. Without profound psychological knowledge or custom, Neanderthal man instinctively buried their dead with ritual and ceremony.

Similar to the natural process are the ways adopted by Parsees in India, who leave their deceased in towers, where they are devoured by vultures; and certain Buddhists in the Himalayas who chop up the corpse, placing it on a rock for the birds to eat.

A group of ancient people customarily put their dead in a cave, as was the case with Jesus or in a long barrow, as with some European Neolithic people, which finds its contemporary version in Italy, Spain, and the US, where the coffin is often placed in a niche inside a mausoleum—a building built to house human remains.

②The Role of Fear

Primitive human beings lived in a world of fear which can be triggered mostly by natural disasters. In their mind, live and death events were the disposal of spirits. Not being able to see or sense these spirits, they lived in a world of unconscious terror.

With an effort to gain peace from these "gods" or "spirits," man invented charms, ceremonies and rituals to placate these spirits. Although we may find many ancient burial customs strange or in some cases unreasonable, they obviously arose for a certain reason.

The first burial customs then, were simple and crude attempts to protect the living from the spirits which caused the death of the person. Fear of the dead caused the burning of bodies to destroy evil spirits. Even today, many primitive tribes just run away from their dead, leaving them to rot. For instance, Zoroastrians allow their dead to rot or be devoured by vultures. The absence of fire in the death ritual is because they view fire as sacred to be applied in disposal of the dead. In addition, burial is considered to be a contamination which will do harm to mother soil.

In others places deep in the jungle, the body is left to be devoured by wild beasts. In Tibet and among the Kamchatkan Indians, dogs are used for this purpose because it is believed that those eaten by dogs will be better off in the other world.

Herodotus, a Greek historian, claimed that the Calatians ate their own dead, which was a sacred honor and duty of the family. To this day, certain African tribes grind the bones of the deceased and mix them with their food.

The Zulus burn all of the belongings of the dead, preventing the evil spirits from haunting in the neighborhood.

Some tribes would set up a fire ring around the bodies to scorch the wings of the spirits so as to prevent them from offending other members of the community.

Other tribes would perform the rituals of throwing spears and arrows into the air to kill hovering spirits, or they would eat bitter herbs to scare off or even kill spirits that may have penetrated their bodies.

③The Role of Religion

This fear of the dead partly contributed to the emergence of religious thought. For instance, the Polynesian word *tabu* means that a creature contacting the dead was isolated and shunned out of a religious or quasi-religious reason. In English this thought is interpreted as "defilement" or "contamination." To most people a dead body is indeed a taboo. Hebrew believed that the dead were considered unclean and whosoever is unclean by touching the dead shall be put outside the camp since they foul the camp in the midst of which the Lord dwells. A similar taboo is expressed in the old Persian scriptures. Anyone contacting a dead body was "powerless in mind, tongue, and hand." This paralysis was imposed upon by the evil spirits associated with the dead body. Sacrifices were also offered in honor of the dead to appease the spirits. In some cultures, these sacrifices were supposed to be used by the deceased in the future world. In some cases, self-mutilation such as the incision of toes or fingers was a kind of sacrifice to pay respect to the deceased.

In some cultures suicide was regarded as the ultimate and extreme respect and sacrifice. The sacrifice of dogs, horses and slaves was commonly practiced in Africa after the death of a king. In Japan, it was the custom for twenty or thirty slaves to conduct Hara Kiri at the death of a nobleman. In Fiji it was once thought necessary for the friends of the deceased as well as his wives and slaves to be strangled.

The strangest and cruelest rite was practiced among the Hindu, India before being outlawed by the British, which was known as suttee, or wife burning. The wife would put on her finest clothing and lie down by the side of her deceased husband on the funeral pyre, waiting to be cremated alive. And it was the eldest son who lit the pyre.

④Funeral Customs by Gender

In many cultures, men and women were treated differently at death. For example, the Cochieans buried their women, but suspended their men from trees. But the Ghonds buried their women but cremated their men. The Bongas buried their men with their faces to the North while their women with their faces to the South.

⑤Modern Funeral Customs

Even in modern times, human being's state of enlightenment does not dispense them completely from the old customs, with death still approaching us from a perspective of fear. Many of our funeral customs found their historical roots in pagan rituals.

Modern mourning clothing evolved from the custom of wearing special clothing to hide identity from returning spirits, who would fail to recognize people when they were in their new attire and therefore, would be confused to ignore them.

The custom of covering the face of the deceased with a sheet derives from pagan tribes who thought that the spirit of the dead escaped through the mouth. Accordingly, they would often hold the mouth and nose of a dying person shut so as to retain the spirits and delay death.

Feasting and gatherings concerning the funeral constituted a necessary part of the primitive funeral in which food offerings were made.

Wakes held today originated from ancient customs of keeping watch over the deceased in the hope that life would return.

The lighting of candles is an evolution from the use of fire mentioned above with the intention to protect the living from the spirits.

Bell ringing derives from the popular medieval belief that the spirits would be kept in confinement by the ringing of a consecrated bell.

The firing of a rifle volley over the deceased found its trace in the earlier tribal practice of throwing spears into the air to protect themselves from spirits hovering in the vicinity. Similarly, holy water was sprinkled on the body to ward off the demons.

Floral offerings were primarily presented to obtain favor with the spirit of the deceased. Funeral music had its origins in the ancient chants aimed to placate the spirits[1].

(2) Different Ways of Body Disposal

There are a number of ways in which humans ritually dispose of their dead.

①Earth Burial

Earth burial is globally typical, with the degree of contact of the corpse with the earth varying. Muslims bury the deceased in a shroud, similar to the ways adopted at certain times in Christian Europe. The British simply place the body in a coffin into the earth. North Americans are firstly conserved before being placed in a solid steel casket, which is put in a concrete-lined grave to ensure that the body is free from the contact with the ground. Accordingly, the decomposition process is more similar to that in an above-ground grave than in a Muslim burial. The funeral afterwards can be conducted years later once the flesh has decomposed and the bones are removed, as in medieval Europe or in Greece today, to an ossuary, or disposed of alternatively[2].

②Cremation

Cremation, followed by ritual disposal of the incinerated remains, is

---

① http: //bartonfuneral. com/funeral-basics/history-of-funerals/
② Davies, D. Death, Ritual and Belief. Cassell, London. 1997.

common worldwide, whose product is not ashes in the form of a powder, but pieces of bone, with the size being determined by the cremator or pyre temperature. In some Western countries, the remains are intentionally pulverized to produce nearly six pounds of ashes. The ways of dealing with remains are various: For instance, they may be ritually thrown into running water for them to mingle with the vast ocean in India; or they may be put in a pot before being buried in a family grave in Japan; or they may be put into a container and interred individually in churchyards in Britain; or they may be buried in an existing common family grave in Finland; or they may be scattered over land or ocean in the US. Mourners participate in the cremation in various ways[①]. Indians circle the pyre, with one crushing the burned skull for the purpose of releasing the spirit; Japanese pick up the cremated bones with large chopsticks before placing them into the burial pot.

Cremationis related with religion for its reflection of various concepts. For instance, in Hinduism and Sikhism, it means reincarnation; in Buddhism, it stands for rebirth, though it is merely in the past century and a half that cremation has become typical in Buddhist Thailand or Japan. In contrast, burial is historically conducted in Islam, Judaism, and Christianity, all of which embody revival of the body. In medieval Europe and still today in Islam, body parts might be missing after cruel wars, arousing great concern since the incompletion might be obstacle for resurrection.

Cremation has increased significantly in some Western countries, which is particularly accepted in secular and Protestant areas. It was in 1965 that the Pope allowed cremation, with the Catholic churches still not approving it. Still, Orthodox Christians do not cremate. In the West, cremation is highest in secularized Protestant countries, and lowest in religious, Catholic, and specifically Orthodox societies. Great Britain (72%), Denmark (71%), and Sweden (63%) contrast sharply with Eire (4%) and Italy (3%). Curiously, the US has a low cremation rate at 24%.

---

① Mitford J. The American Way of Death Revisited. Virago, London. 1999

In the case of cremation, the funeral may follow quite soon, with the products being interred or scattered. Anthropologists have noted that this period of cleansing body corruption may parallel both the period in which the soul is thought of as being in the preparation for its next existence and the period in which mourners reorganize their lives. In general, body, soul, and mourners are all in limbo, the end of which needs to be marked by the final funeral. Many Western funerals, however, consist of only one ritual, or several rituals (cremation, church service, refreshments) on the same day.

③Sea Burial

Sea burial is comparatively rather usual, occurring on the occasions in the history when someone dies on the high seas and it is infeasible for the corpse to return to land. However, other cases are that the deceased might die on land but choose to be buried at sea out of their sentimentally oceanic affection①.

2. Chinese Death Customs

Chinese death rituals contain a rich cultural connotation which can be traced back to the earliest dynasties. Today's Chinese family still follows those conventions with the maintenance of its core value.

(1) Death Customs of Ancient Han Nationality

"Funeral" is a ritual to mourn the deceased and to treat the body remains. Funeral customs bear significant meanings to Chinese despite different time and locations.

①Traditional Rites Before the Funeral

Traditionally, people begin to make preparation for the funeral when their family members are sick into death, cleaning the house with the removal of recreational facilities such as instruments to create a tidy and sol-

---

① Colin Blakemore and Shelia Jennett. "Funeral Practices: Cultural Variation. " The Oxford Companion to the Body. 2001.

emn atmosphere. The body is moved to the hall in the main room immediately after death and new clothes should be put on for the dead. While waiting aside, the families should keep absolute silence and should not make loud noises or even cry so as not to disturb the deceased and to ensure the peaceful passing away.

● Evocation

This is a ceremony trying to call the souls of dead back when they have just died, which is meant to ask them to stay in this world. Ancient people believe that when people die, their spirits stay near the body. Possibility exists to bring them back to life through certain ceremonies.

According to *The Book of Rites*, when a man die, the person who presides over the ceremony will climb up the roof and hold the dead one's clothes in his hand while yelling towards the north which symbolizes the nether world three times: "You are expected to come back!" A male is called by the name while a female is called by the formal name. Then, they roll up the clothes and throw down to the house where there is a servant waiting to catch the clothes with a box, who will take out the clothes and cover them over the body. People believe that clothes that are worn would smell of people's odor, connecting both human body and breath. Thus the soul would be attracted and get into the clothes following the familiar smell or shape.

The custom of calling the soul back prevailed in the Qin and Han dynasties, and has been handed down afterwards with its form and tools changing when people begin to use long narrow flags to call back the soul. If the dead cannot revive after the calling back ceremony, it can be confirmed that the dead have gone forever, and the funeral will be arranged formally.

● Death Announcement

The death of the person should be publicized by the family members, which is known as the death announcement, covering the name, time of birth and death, the date of the funeral as well as the date and placement of interment.

Generally speaking, the announcement can be carried out orally or through obituary, the former being adopted among civilians. Firecrackers have been exploded to announce the death to neighbors since Tang and Song dynasties. Oral message should be sent by the son of the dead personally to close relative and friends, otherwise it will be considered lack of etiquette. Before setting out, the son should first get dressed in mourning or wear a mourning cap and waistband. Arriving at the houses, the son should not enter the door but kowtow to the one coming out to meet him.

- Hastening for Funeral

In rites-governed ancient China, there were strict rules about hastening for funeral. On receiving the death news, one should wail in mourning and rush for the funeral. To attend the funeral of the parents, one should hurry on the journey day and night. On the way they should avoid bustling towns and make a detour so as not to disturb people.

- Condolence

When friends and relatives come to mourn, the mourning sons should meet them while beating the chest, crying with unwrapped hair and bare feet. Wooden memorial tablet is put in the atrium, covered with a flag. Then the sons and daughters keep vigil beside the coffin and wail to mourn respectively according to seniority.

②Rites for Funeral

- Inscription Banner

According to traditional customs of funeral rites, inscription banner, a long piece of silk, is marked with names and identities of the dead. In Chinese history, the inscription exists from the Zhou Dynasty to modern times but has been changing in nature. Originally, it serves as the purpose to identify the dead regardless of its status, however, with the social development, they indicates the ranks of the dead with different length: the higher, the longer.

- Buddhist Ceremony

The Buddhist ceremony is a combination of the religious culture and the traditional culture of rites which used to be adopted in the funerals of

Buddhist only. Later it is gradually accepted by common people and then extends to every social class. The ceremony is particularly popular after *Tang* and *Song* Dynasty, through which the deceased is believed to be exempt from the mortal sin he/she commits and the spirits would go to heaven to enjoy happiness, otherwise they would suffer cruel tortures in hell and their family members could not live in peace and contentment.

If a family member dies, the first process is "shifting chant", where an ashram consisting of monks, *Lamas* and nuns are invited to chant sutras at home, freeing the deceased from sins and comfort the soul as well as changing the fate in the next life through religious ceremonies. The chanting generally lasts three days in a row during mourning. With the completion of the interment, the family should hold memorial ceremonies and invite Buddhists to chant sutra on the death day in the following three years. It is revealed that Buddhism is tightly bound to funerals and imposes a profound influence on Chinese funeral culture especially in the later period of the feudal society.

● Encoffining

Formal encoffining, also called the "undertaking", is to put the corpse into the coffin, bidding farewell to the dead.

At dawn, the coffin will be lifted into the hall, with a bed prepared on which the corpse is to be moved and covered with a quilt before being put into the coffin. While encoffining, the son should hold the body and keep crying sorrowfully. After the corpse is put into the coffin, clothes of four seasons will be filled in the corners. In some cases, some valuable objects cherished by the dead are buried as well. Having finished the above, the coffin cover is put onto the coffin by craftsmen and sealed with nails. At this time, the bed is to be taken away, and the memorial tablet is set up, in front of which is an altar, where offerings of food and drink are placed. Then the memorial is held till the encoffining ends.

After the formal encoffining, memorial ceremonies with wails are held both in the morning and evening, with food offered on the table in front of the coffin. The sons and other younger generation should stand beside the coffin to receive friends and relatives for mourning.

● Funeral Procession

What follows the encoffining is the interment, which is called *Bin* in Chinese. In history, there exist various kinds of customs of the funeral precession among civilians. Traditionally, the family of the dead should invite a geomancer to put down the days of the birth and death, age and dates of funeral on a piece of blank paper, which is to be presented and verified before the coffin is carried out of town. The day before the procession, friends and relatives would come to attend the memorial ceremony and Buddhists are invited to chant sutras. They are to be seated beside the coffin through the night together with the sons, which is called "staying through the night" to accompany the dead. The next morning, the son should wipe off the dust on the coffin with a new broom, and a copper is to be put under the foot of the coffin, a manner called "lifting the coffin" . Then follows the ritual of "biding farewell to the spirit" . The coffin is carried out of the hall and the son heads forward with the long narrow paper flag in hand, followed by the younger generations and so on, crying loudly in mourning. Then coffin is placed on a hearse, which should be pulled with a rope attached to it so that the hearse advances slowly.

In some cases, friends of the dead would collect money to buy some food and liquor as offerings, and serve a feast on the way the coffin is to pass. An elder of high prestige would be elected the host of the memorial ceremony. Once the coffin arrives, all people prostrated themselves, with the host presenting the offerings in front of the coffin and reading eulogy. Finally, the son cries to express his gratitude and the procession moves on. Usually dances and drama performances are also arranged to let the deceased fully enjoy the final worldly pleasure.

Having gone through various rituals, the procession arrives at the graveyard. All the family members cry loudly to pay farewell to the deceased. Coffin and funeral objects are put into the pit, with tomb door closed and earth shoveled. So far the funeral has come to an end.

③Rites after the Funeral

• *Zuoqi*: Seven Weeks

Usually the family members would conduct "seven weeks of mourning" for the deceased, a ritual originated from the concept of Six Realms of Samsara in Buddhism, which advocates that the seven-week salvation will contribute to the happiness of the dead thereafter. Among the 49 days, the "first seven", the seventh day after death, is the first important occasion during the whole mourning process, with the custom differing in various regions. It is widely believed that the soul of the deceased will return home to bid farewell on this very day, then it would be supposed to drink the water of Lethe to erase all the memory about the past before setting foot on the road to the lower world, The family, according to the custom, would prepare a meal for the soul before it comes back and shy away by going to bed with lights off for the purpose of avoiding sentimental moments of the soul, which might otherwise delay its reincarnation. Likewise, the odd number such as "third seven", "fifth seven" and "seventh seven" are also important days to mourn the dead.

• Mourning Observation

As mentioned above, the interment does not mean the end of a funeral, and the family members as well as friends should go on observing mourning for the dead in mourning clothes, the length of which lasts differently from three days to several months or even three days based on the blood relationship, marriage, friendship and political relations. During the time, people in mourning should maintain strict control over food, clothing, shelter and transportation, keeping everything simple in daily life, expressing the so-called "filial piety" in extreme ways of repressing human nature in social activities to show their condolence for the dead.

For instance, fasting is adopted during the mourning, and the children should not eat or drink in three days right after parents' death, only consuming a small amount of porridge barely able to maintain body needs. If mourning people lust for delicious food and eat luxuriously against the rites, they would be criticized by the public or even punished by authority.

(2) Chinese Special Death Customs

①Corpse Driving

In the west part of Hunan Province of China, there exists an old tradition of corpse driving. In traditional Chinese culture, people are deeply attached to their hometown. Therefore, at the dying moment, people always wish to return to their native land. Being buried into the ancestral grave becomes the most cherished desire for those who died away from hometown. Being full of high mountain ranges and precipitous paths with speed currents, west part of Hunan is confined to poor transportation. A profession of corpse driving comes into being under such circumstances.

Corpse drivers should meet three qualifications. First, he needs to be bold since he is required to be with the dead alone, even in the dark. Second, he needs to be strong. Corpse drivers usually live outdoors and have to endure the hardships of travelling. Third, he needs to be ugly that people are afraid to see him, which adds to its mystery. If one wants to be a driver apprentice, his parents should sign a written pledge and he is to be tested by the master personally. Generally speaking, the apprentice should be male above sixteen with a height of 170cm. Meeting the basic requirement, qualified apprentice will be asked by the corpse driver to look at the sun in the sky and spin around with a sudden stop. Those who fail to recognize all directions are eliminated. Then they are required to carry things on shoulders in order to test their physical strength. Finally, there will be a test in which the corpse driver puts a leaf of the phoenix tree on the top of a tomb in a remote mountain and ask the apprentice to locate it alone. Only in this way can the apprentice be proved competent to be a corpse driver.

Arriving at the destination, the corpse driver will take a mouthful of magic water and spray it onto the face of the corpse, which jumps following the driver as if it is brought back to life. Then the corpse driver spray magic water to take back spells for the body to fall into the coffin completely.

②Wizards of the *Nuo* Dance

Nuo is a very ancient Chinese ceremony to meet the deity and dispel ghosts, during which the Nuo dance is performed, a tradition originated from primitive witchcrafts and enjoying a long history among many nationalities. While dancing, the dances wearing a mask will hold a weapon in hand to dispel ghosts and pray for blessings.

In the funeral rites of the *Tujia* Nationality, the mourning hall is often set up in the central hall, with alter in front on which there are two paper men, the god and goddess of *Nuo*, who are regarded as the humane primogenitor of *Tujia*. At night, the headman with a long narrow flag in hand leads four persons with the gong, cymbal or *Suona* to circle around the coffin, and then moves outside the central hall to continue their dancing and singing. At this time, the host may explode firecrackers to entertain both gods and people, releasing souls from purgatory and exorcising the evil spirits. Meanwhile, people will build the *Naihe* Bridge with bamboo wood in the open space of the village road. Under the bridge, they perform the mourning dance and drama for the dead and ancestors. Then, led by the headman, they walk across the bridge to lead the way for the spirit, indicating that the dead goes to the heaven and lives in happiness. Death is highly valued in *Tujia* since they consider death as the beginning of another life.

③Cliff Burial

Cliff burial is the most unique funeral rite in Chinese funeral culture, which is to hang the corpse in a coffin on the cliff. This custom is so mysterious that some specific details remain unknown to the experts. Cliff burial is mostly found in southern China where features mountains and karst landscape. Many minorities live in this area, and most of them hold the *Nuo* culture which might result in this tradition according to historical research. It is believed that the higher the coffin is placed, the more respect is shown to the deceased. In recent years, archaeologists have found many hanging coffins in Jiangxi, Fujian, Guangdong and some other provinces.

Riverside and coastal cliffs are common places for cliff burial. Most are placed about ten meters above water, however, there are some which are placed over a hundred meters above. There are three types of cliff burial. One is to put one end of the coffin in a natural cave or rock cracks and the other end on stakes. Another is to reshape the natural cave in the coastal cliff and then place the coffin inside. The third is to dig a square hole of 1 to 1. 5 meters wide or smaller in riverside cliff and place the coffin in it.

It is extremely dangerous to dig these holes under the conditions of low productive force. According to historical record, most of the holes are dug from top to bottom which is definitely the effort of more than one people. The shape of the coffins resembles a boat, which indicates the widespread use of boat in those places. In the places where cliff burial is popular, people live near water or engage in fishery who often go fishing at sea in groups and many die on the boat. So, making boat-shaped coffins is related to their ancestors' production activities.

④Tree Burial

Tree burial is to put the dead on trees and let it weather, which is connected with the hominids living in the wild field or remote mountains. It is recorded in history that tree burial was very popular among the ancient ethnic group Khitan, who lived in northern China in the *Song* Dynasty. If one member of the Khitan family died, people would first hold a farewell party, then wrap the corpse and put it on a tree in the high mountain to let it weather. The bone would be cremated three years later.

There are mainly three types of tree burial. One is to place the dead body on a tree, which is the most primitive form. In some minorities in southern China, people put the dead on a tree and let it weather into a mummy. Another type is to bind the dead body onto a tree. For instance, people living in the minorities regions of Guizhou Province will bundle their entire body of the dead with vines and bind it onto a tree. The third type is to place the dead into a tree hole either naturally formed or cut by knives and axes. Among the Oroqen Nationality in northeast China, the local people will cut a tree hole as the burial place for the deceased.

Viewing from the history of tree burial, people choose this form mainly because the tree played a very significant role in their concept. In ancient times, due to the limitation of productive force, primitive people think that nature has the spirit and shall be worshiped and tree burial is the perfect example of combination between human and nature.

3. Western Death Customs

The history of funerals is as old as human culture, which can be dated back to at least 300, 000 years ago. For instance, archeologists have discovered Neanderthal skeletons with a typical layer of flower pollen in the Shanidar Cave, Iraq; in Pontnewydd Cave, Wales and at other sites across Europe, an interpretation of the fact that Neanderthals believed in an afterlife. Despite the inexplicit evidence, it revealed that the dead were buried on purpose.

(1) Ancient Western Burial Rituals

An earth mound or a stone heap over the body or ashes of the deceased can be the most simple and universally ancient funeral monuments.

The burial place for ancient Jews was not specifically fixed, which means they can be buried upon the highways, in gardens, or on mountains. However, according to the Christian Old Testament, Abraham was buried together with his wife, Sarah, in the Cave of the Patriarchs in Machpelah; David, king of Israel, and the other kings were buried in the certain field particularly arranged for the kings, allowing them to rest with ancestors.

①Ancient Greece

Originally, Greeks were buried in given places in their own houses. Later on, they established burial grounds in desert islands outside the towns to isolate them from disturbance. Meanwhile, it can reduce the possibility for the people to be infected by those who died of contagious diseases.

The dominating burial custom was interment between the Cycladic civilization in 3000B. C. and the Hypo-Mycenaean period in 1200 – 1100 B. C. It was not until the 11th century B. C. that the cremation of the dead became a new burial practice probably under the Eastern influence. In the

Christian era, both cremation and interment were conducted depending on the choices of certain areas.

Since the Homeric era, the major Greek funerals were the próthesis, the ekphorá, the burial and the perídeipnon which have been performed in Greece till today.

Próthesis is the deposition of the departed on the funereal bed and the threnody of his relatives which were performed in the residence of the deceased. Today the ritual still remains, with the body being placed in the open casket. An indispensable section features Greek tradition is the epicedium, the mournful songs sung by the relatives along with professional mourners, who no longer exist in modern society. The deceased was accompanied by his beloved the whole night before the burial, a compulsory ritual persists nowadays.

Ekphorá is the process of carrying the mortal remains from his home to the church, nowadays, and afterward to the burial place. According to the ancient law, the procession should pass through the streets of the city in silence. Typically certain belongings of the departed were put in the coffin to go along with him. In certain regions, coins are needed to be placed in the coffin to pay Charon, the one who ferries the dead to the underworld. Finally, a farewell kiss is given to the dead by the beloved family members before the casket is sealed.

Cicero, the Roman orator, claimed that the custom of planting flowers in the grave is to ensure the ease of the deceased and the peace of the ground which is maintained contemporarily. The mourners go back to the house of the departed for the perídeipnon, the dinner after the burial following the ceremony. As revealed by archaeological findings such as ash traces, animal bones, crockery shards, dishes and basins-the dinner during the classical era was also conducted at the burial spot. According to the written materials, however, the dinner could be served at home as well.

Another important funeral occasions are "the thirds", two days after the burial and "the ninths", eight days after the burial, when the concerned parties of the deceased gathered at the burial spot, and this custom is maintained presently. In addition, memorial services take place at regular intervals such as 40 days, 3 months, 6 months, 9 months, 1 year after the death and from then on every year on the death anniversary in the modern times. The relatives of the departed are in mourning, during which women are in black clothes and men wear a black armband.

②Ancient Rome

In ancient Rome, before someone's death, the eldest male of the pater families would be summoned to bed, trying to catch and take in the last breath of the deceased.

Funerals of the people with high social status were commonly held by certain undertakers called *libitinarii*. Despite the lack of written description, it was believed that an important part of the funeral rites comprised a public procession to the tomb or pyre to cremate the body, with the family members carrying the image of the family's deceased ancestors. Later on, only the most locally prominent families were entitled to bear the masks. The procession could be rather boisterous with the participation of mimes, dancers, and musicians plus professional female mourners. Besides, there were benevolent funerary organizations undertaking such rites on their behalf.

Nine days after the body disposal, a feast was held and a libation was poured over the grave or the ashes. Because most Romans preferred cremation, the ashes were usually collected in an urn before being placed in a niche of a columbarium, a collective tomb. During the nine days, passersby were warned by Mediterranean Cypress hung in the neighborhood since the house was regarded as being stained. In the end, the house would be cleaned and swept to symbolically remove the taint of death.

Several Roman holidays are associated with a family's ancestors. For instance, the *Parentalia* is held between February 13 and 21 to worship the family's forebears; and the Feast of the *Lemures*, held on May 9, 11, and 13, in which ghosts were said to be active. Therefore, the pater families would appease them with beans offerings.

With the passage of time, an extravagant funeral of the politically or socially dominating kin group would be viewed as negatively influential in

Roman society, which did harm to social fairness since people share the e-
qual right of grief. Therefore, increasing restrictions were established by the
authority concerning the length, expense and manner of the mourning funerals. For example, under some laws, women were inhibited from loud wailing
and limits were imposed on people as to expenditure on tombs and burial
costumes.

Despite the burial limitations, the tombs of rich and the common people still differed which were usually constructed during their lifetime. The
former were typically built of marble, with the ground enclosed with walls
and trees planted around. But sepulchres of average people were built underground which were called hypogea. Niches were cut out of the walls with
urns placed inside which were named columbaria[1].

(2) Western Death Traditions

①Wake

A wake is the custom to watch over a body from death until burial
which derives from Roman Catholics. It is a once common practice in western English speaking countries, specifically in the America and Ireland and
the vigil turned to a religious observance in early Christian England, with
people believing that the dead spirits would return home for a visit after
death.

Wakes consists of prayers for the deceased and comforts to the beloved
family members of the departed. With family members being accompanied by
mourners, most modern wakes are interrupted for the night. The modern version of wake is called the Visitation, in which the departed's family receives friends' condolence and sympathy on the day or night before a funeral.

The conventional "Irish Wake" is a mourning custom conducted in Ireland until the mid – 1970s, which is now practiced only in distant Irish regions that value tradition. Soon after the death, word of mouth will spread

---

① http: //en. wikipedia. org/wiki/Funeral#Ancient_ funeral_ rites the news and neighbors will help in preparing food and drinks and alcoholic beverages. Therefore, it is an occasion for family, friends, and neighbors of the deceased to express their grief. The corpse will commonly be dressed in white linen before being placed in its own bed and it should never been left alone. Briefly speaking, Irish wakes were the combination of joy and sorrow.

In general, the tone of the wake may be varied according to regional-preference. For some, it is a celebration of the passed life. For some, it is an opportunity to honor the departed in a loving atmosphere with stories, songs, and jokes that relate to his or her memory. However, in some cultures, the wake is rather solemn, with the representative being the Jewish rite of sitting Shivah[1].

②Funeral

A funeral, or a memorial service, is often officiated by clergy from the departed's church or religion, which may be performed at places such as funeral home, church, crematorium and cemetery chapel. Besides the location, the date can be chosen following the family's will, usually several days after the death. Such memorial service is primarily common among Christians, with Roman Catholics referring to it as a mass when communion is offered. During the process, a priest says prayers and blessings beside the sealed casket, with the family members making additional remarks. Funerals conducted in the funeral home can be rather simple, chiefly comprising prayers, blessings and eulogies from the family, with a clergy or a close family member directing the ritual.

The typical open-casket service offer mourners the chance to look at the departed for the last time. According to sequence of precedence, the immediate family members often approach the coffin firstly, followed by other mourners, and finally the immediate family may file past again, so they are the last to see their beloved before the sealing of the casket. But for some religions, the coffin is traditionally closed after the wake and is never re-

①   http: //thefuneralsource. org/trad15. html

opened for the funeral service.

Funeral services usually consist of prayers, readings from a sacred text, hymns and words of comfort by the clergy. Typical eulogy is often delivered by a relative or close friend, which chiefly depicts the unforgettable memories and accomplishments. However, in some religious denominations such as Roman Catholic, Anglican and the Churches of Christ, eulogies from loved ones are not encouraged during this service for the sake of tradition preservation. In such cases, the eulogy is simply done by a member of the clergy even though he might never know the deceased. Church bells will probably be tolled both before and after the service.

In the funeral service, the coffin may be covered with a large bunch of flowers, of a casket spray. And for the one ever served in a military or governmental branch, there might be a national flag covering the casket.

All in all, funeral customs vary greatly from region to region, but generally speaking, any kind of noise other than quiet whispering or mourning in the service is regarded as being particularly disrespectful.

③Burial service

A burial service is the ritual to bury or cremate the departed's corpse at the side of the grave, tomb, mausoleum or cremation as the final conclusion. In most cases, the burial service will be conducted soon after the funeral or the burial service will be held at a later time.

In many religious traditions, it is the pallbearer, male close relatives but not the immediate relatives or friends of the deceased, to carry the coffin from the chapel to the hearse and finally to the location of the burial service. During the memorial service, they are arranged to sit in a specifically reserved area.

Sometimes, the important belongings of the departed will be buried or entombed under the ground with their owners. However, it is not the case for Jewish services, which require that nothing of value be buried with the decedent.

(3) Western Special Death Customs

①Europe

Europe, as any other part of world, possesses a large number of death rites.

• Romania

In Transylvania, Romania, it is believed that each person has his/her own tree and his/her star. The falling of a star symbolizes the death of a person. Fir is regarded as the tree of life, which will be placed at the head of a grave.

After the death of a person, young men will be responsible to bring the fir from forest and meet with a group of women at the village entrance. They sing a song telling the relation between the deceased and the tree, with the letter turning dry and rot near the decedent.

In a village named Săpânţa, the local cemetery is pretty unique, known as The Merry Cemetery, which comprise approximately 800 beautiful tombstones with simple paintings. On every piece of tombstone, there is vivid and funny description of the life that the departed used to live.

• Poland

In Poland, when someone dies, the door and windows of the house are supposed to be opened, offering an outlet for the soul of the decedent. Mirrors are covered with a piece of cloth and clocks are put to a stop. The body will be washed and dressed by a professional woman. Following the Tradition, the corpse is put on boards between two chairs or two tables.

The relatives and friends keep vigil during the night, and the body is placed in the casket on the day of funeral. Usually the body will be kept in the house for three days and people sing and pray rosary and litanies. The funeral will be conducted on the third day after the death.

• Ireland

Ireland shares some similar customs. The window is kept wide for the soul to withdraw from the house, with the path completely accessible. Anyone blocks the way will be inflicted with bad luck. But about two hours later, people should close the window, preventing the soul from coming back.

- UK

In certain parts of the UK, it is a tradition to put coins, particularly pennies on the eyelids of the departed.

In the Scottish Highlands, a long-lasted death rite prevails. The decedent is buried with bit of soil and salt placed in a wooden plate on his chest. The former implies the deterioration of the body and its integration with the earth while the letter symbolizes the immortality of the soul.

- Netherlands

In the Netherlands, people used to cover the windows of the house with white sheet if someone dies until the end of the funeral. But this tradition almost goes extinct in the modern society, with no one knowing for sure about the origin of this tradition. One popular explanation is that it is done to drive off the evil spirits.

Another custom is that females produce a night dress named "doodshemd" particularly for her wedding night on which her initials are sewed. After the wedding night the "doodshemd" was washed and reserved in the closet as the "linnenkast".

The second time a woman dress in her "doodshemd" is on the occasion of her death. The needle used in making of the dress would be broken in half and buried with the woman. Otherwise, people simply throw it into the fire.

- Lithuania

When someone dies, in Lithuania, a female family member is responsible for naming all the virtues of the decedent, which is regarded as the opportunity for the relatives to express love and appreciation for all the good deeds the departed did during his/her lifetime.

In the past, various items could be placed in the casket to accompany the departed in the afterlife. Now only certain objects such as rosaries and pictures of saints are put inside the coffin, which is supposed to be taken out of home as long as the corpse is placed inside. Everything must be done neatly so that there would be no more deaths in that house.

Three handfuls of soil is put over the coffin, bringing eternal peace for the departed. A particular dinner is held following the funeral, a treat for the soul of the dead and its companions. With this dinner, the survivals ask the dead to leave the family unharmed and to ask God for blessing as well. The food should remain untouched otherwise may bring another death to the family.

Lithuanian women used to wear white kerchiefs in the mourning, the color of death. Another typical feature is that cemeteries are usually located on some hill. Therefore, in the Lithuanian folklore term, "high hill" is synonymous for cemetery.

● Estonia

In some villages in Estonia, people tend to believe that the dying person is supposed to be fed before death, otherwise he or she could visit the family members in their dreams and demand for food. It is even worse that greater misery could be imposed on those who are still alive.

In Salme, it was said that a sick patient could be healed by a simple touch of a dying person. Meanwhile, the following words needed to be announced: You are departing now and take my misfortune along.

● Russia

Immediately after the death of a Russian, a glass of water covered with piece of bread on it is placed next to the body or in the windowsill. Then, six weeks following the death, every family meal should contain a glass of vodka with slices of bread, as the sacrificed offering for the departed[1].

②North America

● America

The customs mentioned here are the Native American death rites.

The Dakota or Sioux Native Americans live in North and South Dakota Dakota, Minnesota, Montana and Nebraska. The Dakota painted the face of

---

[1]　http: //traditionscustoms. com/death-rites/european-death-rites

the departed with red, which is regarded as the color of life in their culture.

The Navajo or Diné people live in Arizona, New Mexico, Utah and California who possess many different death rites. The Navajo believe the crying of an owl signifies death and the sound of coyote symbolize the impending evil or death.

When someone in the community dies, it will be wrapped in a new blanket before three or four people put it on a horse. Driving the horse northward, they will bury the body in a place far enough. The horse will be killed to carry the body into the afterworld.

Both Navajo and Apache people feared ghosts of the dead who were believed to haunt the living. Burning the body, its house as well as all of its belongings, family members of the decedents chose to moved away so as not to be haunted.

It is the tradition for the Choctaw people to place the corpse on a plate, leaving it to decay by nature. Then the skull and some long bones will be taken apart to be presented at the feast held to honor the decedent two or three years after his death.

The Seminole people live in Florida and Oklahoma who used to put the body of the departed in the *chickee*, an open-sided building with thatched roof, cypress poles and palm fronds. With the body left there, the community withdrew from the place and settled somewhere else.

Another tradition still remains among the Seminole. After people's death, their beloved gather all of the possessions and throw them into the swamp.

The Comanche people nowadays live in Oklahoma and Texas. It was the custom for their group members to discard the old and sick except for their family, which was not conducted out of cruelty but due to their belief that evil spirits would attack the body of old and sick.

With the knees of the deceased folded and tied, the corpse was washed before being dressed in finest clothing and put upon a blanket. The face was painted red with eyes covered by clay.

The relatives bid farewell to their beloved, which was then wrapped in blanket and tied with buffalo-hide rope, with a horse carrying it to the burial place.

The Comanche preferred to bury their dead in a cave, a ravine or a crevice among the rocks. Buried in a sitting position, the body was placed in a hole, on the ground, or around stacked rocks and wooden poles. The survivals also chose to leave the place where the death occurred, looking for their settlement somewhere else.

The Nez Perce tribe lives in the Pacific Northwest region of the United States. It was the custom to sacrifice a horse, wives or slaves in the case of a warrior's death.

The Hopi people today chiefly live in the reservation of the northeast of Arizona. On the fourth day after death, "hikwsi" or "person's breath" is believed to move to a place called Underworld or Lower World, other forms of existence. However, being there does not necessarily mean the disconnections with world of living. Rather, the Hopi consider that *hikwsi* can return in the form of clouds or rain[①].

• Canada

For Canadians with high social status, or for a member of the armed forces or the police, public rituals about funeral arrangements enjoy priority over individual customs and expectations which demand the dominant role of professional organizations. State funerals are organized to pay respect to public officials, offering citizens a rare chance to lament and commemorate national figures.

Concerning death announcement, traditional codes need to be followed. Immediate kin take precedence over other relatives who are entitled to be nearer to the scene of death, and it is a break of etiquette not to reveal the truth to a close relative about a death. With Orthodox Jews, the message of death and arrangement may be suspended since funeral have to wait until after the Sabbath.

---

① http://traditionscustoms.com/death-rites/native-american-death-rites

The preparation of the body is required to be done by the eldest son or by a designated person for certain religious groups, such as Hindus, Sikhs and Muslims, but for most Canadians, it is the responsibility of the funeral director to prepare the body: body wash, blood ejection from the veins and embalming fluid substitution, the chest and abdominal cavity cleaning and disinfection, makeup application, hair trimming and body attire offered by the next of kin. For most Muslims, they usually wrap the body in a shroud soon after body wash and the burial occurs the same day as death following Islamic custom.

Funeral services vary religiously and culturally. If there is no local mosque, the last prayer of the Muslims for the body may be conducted in the decedent's home before being transported to the cemetery. For Roman Catholics, Anglicans and Eastern Orthodox Christians, the normal practice is to perform the service at the church with the body present since the church is the only approved place to hold a mass. However, in other community groups, the church is considered the right location for funerals, despite the denomination. A more recent trend is the memorial service to honor the deceased, usually with particularly poetry or music selected, which is lack of any religious reference.

The interment norm is ground burial even though cremation is increasingly prevailing in Canada. Early Canadian Buddhists, according to creed of the Buddha, unexceptionally cremated the deceased. But now some Buddhists have abandoned this tradition, turning to ground burial, or ashes interment in a grave. Some Orthodox Christians, traditional Muslims, Jews and native people repel cremation for religious reasons. Even among Roman Catholics, the tendency toward cremation is spreading, particularly when the Pope canceled the official ban against the practice since 1983. In addition, interment is important for Sunni Muslims, who are influenced by the norm of facing Mecca. Finally, shortage of burial space has also contributed to the trend of cremation.

Ethnic and religious cemeteries are often seen in Canada, having restrictions according to memberships. Despite the legislated regulations concerning private cemeteries, they still exist besides public ones. A graveyard is viewed legally as a property and a deed is issued for the lot. Most cemeteries have restrictions about tombstones, markers and even flowers. Modern cemeteries usually prefer a park-like setting to traditional rows of gravesites.

As for bereavement period, there is no fixed specification. For instance, traditional Jewish law stipulates one-week-mourning. Widows, in traditions like Coptic Christian, are supposed to be in black for a whole year, with a memorial service held in the end. Some Catholics conduct a mass on the first anniversary of the deceased and some have masses said for the departed, but Protestants have abandoned this ritual of the decedents. Muslims may hold an annual memorial dinner, particularly in the case of the well-known individuals.

Mormons usually perform certain ceremonies to elevate the souls of the dead to a state of grace. Various Orthodox worshippers have an annual occasion to memorize the deceased, with the names of the decedents read, and prayers said, after which the family visit the cemetery.

For Canadians, the interment is probably the last public opportunity for relating to the deceased. Among some native individuals of the Yukon and northern B. C. , small buildings with a fence are erected over a grave, with symbolic sacrifices offered for the journey to the next life. Mausoleums may also be constructed for the wealthy or the distinguished decedents, but heavy expenditure and a reluctance of glorification of the dead has restrained people from practicing it widely. Graveyard visitation may help to promote the memory but, except for those ancestral convention followers, there is little direct link with the deceased[1].

4. Comparisons

Generally speaking, Chinese and western death rituals differ under the following influences:

---

[1]　http：//www. thecanadianencyclopedia. ca/en/article/funeral-practices/

(1) Religion

Religion exerts a significant impact on human behavior, the death rituals are in no exception. Basically, China is a country of polytheism, with a
combination of Confucianism, Daoism and Buddhism, the first being the
fundamental one, of course. In traditional Chinese culture, there has been a
belief in immortality of the soul. Therefore, people are concerned about the
soul of the deceased which is attached to deities and worshipped in ancestor
temples. Later on, the concept of "six metempsychosis and reincarnation of
the afterlife" came into being with the introduction of Buddhism. Daoism,
the native religion, originally had little influence among civilians since it
just advocated Chinese alchemy for people to be immortal; however, it
gradually absorbed many ideas of the above two religions and became similarly important in people's life, especially on the notion of underworld. To
sum up, Chinese funeral rituals primarily reflect Confucian tradition, coupled with the traces of Buddhism and Daoism, resulting in the typical Chinese funeral of grand and costly customs which go through complicated procedures.

On the other hand, western culture is monotheism, with the Christianity taking the dominant role in people's life. Western funerals are essentially
religion-oriented. The soul of each individual Christian is believed to interact
directly with God, hence, the soul, rather than the flash of the deceased
is valued. In this case, western funerals tend to be simple, praying for the
dead to relieve its pain in return for a happy soul in heaven.

(2) Ethic Values

Chinese and western ethic values are distinct as well. The core value of
the former is "filial piety" which is formed since *Qin* and *Han* Dynasty under the influence of Confucianism, a concept elevated to the greatest significance. Therefore, the solemn and grand funeral burial is the perfect manifestation of being "filial" for the children of the dead, otherwise, a rough
procedure will lead to public condemnation, even disgrace the whole fami-

ly.

In contrast, western ethics attach great importance to individualism and equal rights, the same is true as to the parent-child relationship. Particularly since the Renaissance, the value of self-respect is increasingly visible. Thus the point of the death rituals is not to inform others how sorrowful the children are, but to pay respect to the God, bringing peace to the deceased.

(3) Life and Death Philosophy

In Chinese traditional culture, death is viewed from a negative and deceptive perspective, which is generally avoided especially in the interaction to older generations. Being a symbol of misfortune and horror, death is never an acceptable topic in daily conversation. Therefore, people are reluctant to face it, not to mention to treat it rationally. Contrarily, death is treated more philosophically by westerners, who believe that death is the topic worth discussed in daily life', and the education of which can be a part of the primary and secondary education. In this case, the death of relatives and friends can be taken more easily for the common westerners.

What's more, the fundamental value behind life and death is responsibility, with sacrifice being the sublimation of human spirits. However, the center of Chinese philosophy is the loyalty to authority and belief. Being an agricultural society, China has always advocated the combination of human and nature since people chiefly are reliable on the nature, so fatalism is strongly advocated with people being pessimistic towards death. But westerners are more optimistic when facing death, believing that the choice of life and death lies in the hand of each individual.

All in all, the contemporary Chinese and western funeral rituals differ a lot due to the sharply contrasted ideas between the two societies.

Chapter Eight

Customs of Festival

1. General Introduction

A festival is an event primarily initiated by a community, centering on and celebrating some unique culture of that community and its traditions, often observed as a local or national holiday.

(1) Origin

Even though every nation has its own holidays, the origins of them share the following four aspects:

①Production Activity

Productive activities are the fundamentals of people's life. Therefore, many holidays are associated with the industries such as agriculture, forestry, fishery etc. Take China for example, one of the most significant moment: the Spring Festival, is the occasion to celebrate the harvest and pray for the next one.

②Religion

Religion is the common ideology held in every nation. Especially in the days of under-developed science, people were more confined to the belief that they were governed by kinds of spirits, which see its reflection in religion. Generally speaking, a number of traditional festivals are religious or even converted from its holidays. Christmas, one of the western grandest holidays, is the time in memory of Jesus's birthday. People take the opportunities to worship the spirits, hoping for fortune and prosperity.

③Heroes or Events

Throughout history, there are numerous heroes who contribute immensely to the society, regarded as the role models by offspring and there are important events which matter to the survival of the whole nation. Accordingly, the special holidays come into being in honor of the greatest people and events. For instance, the Dragon Boat Festival is the time to honor Quyuan, a Chinese patriotic poet; July fourth, is the day for Americans to celebrate their national independence.

④Social Interaction

Human beings own the strong desire to promote social relationship through mutual interaction. Therefore, assembly activities arise to meet the needs such as Carnival in Brazil and Palio in Italy.

(2) Characteristics

Folk holidays all possess the similar characteristics:

①Periodism

Holidays are characteristic of being seasonal, which cycle based on regular period. The periodism enables people to remember the festivals easily, ensuring the orderly arrangement for the festivals.

②Speciality

Festivals are namely opposite to ordinary days, which are special in aspects that folks might wear certain costumes or eat given foods on that day, doing certain recreations to celebrate the unique occasion.

③Collectivism

No holidays are not collective and individuals can't create a holiday and thus observe it by themselves. Besides, most festivals are national that shared by the same nation, mirroring ethnic economy, culture, psychology and belief. Consequently, some holidays are unique among given nationalities, such as the Shoton Festival of Tibetans and the Memorial Day of west movement of Xibo Nationality in China. What's more, even many nationalities have the same holidays due to cultural blending, each nation has its typical way to celebrate them.

④Entertainment

The majority of the holidays are entertaining, and different kinds of ceremonies are conducted to create the cheerful atmosphere for celebration. Even in modern society, people no more do sacrifices to pray for fortune and prosperity, words of good will are still expressed to bring the best wishes and luck.

(3) Functions

①Prompting

One of the important functions of holidays is to advocate virtues socially such as the Mother's day, Father's day, Women's Day and Children's day to encourage the care for parents, women and kids.

②Comforting

Mentality governs human activities. Aspirations sustain people to live an active life, and comfort is a daily necessity for human beings to pursue satisfaction and security in life. Therefore, folks worship spirits through festival sacrifices in the hope of obtaining happiness and good luck.

③Communicating

Festivals, no matter in the form of family reunions or community gatherings, aim to promote social communication. People are offered the opportunities for mutual understanding in the specific occasions, spreading the fine social atmosphere so as to build up a harmonious and benevolent society.

2. Chinese Festival Customs

Featuring different styles and themes, conventional Chinese festivals are an indispensable section of the country's history and culture, both ancient and modern. Generally speaking, a close relationship exists between many traditional festivals and the 24 solar terms of the Chinese Calendar. Some others are associated with religious beliefs, superstitions and myths. The majority of the festivals took shape around the Han Dynasty.

(1) Festival Customs of Han Nationality

Every festival derived from its own unique origins, with the customs mirroring the conventional practices and philosophy of the Chinese people. The most popular festivals are listed as the following:

①The Spring Festival

Chinese Spring Festival, or Lunar New Year, has over 4, 000 years of history. It is the greatest festival for the Chinese families to hold reunion. Dating back to the Shang Dynasty, Spring Festival comprises colorful activities.

It is the custom of Chinese to present offerings to ancestors in the last month of Chinese lunar calendar, with people doing utter cleaning, having bathes and so on. Gradually, people commence to honor different deities as well on that occasion, when all the farm works completed. Therefore, the sacrificing time altered based on the farming schedule and began to be fixed from the Han Dynasty. The customs of worshipping deities and ancestors remains even though the ceremonies are not as grand as before. It is also the time that spring is coming, so people held all kinds of ceremonies to welcome it.

According to folk custom, this traditional holiday actually lasts from the 23rd day of the twelfth month to the 15th day of the first month (Lantern Festival) in the lunar calendar, which can be roughly divided into three periods: the days before the festival, the festival days and the days after the New Year Day, with various rituals conducted in each phase.

• Preceding Days

—Preliminary Eve

The 23rd day of the twelfth lunar month is regarded as Preliminary Eve, when people used to offer sacrifice to the kitchen god. However, in modern times, most families, particularly those living in urban areas, simply make delicious food to enjoy themselves.

Individuals start to prepare for the coming New Year following the Preliminary Eve, which is called "Seeing the New Year in" as well.

—Cleaning and Purchasing

Prior to the New Year, cleaning is usually done in Chinese culture, including the grounds, the walls, and every corner of the house. The origin of this ritual is that in Chinese, the pronunciation of "Dust" resembles that of the word "old" (Chen) . Therefore, cleaning means a farewell to the bad luck or the old stuff to embrace a new start.

Meanwhile, people tend to buy new items, especially new clothes for the coming festival, a gesture to welcome new things and get ready for a new year.

—Couplets

Chinese couplets are usually pasted on doorways as a symbol to celebrate the New Year, with the original form being "Taofu", a piece of peach wood to protect against evil spirits without any inscription. Later, In the Song Dynasty, people began to write antithetical couplets on the wood to express good wishes apart from the decorative function. Gradually, peach wood was replaced by the red paper. And the final couplets form include antithetical on the right and left sides of the door and a horizontal scroll hanging on the top.

—Pasting the "Fu" and Paper Cut

The character "Fu" means good fortune in Chinese, symbolizing people's good wishes for the future, therefore, people always paste it on gates or furniture during the Spring Festival. Pasting the "Fu" upside down, meaning the arrival of happiness, is a widely accepted convention among Chinese. Other auspicious words or pictures are cut on red paper and pasted on windows to express good wishes for the future in the coming new year.

In the ancient time, these characters and the patterns were written by hand, but now, they were typically replaced by printed ones.

—New Year Paintings

New Year paintings originated in Tang Dynasty, with the purpose of casting the evils away by simple patterns, which also serve as a decoration for the festival, and the patterns of the pictures vary from region to region. Particularly in Taoism and folk-custom, the Gate Gods, as one of the most popular gods, serve the role to guard houses. Ancient people used to paste their pictures on the door to bring safety to the houses by driving a-way evils. Now this custom still remains in most rural areas.

—Chinese Knots

Chinese knots are typical decorations during the festival, which were o-riginally used to string jade pendants on clothes and some musical instruments such as flute, Xiao (a vertical bamboo flute) and so on. Now these knots are used to express the blessing and best wishes for other people.

• New Year's Eve & Day

These two occasions are viewed as the peak of the Spring Festival which is embodied by typical activities such as family reunion dinners, eating dumplings, staying up all night, setting off firecrackers and so on. Besides, visiting relatives is common during the first day of the New Year.

—Family Reunion Dinner

Family reunion dinner is the most important feast for the family to get together, particularly those who are not able to be with each other during the year due to various reasons. With all the family members sitting around the table and toasting best wishes for each other, the family is surrounded by the warm festive atmosphere.

—Staying Up

The custom of staying up all night dates back to the Northern and Southern Dynasties as the product of an ancient legend. It was said that there was a fearsome demon called "*Sui.*" Every year on New Year's Eve, the demon would emerge to harm the children. Therefore, parents would keep the lights on and stay up the entire New Year's Eve to keep the demon away.

—Lucky Money

The custom of giving lucky money to children was related with a story. A couple put eight coins in a red wrap before placing it below the child's pillow accidentally on New Year's Eve. When "Sui" was about to touch the child's head to attack him, the eight coins magically beamed bright light and scared it away. It turned out that the eight coins were eight immortals who were secretly protecting the children. Therefore people named this money as "lucky money for the New Year's Day. " And this custom passed from generation to generation.

—Firecrackers and Fireworks

Firecrackers are always set off at 12 o'clock in the midnight to welcome the arrival of the new lunar year. The custom is associated with a fierce monster called "nian" (year) who was believed to eat human beings. Firstly, people were scared of it so they hid on the evening when the creature e-merged. Later, it turned out that "nian" was afraid of the red color, fire and loud sound. Accordingly, people threw bamboo into the fire to drive the monster away. After the invention of gunpowder, bamboo was replaced by firecrackers nearly 2, 000 years ago. In folk culture, the Spring Festival is also named "*guonian*" (meaning "passing a year") and the custom of using red color and setting off fireworks exists till now.

—Eating Dumplings

The typical food during spring festival is the dumpling (*jiaozi*), especially in northern China. Made with flour and stuffed with different fillings, dumplings are usually shared by the family members on the Eve of the Spring Festival. Resembling the Chinese *Yuanbao*, money used in ancient times, dumplings are considered to bring people wealth in the coming year. Sometimes, people put coins, candy, peanuts, or chestnuts randomly in some of the dumplings, and the people who accidentally eat them are believed to be blessed. For example, a coin means wealth, candy for sweet life, peanuts stand for health and longevity, and chestnuts symbolize vig-or. In addition to the New Years Eve, it is also a convention in many re gions of China for people to eat dumplings on Jan. 1st and Jan. 15th of lu-nar calendar.

• Following Days

—Paying New Year's Visits

It is customary for individuals to visit their relatives to express good wishes to each other in the beginning of lunar new year. In ancient times, younger people were required to salute the elderly by kowtow; however, to-day they salute them simply by offering good wishes. And the older genera-tion gives them lucky money wrapped in red paper in return.

People usually drop in at relatives and friends'houses, greeting one an-other with "Happy New Year". In certain big extended families in rural areas, this activity lasts for several days. It is common for people to visit others with gifts without such as local products, fruits, desserts, wines and so on. Although in the modern society some people tend to send greetings by telephone or e-mail, the convention of paying visits still prevails.

—Temple Fairs

Being another convention in the Spring Festival, temple fairs were pri-marily a worship of temples, but now they turn into carnivals which can be held in parks, including activities such as dragon dances, lion dance, stilt walking, worship dances, Chinese magic and other kinds of traditional folk art. In addition, people can purchase all kinds of daily merchandise at rea-sonable prices.

Various snacks, such as sugarcoated haws and roasted skewered mutton are popular food in the joyful temple fairs.

In certain regions, particularly in Beijing, temple fairs are held almost every day in different places such as Wangfujing, Altar of the Earth and Dragon Pool Park during and after Spring Festival.

—Burning Incense at a Temple

On the first day of lunar New Year, people usually go to the temple to burn incense which is believed to bring the whole family good fortune in the coming year, making New Year wishes come true. On the fifth day of the Spring Festival, temples are crowded with individuals who worship Kuan Kung, the God of Wealth by presenting fruits and various foods or by burn-ing worship paper.

②Lantern Festival

Lantern Festival is the first significant holiday after Spring Festival, falling on the 15th day of the first lunar month, on which night people gather in the street to watch various colorful lanterns. It is also called

Yuanxiao Festival because every household eats *yuanxiao*, a rice ball stuffed with different fillings. Featured with recreational atmosphere, it is also the occasion for family reunion.

With more than 2,000 years history, various traditional activities are conducted during Lantern Festival.

● Watching Lanterns

Lantern appreciation is related with Buddhism, which flourished in China during the Han Dynasty. To further popularize this religion, the emperor ordered to light lanterns in the imperial palace to pay respect for Buddha on the 15th day of the first lunar month. During the following dynasties such as Tang, Song, Ming and Qing, lighting lanterns gradually became a widely accepted tradition among Chinese.

In modern society, when the festival comes, red lanterns are hanged everywhere in the street. In the parks, lanterns of various shapes and types appeal to a sea of visitors and they are amazed by the objects which so vividly embody traditional Chinese folklore.

● Guessing Lantern Riddles

Dated back to the Song Dynasty, guessing riddles is viewed as a typical recreational activity of the Lantern Festival. Originally people write the riddles on the lanterns, but now they are just written on pieces of paper and are pasted them on colorful lanterns for visitors to guess. If one has got the answer, he can pull the paper, reaching out to organizers to verify it. Gifts are presented to the correct guessers, with people from all walks of life enjoying it just because of its challenge to intellectuality.

● *Shehuo*

As a part of the Lantern Festival, particularly in Northwestern China, *Shehuo*, originated from Shaanxi operas, is a popular form of worship which comprises performances and parades such as the dragon and lion dances, *yangko* (a popular rural folk dance), and stilts walking.

Derived from the Three Kingdoms Period, the lion dance is a typically traditional art that adds unique fun to the Lantern Festival. The characteristics of northern and southern lion dance are different, with the former paying more attention to skills and the latter focusing on animal resemblance. Usually one person manipulates a small lion made of quilts resembling a real one, and with two persons acting like a big lion, one manages the head part and the other, the rest. Under the guidance of a director, the lions sometimes jump, leap, and do difficult acts such as walking on stilts.

According to Chinese ancient custom, the lion stands for power, boldness and strength which is capable of protecting people. Therefore, by doing the lion dance, everyone prays for auspiciousness.

Stilts walking, another folk art, traces its origins to the Spring and Autumn period. Performers not only walk on stilts by binding them to their feet, but also do some extremely difficult moves. As actors act as different characters like monks, clowns, and fishermen, the art entertains people by vivid and humorous performance.

- Eating *Yuanxiao*

Yuanxiao, or *tangyuan*, is a dumpling ball made of sticky rice flour stuffed with different fillings like sugar, rose petals, sesame, sweetened bean paste, and jujube paste. Eating *yuanxiao* is indispensable for people during the festival. The way to cook *tangyuan* can be various since it can be boiled, fried or steamed, and each has a unique taste. The reason why people consume *Yuanxiao* is because of its round shape which stands for reunion, harmony and happiness. During the night of the festival, family members sit together to taste *yuanxiao* and appreciate the full moon.

③*Qingming* Festival

Qingming Festival, which is also known as Pure Brightness Festival or Tomb-sweeping Day, is one of the Chinese Twenty-four Solar Terms, falling on either April 4th or 5th of the Gregorian calendar. It is typically a turning point that temperatures begin to grow and rainfall increases, an indication for plowing and sowing in the spring. Besides being a seasonal symbol, it is an important day to pay respect to the dead. And in the modern times, it is also an appropriate time for a spring outing.

- Origin

Qingming Festival was said to honor a loyal man named *Jie Zitui* in the Spring and Autumn Period. *Jie* cut a piece of flesh from his own leg to save his hungry lord. Nineteen years later when the lord decided to reward him for his loyalty, he just refuse to take it and hermit himself in a mountain with his mother. To force him to emerge, the lord ordered that the mountain should be set on fire. And *Jie* was found dead with his mother as a result. In order to commemorate *Jie*, the lord commanded that the day *Jie* died was *Hanshi* (Cold Food) Festival-the day that only cold food could be consumed.

The next year, when the lord went to the mountain to sacrifice to *Jie*, he found willows revived, so he ordered that the day after *Hanshi* Festival was to be *Qingming* Festival. Gradually, the two festivals were incorporated as one.

The main activities that people conducted in *Qingming* Festival are tomb sweeping, taking a spring outing, and flying kites. Some other lost customs like wearing willow branches on the head and riding on swings brought additional joy in past days. Generally speaking, it is a mixture of sorrow and happiness.

● Tomb Sweeping

Tomb sweeping is considered the most important custom in the *Qingming* Festival from which Tomb-sweeping day got its name. Cleaning the tomb and paying respect to the deceased with offerings are the two major activities to commemorate the dead. Weeds around the tomb are cleared away and fresh soil is added to show care of the dead. The decedent's favorite food and wine are presented as sacrifice. Paper resembling money is burned to ensure that the deceased have sufficient money to use in the afterworld. Finally, people kowtow or bow before the tablets.

Today, with cremation replacing burying, the custom has turned simper in urban areas. Usually only flowers are presented to the dead.

● Spring Outing

Apart from being the occasion to commemorate the deceased, it is also a time for people to go outing. In April, trees turn green, flowers blossom, and the sun beams. It is a good time to go sightseeing, appreciating the beautiful natural scenes. This custom can be dated back to the Tang Dynasty and remains till now. Therefore, visitors are rather crowded during the month of the festival. Spring outings not only add joy to life but also promote a healthy body and mind.

● Flying Kites

Flying kites is another activity favored by individuals during the *Qingming* Festival. Kites are flown during the day time as well as in the evening, with small lanterns tied to the kite or to the string that holds the kite. Unlike flying kites during common days, people usually cut the string of the flying kite to set it free on this day, which is believed to bring good luck and to get rid of diseases that might have bothered people.

To sum up, the *Qingming* Festival is a special occasion with a combination of sorrowful tears for the deceased with the joyful laughter from the spring outing.

④Dragon Boat Festival

Falling on the fifth day of the fifth month of Chinese lunar calendar, the Dragon Boat Festival has been held annually for over 2, 000 years and is special for its educational impact. The festival was originally to commemorate the patriotic poet *Qu Yuan*.

● Legend of *Qu Yuan*

Qu Yuan was a minister in the State of Chu-one of the seven warring states before Qin in China's first feudal dynasty. He advised to the authority to fight against the powerful State of Qin (one of the seven states during the Warring States Period together with the State of Qi) . His proposition was not favored and he was exiled by the emperor. To show his national affection, he wrote many enduring poems such as *Li Sao* (The Lament), *Tian Wen* (Asking Questions to the Heaven) and *Jiu Ge* (Nine Songs) and is therefore regarded as a famous poet in China's history. In 278 BC, after finishing his last masterpiece-*Huai Sha* (Embracing the Sand), he drowned himself in the river since he would never bear to see his country occupied by the rival State of Qin.

Upon hearing the death of Qu Yuan, all the local citizens were in great sorrow. Fishermen sailed their boats down the river to look for his body and others threw food into the river to attract fish and other animals, preventing them from destroying Qu Yuan's body.

Because Qu Yuan died on the fifth day of the fifth lunar month, people chose to memorize him on that day every year, with dragon boat racing and eating *zongzi* becoming the core customs of the festival. For two thousand years, Qu Yuan's patriotism has affected generations and he remains respected by the individuals from all over the world.

Many traditional activities are conducted on the special day by Chinese and even by some people in neighboring countries.

• Dragon Boat Racing

As is mentioned in the above, the race derived from the story in which people rowed their boats to save *Qu yuan* after he drowned himself in the river. Dragon boats are thus named because its shape resembles traditional Chinese dragon. A team of people struggle to work the oars unanimously to reach the destination prior to the other teams. Particularly, one team member sits at the front of the boat, beating a drum to promote morale and ensure that the rowers keep the same rhythm. Besides the competitiveness, the winning team is said to bring harvest and happy life to the regional people. Meanwhile, some of ethnic minorities in China also hold dragon boat races like Miao and Dai.

• Eating *Zongzi* (pyramid-shaped glutinous rice wrapped in reed or bamboo leaves)

Many Chinese festivals associate with particular customary food and the Dragon Boat Festival is one of them. *Zongzi* is made with sticky rice wrapped in pyramid shape but with various fillings. Roughly speaking, northern people favor the jujube as filling while the southerners favor sweetened bean paste, fresh meat, or egg yolk. Many families prefer homemade *Zongzi* by soaking the glutinous rice, washing the reed or bamboo leaves and wrapping *Zongzi* with leaves. Today, this custom still remains.

• Wearing a Perfume Pouch and Tying Five-color Silk Thread

Perfume pouch, according to folklore, is capable of protecting children from evil. Thus on this occasion, parents have children's clothes decorated with various fragranced pouches, a small pouch made of colorful silk cloth stringed with five-color silk thread.

Another custom is to tie five-color silk thread, an item which is believed to own magical and healing function, to a child's wrists, ankles, or around their neck. Children are not supposed to make noise when their parents tie the thread for them, neither should they remove it until a given time. Only after the first summer rainfall can the children toss it into the river to protect themselves from plague and diseases.

• Hanging Mugwort Leaves and Calamus

Summer is the season when all kinds of diseases prevail. Therefore, people do house cleaning, placing mugwort leaves and calamus on the top of the doors to discourage disease on the particular festival since the roots and leaves of these plants can purify the air by releasing an aroma to dispel the annoying insects such as mosquitoes and flies.

⑤Double Seventh Festival

Chinese Double Seventh Festival, the seventh day of seventh lunar month, is what Valentine's Day to the westerners which is associated with one of the Chinese four folk love legends: *Niu Lang* and *Zhi Nu*, labeling the festival with great romance.

It is said that *Niu Lang* was a kind-hearted cowherd who accidentally take good care of a sick cattle from heaven. To express gratitude to *Niu Lang*, the cow helped him get acquainted with a fairy named *Zhi Nu*. They married to live a happy life with *Niu Lang* planting in the field while *Zhi Nu* did weaving at home. However, the king of the heaven disapproved of their marriage, taking *Zhi Nu* back to heaven. With the help of the cow, *Niu Lang* flew to heaven together with his two children as they chased their wife and mother. Unfortunately, it was before he could reach *Zhi Nu* that the queen of the heaven created an immense river between them. Tears from the couple flowed unceasingly that even win sympathy from the queen. Eventually, she permitted them to meet only on the seventh day of the seventh lunar month every year with magpies forming a bridge for them to cross the river. Gradually, the day that *Niu Lang* and *Zhi Nu* meet becomes the Double Seventh Festival of today.

Frankly speaking, in contemporary Chinese urban areas, the festival is somewhat neglected compared with western Valentine's Day especially among young people. In rural regions at night, girls sew some articles to compete with each other. In addition, they prepare some sacrifices to worship Zhi Nu in the hope of being endowed with the masterly sewing skill. Besides, they also pray for a sweet lover.

Although some conventional customs have been changed or been lost, the legend of *Niu Lang* and *Zhi Nu* still remains among generations.

⑥The *Zhongyuan* Festival

Zhongyuan Festival, also known as the Ghost Festival, *Yulanpen* Festival or the Mid July Day, is on July 15th in the lunar calendar, an occasion observed by the Chinese to sacrifice their forefathers.

● Origin

The festival originated from Taoism which believes that the three *Yuans*, namely heaven, earth and water, are the basis of everything; and the Heaven *Guan* (Governor), Earth *Guan*, Water *Guan* are established accordingly. The Taoists call the 15th day of the 1st, 7th, and 10th lunar month respectively as Shang (upper) *yuan*, Zhong (Middle) *yuan* and Xia (Lower) *yuan* in memory of the three Guans. *Zhongyuan* Festival or Ghost Festival is made to forgive the sins of the dead. Dozens of grand religious ceremonies are held on *Zhongyuan* Festival to pray for favorable weather, prosperity and peace.

Zhongyuan Festival is also named *Yulanpen* Festival, with *Yulan* derived from the Sanskrit with the meaning of Suspend. And *Pen* is a ware for collecting worshipping gifts in Buddhism. It comes from a Buddhist story called *How Mulian saved his mother*. When Mulian was ten, he was appointed to be a monk by Kshitigarbha. A few years later, his mother died and was sent to the Hell because of her sins. When Mulian knew that his mother was suffering from the punishment of "hanging upside down" in the sixth layer of the Hell, he brought food to his mother. Mulian tried to feed his mother but the food turned into ashes whenever it was close to her mouth. Mulian went to Sakyamuni for help. Sakyamuni told Mulian about her mother's sins and told him that if he wanted to help his mother, he must prepare vegetable foods for all the spirits on the fifteenth day of the seventh month of the lunar calendar. Mulian did it and saved her mother from being a hungry ghost.

Chinese folklore gives the festival another name: Ghost Day. It is said that, ghosts and spirits, with the permission of the king of Hell, would come out to see whether people good or evil on July 1st. They are believed to visit the own former houses, enjoying the ritualistic food offerings and fetching paper money burned by their family. And July 15th is the deadline on which all departed ghosts had to return to hell since the door between the world and the hell would be closed, otherwise, they would be abandoned. On this day, water lanterns are floated along the river by people to direct the ghosts back to their own world.

● Ancestors' Worship

Zhongyuan Festival is the transition from summer to autumn. The deceased ancestors are believed to go back home to see the descendants, thus, ritualistic offerings, spirit paper money will be offered. According to multifarious rituals, ancestral tablets could never be moved while being worshipped except for the festival. They are moved respectfully on the alter for sacrifice and the incense is burnt with three meals being served. A portrait of the deceased will be taken out and hung in the hall. The family members kneel down to worship ancestors in turns according to their ranks in the family. What happened in the last year must be reported to ancestors by the elders, who also beg the ancestors to bless the whole family.

● Lantern Floating

One of the local folk tales is that the lantern floating is a religious ceremony started in temples for the purpose of transmuting and absolving the sufferings of ghosts. Later, people commemorated the deceased through floating lanterns as the custom became popular. The designs of the lanterns are varied, and the most common style is the lotus lantern, and there are also cabbage and watermelon lanterns. One of the lanterns' making processes shows that one should prepare many large pieces of colored-paper at first, then cut bright red, pale red, yellow, green, purple paper into square pieces of the same size, and fold them into square, stretching the four corners out to form a lotus lantern is made. The paper lanterns' bottom should be put into pine oil for a while and dry it in the yard to reinforce the shape to make it waterproof. After finishing the lanterns, people float water lanterns along the river while Taoists or monks playing folk tunes with the mouth-organ (*Sheng*) and panpipe (*Xiao*).

⑦The Mid-Autumn Festival

Mid-Autumn Festival is celebrated on the 15th day of the eighth lunar month. The full moon on that day is a symbol of reunion, therefore, it is also called *Tuanyuan* (reunion) Festival in China.

● Origin

Mid-Autumn Festival is a traditional moon sacrificial custom which could be traced back to ancient times when people observed that the lunar movement was closely related with seasonal changes and agricultural production. Therefore, to demonstrate their respect to the moon and to celebrate the harvest, they sacrificed to the moon on autumn days.

Roughly speaking, this custom dated back to the *Zhou* Dynasty and was firstly practiced among the royal families on the Autumnal Equinox which was far from being a great festival. In the following dynasties of *Sui* and *Tang*, social growth gradually prompted the custom of moon appreciating on the moon sacrifice day to be widely conducted among the civilians, who practiced their faith more freely than the royal class without strictly conducting their activities on the Autumnal Equinox. Gradually the closest full moon day to the Autumnal Equinox, August 15th of the Chinese lunar calendar, became a preferred fixed festival. Finally Mid-Autumn Festival became a commonly celebrated folk festival by the time of the Northern Song Dynasty.

● Moon Sacrifice

As mentioned above, moon sacrifice dates back to the Zhou Dynasty when the emperors typically offered a sacrifice on the Autumnal Equinox at the Altar of the Moon. With the passage of time, this ritual has entered into folk lore and now the sacrificial ceremony is usually held in family bases. However, in the modern society, this activity only remains in certain countryside or at given places of interests to attract tourists but no longer exists among most of Chinese families.

Traditionally, the typical sacrificial offerings were moon cakes or any other food such as watermelons cut into the shape of a lotus flower, grape-fruits, boiled green soybeans, oranges and wine etc, with most of them made in round shape since the Mid-Autumn Festival was regarded as a day for family reunion and the Chinese pronunciation of "round" is the same as that of "reunion". The offerings would be put on a table under the moon-light. Besides, an incense burner was placed in front of the table between two lighted red candles.

When the ritual began, two deacons walked and stood on each side of the offering table, followed by the officiant (usually the oldest woman in the family or the hostess) and the other family members who knelt down in front of the offering table. Then the officiant took over three burning joss sticks from the deacon and made some wishes before placing them in the burner. Later, the officiant would pray loudly towards the moon after pouring a cup of wine in front of the offerings. Written prayer paper and moonlight papers (the incense papers painted with the moon palace and goodness of the moon) burnt, all attendants genuflected three times. Finally, the attend-ants burnt the incense and worshiped to the moon successively.

- Appreciating the Moon

Unlike the declining moon sacrificial ceremony, moon appreciating is much more prevailing among common people. All the families sitting around a table, they chat with each other and eat various foods (the offerings from the ceremony) while appreciating the moon, which virtually derived from the sacrificial ceremony, but just turned a serious event into a relaxa-tion. Firstly originated from the Three Kingdoms Period, the phenomenon be-came very popular in the Tang Dynasty, with numerous literary works praising the moon and expressing yearnings and affection to distant relatives and friends. It was during the Song Dynasty that the earliest official Mid-Autumn Festival, a folk festival, took in shape.

● Eating Moon Cakes

The origin is related with the victorious revolters of the Yuan Dynasty who were said to pass messages by hiding notes in moon cakes. Later on, the leaders distributed moon cakes to his followers on the coming Mid-Autumn Festival. Since then, eating moon cakes on Mid-Autumn Day became formally established. Usually after the moon sacrificial ceremony, the officiant cut the largest moon cake into even pieces and passed them to every family members. Even for those who could not make it home at night, there was a piece reserved for them since it symbolized reunion and the sacrificed cake was viewed as auspicious. Nowadays, although the sacrificial ceremony vanished among most families, they still gather together to share the moon cakes on the festival night.

⑧*Chongyang* Festival (Double Ninth Festival)

Falling on the 9th day of the 9th lunar month, *Chongyang* Festival is also named as Double Ninth Festival, an occasion when overseas Chinese feel strongly homesick, and the time to pray for longevity as well.

● Origin

The origin of the word *Chongyang* derives from *The Book of Changes* or *Yi Jing*. Ancient Chinese regard "nine" as the number of *Yang* which means masculine as opposed to *Yin*, feminism. The ninth day of the ninth month is the day that contains two *Yang* numbers, and "*chong*" in Chinese means double which is how the name *Chongyang* came from. Meanwhile, double ninth was pronounced the same as the word of "*Jiu Jiu*," which means "forever" . Therefore, the Chinese ancestors considered it an auspicious day associated with longevity and the festival can be dated back to the pre-Qin period.

● Legend

Like some other Chinese traditional festivals, *Chongyang* Festival has its own story. A devil was said to appear in the Nu River during the Eastern Han Dynasty, causing diseases in the neighborhood. A young man named *Hengjing* was deprived of his parents due to the plague. Therefore, he went to great lengths to learn swordsmanship from an immortal to expel the devil.

On the eighth day of the ninth lunar month, *Hengjing* was told it was time to rid people of the devil. Taking a bag of dogwood and some chrysanthemum wine, *Hengjing* returned to his hometown. In the next morning, all the villagers held a piece of dogwood leaf and a cup of Chrysanthemum to the nearest mountain under the leadership of *Hengjing*. At noon, when the devil emerged from the Nu River, the devil's magician was somewhat weakened because of the fragrance of the dogwood and the chrysanthemum wine, which led to its surrender to the hero.

Since then the custom of climbing mountains, drinking chrysanthemum wine and holding onto dogwood on the ninth day of the ninth month have become popular.

● Ascending a Height

The activity of climbing mountains to avoid epidemics was passed down from centuries ago. So the Double Ninth Festival is also named "Height Ascending Festival". Commonly people will climb up a mountain or a tower during this day, with ancient poets writing large amounts of poems depicting the custom. Even in the modern ages, people still swarm to famous or nameless mountains to observe the festival.

● Eating *Chongyang* Cake

Chongyang Cake, a steamed cake of two layers with nuts and jujube sandwiched in between is the popular food of the festival since the pronunciation of cake in Chinese is identical to that of the word "height" . Hence personal achievement is likely to be made in the following days once one consumes the cake.

● Wearing Dogwoods

The custom of wearing dogwood to ward off the disaster or dispel bad luck was prevailing in ancient times. Particularly in *Tang* Dynasty, women and children have the custom of wearing a fragrant pouch with dogwood sewed in. But with the progress of times, this custom is fading away and rarely exists.

● Appreciating Chrysanthemum and Enjoying Chrysanthemum Wine

The Double Ninth Festival is always the season when chrysanthemums bloom. And the custom of eating this flower was recorded in *Quyuan's* poem *Lisao*, as people believe the consumption of it contributes to health and longevity, making it a symbol on people's pursuit of long life for its great medicinal properties. Chrysanthemum wine is an indispensable part of the festival since it is thought to be capable of preventing and curing all kinds of diseases and disasters.

Meanwhile, its auspicious meaning helps it guard against the evil, being equally important as the dogwood. Therefore, chrysanthemum appreciating had become one of the most important customs as early as the *Jin* Dynasty. In modern times, as chrysanthemums blossom during the festival, it is a pleasure to admire the various chrysanthemums in parks. Grand chrysanthemum exhibitions are held in big parks that attract numerous visitors.

● Respecting the Seniors

In 1989, *Chongyang* Festival was designated by the authority as Senior's Day-a day to particularly pay respect and show care to the elderly as nine is pronounced " *jiu* " meaning long, hence longevity in Chinese. Activities are organized for retirees to go out to climb mountains or on outings. Younger generations of a family also accompany their elders to have a relaxation while wishing health and happiness upon them.

⑨Winter Solstice Festival

As early as 2, 500 years ago, during the Spring and Autumn Period, Chinese identified the point of Winter Solstice by observing movements of the sun with an ancient tool named an Earth Sundial. Being the earliest of the 24 seasonal division points, the time will be each December 22 or 23 according to the Gregorian calendar. The Northern hemisphere on this day has the shortest daytime and longest nighttime, after which days will become increasingly longer. Since ancient Chinese believe the *yang*, or muscularity will be much stronger afterwards, this day is an occasion worth celebrating.

● History

According to historical records, Winter Solstice was viewed as the starting point of a new year during the Zhou and Qin dynasties, which persisted and was called the Small New Year, when ancestor worshipping ceremonies and family reunions usually were conducted. Then it became a festival during the Han Dynasty for which people had official holidays. Officials would organize celebrating activities. The army was stationed in, frontier fortresses closed and business and traveling temporarily ceased. Common people exchanged various gifts for celebration. Then the Tang and Song dynasties witnessed its prosperity, during which people offer scarifies. Emperors worshiped heaven and their ancestors on that day to pray for a good harvest while people kowtowed to their parents and offered sacrifices to their ancestors. By the Ming and Qing Dynasties, the well-preserved Temple of Heaven in Beijing was constructed for that reason. And there was a saying that "Winter Solstice is as important as the Spring Festival", implying the great significance attached to this day.

● Typical Food

Dumplings are the most essential food for Winter Solstice, which is believed to keep the eaters from frost in the upcoming winter, particularly in northern China, Nowadays, there are different customs in southern and northern China. However, sticky puddings or sweet dumplings and Tsampa, the symbol of a family reunion, are more popular among southern residents. For instance, in the southern part of the middle and lower reaches of Yangtze River, people have ormosia glutinous rice food and in Hangzhou, rice cakes with various flavors are most welcomed.

The Taiwanese even keep the custom of offering nine-layer cakes in the shape of chickens, ducks, pigs and so on as symbols of auspiciousness to their ancestors. People of the same family clan assemble at their ancestral temples, worshipping their ancestors in age order. Then a grand banquet is served following the sacrificial ceremony.

In addition, people also have hot foods such as mutton, noodles or winter wine for celebration to help themselves keep warm in winter.

⑩*Laba* Festival /Rice Porridge Festival

The *Laba* Festival is a Chinese conventional festival falling on the eighth day of the 12th lunar month. The 12th lunar month is called *La* in Chinese and eight is pronounced *ba*.

- Origin

Laba Festival was primarily a time for individuals to give sacrifices to their ancestors, praying to heaven and earth for a good harvest and good luck for the family. Besides, it is also the day on which Sakyamuni, founder of Buddhism, realized truth and became a Buddha.

- Eating *Laba* Rice Porridge

Laba rice porridge is said to be originated from India. Sakyamuni, the son of a king in northern ancient India, tried to enlighten himself according to religious doctrine. After six years of a very tough life and self-torture, with only rice being consumed daily, he realized the truth of Buddhism while sitting under the bodhi tree on the 8th day of the 12th lunar month. Therefore, people memorize him by eating porridge on the eighth day of the 12th month annually.

The custom started in the Song Dynastyand became popular in the Qing Dynasty, therefore, Chinese have been eating *Laba* porridge on *Laba* Festival day for more than one thousand year. It is well known that since ancient times Chinese people have attached great significance to growing crops, so when they reap great harvest after years of labor, the farmers will offer sacrifice to the ancestors, heaven and earth, making *Laba* porridge being one of the way to celebrate.

The ingredients of *Laba* porridge are various and nutritious materials, which consists of diversified rice (glutinous rice, oats, corns etc.), beans (soy beans, mung beans, kidney beans, cowpeas etc.), dried nuts (chestnuts, almonds, peanuts, etc.), bean curd and meat. Melon seeds, lotus seeds, pine nuts, sugar, and other preserved fruits are added to give more flavors.

After hours of cooking, the porridge is presented as a sacrifice to the ancestors and is offered to other eaters before noon. Usually *Laba* porridge will not be consumed all but some are left to indicate a good harvest in the coming year. Some lenient people share the porridge with the poor on this specific day.

(2) The Typical Festivals of Chinese Ethnic Minorities

Roughly speaking, there are over 1, 700 festivals in China, among which 1, 200 belong to the ethnic minorities with their own origin or legend. Some of them are closely associated with religious beliefs, such as the Corban and Kaizhai Festival, while others are related to entertainment activities, such as the Nadam Fair of Mongolia and the Tibetan New Year.

Some of the ethnic minority festivals are grand and influential, appealing to spectators from far away. The following are some of the typical ones:

①March Fair of Bai Nationality

The March Fair is held annually on the 15th to 21st day of the third lunar month as the conventional great event for Bai ethnic minority who mainly live at the foot of Mt. Cangshan in Dali, Yunnan Province. Primarily an event to recite the lections and to offer sacrifice to Kwan-yin, a female Bodhisattva, it has now become a thriving fair that thousands of people from different regions would be happy to attend.

In the fair, all kinds of merchandises are available including medicinal ingredients, teas, livestock, and other goods for daily use. Besides, Street for foreigners and local foods are also set up, offering even more varieties to attract visitors. Not only can people trade goods with each other, the fair is also full of rich and colorful activities including singing, dancing, horse races, wrestling, flowers show etc①.

②Nadam Fair of the Mongolian

In Mongolian, Nadam means "entertainment or game"; thus Nadam Fair is the annual conventional pageant which is held between July and August when the grass thrives and the livestock is strong. Historically Nadam

---

① http: //www. travelchinaguide. com/essential/holidays/minority. htm

Fair was the occasion for various sacrificial activities, with people praying for blessings from Manito. Currently, competitive sports such as wrestling, horseracing, and archery, the three skills that all Mongolian males master, are the most important events of the fair. In addition, track and field sports, tug-of-war, basketball and volleyball matches are added as well to bring more interest to the fair. Usually the fair finishes with a bonfire party during the night with people singing and dancing happily.

③End of Ramadan of Hui, Uygur, Kazak etc.

The ninth month, according to the Islamic calendar, is the fasting month of Ramadan during which every Muslim should have breakfast before sunrise. Food and water are not allowed until after sunset. After nearly a month of fast, comes the three-day traditional End of Ramadan Festival.

Muslims need to dust the houses in the early morning on the first day of the festival and they will go to mosques to pray to Mekka, halidom of Islamism after bathing despite the weather. Visiting the ancestor graves to mourn for them is also a necessary ritual. Traditional festival food and colorful activities like wrestling add more enjoyment to the festival[1].

④Corban Festival of Hui, Uygur, Kazak etc.

Celebrated mainly among the Hui, Uygur, Kazak, Uzbek, Tajik, Tatar, Kirgiz, Salar, Dongxiang, and Bonan minority groups, the Corban or "Zaisheng Festival" is one of the most significant annual events on the tenth day of the twelfth month by the Islamic calendar. Houses should be utterly cleaned and different kinds of traditional cakes are made even before dawn. On the day of this festival, Muslims wear neat clothes after a morning bath before going to the grandest mosque in the neighborhood to pray.

Livestock like sheep and ox are slaughtered as gifts to present to relatives, friends, and guests for which the name of "Zaisheng Festival" is given. People gather together to eat mutton, cakes, fruits and other delicious food while chatting with each other. Activities vary according to customs of different minority groups. Singing and dancing assemblies are held a-

---

① http: //en. wikipedia. org/wiki/Ramadan

mong the Uygur in Xinjiang Province. Activities like horseracing and wrestling are conducted among the Kazak, Uzbek, Tajik and Kirgiz minorities. Whatever the forms of celebration are, the day of Corban festival is full of joy and delight[1].

⑤Water-Splashing Festival of Dai Nationality

Water-splashing Festival is regarded as the most influential feast of Dai nationality, an occasion as important as the Spring Festival of Han nationality on the 14th to 16th of April. To celebrate the great event, people slaughter pigs and chickens, preparing wines and other foods in advance. Different activities are conducted during the three-day festival. Dragon boat racing and peacock dances are held on the first day. The representative water-splashing event is usually held on the second day by the banks of the *Lancang* River, one of the main rivers of southwest China. Girls of Dai ethnic minority dip branches into the river, sprinkling the water onto others to clean the filth of people and to convey their best wishes. Then participants of different ethnic groups attend it and use the basins and buckets to contain the water before splashing it onto other individuals, bringing the gatherings to the climax. Although all the people are soaked to the skin, they happily enjoy the event. On the last day, young people would play certain games, taking the opportunity to express their affections to the one they love.

⑥Torch Festival of Yi Nationality

Torch Festival is viewed as the greatest conventional holiday of the Yi ethnic minority on the 24th to 26th day of the sixth lunar month. On the first day, people always worship ancestors and visit relatives and friends to express their best wishes. Entertaining activities such as bull and sheep fighting, horse racing, cockfighting, singing competition, beauty contest, wrestling and tug-of-wars etc are held on the following day. Then comes the biggest event in the evening of the third day when large bonfires are lit while people sit, sing, and dance around them the whole night since Yi

---

① http://www.travelchinaguide.com/essential/holidays/minority.htm

people view the torch as the symbol of happiness and purity which brings good fortune to the people. In the eyes of the foreigners, it is the Carnival with Chinese characteristics due to its frantic and ardent atmosphere.

⑦Knife-Pole Festival of *Lisu* Nationality

Nowadays, climbing knife poles is viewed as the traditional sport of the *Lisu* people. In China, a saying goes that "climbing the Knife Mountain and diving into the Fire Sea" to encourage people's bravery which is exactly embodied by the Knife-Pole Festival, a traditional gala of *Lisu* nationality. On the festival eve, a huge bonfire is lit with people dancing around. Then some of the men leap in the fire and extinguish it with barefoot which is widely believed to have the function to avoid all disasters.

On the second day of lunar February, there comes the highlight of the festival that appeals to a large number of audiences. There are poles that are 20 meter in height, each affixed with 72 sharp knives for the warriors to ascend via the sharpened blades. Once reaching the top, they are rewarded with loud applauses before they light firecrackers, throwing small red flags to the crowds to shower good fortune upon everyone. The rest of the day is for the young to throw pouches to each other as a way of conveying mutual love.

⑧Bullfight Festival of Miao Nationality

The Miao people are originally farmers, viewing cattle as an indispensable asset who helps the owners in their daily lives. The traditional Bullfight Festival is usually on the 25th day of the lunar January when hosts feed the animals well, with wine even being given for a better performance. An even meadow is always preferred as the right location for the event and Miao people will present with their best dresses on this auspicious occasion.

When the bulls fight, audiences around the meadow cheer and scream, adding the fierce and intense atmosphere to the activity. For the winning bull, they are adorned with red silk sashes and flowers. After the game, people light bonfires within the bullfighting ring with young men playing *Lusheng*, a homemade reed mouth organ with five or six pipes, played by various ethnic groups in southwest China, girls dancing the whole night. By holding the Bullfight Festival, Miao people express their wishes for good health and a favorable harvest in the forthcoming year①.

3. Western Festival Customs

(1) Typical Western Festivals

①Valentine's Day

● Origin

Valentine's Day, also known as St. Valentine's Day, is on February 14th for people to convey their love with greetings and gifts. Although several Christian martyrs named Valentine, the day is said to have its name from a priest who was martyred about 270 A. D. by the emperor Claudius II Gothicus. According to the story, the priest signed a letter to his jailer's daughter whom he had fallen in love with, "from your Valentine." Another version is that the holiday is associated with the Roman festival of Lupercalia, held in mid-February. The festival was primarily to celebrate the arrival of spring which included fertility rites and the pairing game between women and men by lottery. At the end of the 5th century, Pope Gelasius I replaced Lupercalia with St. Valentine's Day, a festival gradually evolved into the occasion related with romance almost ten centuries later.

Traditional holiday gifts are valentine cards, candies and flowers, especially red roses to symbolize beauty and love. The day is popular in the West such as United States, Britain, Canada, and Australia; and it also is celebrated in other countries, including France and Mexico. Recent years the holiday also becomes prevailing in the East.

● Valentine's Cards

Formal message cards, or valentines, emerged in the 1500s. Two hundred years later, commercially printed cards were being used. Valentines typically depict Cupid, the Roman god of love, coupled with hearts, the traditional seat of emotion. Birds also are the symbol of the day since their

---

① http://www.travelchinaguide.com/intro/festival/minority.htm

mating season is thought to be started in mid-February. Hand-made valentine cards feature lace and ribbons with the pictures mentioned above. It was not until the 1840s that the commercial Valentine's greeting cards began to catch on in the U. S.

Today, Valentine's Day is one of the major holidays celebrated in the west. According to the American Greeting Card Association, one quarter of all cards sent annually are Valentines. But in the west, apart from lovers' affection, it has been expanded to emotions among relatives and friends. Besides, many school children are encouraged to exchange valentines with one another on this day[1].

②Easter

Primarily a non-religious festival, Easter turned into a holy celebration in the second century, with the religious side fading among common western civilians later on.

• Origin

Easter, used to be spelled as Eastre, is primarily an uproarious festival for the ancient Saxons to celebrate the return of spring and to commemorate their goddess of offspring. When the Christian missionaries met the northern tribes with their pagan celebrations, they attempted to convert them to Christianity, but in a secret manner.

However, it would be extremely dangerous forearly Christian converts to observe their holy days in a way that differs from the existed celebrations, which might otherwise arouse others' anger and disgust. To protect them, the missionaries decided to spread their religion gradually among people by encouraging them to keep on celebrating pagan feasts, but in a Christian manner.

Therefore, the pagan festival of Eastre was at the same time of year as the Christian observance of the Resurrection of Christ. And finally, the early name, Eastre, was replaced by its modern spelling, Easter.

• The Date of Easter

---

① http: //www. gifts2015. com/valentines-day-celebration/

Easter was originally celebrated on different days of the week. In 325 A. D. , the authority issued that Easter shall be celebrated on the first Sunday after the first full moon on or after the vernal equinox. However, the "full moon" in the rule refers to ecclesiastical full moon defined as the fourteenth day of a tabular lunation, not the same date as the astronomical full moon. Accordingly, the ecclesiastical "vernal equinox" is always on March 21. Therefore, Easter must be celebrated on a Sunday between the dates of March 22 and April 25.

● Easter Bunny

The Easter Bunny is not a modern invention but a symbol derived from the pagan festival of Eastre which is also the goddess worshipped by the Anglo-Saxons through her earthly symbol, the rabbit.

The Germans brought the symbol of the Easter rabbit to America and Easter was not widely celebrated in America until shortly after the Civil War.

● The Easter Egg

The Easter Egg predates the Christian holiday, the same as the Easter Bunny and the holiday itself, and the custom of exchanging eggs in the springtime can be dated back to many centuries before when Easter was first celebrated by Christians.

From the ancient times, the egg symbolizes rebirth in most cultures with eggs being wrapped in gold leaf or being colored brightly after being boiled with the leaves or petals of certain flowers.

Today, children play interesting game by hunting colored eggs and place them in Easter baskets together with the modern Easter eggs, those made of plastic or chocolate candies①.

③Halloween

Halloween, the shortening of All Hallows 'Evening or All Hallows' Eve, is a festival celebrated on the night of October 31. Traditional attrib-

①　https：//www. cbn. com/spirituallife/onlinediscipleship/easter/the ＿ traditions ＿ of ＿ easter. aspx？ option ＝ print

utes are trick-or-treating, costume parties, "haunted houses" and jack-o-lanterns etc, which is said to be brought to North America by Irish and Scottish immigrants in the 19th century. It is celebrated in other western countries in the late 20th century such as the United States, Canada, the United Kingdom as well as of Australia and New Zealand and so on.

● Origin

The origin of Halloween is the ancient Celtic festival known as Samhain (a time named by the ancient pagans to preserve stock of supplies and prepare for winter), a celebration of the end of the harvest season among ancient Gaels who held the belief that the boundaries between the living worlds and the dead overlapped and the decedents would come back to life, causing disasters such as sickness or damaged crops on October 31.

The festival later would frequently features bonfires since it is believed that the fires attracted insects and bats to the area, bringing additional elements of the Halloween. Besides, masks and costumes were worn to imitate the evil spirits so as to appease them.

● Trick-or-treating

As one of the major traditions of Halloween, Trick-or-treat, is an activity for children in which they go from door to door in the neighborhood in costumes, demanding for treats like candies with the question "Trick or treat?" . Otherwise, they threaten to play a trick on the homeowner or his house if their request is rejected. Therefore, it has become commonly accepted that if one lives in a neighborhood with children, one is supposed to prepare treats in advance for trick-or-treaters.

As to Halloween costumes, it is believed that the practice of dressing up in costumes and begging from house to house for treats traces back to the Middle Ages. In a sense, trick-or-treating is similar to the late medieval practice of "souling," which originated in Ireland and Britain when the poor go door to door on Hallowmas, November 1, receiving food in return for prayers for the dead on the following day, All Souls Day[1].

---

[1]   http: //www. halloweenhistory. org/

- Jack O'Lantern

Jack O'Lantern had its name from Jack, a drunk, according to an ancient Irish legend. One day he was out in the forests and tricked Satan into a tree to throw down some fruit. Once Satan had helped him, he carved a cross into the tree and trapped him there. He then made a deal that Satan would leave his soul alone when he died. And because of that, heaven would not take him either when he died. As he kept bothering the Devil to let him in, the Devil gave him a burning ember instead. He carried the ember in a hollowed out turnip to light his way as he wandered through eternal darkness on the earth. It gained popularity as house decorations in the U. S. after immigrant Irish discovered how much easier pumpkins were to carve than turnips. Eventually former replaced the latter in America and became the modern version of Jack-o-Lantern, which really possesses a spooky touch, particularly when the glowing faces emerge from the dark.

- Halloween Witches

According to various legends, witches have long been related with Halloween, who gather twice a year when the seasons changed, on April 30—the eve of May Day and the other was on the eve of October 31—All Hallow's Eve.

When the witches arrive on broomsticks, they start to celebrate a party hosted by the devil. They love to conduct magical mischief such as casting spells on people or transforming themselves into different forms.

It is said that to meet a witch, people deliberately wear the clothes on wrong side out and walk backwards on Halloween night①.

④Thanksgiving Day

Thanksgiving Day is originally celebrated on the fourth Thursday of November in the United States and on the second Monday of October Canada as a national holiday to express thanks for the blessing of the harvest and of the preceding year, with its historical roots in religion and culture, but has long been celebrated in a secular manner as well.

---

① http://www.ibuzzle.com/articles/halloween-witches.html

● History

Prayers of thanks and thanksgiving rituals are not uncommon among nearly all cultures after harvests or at other times. Historically speaking, the Thanksgiving holiday's history in North America is derived from English traditions since the Protestant Reformation in the reign of Henry VIII and in reaction to the large number of religious holidays on the Catholic calendar.

Before 1536, there were 95 Church holidays in addition to 52 Sundays, requiring people to go to church without working, sometimes a burden since people need to pay for expensive celebrations. The 1536 reforms witnessed the reduction of church holiday numbers to 27, but some Puritans wished to thoroughly abandon all Church holidays, including Christmas and Easter.

In 1620, the Pilgrim settlers sailed to America on the May flower, seeking a place to enjoy freedom of worship. After a two-month tough voyage they landed at what is now Plymouth, Massachusetts in icy November. During their first winter, starvation or epidemics deprived over half of the settlers of their lives, with the survivors sowing in the first spring with the help of the natives. Eventually the fields yielded a rich harvest beyond expectations. To show gratitude to the Lord, Thanksgiving holiday was observed among people, which was officially proclaimed as a national holiday by President Abraham Lincoln in 1863. On this occasion, a splendid thanksgiving meal is served, with families gathering together and talking, while others watching a game or a parade filled with pilgrims, Indians and other colonial figures[1].

● Holiday Feast

The typical Thanksgiving menu of turkey, cranberries, pumpkin pie, and root vegetables originated from New England fall harvests. In the 19th century, local cooks modified the menu according to their own choices and necessities with its popularity among the nation. For instance, in Minnesota, the turkey might be stuffed with wild rice while in Washington State, local-

---

[1] http://en. wikipedia. org/wiki/Thanksgiving

ly grown hazelnuts are featured in stuffing and desserts. In a word, most of these local variations have remained largely a regional phenomenon. However, it is undeniable that the contemporary Thanksgiving menu is highly influenced by southern Thanksgiving trends in the U. S. Roughly speaking, corn, sweet potatoes, and pork constitute the major part of traditional southern home cooking, and these staple foods provided the main ingredients in southern Thanksgiving additions like ham, sweet potato casseroles, pies and puddings, and corn bread dressing which spread across the country with southerners' relocation.

• Cracking the Wishbone

One of the strange Thanksgiving traditions for many families is to "fight" for the opportunity to crack the turkey's furcula, or wishbone. It is said that whoever gets the bigger piece will have his or her secret wish come true.

The custom is associated with the Etruscans, an ancient Italian civilization, who believed in chickens' oracles, using the birds to predict the future. Once a chicken was killed, it was laid out to dry so that individuals still had access to its powers.

The wishbone was then picked up, stroked and revered, for people to make a wish, giving it its current name. In Medieval Europe, people claimed that it was a goose bone that was used[1].

⑤Christmas

No one can imagine that from its modest origins, Christmas has developed into the grandest global celebration.

Christmas, primarily the fourth most important Christian date after Easter, Pentecost, and Epiphany, is the festival to honor the divinity of Jesus. Roman Catholics and Protestants celebrate the birth of Jesus on December 25 while Orthodox Christians observe Christmas around January 6, according to the Julian calendar.

---

① http://www.theblaze.com/stories/2013/11/28/5 – thanksgiving-traditions-americans-love-a-brief-history-of-turkey-wishbones-football-and-more/

● Origin

For modern Christians, Christmas originated from the birth of Jesus Christ, as written in the Bible. However, most of the Christmas conventions actually predate the Jesus' birth, and many of them are completely deceptive in their meaning and origin.

The date of December 25th is said to be associated with the ancient "birthday" of a pagan deity, Mithra who influenced the Roman Empire religiously during the first few centuries A. D. Mithra was related to the Semitic sun-god, Shamash, whose worship spread throughout Asia to Europe in which he was called Deus Sol Invictus Mithras. Being well-known for absorbing the pagan legacy of its widespread empire, Rome further converted this pagan religious ritual to a celebration of the god, Saturn, and the rebirth of the sun god during the winter solstice period, which was recognized as Saturnalia and began the week prior to December 25th. To honor the festival, the priests of Saturn carried wreaths of evergreen boughs in procession throughout the Roman temples, and the civilians celebrated it with gift-giving, feasting, singing and even debauchery.

Variations of this pagan holiday sprang out throughout the first few centuries after Jesus Christ, and it was in 336 A. D. that Emperor Constantine officially transformed it into the "Christian" holiday, the Christmas.

● Santa Claus

The prototype of Santa Claus is believed to be Saint Nicholas, Bishop of Myra, a place in present Turkey, who was generous and particularly caring to children. He was buried in Myra after his death around 340 A. D. , but Italian sailors stole his remains before removing them to Bari, Italy in 1087, ironically contributing to St. Nicholas' popularity throughout Europe.

His reputation for being kind and generous snowballed, making him a saint who possesses the power to create miracles. Later, St. Nicholas became the patron saint of Russia, an image portrayed as a jolly man with red cape, flowing white beard, and bishop's mitre.

Throughout Europe, he served as patron of various kinds. For instance, in Greece, he is the patron of sailors; in France, the patron of lawyers;

and in Belgium, the patron of children and travelers. In addition, numerous European churches were dedicated to him and some time around the 12th century an official church holiday, the Feast of St. Nicholas, was invented in his honor, which was celebrated on December 6 featuring gift-giving and charity.

The number of European followers of St. Nicholas shrinked after the Reformation, but the legend was kept alive in Holland where the Dutch spelling of his name was Sinterklaas. Dutch children were told to leave their wooden shoes by the fireplace in which treats would be placed as a reward to them. With the tradition being brought to America in the 17th century by the Dutch colonists, the Anglican name of Santa Claus finally came into being.

- Christmas Trees

In 16th century Germany, fir trees were decorated both indoors and outdoors, with apples, roses, gilded candies, and colored lights. A fir tree hung with apples was viewed as the Paradise Tree, representing the Garden of Eden. In addition, Protestant reformer Martin Luther is said to be the first to adorn trees with light.

It was Queen Victoria's husband, Prince Albert, who brought the notion of Christmas tree to England in 1848. The well-known picture of the Royal Family of Victoria in which Albert and their children gathered around a Christmas tree in Windsor Castle, contributed to the popularization of the tree throughout Victorian England. Brought to America by the Pennsylvania Germans, the Christmas tree eventually got accepted among Americans by the late 19th century.

- Christmas Stockings

A popular story has it that nobleman grew desperate over his wife's death and foolishly abandoned his fortune, leaving his three young daughters without dowries who probably would face a life of spinsterhood in the future.

The generous St. Nicholas was glad to lend him a hand while remaining anonymous. He rode his white horse by the nobleman's house before threw

three small bags of gold coins down the chimney where they were accidentally contained by the stockings that were hung by the fireplace to dry.

  • Mistletoe

Mistletoe, a plant favored by Druid priests 200 years before Christ
birth in their winter celebrations because it can remain green during the
freezing winter despite its rootlessness.

What's more, the ancient Celtics applied it as an antidote for poison,
infertility and even to scare off evil spirits since it was believed to possess
magical healing powers. Meanwhile story had it that when ancient Roman enemies met under mistletoe, chances were that they would lay down their
weapons and embrace. Therefore, it was regarded as a symbol of peace.

Scandinavians related the plant with their goddess of love named Frigga
which may account for the reason why westerners form the custom of kissing
under the mistletoe. Those who kissed under the mistletoe would be blessed
with happiness and good fortune in the forthcoming year[1].

(2) Special Western Festivals

①Carnival, Venice, Italy (February/March)

The Carnival of Venice is the most celebrated Carnival in Europe due
to its distinctive masks. Being a festival associated with Easter, the exact
dates of the Carnival is unfixed in some time around Feb or Mar. Carnival
runs for two weeks which lead up to Fat Tuesday, a celebration meant for
Christians to indulge themselves before Lent.

The greatest feature of the Carnival is the masks originally invented to
make the wearers anonymous. Nobles used to walk among the regular citizens, indulging in wild activities without being revealed who they
were. Currently, the masks are still important but are more valued for its
artistic attributes.

During the festival, various activities are conducted such as gondola
parade, concerts, and gala balls which appeal to visitors around the world

---

① http://www.allthingschristmas.com/traditions.html

for appreciation.

Figure 8 – 1   Carnival

②Oktoberfest, Munich, Germany (mid-September to October)

Oktoberfest is the world's biggest beer festival held annually in Munich, Germany. The grand party usually lasts for 16 days which begins on late-September and ends during the first week of October. It is viewed as the world's largest fair as one of the most famous events in Germany.

The first Oktoberfest was celebrated in 1810 in an area named Theresienwiese located near Munich's center. Visitors gather for the vast mugs of beer, würstl (sausages) and brezn (pretzel). Besides traditional foods, there are also conventional family costume parades and rides.

The beer served at Oktoberfestis supposed to be brewed within the city limits of Munich. Every year, about 7 million liters of beer are consumed by locals and more than 6.5 million visitors. During the festival, there are 14 large tents at Oktoberfest among which the Hippodrom is one of the trendiest in which the Oktoberfest band plays all the Oktoberfest classics at nights. Besides, Schottenhamel is the most important tent that is very popular among younger generation.

Figure 8 – 2   Oktoberfest

③St Patrick's Festival, Dublin, Ireland (March)

St. Patrick's Day, a religious and cultural festival honors St. Patrick, the patron saint of Ireland, has been an official feast day since the 17th century, gradually becoming a celebration of Irish culture in general and observed internationally on March 17.

Music and dancing, a boat race, a treasure hunt, particularly the colorful parade are the highlights of the festival.

Figure 8 – 3   St Patrick's Festival

④Running of the Bulls, Pamplona, Spain (July)

Every year between July 6 and 14, Pamplona becomes the international focus since it is the home of the Festival of San Fermin, which is most well known for the Running of the Bulls, a 800 – meter run with dozens of angry bulls chasing the brave runners in which injuries and deaths are not uncommon.

The custom derived from the procession when bulls had to be moved from the off-site corrals to the bullring for the evening shows. Young people would jump among the bulls so as to show their bravery. Another version is that this festival originated from the transportation of the bulls to the market with men attempting to speed the process by applying various strategies, which gradually became a competition as youngsters always try to race in front of the bulls.

Figure 8 – 4   Running of the Bulls

⑤Edinburgh's Hogmanay Festival (December 30 – January 1)

Edinburgh's Hogmanay is a 3 – day winter festival taking place at the end of each year. It starts early in the evening of December 30. At midnight the bells ring, with people singing the old folk song Auld Lang Syne together. The festival features the torchlight Procession, concerts, movies, and street parties.

The celebration derived from the early pagan worship of fire and sun a-
mong the Vikings. As time goes by, it turned to the Roman Saturnalia Festival, while Viking Yule became the 12 Days of Christmas①.

Figure 8 – 5   Edinburgh's Hogmanay Festival

4. Comparisons

(1) Civilization Degree

Deeply influenced by the conventional economic mode of "men till the
land and women weave cloth" in the feudal society, Chinese people have
always regarded agricultural activities as their life center, creating the "Solar terms" in Han Dynasty, which turned out to be the prerequisite and
foundation of most Chinese traditional festivals. Gradually, various kinds of
cultural activities including dramas, folk songs, poems, and other sacrificial
ceremonies etc. emerge, bringing rich agricultural connotation to different
Chinese festivals.

---

① http://www.bootsnall.com/articles/12 – 03/best-festivals-and-events-in-europe.html

Unlike China, western countries are mainly highly industrialized whose national economy is dependent on manufacture or technology rather than agriculture, which simply takes up a small proportion. Therefore, the agricultural characteristics of the festivals are comparatively weaker than Chinese counterparts. And even the Thanksgiving, the most tightly related agricultural festival, is hardly a festival to celebrate the harvest, but an occasion for family reunion and for folks to express their gratitude to the God.

(2) Religious Influence

Confucianism is a Chinese ethical and philosophical system derived from the instructions of the Chinese philosopher Confucius (551 – 479). As a complicated integration of moral, social, political, philosophical, and quasi-religious ideas, it has had massive impact on the culture and history of China, with the core value concerning traditional festivals being manifested as "filial piety" and "benevolence".

The Confucianism advocates four virtues of loyalty, filial piety, continency and righteousness, among which the second is of great social significance. Primarily the term "filial" means the respect of a child to parents, but later this relationship was extended to a wider scope: subject to ruler, son to father, wife to husband, younger brother to elder brother and friend to friend. With the passage of time, "filial piety" has penetrated into the Chinese morality and becomes an essential moral maxim to judge a person. Particularly, it has always been emphasized in traditional festival celebration, enriching the implication of the festivals.

As a result, reunion is the primary theme in most Chinese traditional festivals. For instance, ancient Chinese people used to observe the Mid-autumn Day to worship the moon, but over time this purpose fades but focuses more on family reunion. The Spring Festival, being the biggest time celebrated over a whole year, also values the significance of reunion greatly. Therefore, people travel thousands of miles to rush home so as to get together with their family members. All in all, the happy reunion with the family is an utter reflection of "filial piety". Confucian philosophers once contended, "While your parents are alive, it is better not to travel far away." In a sense, the reunion at festivals is a demonstration of people's cultural identification with "filial piety", displaying respect to the ancestors and parents. Additionally, younger generation is supposed to pay New Year calls to the older relatives with gifts is another good exemplification of "filial piety".

Besides, benevolence is another core value of Confucianism which undoubtedly influenced the Chinese traditional culture, with the key word of "blessing" embodied at festivals. For example, the elder, according to the tradition, gives "red envelops" to the unmarried juniors to bless them with good luck as well as to ward off evil spirits during the Spring Festival. Blessings demonstrate the affection and concerns for others which contribute greatly to the maintenance of the intimacy among people.

However, western religion is a complication with multiple branches, among which the largest one is Christianity. In a sense, the western culture has evolved under the huge influence of Christianity, with a number of traditional festivals being directly the products of religious beliefs.

Briefly speaking, the philosophy of Christianity mainly comprises the life, death and revival of one person, Jesus Christ, the son of God. For example, Christmas is believed to be a celebration to commemorate Jesus' birth; Easter is celebrated in the honor of his resurrection. Other festivals have also been labeled by Christianity, such as the Valentine's Day and the Halloween. With the former memorizing the saint Valentine, and the latter being a day in the memory of all the saints. There is no denying that Christianity has profoundly taken root in western culture, so as to exert great influence on various traditional festivals.

(3) Collectivism Philosophy

Close family bond has always been emphasized in Chinese traditional culture, a concept sustains the whole national spirits. To a large degree, family serves as the perfect representative of collectivism in people's mind since it is viewed as the basic social unit. Mirroring the social value, festivals such as Mid-Autumn Day and Spring Festival emphasize the intimacy between family members, which in turn, actively promote the advance of the whole nation. There is no doubt that collectivism is pretty preserved in spite of the speed social progress among Chinese, home and abroad.

On the contrary, with the impact of religion and individualism, western holidays tend to be taken as the opportunity to relieve people from heavy social and emotional stress, with people breaking the rank boundaries and behave wildly and even abnormally to pursue original entertainment and simple individual satisfaction. In this case, western festivals highlight social interaction, collectivism and revelry to demonstrate their wishes of collective participation in the whole festival.

To sum up, different cultural traditions and ideology determine the distinct features and characteristics of Chinese and western festivals.

Chapter Nine

Customs of Folk Beliefs and Taboos

1. General Introduction

(1) Definition

Folk beliefs are the common beliefs that are not scientifically grounded but are widely accepted as truth within certain communities, ranging from the weather to childbirth. Some of these beliefs are merely light-hearted precepts, whereas others contain important social rules, once broken, will be regarded as a serious violation of mutual respect and even do harm to the group members' well-being.

Folk beliefs take in different forms within a culture. Some remain secret and private, known only within a limited society while others take more public expression. The latter often appear in the form of colloquialisms, or "hard sayings", which are deeply rooted in culture. For instance, the frequently heard weather-related saying "red sky at morning, sailor take warning; red sky at night, sailors delight." is the popular belief among people.

Sports and recreation also have their own folk beliefs. Football, basketball and baseball players often maintain a strict set of practices or superstitions about playing. Even the coaches might insist on wearing certain clothes which will bring them good luck.

Despite the fact that technology and science have become increasingly important in modern society, different folk beliefs remain prevailing among individuals and still serve as behavioral guidance in their daily activities. Another case is that the actual practice associated with the belief may have declined, but its verbalization still exists.

Meanwhile, at early times when the society was scientifically underdeveloped, human beings tended to be confined in their personal understanding of the universe. Therefore, irresistible natural power such as ghosts, evil spirits, demons and monsters are strongly believed to harm human life. Taboos came into being as a vehement prohibition of an action based on the belief that such behavior is either too sacred or too accursed for ordinary individuals to undertake, under threat of supernatural punishment.

Such taboos exist in almost all societies, ranging from strong prohibitions concerning human activity to custom that is sacred or forbidden according to moral judgment and religious beliefs. Breach of a taboo will always incur objection by society in general, not merely a limited group subset. Roughly speaking, taboo culture is an aspect of folk belief[1].

(2) Worshipped Objects

The worshipped objects in folk belief are categorized into the following types:

①Souls

• Ancestors

In certain countries, such as China, respects for ancestors are highly valued since ancients believe that the souls of ancestors can bless the offspring generation for generation, which gives rise to traditions of worshipping, funeral etc.

• Ghosts

The ghosts are the souls of the dead. The wandering ghosts without certain shelters are considered evils. Once the souls leave the flesh, people would suffer illness or death. The customs of exorcism and evocation are based on the above belief.

• Divinities

---

① Lisa Abney, "Folk Beliefs," Encyclopedia of Oklahoma History and Culture, www. okhistory. org

In human history, the heroes are regarded as divinities by common people such as Buddha, *Li er*, the supreme god of Taoism or *Guan yu*, the God of wealth in China, who were great men when they were alive, and their souls become spirits after death, exerting huge influence on folk's life. A series of activities of God worshipping emerge out of the admiration towards them.

②Creatures

Many natural objects such as the sun, the moon, the star, the mountains etc. are believed to be God. Besides, certain animals are treated as spirits in given culture. Therefore, there exist kangaroo spirits in Australia, and crocodile and snake spirits in Africa.

(3) Characteristics

Despite different countries and cultures, the folk beliefs share some common features:

①Mysterious

Mysteryis the foundation and basic elements of all folk beliefs, through which the unknowability is deepened even to the level of superstitions. Therefore, omnipotence is enhanced to ensure folks' admiration.

②Utilitarian

Utilitarianism is evidently expressed in folk beliefs. After all, people's beliefs are held for the sake of avoiding misfortune and pray for happiness, no matter for themselves or the whole families.

③Regional and National

Folk beliefs are the fruits of the combination of nature and society, so it is natural that the birth of certain beliefs is immensely influenced by the nature. For instance, people living by the seas might feel deeply about the power of sea while mountain inhabitants might worship mountains, trees etc, being quite ignorant of the spirits of sea. Meanwhile, different races will naturally develop diverse beliefs out of different national psychology.

④Contraindicated

Every folk belief encompasses two parts: what should be done and what should not be done, the latter being the taboos. The beliefs without taboos do not exist. For example, for Chinese who worship the God of Sea, they should avoid the words of "fan (capsize)" for fear that the ship might really be turned over in the sea. It can be put that taboos reinforce folk beliefs from the opposite angle.

2. Chinese Customs of Folk Beliefs

(1) Folk Beliefs of Han Nationality

Chinese folk beliefs, or Chinese folk religion, are difficult to define. In the past, Chinese folk religion was once mistakenly judged as a combination of Confucianism, Taoism, and Buddhism, but it is now widely accepted as an individual system of belief and practice. Objectively speaking, those Chinese who self-consciously claim to possess no religious identity are virtually often adherents of Chinese Folk Religion. Furthermore, the Chinese folk religion is not enclosed thanks to the confluent feature, but rather embraces easy incorporation of certain local beliefs and practices, which also contains shamanism, ancestor worship, magic, ghosts and other spirits, and aspects of animism[1]. All in all, such folk religion may overlap with one person's philosophy in Buddhism, Taoism, Confucianism, or other traditional Chinese religions, coupled with other folk complements.

①Ancestor Veneration

The ancestor worship is undoubtedly an indispensable part of the belief system among Chinese people, the cult based on the common belief of reciprocity between the living and the deceased. The living have the obligation to sustain the spirits of the ancestors by maintaining their graves so as for the dead to bring blessings and good fortune to their living descendants. If their offspring fail to attend to their ancestors, chances are that the ancestors will become a hungry ghost, who can be vengeful and dangerous, wan-

---

① Ching, Julia, Chinese Religions. New York: Orbis Books, 1993.

dering in the spirit world. Accordingly, it is highly essential for the living to pay attention to the dead for the sake of their living prosperity.

The history of ancestor worship can be traced back to Shang Dynasty when people believed the existence of many gods who possessed the power to bring them gifts and blessings. However, the living were incapable of contacting these gods directly whereas the ancestors were able to bestow their living predecessors with good fortune through those gods.

From time to time, large numbers of sacrifices such as oxen, sheep, pigs and dogs, even humans were offered to dead kings, sometimes queens. Besides, food and drink served in bronze vessels would be presented to the ancestors at regular ritual ceremonies.

Royal funerals also feature sacrifices. The royal coffin would be placed above a central pit where a dog had been sacrificed. Often the royal person's closest servants would be killed in order to be buried in the tomb to accompany the master. Human sacrifice was also practiced to consecrate new buildings. The Shang king would like to apply divination through oracle bones to determine the best day to present sacrifices to their ancestors.

Then, as time advances, ancestor worship becomes more common with offerings to the departed for their afterlife welfare, which is assumed to be similar to the earthly life. Ancestor worship starts at the dead kin's funeral where necessities are put in the coffin or burned as a sacrifice.

Following the funeral, daily or twice-daily offerings are given which are expected to bring the family members a good life in the afterworld. Necessities and luxuries such as the fruits, wine and other favorite foods of the dead are arranged on the altar, usually in bowls. Small sums of money, symbolic pieces of paper called "spirit money," are burned in front of the altar. Family members bow successively before the altar with respect.

After the funeral, Chinese families normally establish a home altar for ancestor worship. The altar typically consists of a portrait or a photograph of the deceased, a commemorative plaque and cups for offerings. Commonly altars are worshipped for 49 days, after which the deceased is honored together with all the other kinship ancestors[1].

Once the home altar is with drawn, the ancestors are thought to dwell in commemorative tablets, pieces of wood inscribed with the name and dates of the deceased, which are kept in a small shrine at home and in the clan ancestral temple, with incense being lit and offerings of food and prostrations being presented.

All in all, Chinese weddings and funerals often comprise elaborate rituals to memorize deceased family members and periodical rites are also conducted at the family cemetery. In addition, ancestor worship is indispensable to the Chinese conventional festivals such as Ghost Festival and Tomb Sweeping Festival[2].

②Buddhism, Taoism and Confucianism

Confucianism, Taoism and Buddhism are the three mainly worshipped religions among Chinese who were sometimes opponent but sometimes complementary throughout history, with the first being more dominant[3].

Confucianism and Taoism appeared almost at the same time in Chinese history-near the end of the Zhou dynasty, which had a profoundly impact on the progress of the core value of Chinese culture.

● Confucianism Worship

Confucius (Kongzi, 551 – 479 B. C.), founder of Confucianism, advocates "Ren" (benevolence, love) and "Li" (rites), particularly stresses the respect for social hierarchy. Being famous for instructing students based on their intellectual inclinations, his teachings were later recorded by his students which was entitled "The Analects."

Mencius (Mengzi, 389 – 305 B. C.), another great mind of Confucianism, believed that human beings were innately virtuous and the government should be benign to its people. Supported by the emperors and absorbing the

---

① Keightley, David N. , Heritage of China. Early Civilizations in China: Reflections of How It Became Chinese. Ed. Paul S. Ropp. San Francisco: University of California Press, 1990.

② http://www. religionfacts. com/chinese-religion/practices/ancestor-worship

③ Soothill, W. E. The Three Religions of China. New York: Hyperion Press, 1923.

ideas of Taoism and Buddhism, Confucianism gradually grew into the orthodox ideology in feudal China. By the 12th century, Confucianism had e-
volved into a firm philosophy that promoting heavenly law preservation and
human desires suppression[1].

Rather than enacting severe laws to prevent people from committing
crimes, Confucius called for self-discipline among citizens for them to behave legally since people always try to avoid losing face with improper behavior. Therefore, the government would not bother to establish many coer-
cive laws required for smooth functioning of the society.

To commemorate Confucius, a grand ceremony would be conducted
regularly in the Confucius Temple, regarded as "the national ceremony" in
ancient times which consisted of music, songs, dances and rituals. The most
significant one was three-gift-presenting ceremony, with the first gift presented being yellow silk, second incense, and finally wine[2].

● Taoism Worship

Taoism has exerted great impact on Chinese thinkers, writers and art-
ists, which was founded by Lao-tzu in approximately the sixth century
B. C. , whose masterpiece is "The Classic of the Virtue of the Tao. ", or
" Tao-teching ", stressing the dialectical philosophy of inaction. Zhuang
Zhou, the main advocate of Taoism during the Warring States period, crea-
ted a relativism calling for the entire freedom of the subjectivity.

Being the most important concept in Taoism, Tao is described as
"There was something undefined and complete, coming into existence before
Heaven and Earth" . Or in other words, it is the creator and sustainer of
everything in the Universe. Being the conductive model followed by the Taoist disciples, Taoism is always connected with non-doing and emptiness.

Taoist deitiesare various, and famous ones include Kitchen God and

---

① Yang, C. K. "Chinese Thought and Institutions." In The Functional Relationship Between
Confucian Thought and Chinese Religion. Ed. John K. Fairbank. Chicago: The University of Chicago
Press, 1957.

② http: //www. cultural-china. com/chinaWH/html/en/History140bye566. html

Guan Yu, revered as Saintly Emperor Guan. The highest Taoist deity, the Jade Emperor, adjudicates and allocates rewards and punishments to actions of saints, the living, and the deceased based to a merit system.

Unlike the Confucianism of social reform through morality, ritual, and authoritative regulation, the genuine way of Taoists restoration lied in the abandonment of learned sage wisdom. Ideas such as to manifest the simple, embrace the primitive, reduce selfishness, and have no desires are particularly urged by Lao-tzu[1].

- Buddhism Worship

Around the 6th century B. C. , Buddhism was founded by Sakyamuni in India, with spiritual liberation being viewed as the top goal since human life is full of misery. It was spread into China through Central Asia in Han dynasty, around the time when Christ was born.

The early Chinese Buddhists assumed the indestructibility of the soul. During the 5th and 6th centuries A. D. , Buddhism developed into a powerful intellectual force in China, with monastic establishments being sharply increasing. In Sui dynasty, Buddhism thrived as a state religion which was applied to rule over the whole reunified China and peaked at Tang dynasty when the authority extended its control over the monasteries and even the ordination of monks.

The elementary belief of Buddhism is that all suffering derives from worldly desire, and people should strive to get rid of it to secure happiness. Meanwhile, Buddhism believes in reincarnation of human beings. Therefore, one's behavior in previous lives, known as karma, determines the type of existence of the next life that person owns. The highest status of Buddhism is to be free of the cycle of death and rebirth through enlightenment, achieving nirvana, a timeless state, in which one has no desire.

With the incorporation of some Taoist and original ancient Chinese gods, Chinese Buddhism are more sophisticated than Indian Bud-

---

① http：//www. nationsonline. org/oneworld/Chinese_ Customs/taoism. htm

dhism. Among all the Chinese Buddhist deities, the most popular ones are Tathagata, ruler of the Western Paradise and Guan Yin, the goddess of mercy①.

③Folk Taboos

Taboo is the explicit prohibition of social behavior that keeps changing and varies from region to region. Chinese Hans possess their share of taboos, some of which are listed below:

● Table Manner

People are supposed to place chopsticks horizontally over their bowls. They should never lay them on the table or stick them vertically into the rice bowl which otherwise would be regarded as a sign of offering a sacrifice.

In addition, when one proposes a toast, it is disrespectful to raise his glass higher than the rim of a senior.

If one is thirsty and no one has poured him a drink, it is very impolite to just pour it for himself. On the contrary, he should offer to pour for a neighbor first and then himself.

● Taboo Words

In ancient China, the names of the emperors and seniors were viewed as taboos. It was utterly forbidden to write the name of an emperor in black and white. To common people, they have several ways to avoid taboo words. For example, use any word element morpheme of a taboo word as one's name; replace the taboo word with its synonyms; use homophones to substitute the taboo word; alter the pronunciation of the tattoo word; apply characters in similar shapes; add components to the taboo character to invent a new word.

● Numbers

The "four" in Chinese is pronounced phonetically similar to "death", so the No. 4, 14, 44 and so on are always avoided. For example, a Chinese would not buy house No. 4 or the 4th floor. Besides, fortune comes in

---

① http://www. chinamonitor. com/pages/HistoryCulture. html

pairs so odd numbers are avoided for special occasions such as birthdays and weddings. Meanwhile, to stop bad issues from reoccurring, burials and offering presents to the sick usually are not chosen on even numbered days.

• Birthdays

Noodles are usually eaten on people's birthday to symbolize longevity, they should not be bitten or cut which otherwise may represent a short life span.

(2) Folk Beliefs of Chinese Minorities

①The Mongol Nationality

The dominant belief of the Mongols used to be Tengrism, the worship in heaven, which prevailed among Turks, Mongols, and Hungarians, as well as the Huns. With the passage of time, Tengrism evolved into a religion prevailing among Central Asian with the combination of shamanism, animism, totemism, both polytheism and monotheism, and ancestor worship. Meanwhile, it still remains to be an important element of Mongolian mythology.

Historically, particularly in the era of the Great Khans, Mongolia practiced free worship. In the 17th century, Tibetan Buddhism took the dominance, with conventional Shamanism being suppressed and marginalized apart from some remote regions. At the same time, several shamanic practices like ovoo worshiping, were gradually absorbed into Buddhism rituals.

Briefly speaking, Tibetan Buddhism owns a lot of deities, contributing greatly to the creation of religious works in the form of painting and sculptures.

Traditionally, Mongolians believe in various good and bad omens. They tended to hold the idea that misfortune might be caused as the product of frequent negative talk. Misfortune might arrive due to the violation of some taboo, say stepping on a yurt's threshold, desecrating waters or mountains, etc.

The most threatened family members were children, therefore in order not to arouse the attention of the evil spirits, boys might be dressed up like girls, or they would even sometimes be given non-names. Before going out at night, parents would sometimes paint young children's foreheads with soot to deceive evil spirits into believing that this is a rabbit with black hair on the forehead rather than being a child. As to names, their selections are symbolic with several meanings; most importantly, the name might have great influence on its future character, fate and destiny.

Mongolians worship ovoos as well, which should be circumambulated when passed by, with some sweets being presented as sacrifices for the sake of a further safe trip. Certain ovoos, particularly those on high mountains, are sacrificed to ensure good weather and to avoid misfortune[①].

Other taboos mainly related with fire, water and childbirth.

Mongolians admire fire, the fire god and the kitchen god, which are related with many taboos. For instance, it is forbidden to dry their feet or shoes over the furnace inside the yurt. It is also taboo to insert a knife into the fire or to throw dirty objects into the fire.

Water is believed to be the purest deity, so it is taboo to wash their hands in or bathe in the river. It is also taboo to place dirty objects into the river.

After ethnic Mongolian women give birth, a sign indicating the sex of the baby—bow and arrow for a boy; red cloth for a girl—must be placed where it is visible to let visitors know to keep their distance.

②Tibetans

According to Tibetan legends, the deities they worship reside at the top of the mountains. Various individuals want differently from them. The seniors make offerings praying for longevity while the youth hope for beauty. Besides, those Gods were believed to possess the power to control the weather such as wind, rain and thunder, thus herders pray for the ownership of considerable herds and farmers expect substantial harvests.

Besides, Tibetans worship yak head due to its indispensable role in their nomadic lives. Yaks are treated as "Norbu" or treasures, finding their

---

① http: //en. wikipedia. org/wiki/Culture_ of_ Mongolia

way into artworks like monastery murals, rock carvings and home decorations. For another, according to classics of the Bon religion, yaks came from heaven to the top of Gangdese Mountains to act as the protector, with one of the Buddhist warriors having a yak head.

In addition, rocks which are commonly found in the plateau are worshipped. Therefore, people accumulated stones with multicolor sutra streamers on the mountains and regard them as the mansions of mountain gods. When passing by, individuals make a clockwise rotation of the stone heap, adding stones to it and muttering the Six-Syllable Prayer for the purpose of dispelling disease and other personal misfortune, as well as taming the monsters and devils. Once the stone is carved with sutra lines, it turns to something holy. Stones carved with the Six-Syllable Prayer or sutra lines are called Mani Stone Mounds with uncertain shape, size and amount. Different items can be placed above the mounds with different meanings. For example, golden ball represents treasure and a silvery cluster of arrows stands for divinity.

Apart from the beliefs in natural objects, Tibetans are greatly pious to Buddha compared with other nationalities, with many corresponding rituals arising.

One ritual is prostration: lying face down in devotion usually with the following procedures. First, people stand upright, chanting the 6 – character sutra meaning "merciful Buddha". Then putting his palms together, one raises his hands up over his head and take a step forward. After that, people lower his hands down in front of the face before taking another step forward. Next one lowers his hands down to the chest and separate both hands, stretching them out with the palms down and kneeling down to the ground, and finally prostrate with the forehead knocking the ground slightly.

Devout Buddhists can be seen prostrating during the whole journey from their home to Lhasa. People move forward with determination and faith by prostrating forward every three steps for months or for years, never giving up despite the extreme exhaustion. In case of some irresistible factors, they draw a line with pebbles instead of prostrating.

Making pagoda models is another religious custom in Tibet, in which people place spell written on a small piece of paper, coupled with a small amount of highland barley. People usually put the models around a real pagoda or a statue as sacrifices to the Buddha. For example in Aba, Tibetans place their model pagodas at the road side or in a village to pray for a good harvest. Or they are buried in the farmland due to their magic of killing harmful insects.

In sum, pagodas are significant symbols of Buddhism, with the Buddhists walking around them in a clockwise direction while chanting the 6 - character sutra, rotating the beads between thumbs and the index fingers, and praying for peace. Some walk around it repeatedly and some offer sacrifices in front of it.

It is a routine for the religionists to recite or chant Buddhist scriptures as believers in Lamaism. Turning the prayer wheels with scriptures inside serves the same function. Many Tibetans keep portable prayer wheels at home, with followers of the Yellow sect turning the wheels clockwise but followers of the Black sect counterclockwise[1].

As to taboos, there are still many that should be noticed:

People should sit cross-legged in a house or a tent, with men on the left and women on the right since they are not allowed to sit together.

It is forbidden to make a racket while crossing snowy mountains and passing by lakes, nor is it allowed in monastery and near monastery.

When pouring tea, it is tabooed to use dirty bowls or to finger the rim of the bowl.

It is not allowed to whistle indoors or at night, which is believed to arouse the attention of ghosts and nocturnal spirits.

People should not accept gifts with dirty hands.

It is tabooed to step over others' foods and kitchenware.

When presented with a cup of wine, people should dip their ring fin-

---

[1]   http://www.chinatravel.com/facts/tibetan-ethnic-minority.htm

ger in the wine and flick it to the sky, the air and the ground respectively to show their respects to the heaven, the earth and the ancestors before tasting it.

It is banned for Buddhist, especially monks and nuns, to kill; and it is also tabooed to kill creatures in the face of them.

In the temple, behaviors such as wearing a hat, smoking, touching statues, turning over the Buddhist books and knocking bells and drums are not allowed.

Pointing to Buddha statues, Thangka, scripture and fresco with fingers is impolite. Use palm to show respect.

When meeting a lama, it is unacceptable to hug him or shake hands with him. The proper way is to hold the two palms upright in front of the chest, and lower the head[1].

③Hui Nationality

The Hui people practice the Islamic religion, which is an indispensable part of the Hui Nationality, with the followers being called Muslims whose scripture is called Koran. They abide by a traditional Islamic life such as the exclusion of pork in their meal. Mosques, the sacred place worshipped by Muslims are constructed to conduct religious services in the charge of I-mam. Some mosques also serve the function of spreading religious knowledge as well as cultivating Islamic clerical practitioners.

The tenth day of the twelfth month of the Islamic calendar is Edi Al-Adha Day, the Feast of Sacrifice, with animals like camels, oxen and sheep being killed in sacrifice to their God Allah. Besides, the ninth month on the Islamic calendar is Ramadan, a month of fasting during which all Hui Muslims must abstain themselves from drinks, food and sex, giving people the opportunity to reflect on their own sins as well as the experience of starvation. Following the fasting is the tenth month called Hari Raya Puasa, which features grand galas to celebrate the fulfillment of the fasting. On this day, all Muslims get up early, taking a bath and lighting incense be-

---

① http://www.intochinatravel.com/etiquettes-and-taboos-in-tibet/

fore going to the mosque in formal clothes to listen respectfully to the lectures and sermons of imams. Finally, they go to their cemeteries, worshipping the deceased to commemorate them.

The *Hui* people are known to value hygiene in their daily life. Whenever possible, people always wash hands both prior to and after meals with flowing water. The majority of the *Hui* do not smoke or drink. When dining together, the seniors would be invited to sit at the honorable seats, with juniors sitting at the edge or just on benches on the floor.

For *Hui* Nationality, certain kinds of food are forbidden, such as pork, dogs, horses, donkeys and mules. For seafood, only fish and shrimps can be eaten. Animals killed by people from other nationalities or die naturally are not edible to the *Hui* people. Only those killed by the cook or the imam from the mosque can be consumed. In addition, one should not reveal his or her bosom and arms in front of others.

All livestock should be kept away from drinking sources such as wells and springs which are not allowed to be contaminated by people washing their hands, faces, or clothes in them. Particularly, any remaining water of a container should never be poured back into the source[1].

④*Zhuang* Nationality

The Zhuang nationality admires the nature as well as the ancestors, with each house having shrines to worship. As to religion, the Zhuang people take *Moz* as their main religious belief under the influence of both Buddhism and Daoism. Besides, they also worship various Gods, including Nature God, Social God, Patron God etc; and the religious rituals vary accordingly.

Buluotuo, a half-man and half-God mythology ancestor in the Zhuang oral literature, is considered to be the world creator as well as the Moral God.

Huapo, the wife of *Buluotuo*, is the goddess in charge of the child

---

① http: //www. chinatravel. com/facts/hui-ethnic-minority. htm

birth, also known as the Virgin Goddess. After a baby's birth, the parents make a paper flower, hanging it on the top of the bed. Mothers, together with the children will worship *Huapo* on important festivals or in the case of children's illness, praying for her protection.

The Zhuang nationality also admires the land god who is thought to be in charge of drought, flood, disease as well as livestock, with the temple of land god being built in each village. Without statues inside, the characters of which is written on a red piece of paper, pasted on the wall in the central for the locals to worship. On the occasions of festivals or important events, the villagers go to the temple, praying for protection.

Shegong is also regarded as the protector of the Zhuang villages. The folks usually have an altar under the big trees, with several stones or a stone statue of dog putting inside. On New Year's Eve, each household prepares wines and meat to worship *Shegong*. In the annual ceremony, all the respectable seniors meet in front of the altar, discussing the big events of the village in the forthcoming Year. Younger generations also gather to the altar to pay respect to the old villagers. Newly married women, accompanied by their husbands, need to return to her parents' village to attend the ceremony. The host of the ritual will present jewelry to the new-born babies, blessing them with peace, health and fortune, and his parents distribute red eggs to the villagers.

Three-year-old children will be taken to the alter by parents, who offer sacrifices of wines and chickens. The child kneels down, requiring the uncle to give him/her a name. Finally, the parents hand out chicken which is cut into small slices, coupled with a piece of brown sugar, to other families, informing them the baby's name. The young girls will get their ears pierced and put on earrings in front of the altar. At night after the ritual, all families put meat, soups, sticky rice dumplings and red eggs that were ever presented to the altar in front of the doors of women's rooms who have children to redeem the souls of the children. In the end, the soup and food will feed the livestock and poultry, a way to make them much stronger. If insects do harm to their crops, the Zhuang people will assemble, killing pigs, sheep and chickens, and take the offerings to worship *Shegong*. The blood of the animals are used to dye paper strips, which are later hanged on sticks in the field, representing the presence of *Shegong*, to put the insect damage to a stop.

June 6th is the day for Zhuang families to kill chickens to worship the God of Crops, with all villagers meeting and singing together. Small paper flags are placed on the edge of the field in the hope of bringing in a good growing of the crops. In the case of insect damages, Yellow Dragon Dancing will be performed to drive them away. When sowing seeds, villagers always throw grains or peanut shells at the entrance of their village to pray for a good harvest. During July, some Zhuang villages conduct the ceremony of Worshipping Young Crops. Preparing some wines and pork, people, both young and old, will meet outside their village, drinking and singing agriculture songs to ensure a good harvest. Following autumn harvest is the ceremony of Eating New Rice. Folks pick some new rice from the fields before cooking it; then, they reap the rice after killing chickens and ducks as sacrifice for the worshipping ceremony.

Zhuang people also worship God of Ox, believing that ox is sent by God of Heaven down to the earth to help them with their farm work. Accordingly, May 5th is the birthday of ox, known as Ox Day, when ox slaughtering is forbidden and incense is burned to worship God of Ox. Oxen are fed with colorful sticky rice, even wines. When the spring ploughing begins, ceremony of Summoning Ox Souls will be held, with chicken, fish, meat, and colorful sticky rice being made as sacrifices. Firmly believing that oxen are laborious in the farm season and tiredness may result in their souls flying away, people need to perform rituals to summon the Ox souls back.

Some typical taboos are listed in the following:

It is not allowed for the *Zhuang* nationality to kill animals on the first day of the lunar January. Strangers are forbidden to enter the courtyard of the family which just has a new born baby during the first three days, or even the first seven days. As to the mother of a less than one month old baby, she is not allowed to visit other families. Ascending the bamboo building of a *Zhuang* family, one should take off his shoes. People who wear a bamboo hat or carry agricultural devices such as a hoe are not welcome by other families.

As to the pregnant women, there are also some taboos. For instance, pregnant women are not welcome to be a guest in the wedding ceremony. In addition, she should never glance at the bride. And they are forbidden to go to other pregnant women's houses. If a family member gets pregnant, a sleeve, a branch of trees, or a knife should be hanged on the gate to inform others of the news. If anyone enters the courtyard of the family unconsciously, he/she should name the baby, or offer a piece of clothes or some other gifts. More interestingly, he/she should burden the responsibility to be the new baby's godfather or godmother.

The fire place and kitchen stove are the most sacred places in the Zhuang family, as a result, it is not allowed to tread the tripod on the kitchen stove[1].

3. Western Folk Beliefs and Taboos

(1) Europe
①Russia
● Religions

In Russia, pre-Christian polytheism such as Orthodoxy, Islam, Buddhism, Protestantism, Catholicism, Judaism, and shamanism coexisted for hundreds of years, with churches being built normally on ancient sacred sites. The state has returned thousands of churches, mosques, and temples coupled with icons and other religious objects to their respective communities. Tradition such as the curative adoption of "holy water" from a church as well as many animistic rituals and feasts based on the agricultural calendar remain. Conventions about forest and house spirits and metaphysical

---

① http://www.chinatravel.com/facts/zhuang-ethnic-minority.htm

healing practices still exist among individuals, particularly among rural residents.

The modern times witness the religious prosperity since monasteries and religious schools for all faiths have emerged, and the number of religious practitioners has approximately doubled since the 1970s. There has also been an explosion of alternative and New Age spiritual movements, publications, and practitioners.

The majority of ethnic Russians regarded themselves as Orthodox Christians, with the number of the active participants of the church activities being on the declining compared with the growing numbers of the key religious holiday observers. Among the various religions, the Russian Orthodox Church takes the comparative dominance, aligned with the state power since Kievan times and even in the Soviet period, which was allowed to operate within certain limits, enabling the security and control of the state to be achieved through the administrative networks and ideological influence of the Orthodox Church.

Besides, Islam has always been important throughout Russian history, dominating the northern Caucasus and the Volga region since the eighth and the tenth century respectively. Contemporarily, Islam belongs to one of the large religions, only secondary to Russian Orthodoxy, with at least 19 million practitioners, most of them being Sunni Muslim from Tatars, Bashkirs, Kazakhs, Chechens, and Avars etc. Moscow, the capital city, acts as the Islamic center in Russia, with many active mosques and organizations serving the millions of Muslims in Moscow. Meanwhile, there are impressive populations in many other large cities as well[1].

● Superstitions and Taboos

The folk beliefs, or so called superstitions, are indispensable part of people's daily life. For example, Russians believe that to return safely from a journey, they had better to sit on their luggage for a few moments. When presented others with a wallet gift, they should place some money inside or

---

① http://www.everyculture.com/No-Sa/Russia.html

the gift receiver might suffer poverty.

Russians always prefer to give odd number of flowers, the only exception being the occasion of funerals. Russians must not stand on the threshold of an apartment, Walking across it or handing anything across it since the ancient Slavs considered the threshold a place occupied by demons.

Items like knives, clocks and scarves should never be offered as a gift, which represent enemies, separation and tears respectively. If one does receive such present, he might give a small coin in return, meaning that it is bought rather than got for free, to remove the effect of bad omen.

People with any empty container such as bucket or a cart is considered unlucky. Therefore, street cleaners always put brooms, rakes or other devices in their empty carts.

Another interesting taboo is that never offer unmarried girls corner seats. The reason is that it was normally the old maids, poor relatives taking the humblest places at the table in ancient Russia. Therefore, it is believed that a girl sitting at the table corner can hardly find a desirable husband.

In general, the traditional taboos usually derive from old beliefs. For instance, whistling indoors or praising the child in the face of others may arouse the attention of evil spirits, so the Russians always avoid such behavior.

②United Kingdom

● Religions

Roughly speaking, Religion in the United Kingdom has long been dominated by different forms of Christianity throughout history, despite the fact that routine church attendance has fallen sharply since the middle of last century, and immigration as well as demographic transfer have resulted in some shift to other faiths.

The various Christian sects in the United Kingdom have divided the church for centuries. Particularly in the 16th century, Henry VIII rejected the supreme authority of the pope, contributing to the appearance of some Protestant tenets and the founding of the Church of England. In Scotland, the Reformation led to the Church of Scotland governed by presbyteries rather than by bishops, similar to the case in England. In the 17th century the Church of England got separated under the influence of the Puritan movement, giving rise to Nonconformist denominations, a reflection of the Puritan desire for simpler worship forms.

In the middle of the 18th century, the Presbyterian Church of Wales remains the most powerful religious branch in the principality. The great Evangelical revivals, closely related to John Wesley and others, contributed to the emergence of Methodist churches, especially in the industrial areas, with Northumberland, Durham, and Yorkshire in northeastern England and Cornwall in the southwestern peninsula occupying the largest proportion of Methodists.

In the 19th century the Salvation Army and various fundamentalist faiths evolved. Denominations from the United States also gained adherents, coupled with a significant rise in the practice of Judaism in Britain. In the 17th century, the first Jewish community was founded in London, and many Jews settled in large provincial cities till last century. It is estimated that Britain currently owns the second largest Jewish community in Europe.

All in all, the British is a highly religiously tolerant country, with increasing number of immigrants introducing other religious beliefs since the 1950s, Islam, Hinduism, Sikhism and Buddhism. The majority of Muslims originated from Pakistan, Bangladesh, India, Cyprus, the Arab world, Malaysia, and parts of Africa. In addition, the large Sikh and Hindu communities came from India[1].

 • Superstitions and Taboos

According to a survey, almost one in five Britons believes in superstitions. And the following are the typical ones:

Some behaviors might bring about misfortune. For instance, walking under a ladder. In medieval times, ladders were leaned against the gallows for people to dispose the bodies. Therefore, people assume that walking beneath a ladder may result in their death.

---

[1] http: //kids. britannica. com/shakespeare/article - 44685

Breaking a mirror is considered unlucky as well, with the origin derived from ancient Greece when mirrors could be very expensive since they were firstly invented. Any servant who broke one would have to offer seven years of labor to pay back the debt.

Opening an umbrella indoors is considered a taboo. In ancient Egypt beautiful umbrellas decorated with papyrus and peacock feathers were used to protect the nobles and religious leaders from the sun heat. The shadow beneath the umbrella was viewed sacred, thus stepping into it was considered sacrilegious. But it is generally accepted that bad luck does not befall if the umbrella has first been opened outdoors and brought indoors to dry.

Putting shoes on the table is unlucky. When miners in the northern England died in mine accidents, their shoes were placed on the family table as a mark of respect. Therefore, placing shoes, whether new or old, on a table was associated with misfortune.

On the contrary, certain behaviors will bring good luck. For instance, touching wood. Early pagans believed that deities dwelled on trees; so knocking on a tree can help people to gain protection from these spirits. Later such beliefs were absorbed into Christianity, with knocking on wood being similar to obtaining the guard of the cross.

Finding a penny on the floor is definitely lucky. Conventionally it is believed that metal was a gift from the gods, protecting people against evil spirits. Accordingly, metal, may it be a penny, a button, or something else can bring fortune. A horseshoe is hanged over a door frame to serve the same function.

There are some other interesting folk beliefs. For instance, burning ears indicates being talked about and English literature from Chaucer to Dickens abounds with references to burning ears. Other body sensations might have a similar predictive ability: a flickering right eye predicts a friend's arrival whereas a pricking in one's left thumb means something evil will appear.

③Germany

• Religions

Being a religion existed in Germany for over 1300 years, Christianity is still the major religion in this country and is regarded as its cultural heritage, with approximately 65% to 70% of the population being Christian followers.

Due to the Protestant Reformation and the following Thirty Years' War in the 15th and 16th centuries, the religious distribution was formed according to the preferences of local rulers: most regions in the South or West are Catholic whereas the North and East are primarily Protestant.

Other sects of Christian religion in Germany are Free Evangelical Churches, which is a loose union of congregations attached to Baptism, Methodism and relative faiths like the Mennonites and the two Orthodox churches. Christian evangelism in Germany was attributed to American missionary efforts in the 19th century. Both the Greek-Orthodox and the Russian-Orthodox religion in Germany grew with the increasing number of Greek and Serbian immigrants in the 1960s and 1970s.

In addition to these minor Christian congregations, other small religions in Germany are Islam, accounting for roughly 4 % of the German inhabitants; Judaism, and Buddhism, both of which take up less than 1% of Germany's population[1].

• Superstitions and Taboos

Germansare considered to be calm and reasonable. However, it is also a culture full of myths and folk-tales.

Chimney sweeps are definitely the symbol of fortune. After all, there's nothing more lucky than cleaning out soot from a confined area. In Germany, especially on New Year's Day, Germans would find chances to shake hands with their friendly neighborhood sweeper.

When saying hello to friends in the bar, instead of waving or other gestures, Germans would like to knock on the table, which is believed to be able to guard them against evil spirits since the table in the tavern is normally made of oak, a holy tree.

Offering knives as gifts is a taboo, which is believed to bring the re-

---

[1]   http: //trendwave. com/spirituality-and-religion/religion-in-germany——internations. org

ceiver and his family injury and death. This superstition derives from an ancient story that a knife smith made a wrong deal with the devil, leading to the curse to all his family.

There are also a series of German superstitions associated with old ladies, who are commonly viewed as evil. According to ancient medieval custom, one of the greatest misfortunes is to pace between two of them on the road.

④France

• Religions

In the past thousand years, France has always been remarkable for being a European "Catholic" country.

From the era of Charlemagne to the uprising of Protestantism in the 16th century, France was one of the principal nations in a continent in which Catholicism was the most important branch of Christianity, except in orthodox areas. After that, most of France, especially the French monarchy, insisted the Catholic faith whereas many other areas of Europe, such as England, Switzerland, the Low countries, and much of Germany and Scandinavia, shifted to various forms of Protestantism.

The French Resolution in 1798 resulted in the national control of religion, with monastic orders being abandoned. But in 1801, Napoleon reached an agreement with the Vatican, restoring the church's previous status substantially.

Therefore, France was primarily a Catholic country during the 19th century; but in 1905 the milestone law was established, confirming the division of the State and the Church. Ever since, even though Catholicism still remained the major religious belief in France, the Catholic Church is actually one among a number of religions. Citizens were entitled the freedom to practice whatever religion they worship. So in contemporary France, Catholicism exists together with Protestantism, Islam, Buddhism, Judaism and several other minor cults.

Anyway, it is true that compared with Britain or the United States, the position of religion is obviously weakened, with public figures being likely to keep themselves away from religious ceremonies[1].

● Superstitions and Taboos

The French are renowned for the good taste of their bread, but an up-side-down loaf given to them might be regarded as an offence. Apparently handing someone a loaf of bread upside-down or placing it on the table up-side-down is believed to bring both the giver and the receiver hunger and misfortune.

Another old superstition is that an encounter with an owl for a pregnant during her pregnancy will signify the birth of a girl. Even though no expla-nation is offered for such unreasonable connection, it still prevails in some areas.

Unlike Britains, Friday the 13th is considered a somewhat fortuitous day on which people will buy stocks or lottery in the hope of gaining good fortune.

However, having 13 people around a dinner table is considered a ta-boo. Accordingly, for people holding parties, they had better keep the num-ber of the participants lower or higher than this figure.

Hanging a horseshoe over a doorway is a generally adopted way to in-vite good luck to a home, but opinions divided among nations the way to deal with it. For the French hanging it upside down is lucky, otherwise bad fortune will befall.

Maybe the oddest of all, in some cultures, say British culture, being hit by bird's droppings is lucky; but in France, stepping on dog poo is good since it is believed to represent magic blessings.

⑤Italy

● Religions

Ancient Romans worshipped a number of gods and goddesses who were responsible for protecting various worshippers' lives. For instance, the god-dess Juno was regarded as the protector of Roman females, coupled with Minerva, the goddess of wisdom. Mars was worshipped as an important im-

---

① http://about-france.com/religion.htm

age, being the God of war; and Jupiter was the god of the sky.

With Christianity increasingly introduced to various areas of Rome, the cult for these gods and goddesses invariably faded. Gradually, the Roman Catholic Church is gaining the greatest power in Italy. The Vatican, where the Pope, the head of the church, resides, is located in Rome. Generally speaking, the history of the Roman Catholic Church is based on politics as well as on religion.

At one point, religion began a rather hasty descent and continued to spiral downhill until the counter-Reformation Movement. Due to the Protestant Reformation Movement and the many abuses that went on within the Catholic Church, a need arose for a turn around and a resurrection of truly religious beliefs within the church. Pope Paul III was able to begin leading the church away from the political games that had taken such an active role in the past. The Jesuits, a newly created religious order, was created, along with the Council of Trent, which was made up of men willing and ready to deal with the doctrinal dilemmas created by the influx of the Protestant religion.

The Roman Catholic Church experienced a resurrection in the 16th century, a sect always in opposition of the Protestant religion. However, Lutheranism became a problem in the mid to late 1500s, resulting in the arising of the Roman Inquisition led by Pope Paul III which helps greatly to bring the Catholic religion to the people. Bishops were encouraged to make frequent presence known among people, seminaries were conducted to train a large number of clergies, and church buildings sprang up, despite the still strong influence of Protestant religion.

Meanwhile, the Jewish belief takes up a part in Italian religion. Approximately 2, 000 years ago, a few Jews settled in Rome, with accumulation gradually formed in southern Italy. Being the first group of people who lend money with charge of interest, the Jews exerted great influence in trade and merchandising. Believing in Messiah rather than Jesus, the Jews has long been suffered persecution. For instance, they were required to live in segregation, and they were forced to wear a religious symbol visible to all during the Holocaust, with over 7, 000 Jews being slaughtered during World War II. Despite the sufferings, their lineage survived with more than 40 thousand Jewish Italian citizens today.

Nowadays, the Roman Church still dominates, with people of the Church looking up to the Pope for life guidance[1].

● Superstitions and Taboos

The major superstition that Italians hold concerns Malocchio, or Evil Eye, which may be regarded as a curse, even though strangely it might be caused by a compliment. For instance, an Italian is told that his baby is beautiful, which might result in a tempted fate. To guard the child, he must put on a horn sign or the hand sign of extending pinkie and index finger, while keeping the others folded back, to scare off the evil spirit that probably will befall.

A lot of Italians wear a corno, horn-shaped charm as a piece of jewelry for protection as well as hanging one in their cars.

If a Malocchio occurs, the person may be inflicted with a serious headache, and a baptized, communed or confirmed Catholic might help.

On New Years Eve, Italians may perform a private prayer, which is similar to an initiation rite to empower them for the sake of removing Malocchio. Meanwhile, on this day, consuming lentils at midnight is believed to bring fortune. Ladies wearing red undergarments will be blessed with love in the coming year.

Birds and bird feathers, particularly peacock feathers, are considered to have the Evil Eye on them, which should be avoided in home decoration.

Apart from the first Friday in March, it is believed inappropriate to shave on a Friday. In addition, Friday the 17th, rather than Friday the 13th, is considered an ill-fated day.

No housework should be conducted on January the 6th, the day of Epiphany, a holiday related with La Befana, a witch who refuse to visit the

---

[1]   http: //en. alzakera. com/2015/02/12/italian-culture-religions-of-italy/

baby Jesus because of the unfinished housework. Every year on the January 5th, La Befana goes from door to door to send gifts to the Christ child.

(2) North America

①America

In this section, due to the limitation of space, the religions of Indigenous Americans are introduced here.

● Overview

Native American religions are the spiritual practices of the locals in North America. Generally speaking, conventional Native American rituals can differ significantly, according to the histories and beliefs of various tribes, ranging from monotheism, polytheism, henotheism to animism. Traditional beliefs are commonly passed down in forms of oral histories, narrations, allegories etc, through face to face instructions within families and communities.

However, from the 1600s, European Catholic and Protestant denominations sent missionaries to convert the American native tribes to Christianity. From the mid 19thcentury to mid 20th, the efforts reached a peak as the authority and Christian churches made joint efforts to force Native Americans to register as Christians. In addition, native children were forcibly taken from their families to Christian-US government cooperated system of American Indian boarding schools where they were instilled with European Christian beliefs, mainstream American culture and the English language, a cultural suppression that continued through the 1970's. What's more, a series of US Federal laws were established to ban traditional ceremonies such as sweat lodge and sun dance ceremonies etc, for over eighty years, which ended in 1978 thanks to the passage of the American Indian Religious Freedom Act.

● Major Native American Religions

—Bole-Maru Religion

The Bole-Maru, the dreams of medicine people, was a religious revitalization movement of the Maidu, Pomo, Wintun, and other tribes of north-central California in the 19th century which absorbed traditional and Christian beliefs and ethical guidelines, with revelations from dreams playing a central role. Some of the typical dances of this religion were the Bole or Maru dance, the Bole-Hesi Dance, and the Ball Dance in which dancers typically wore large headdresses.

—Christianity

As previously mentioned, Europeans brought their Christian religion to the Americas, with the characteristics of Native American Christianity being "fundamentalist in theology, conservative in their practice, and often revivalistic and evangelical. "①

In a sense, the US government has long been applying Christianity as an instrument in cultural assimilation, as a result, many Native American Christians believe both their traditional beliefs as well as Christianity, as with the Native American Church. Therefore, Native American Christians "have constructed and maintained their. . . religious identities with a variety of considerations in mind. . . . Many native Christians accomplish this identification without abandoning or rejecting native religious traditions. "②

—Drum Religion

The Drum Religion, or the "Big Drum", "Drum Dance", or "Dream Dance", originated around 1890 among the Santee Dakota. Spreading through the Western Great Lakes region to other Native American tribes such as the Ojibwe, Meskwaki, Kickapoo, Menominee, Potawatomi, Hochunk and others, it created a sense of unity through ceremonies as a result of the religious revitalization movement which encompassed playing sacred drums as well as passing sacred knowledge between tribes.

—Earth Lodge Religion

The Earth Lodge Religion, also known as the "Warm House Dance"

①　Neusner, Jacob. *World Religions in America: An Introduction.* Louisville: Westminster John Knox Press: 2003

②　Ellis, Clyde. "American Indian and Christianity" in Oklahoma Historical Society's Encyclopedia of Oklahoma History and Culture. Retrieved 25 May 2013

among the Pomo, was founded in northern California and southern Oregon tribes, then spread to tribes such as the Achomawi, Shasta, and Siletz etc. Foreseeing occurrences similar to those predicted by the Ghost Dance, such as the return of ancestors or the world's end, the Earth Lodge Religion influenced the later religious practice, the Dream Dance, which belonged to the Klamath and the Modoc.

—Feather Religion

Absorbing aspects of the earlier Indian Shaker Religion and the Waashat Religion, the Feather Religion, founded in 1904 by Jake Hunt, is a religion of the Pacific Northwest due to revitalization movement. It is also labeled as the Feather Dance or the Spinning Religion, with Sacred eagle feathers used in rituals.

—Ghost Dances

Ghost Dances exerted huge impacts on many native American religions, a general term including different religious revitalization movements in the Western United States. In 1889 – 1890, a Ghost Dance Religion was founded by Wovoka, a Northern Paiute, which is intended to combine primary ways of life with the death while predicting their revival.

The earliest Ghost Dance impacted religions such as the Earth Lodge, Bole-Maru Religion, and the Dream Dance, with The Caddo Nation still practicing it today.

—Indian Shaker Religion

The Indian Shaker Religion, or Tschadam, was founded by John Slocum under the influence of the Waashat Religion. The name originates from the shaking and twitching motions applied by the performers to get rid of their sins. A combination of Christianity and traditional Indian teachings, it is still practiced today in the Indian Shaker Church.

—Longhouse Religion

The Longhouse Religion was founded in 1776 by Seneca Handsome Lake in order to revitalize Native American religion among the Iroquois till today. The creed *of the Longhouse Religion is the Gaiwiio, or " Good*

Word", a combination of Christianity with long-standing Iroquois beliefs[1].

● Superstitions and Taboos

Common Native Americans, except for some trained specialists, are not allowed to kill an eagle, wolf, or rattlesnake. Besides, the cutting of evergreens is typically avoided but sometimes they are harvested and utilized for ceremonial purposes.

Some Native American families put sprigs of cedar or pine needles into a pot of hot coals for a smoldering effect of pungent smoke to achieve purification.

Ginseng, like Evergreen wood, is seldom applied as firewood since it is respected as being sacred. When seeking ginseng, the firstly found plants are passed by. When the desired one is located, people uproot it with proper prayer before placing some beads in the hole as offerings.

If a hunter kills a deer, he is supposed to cut out the hamstrings and leave them behind. But it is a taboo for him to leave them in the meat, nor should he leave without praying to the deer. Rather, since it is a common practice for people to throw meat to the fire as offerings, he should cast the tip of the deer's tongue to the fire as an offering of thanks.

Pregnant women should not consume squirrel, speckled trout, rabbit. In addition, they should not linger in doorways or wear stuffs tied around their neck, say a neckerchief.

Women in their moon time, which means going through the menstrual cycle, should be kept in isolation, during the duration of their bleeding, staying in a house built particularly for this purpose. Furthermore, they should avoid men, never touching them or preparing food for them. In a word, they should never participate in any community ceremonies. At the end of their menstruation, they are required to be purified by sweating and going to water before returning to the community.

Foods from the opposite fields of this world should never be mixed. For instance, birds should never be eaten with fish, since they are from the

---

① http://en. wikipedia. org/wiki/Native_ American_ religion

upper world of sky and the lower world of water and underground respectively.

The mourning period of a deceased lasts for one year during which it is a taboo to name the dead orally.

②Canada

• Religions

Christianity is the dominating religion in Canada, with 70% citizens claiming themselves as being either Roman Catholic or Protestant. Traditionally, native peoples practiced a wide range of religions prior to European settlement. Many native individuals and groups were converted to Christianity through missionary work that began in New France, but in recent years there has been a revival of Aboriginal religions.

During the 19th century, especially due to the immigration wave in 20th century, religious pluralism is common in Canada, with the representatives being Judaism, Buddhism, Sikhism, Hinduism, Islam, and the Baha'i faith etc, which, Briefly speaking, can be divided according to their sense of the sacred based on historic events (Judaism, Christianity, Islam, Sikhism and the Baha'i faith) or on the natural cycle and rhythms of life (Hinduism, Taoism and, to some extent, Buddhism).

The Protestant Reformation of the 16th century contributed to the reaction against priestly religion under the influence of scholars like Martin Luther and John Calvin. The former stressed what God does for humanity through Christ, rather than how human beings prove themselves to God, with the result that faith, or trust in God's action, rather than ritual or human routines, developed as the core of what Protestants regarded as true religion. Being the theists, Christians firmly believe that God is the creator, redeemer and judge of the world.

Among Roman Catholics, the church was dominantly influential in Québec until the Quiet Revolution of the 1960s due to its institutional base for nationalism. Anti-English sentiment was targeted on Irish prelates in Ontario and Protestant business leaders in Montréal. In the West, the "left wing" of the Reformation was chiefly embodied by colonies such as Mennonites and Hutterites while immigrants from Eastern Europe included Russian and Ukrainian Christians from the Orthodox Church, with Jewish worship conducted by rabbis from the Orthodox, Conservative and Reformed traditions[1].

● Superstitions and Taboos

There exist some superstitions and taboos among Canadians, just to name a few.

In Alberta, picking blackberries after October 11 is perceived as bringing bad luck since by this time in the year, the devil has already laid curse to the remaining berries.

A First Nations ritual is believed to bless a new home by taking lit sage from door to door and saying prayers to get rid of evil spirits and misfortune.

In Saskatchewan, a red sky at night in the springtime means that the next day would be a windy one which was not appropriate for farmers to seed.

4. Comparisons

Folk religion primarily consists of certain ethnic or regional religious traditions which are performed under the constraints of an established religion, but is beyond the limitation of official doctrine and practices. Folk religion's beliefs are held all over the world, ranging from nation to nation.

(1) Core Value

One of the dominating religions in the west is Christian, the core value being original sin. Because Adam and Eva, human ancestors, committed sin and transmitted corrupted morality to their descendants, because of which people are bound to die, and will be punished all their life. It is revealed that all things of Christianity are classified into two worlds: the human world and God's world, which are separated but dependent. Obviously,

---

[1]   http://thecanadianencyclopedia. ca/en/m/article/religion/

Christianity preached that man and God, the separation of man and nature. However, Chinese religion would emphasize the harmony between man and nature, solving problems in a people-oriented way.

(2) Variety

Christianity is monotheistic, advocating that there is only one master of the universe, Jesus. According to predetermined order and purpose, the God arrange the whole universe who acts not only as God, but also as the Father, Son and Holy Spirit. Therefore, the Christian establishes a complete doctrine including Doctrine of God, creationism, human nature, original sin of Christ, and salvation. Therefore with the formation of Christianity, it gradually established a fixed, unified values and outlook on life. In practice, Christianity also establishes unified church organization such as church in urban and rural areas for Christians to pray.

China's religions, however, has given people great freedom to hold religious sentiment in their hearts. Therefore, the Gods that most Chinese people worship are not uniform. Most Chinese people do not belong to a certain religious organization, but to follow a unified spirit from Confucianism, Buddhism and Taoism. The religious tradition in China, Confucianism, has constituted the soul of Chinese culture in the long course of historical development. Many thinkers and politicians in China are based on the Confucian sense of responsibility to pursue truth, to maintain the orthodox and to implement reforms.

In addition to Confucianism, Buddhism and Taoism, the Chinese folk religion and worship of spirits are also very much prosperous and universal. The sharp contrast between the conceptual life and practical life resulted in the loss of religious values in China, and also led to the emergence and spread of a variety of primitive superstitious beliefs.

(3) Faith Degree

Christians believe that God created the human ancestors: Adam and Eve, but they rebelled against God, so every human being is guilty, and the purpose of human life is for redemption. To win God's favor, men need to conquer the nature and to transform themselves. The transcendence that Christian pursues is the baptism of the soul. The God-person relationship is superior to all earthly relationships. Christians are in the pursuit of spiritual purification with the cost of divisional dual suffering between spirit and flesh. Worldly pain is regarded as the bridge to the happiness which simply forms the basis of the western religions.

However, the diversity of Chinese belief comes from its inherent agricultural social structure. With farmers being China's majority, agricultural production is given priority in daily life, therefore, people believe in spirits but do not rely entirely on them. In a sense, Chinese formed secular utilitarian attitude towards religious tradition. Accordingly, unlike Westerners who go to church every Sunday, Chinese seldom go to worship the spirits unless they have certain concrete purposes, say, pray for the birth of a son, or fortune or recovery from diseases, etc. , except for the common religious festivals. What's more, unlike western Christians who are quite familiar with the relative religious values, the believers of Buddhism or Taoism, are not acquainted with the main content of religious doctrine. Those believers do not seek spiritual pillar in the religion, just hoping to have their desire satisfied.

(4) Degree of Exclusiveness

Western religions are henotheistic-that is, requiring exclusive adherence-while eastern religions often are not exclusionary but incorporate different belief systems.

Still take Christian as example, it was developed against other religions in the middle ages in Europe. After the decline of Roman Empire, the Christian (Catholic) leader first forced the pagans to convert to Christianity, and gradually politically and militarily expand it to the whole continent, with the Pope as the core of the European feudal theocracy. Thus inquisition was set up to attack other "pagans", including the Jews who believe in Old Testament, coupled with hundreds of years of Muslim Crusade. Even during the immigration process after the discovery of new continent, the colonists also forced indigenous peoples to join Christian communities through legislation.

After discovering the new continent in the process of immigration, the colonists also forced indigenous peoples join Christian groups in the form of legislation. What's more, the combat among different sects were intense within the Christianity. With the development of modern society, western countries have implemented the policy of free religion.

Firstly, the Declaration of Independence in the United States established the relevant legal provisions, with other western countries following suit. As a result, the concept of exclusive sect has subsided and the word "pagan" is rarely heard. But still, the conflict might trigger some regional war in the world, especially when the ethnic contradiction weaved with religious ones. Bosnian issue, Northern Ireland issue and the conflict between Armenia and Azerbaijan, particularly the Middle East conflict are the typical cases of such problem. After all, it is evident that the western religious exclusiveness is much severer than the situation in China.

Conversely, there has been no state religion throughout Chinese history under the rule of imperial power, with the dispute between Buddhism and Taoism peacefully conducted. The reason why Foreign Buddhism can gain more prosperity than native-born Taoism is mainly due to its adaptation to the Chinese traditional beliefs, for instance, "the cycle of cause and effect" is apparently more popular than Taoism's pursuit of immortality among people. As to Islam which is accepted by over ten Chinese minorities since its introduction to China in Tang Dynasty, has never fallen into serious conflict with other religions.

In short, China's religions and beliefs possess great tolerance to each other, as the result of its relative closed geographic location. It is the Chinese historical tradition that all different religions coexist harmoniously in this land.

To sum up, the above four aspects are not isolated, but closely related and form corresponding religious modes, with the western being institutional while the Chinese being diffused.

Chapter Ten

Customs of Etiquettes

1. General Introduction

(1) Definition

The word "Etiquette" is derived from French. Wikipedia defines Etiquette as a code of behavior that delineates expectations for social behavior according to contemporary conventional norms within a society, social class, or group[1].

Etiquette can also be regarded as general social behavior observed in multiple situations, ranging from nation to nation. Learning those behavioral codes can be particularly difficult to handle for new arrivals of a given culture, even old hands sometimes misconduct under certain circumstances. .

Generally speaking, the rules of etiquette govern people's manners. For instance, greeting people with politeness and respect is universally accepted in many cultures, but the ways to demonstrate respect vary. In some countries, people may bow or clasp their hands together when greeting others whereas in the United States, people often shake hands, or hug even kiss each other. Meanwhile, since the social norms are so different, individuals may study etiquette for the sake of not offending others or embarrass themselves.

(2) Characteristics of Etiquette

①Universality and Nationality

Human beings are social animals and interpersonal etiquette is the sym-

---

① http: //en. wikipedia. org/wiki/Etiquette

bol of human civilization. Every ethnic group and nation has its own conventional etiquette. However, those nations vary in different aspects, such as productive modes, social developing phases, beliefs and religions etc. Therefore, the social etiquette differs greatly with its national uniqueness.

②Variability and Hierarchy

Etiquette may vary with the passage of times. Meanwhile, in class society, etiquette is originally a representative of class difference, a customary and institutionalized form to legalize the class oppression. In slave society and feudal society particularly, people's manner need to follow the rigid protocols in the interpersonal interaction. Anyone who violates them would be despised and condemned, or even punished legally to maintain the governors' authority and consolidate their surveillance. Up to now, in the contemporary society, even though the human equality is legally established, the interpersonal courtesy is still based on different ranks; for instance, the respect needs to be shown by the young to the senior, the subordinate to the supervisor. In a word, following hierarchy difference is the essential principle of the etiquette.

(3) Functions of Etiquette

①Social Harmony

The primary function of etiquette is to show respect to people, enabling them to have a sense of recognition. Meanwhile, bidirectional courtesy plays an important role in interpersonal intimacy, facilitating social interaction and harmony.

②Social Stability

Etiquette is a moral convention. How to interact with others is an inevitable problem that people need to learn during the process of growth. Everyone is exposed to interpersonal communicative convention, consciously or unconsciously, growing to a courteous human being. Good-mannered behavior, not only can perfect a person's character, but also elevate the whole nation's quality, reducing social conflicts and resistance, contributing to the formation of a stable society.

2. Chinese Etiquette Customs

(1) Etiquette Customs of Han Nationality

①Greeting Manners

Ancient Chinese traditions were very much rooted in the teachings of Confucius which dictated how each Chinese must behave towards one another with regards to their positions and status in society.

Traditional Chinese greeting customs are listed as the following:

● Saluting with Folded Hands

According to relative research, the etiquette of saluting with folded hands can be traced back to Zhou Dynasty, a gesture used to express respect to others, with both hands clasping, one hand over the other, and raised in front of the chest.

● Kowtow

Kowtow, a conventional custom for worship on bended knees, can be dated back as early as the legendary Emperor Xuan Yuan. Interestingly, the concept of "to sit" in ancient times was utterly different from what we know today, a gesture can rival the frequency and importance of kowtow today. With both knees bent down on the mat, the buttocks rest on the heels. When meeting a guest, the host had to stretch the upper part of the body with respect. Slowly, the custom of kowtow evolved as a part of daily life.

There are two common situations in which people conduct kowtow. One is that everyone would do so in the presence of the emperor. The other occasion is during the Spring Festival that younger family members were supposed to kowtow to the seniors.

● Bow

The custom of bow derived from a heaven worshipping ritual in the Shang Dynasty, when sacrificial offerings were bent into a circle to show respect and piety of the worshippers. Gradually, people start to express their esteem to those with high social status or the elder. Today, it is still a typical way of showing gratitude or respect.

Besides the above mentioned manners, traditional greeting etiquettes of ancient China also comprise making a *wanfu*, a form of greeting by women with folded hands moving about at the lower right side.

To sum up, most of the etiquettes are no longer performed, but saluting with folded hands is kept alive owing to its features such as being hygienic, easy and graceful. It adds up to the festive atmosphere as an exchange of greetings between close friends and relatives in traditional holidays.

● Handshake

The Chinese are not originally hand-shakers, but the custom is now commonly conducted among people. Sometimes, in the eyes of the Westerners, Chinese shake for too long, and the handshakes are rather limp instead of being firm which is perceived as an attitude of humility and respect.

②Table Manners

A number of etiquettes occur when people eat in China.

● Round Table

Chinese prefer to eat around a round table, rather than a rectangular or square one, since they can be seated conveniently, facing one another. The chair towards the entrance, or the east, is reserved for the most honorable guest. In a formal setting, the closer that people sit next to the person of highest status, the higher their rank is.

Typically, on a Chinese dining table, there are always a cup, a bowl on a small dish, the chopsticks, and spoons, with dishes being served in the center.

● Chopsticks

Except for soup, all dishes are supposed to be consumed with chopsticks, about which there are many etiquettes. For instance, twiddling with chopsticks, licking chopsticks, or stirring up food with them, gesturing with them or pointing them at others are all viewed as inappropriate table manners. Particularly, it is tabooed to stick chopsticks in the center of rice, which is regarded as inauspicious since it is the way to offer sacrifice.

• Serving Drinks

A characteristic dining meal is always accompanied by tea, beer or distilled spirit. It is the convention for the one who sits closest to the teapot or wine bottle to pour them for others, from the senior and superior to the junior and inferior. It is offensive to let guests pour tea or wine themselves.

• Toast

A toast to others is a typical Chinese dining manner. All people seated and all cups filled, the host would toast others first by saying simple prologue. During the dining, after the senior's toast, people can toast anyone from superior to inferior at their will. When offered a toast, the receiver is expected to cease eating and drinking to accept and toast as a response.

Usually, all the dishes should not be eaten up thoroughly in a formal banquet; otherwise, the host might think that the guests are not well treated by the presence of insufficient food.

(2) Etiquette Customs of Chinese Ethnic Minorities

①Tibetan

In Tibet, presenting *hada* is a conventional Tibetan courtesy, particularly on the occasions of weddings and funerals. Besides, it is also presented when people visit seniors, worship Buddha, and bid farewell to guests. In a monastery, only after presenting *hada* can people pray to the Buddha statues; otherwise, they are not allowed to visit the different halls. Before leaving, they will place a *hada* beside their seats, representing their undivided souls.

Hada is made of silk, and is loosely weaved, which feature different auspicious patterns including lotuses, bottles, umbrellas, and conches. Expressing good wishes, they can be in different lengths, as long as 3 or 4 meters or as short as half a meter. Tibetans view white as the symbol of purity and fortune; therefore, *Hada* is normally white. However, there is a special *hada* of five colors: blue, white, yellow, green, and red, which respectively representing the sky, clouds, land, river, and the God in charge of Buddha dharma. The five-colored *hada* is an extremely valued gift which can only be presented during special occasions such as to Buddha statues or intimate relatives.

The common way that people present a *hada* is like this: The presenter takes the *hada* with their both hands, lifting it up to the same level as the shoulder, and reaching out their hands before bending over and passing it to the guest. The top of one's head should be as high as the *hada* to exemplify the presenter's respect and best wishes while the receiver is expected to receive it with both hands. In addition, to seniors, it can be lifted over the head with body bent slightly forward and put in place in front of the seats. For peers or those younger, it is just hanged around receivers' necks.

As to the origin of *hada*, there are several versions, one of which is related with Zhang Qian, a respectable diplomat in the Han Dynasty. Zhang Qian was assigned as the ambassador to the west neighboring nations of China. When passing Tibet, he presented silk to the chief of local tribe since silk was rare and therefore regarded as precious gifts in ancient China. The tribes then learned that giving silk was a courtesy to promote friendship. Gradually it became a custom extended to all areas in Tibet.

Another version is associated with the ancient Tibetan king, Wangbasi who brought *hada* back after the meeting with the emperor Khubli Khan of the Yuan Dynasty. Having the pattern of the Great Wall and the Chinese characters "*ji xian ru yi*" (good luck and happiness to you), *hada* was regarded as the ribbons in fairy maidens' clothes to demonstrate purity and authority, which later contributed to its religious connotation[1].

②*Zhuang* Nationality

The Zhuang ethnic group is remarkable for its hospitability to guests. In the past, a family's guest could be treated as the whole village's guest, who was invited to eat in different families. When one family kills a pig,

---

① http: //www. chinatravel. com/facts/tibetan-ethnic-minority. htm

they will invite the whole neighborhood to enjoy the feast.

For Zhuang people, wine is indispensable on a dinner table to demonstrate their value to the honorable guests. A custom named "Union of Wine Cups", particularly, is practiced: the guest and the host cross and twist their elbows with each other, drinking not with the cups, but with the white ceramic soup spoons. Usually, the host family provides the best food and accommodation, especially to the elderly and the new guests.

While having dinner, the juniors cannot eat first until the dishes have been tasted by the seniors. When serving tea or food, one should use both hands, and he is not allowed to pass the tea or food to the other who is behind him. The person who finishes eating first should tell others to take their time. Meanwhile, it is impolite for juniors to be the last to finish the dining when all others stop eating.

To sum up, it is conventional for the Zhuang nationality to respect the seniors. For instance, it is inappropriate to sit cross-legged in the presence of an old person. Foul words should not be uttered to the old. In the feast, the heads and wings of the chickens are supposed to be offered to the seniors first. When a senior carries heavy load, a passerby should offer help and escort him back home[1].

③*Hani* Nationality

The fireplace is the center of folk life for the Hani nationality, with which there are some certain etiquette. For example, the spider that is above the furnace should never be trampled. In addition, people ought not to spit at or stride over the fire place. Touching the firewood with one's foot is also forbidden. Doorsill is sacred, so one should not stand or sit on it or cut it with a knife.

When visiting a Hani family, the guests will be served with the homemade cigarette pipe as the symbol of the host's warm-heartedness. A nonsmoker can decline it courteously or the host will be offended. The young should not fold their arms or legs, blow whistles, or make noises in front

---

① http://www.chinatravel.com/facts/hani-ethnic-minority.htm

of the seniors. At a banquet, the host may offer the guests the chicken head and liver, and the young guest is expected to present it to the eldest. Religious rituals and family banquets usually begin with some blessing from the old.

An interesting Hani custom is called "recognizing the uncle" since in their belief, the brothers of mother is the most important relative. If a baby does not get intimacy with the uncle, the child can't be blessed with a good future during his growth. On the exact day to recognize one's uncle, the mother and young baby rise early in the morning. Face washed and dressed neatly, the baby is ready to see the uncle. Normally, the mother would also mark the baby's forehead black and tie some garlic to the baby's hat, aiming to scare off the evils. Setting off to the uncle's home, the mother carry many fried stirred yellow beans, steamed chicken eggs and sticky rice pies in her bag. On the way, whoever they meet, the mother should offer them some beans regardless of their sex, age and nationality①.

④Mongolian

One of the typical etiquette in Mongolian culture is to present the snuffbox to the guest. Once being visited, the host will take out his snuffbox and pass it to his guest after uncover it. Receiving it, the guest is expected to put it under the nose to sniff the aromatic tobacco or herbs, nodding head to express compliment. The interaction is indispensable which forms the foundation for future relationship.

Meanwhile, when welcomed in a Mongolian home, the guest should offer the host his pipe. Anticipating this, the host accepts the pipe and fills it with his own tobacco. The host then passes his own empty pipe to the guest, who accepts it and fills it with his own tobacco. Then the two of them each enjoys his own tobacco, but smokes in the other's pipe.

---

① http: //www. chinatravel. com/facts/hani-ethnic-minority. htm

3. Western Etiquette Customs

(1) Europe

①France

Certain social customs exist in every country, with France being no exception. Generally speaking, courtesies in France are rather formal than most other countries.

- Meeting and Greeting

Whether to kiss or not, that is a complicated problem. The common strategy is to observe how the others behave by taking the cue from the French. One usually does not kiss in the first encounter with to an adult. If a woman allows herself to be kissed, she will lean forward, offering her cheek. Not being a real kiss, the social one is deposited high up on the cheek. To be more specific, it is just a delicate brush of the cheeks accompanied by kissing noises.

Usually, the number of kiss that people conduct varies, ranging from region to region. Four kisses are the norm in northern France, three in the mid-west and southern central areas and two in the west, east and extreme south.

- Dining and Entertainment

If invited to dine in a French home, it is appropriate to bring a small present of flowers, a plant or chocolates. One shouldn't serve any drinks before all guests have arrived. If offered a drink, one should wait till the host has toasted everyone's health (santé). He is not expected to pour himself own drinks during the dinner except for water. The French normally say "bon appétit" before a meal and one shouldn't start eating unless the hosts do. It's polite to eat everything that's put on the plate.

- Conversation

The French would love to be involved in detailed and heated discussions, but certain topics should be avoided. For instance, how much a person earns. Therefore, it's considered a faux pas to ask a new acquaintance what his occupation is since his job title will often reveal information of his salary. It is advisable and safer to stick to discussions of food and drink. When talking, one should avoid raising voice, an indication of being abrupt. The French often stand close when conversing, which may cause discomfort to the listeners.

Noise restriction is imposed in French towns and villages, especially concerning the use of lawnmowers and other mechanical devices. Despite the variety, noisy activities are forbidden before 8 or 9 a. m. every day, after 19p. m. on weekdays and Saturdays and after 12p. m. on Sundays, and additionally at lunchtime on Saturdays.

● Body Language

Like the Italians, the French talk with variety of body languages, but the art of gesture manner can be difficult to master. For example, never point to a Frenchman with index finger, but use an open hand for not to be regarded as rude. Likewise, beckon with four fingers, palm down. When counting, the thumb is used to mean "one", not the index finger. To express boredom, Frenchmen usually rub their knuckles against the cheek. To show surprise, they shake their hand up and down, and they pull down their lower eyelid to convey feeling of disbelief[1].

②The United Kingdom

The United Kingdom consists of England, Scotland, Wales and Northern Ireland, with residents of these countries being called "British." While those four countries share many cultural conventions, each has its own cultural distinctions.

The English are courteous and restraint, since politeness and humbleness has always been admired as desirable qualities by the Britons.

Being proud of its uniqueness and unwilling to go along with English ideas, Scots are passionate about their history, who are particularly sentimental about their family as well as their country. Generally, Scots do not take much notice of class consciousness and social elitism, except in the

---

① https://www. justlanded. com/english/France/Articles/Culture/Social-customs-in-France

field of religion.

Wales has been an ingredient of the United Kingdom for over 400 years, but its own language, literature and traditions are still well preserved. Most inhabitants of Wales are of Welsh or English roots, with multitude immigrants coming from former British colonies and other areas of U. K.

Two-thirds of the Northern Irish possess Scottish or English heritage, others being of Irish descent. Irish do not approve of pretentiousness and have a strong work ethic. Besides, family ties are highly valued in Northern Ireland.

● Meeting and Greeting

The British are reserved, looking overly formal in the exterior.

They shake hands in the business and social meetings and shake hands again when leaving, but handshakes are normally light—not firm, with women extending their hands to men first. One is supposed to use last name and appropriate title unless he is particularly required by the British hosts or friends to use his first name.

● Body Language

The British generally do not reveal affection publicly. Intimate gesture such as hugging, kissing and touching is normally reserved for family members and extremely close friends.

The British value personal space. It is inappropriate to stand too close to another person or put the arm around one's shoulder. Staring is extremely impolite.

● Dining and Entertainment

In the dining places, they will politely raise their hand to seek the attention of the waiter rather than by waving or shouting. The business entertaining is commonly done in restaurants or pubs over lunch. Prestigious events such as cricket playing or the regatta can be good occasion for the Briton to extend their friendship.

An invitation to someone's home is not uncommon in England compared with the rest of Europe. But the guests should not discuss business during dinner unless the host initiates the conversation. Time consciousness also varies. In England, when invited to others home, it is desirable to arrive 10 to 20 minutes after the due time and it is not appropriate to arrive early. In Scotland and Wales, however, people are expected to arrive on time. As to the sitting arrangement, a male guest of honor is normally seated at the head of the table or to the right of the hostess while a female guest of honor is seated to the right of the host. In a formal dinner, host or hostess always initiates first toast.

As to the table manner, the diner should keep his hands on the table instead of on his lap all times during the meal. Meanwhile, the elbows should be placed off the table. When done with eating, eaters need to place knife and fork side by side on the plate at the 5:25 position, with a very small amount of food being left on the plate. The host's folding his napkin signals the end of the meal. Usually the guest of honor should initiate leaving a party.

● Others

Men are expected to open doors for women when they enter a room. The Britons always hold the door for a person following behind them. It is inadvisable to insult the royal family or be extremely interested in their privacy. Do not mess a queue because it is regarded as being crude to push ahead in a line. Britons rarely shout or speak loud in public, and excessively demonstrative hand gestures should be avoided in a speech. The English seldom apply superlatives in speaking. For instance, sentence like "I am quite pleased" can be the way to show their intense happiness.

A new arrival should not try to mimic the British accent deliberately. Humor has been indispensable in English life, with the forms being various, such as self-deprecating, ribbing, sarcastic, sexist or racist. When being joked, try not to take it as an offense because normally they are not doing these out of ill intention. In Scotland, kilts are worn by men at formal occasions, a common phenomenon that should not be taken as the object of jokes. Being the sources of conversational conflicts, certain topics such as religious beliefs and politics are among the not-discussed lists which should be unmentioned in the conversation①.

③Italy

Cultural achievement is Italians' greatest pride and they are proud of their imagination and intelligence.

● Meeting and Greeting

Italians usually greet each other with a kiss on both cheeks. In business and on legal documents, females always are labeled with their maiden name. However, on other occasions, they prefer to use their married names or a combination of their married names and maiden names.

● Body Language

Keep eye contact during the conversation, or Italians might think you are insincere. To summon a waiter, they always raise their index fingers while making eye contact. Generally, Italians are known for their rich body language within Europe.

● Dining and Entertainment

Cocktail drinking, especially drinking without eating is uncommon in Italy. Hard intoxication is definitely ill-mannered, since even mild drinking is considered inappropriate. Women hardly drink in Italy. Even on formal occasions, women do not propose toasts.

Italians are cautious about table manners. For instance, people roll pasta with their fork on the sides of your pasta plate instead of using spoon. They use knife, rather than fingers to apply cheese to bread or cracker. When eating fruits, they use a fruit knife and fork, except for grapes and cherries. It is desirable to keep the wineglass almost full when a refill is unwanted.

Burping is perceived as very vulgar in public. When invited to a home, guests usually arrive 15 to 30 minutes later than the stated time. A home tour request to the host is encouraging since they are proud of their homes and would be glad to give tours.

● Gifts

---

① http://www. ediplomat. com/np/cultural_ etiquette/ce_ gb. htm

Italians are typically fond of being gift givers. Gifts are always elaborately wrapped before being opened in the presence of the giver. As to gift choices, high quality liquor, desk accessories, music and books are appreciated. When invited to a native's house, it is a convention to bring a small gift. Other gifts such as a bunch of flowers could be presented to the host's home the day of or the day after a visit. Knives and scissors are inappropriate as a symbol of bad luck. Never wrap a gift in black with gold ribbon because it just symbolizes funeral mourning.

● Others

Italians are known for their tolerance of others' uniqueness. Also, they do not easily reject others because of their lateness, inefficiency and minor mistakes. But they resent arrogance and abruptness. Italians are capable of self-deprecating. There are other social manners such as cover mouth when yawning. Removal of shoes is viewed as being indecent and males should always take off their hats when entering a building[1].

④Russian

Russia differs from most of the other European nations due to its different social ideology. However, it is a nation with its characteristic social manners.

● Meeting and Greeting

For Russians, no matter when greeting or departing, a handshake is always appropriate, but not obligatory, regardless of the relationship. Handshaking with one's gloves on is impolite. And shaking hands over a threshold should be avoided since it is believed to bring conflict.

● Body Language

Russians are very demonstrative people, therefore, hugs, backslapping, kisses on the cheeks are common in their public interactions, especially among friends and acquaintances of the same gender. Russians tend to stand close when talking. Gestures such as putting the thumb through index and middle fingers or making the "OK" signal are viewed as being coarse.

---

① http: //www. ediplomat. com/np/cultural_ etiquette/ce_ it. htm

• Dining and Entertainment

Russians are great hosts and they love to entertain guests. They usually present surplus food on the table than can be consumed as an indication of abundant food. Guests usually leave some food on their plates to honor their host that they are excessively treated.

Once invited to a Russia's home for dinner, the guest is expected to spend time socializing after the meal. Besides, an invitation to a Russian dacha, a typical country home is a supreme honor.

Russians are well-known for their capacity for liquor. Given their hospitality, it is considered rude to decline their offers of alcohol. Drinking is often an all-or-nothing activity, and moderation is never understood.

Toasts are common over dinner, which can sometimes be lengthy. The host initiates then the guests respond. It is not decent to drink unless the first toast has been offered, following which most Russians like to clink their glasses to each other. A non-alcohol drinker is not necessary to join them.

• Others

Russians are extremely content with their culture, seeking every opportunity to talk about their music, art, literature and dance. Therefore, they really appreciate those who know about their art, music, history, particularly their language[①].

(2) North America

①The United States

Throughout its history, the United States feature great number of immigrants. The ethnic structure basically consists of approximately 83% white (generally of European descent, but also from the Middle East and Latin America), 12% African-American, 3% Asian and about 1% Native American, the modern biggest immigrant groups being those from Latin countries.

• Meeting and Greeting

---

① http: //www. ediplomat. com/np/cultural_ etiquette/ce_ ru. htm

American greetings are generally quite informal, not out of disrespect but due to a relaxed life attitude.

Although it is conducted in business occasions, some Americans do not shake hands in social encounters. Rather, they may greet others with a casual "Hello", "How are you?" or even simply a "Hi. " And they seldom shake hands upon leaving. But if handshake is practiced, it is brief and firm with direct eye contact.

Normally, Americans may end the meeting with remarks such as "We'll get together some day" or "Let's do lunch sometimes" . But this is simply a friendly gesture unless a specific date is specified.

It is a must to stand when being introduced. Only the seniors, the ill and the disabled remain seated while being greeting. Meanwhile, when introducing, they prefer to offer some information such as the professional titles but not in the case of self-introduction.

• Body Language

When communicating, Americans prefer a certain physical distance. If they feel they are approached too close, they may step back instinctively.

Generally, Americans are uncomfortable with physical contact between the same genders, particularly between males.

Americans smile a great deal, even at strangers. And they would appreciate being returned with smiles. In addition, Americans are known as "back slappers", which means they always like to give others a light pat on the back as an indication of intimacy.

Holding the middle finger up by itself is regarded insulting and vulgar, a gesture should definitely been avoided. Besides, Americans are quite uncomfortable with silence in social or business communications.

Americans do hate to be interrupted when they are speaking. So they prefer not to do so in their social interactions.

• Dining and Entertainment

Americans tend to eat more quickly compared with people from other nations due to their acute sense of time consciousness. Therefore, dining in the United States is rarely a long and time-consuming activity.

The fork is usually held in the left hand, with tines facing down. Meanwhile, the knife is held in the opposite hand. With food having been cut, the knife is put aside and the fork is switched to the right hand to eat the food. Continental style, in which the fork remains in the left hand to eat the cut food is widely acceptable due to their European heritage.

The napkin is placed on the lap during the meal and the Americans do not tuck it under the chin.

The Americans value honesty. Once invited, it is imperial to call to inform the host of the presence or otherwise. They will be offended if they get the promise of arrival but then disappointed by the absence.

● Gifts

Typically, Americans do not have as many customary taboos concerning gifts giving as many other cultures. Cash gifts are by no means appropriate.

● Others

In the States, it is offensive to stare, ask personal questions or otherwise bring attention to one's physical defects.

Smoking is very unpopular in the United States. Accordingly, Americans rarely smoke anywhere without obtaining permission from others who present.

"Please" and "thank you" arecommonly heard in the United States on almost every occasion for even the smallest kindness and they expect others to do the same.

"Pardon me" or "Excuse me" is uttered for unintentionally physical contact. Americans also say this if they sneeze or cough or fail to understand something someone has said.

Social conversation in the United States is somewhat relaxing, with there being a standard for small talk. People ask questions briefly and simple answers are expected. Americans become ill at ease when others talk for lengthy time in a social interaction[1].

---

① http: //www. ediplomat. com/np/cultural_ etiquette/ce_ us. htm

②Canada

The majority of Canadians claim European blood such as British, French, Italian, German and Ukrainian etc, specifically in the prairie states.

Broadly speaking, Canada has been geographically divided into two societies: one is French-speaking, like Quebec and the other being English-speaking. The latter is normally considered more reserved and less aggressive than their southern counterparts.

● Meeting and Greeting

Compared with Americans, Canadians are generally more courteous and polite than Americans by taking etiquette more seriously.

They would prefer handshaking and self introduction in the first meeting and eye contact is indispensable.

When a woman enters or leaves a room, Canadian males will typically stand up to acknowledge her and it is men who normally extend their hands firstly.

In Quebec, cheek kissing in the French manner is not uncommon. When close friends and family members meet, they call each other first names and kiss both cheeks.

Besides, an older French Canadian gentleman may kiss the hand of a woman. But a foreign man is not expected to kiss the hand of a French Canadian woman which would be viewed as inappropriate and offensive.

As to names and titles, Canadians are more formal than Americans. First names are usually called by intimate friends and family. Besides, Western Canadians may use first names more frequently than other Canadians. Academic titles and degrees are valued by French Canadians which should be introduced formally and properly.

● Body Language

Generally speaking, Canadians are reserved who seldom touch during conversation. Therefore, certain personal space should be maintained in social interaction. In addition, hats and sunglasses should be removed if a person is involved in a face to face communication.

Usually, French Canadians are more animated than other Canadians who are expressive with certain gestures in Quebec. For instance, "thumbs down" is regarded as being impolite, slapping an open palm over a closed fist is considered offensive as well. Like the rest of their fellows, French-Canadians use the "thumbs up" sign to mean "okay. "

Sitting with legs apart, or with feet propped up on tables are rather rude.

Talking with hands in pockets is not appropriate. Certain gestures should absolutely being avoided in public like yawning, scratching, sneezing or blowing nose, toothpicks and nail clippings.

● Dining and Entertainment

When beckoning a waiter in Quebec, they quietly say "Monsieur" or "S'il vous plait" . To beckon a waitress they would Say "Mademoiselle" . They never beckon them by snapping fingers or shouting.

In Quebec, wine usually goes with meals; and it's believed inappropriate to require a martini or scotch before dinner. Typical before-dinner drinks include Pernod, kir, champagne, and vermouth. After-dinner drinks commonly are Cognac, Grand Marnier and other liqueurs.

While continental style table manners are widely adopted in Quebec, American style table manners are applied in other areas of Canada. In particular, dining while walking or standing on the street is considered ill-mannered in Quebec.

Early arrival for a social occasion is rarely encouraged. Instead, people prefer being "fashionably late. "

● Others

Québécois arc particularly proud of their language. Term of "Native A mericans" is unsuitable to refer to native people since it is considered offensive; instead, they are called "people of the First Nations" .

Canadians always try not to get involved in debates about controversial political issues such as the status of Quebec, the superior status of French and English languages in Canadian society, etc①.

4. Comparisons

The major differences between Chinese and Western etiquette are listed as follows:

(1) Origins

In ancient China, etiquette is equivalence to courtesy and ceremony, which was originally to deal with ghosts and spirits since people used to assume that the world was in the charge of invisible spirits. Being a state of ceremonies, etiquette was the core of traditional culture back to 5, 000 years ago. With the social progress, it turned into rituals of modern civilization. Despite that, it is still believed that etiquette was formed as a product of human activities and the primitive religions.

However, the word "etiquette" primarily means "keep off the grass" in the west. The story has it that Louis XIV's gardener noticed that the aristocrats were tramping over the garden, so he put up sign of "etiquette" to warn them off. Therefore, the king of Versailles ordered that no one was able to pass the bounds of the etiquettes. The definition of etiquette later evolved from "list of ceremonial observances of a court" into "the customary code of polite behavior in society or among members of a particular profession or group"② . Until the 1960's, the significance of good manners was highly valued, but with the liberated 1970's, the instruction of proper etiquette declined. Entering the new century, a new emphasis has been put on the revival of traditional values.

(2) Modes of Social Interaction

Chinese and western cultures have attached great importance to inter-

---

① http: //www. ediplomat. com/np/cultural_ etiquette/ce_ ca. htm

② http: //www. oxforddictionaries. com/definition/english/etiquette

personal relationship, but in different way. Chinese are known for their hospitality and their lack of consciousness of privacy interference. For instance, when Chinese are interested in the belongings of their friends, they tend to inquire about the prices. However, the westerners would not do the same since the activity might be regarded as the curiosity about others' economic conditions. Another example, Chinese prefer to ask "where are you going?" when they meet others, a common form of greeting; but in the west, this question might be regarded as embarrassing since it is viewed as privacy intrusion.

In addition, the distance of the interaction between people can be roughly divided into four types: close distance, individual distance, social distance and public distance. Chinese relationship belongs to the first while westerner's belong to the second. For instance, we often see two Chinese girls walking on the street hand in hand, a rare phenomenon in the west. The westerners think that the Chinese are too intimate whereas the Chinese feel that the westerners are relatively cold, arrogant and distant with others. So if Chinese find a thrum in other's clothes, they will naturally pick if off. But it might make westerners uncomfortable.

(3) Personal Philosophies

The westerners take pride in the individual achievements that they rarely conceal their self-confidence when they make contribution to the group. On the contrary, the Chinese culture does not favor the emphasis of personal honor. Normally, Chinese despise those who are proud of themselves. However, the westerners harbor reservations towards the Chinese typical self-humbleness or self-modesty. The usual response to other's compliments is always self-denial. For Chinese, it is simply a modest gesture. But for the westerners, it is not only denying himself with an air of hypocrisy, also an insult to people who expresses appreciation, which gives rise to distinct attitudes to modesty.

In addition, in western world, people are encouraged to be explorative and innovative, leading to inevitable conflicts. However, traditional Chinese culture requires people to be willing to achieve moderation. Accordingly, they are more content to maintain the status quo and harmony. It is undeniable that Chinese have to attain the goal of being moderate rather than being different at the cost of uniqueness.

(4) Social Customs

In Chinese culture, due to thousand years of feudalism, men are superior to women, who are somehow subjected to discrimination. But in the west, respecting for women is their custom. Lady first has become one of the main social principles. It is men's responsibility to take care of women. In fact, modern China attaches importance on gender equality, and western etiquette is gradually becoming more global.

Moreover, China is the representative of the Eastern countries to treat the elders with respect, and the younger generation should shoulder the responsibility to attend to the seniors. In western countries, however, people are educated to advocate self-reliance, so the bond between parents and adult children are somewhat declining with the passage of time, making many elders to feel lonely and miserable in the west.

(5) Status Hierarchism

Chinese culture features a strong sense of hierarchism. No matter in the organizations or in the families, people who take no notice of the hierarchy differences will be regarded as being coarse. The conventional submissive attitudes between officials to monarchs, sons to fathers are still deeply rooted among Chinese. Fathers are thorough authority in the family. Likewise, the teachers also exert absolute authority on the students. Under such condition, the elders tend to guide and assist the young parents to raise and discipline the children. The latter grow up to help their parents to provide for the elders, which forms interdependent relationships among people. On the other hand, the western countries, except for Britain and a few other countries which possess a rigid hereditary system, advocate the concept of equality, the United States in particular. It is normal for parents to address the children's names, and vise versa. The consciousness of the extended family connection is comparatively weak.

All in all, Chinese and western etiquette vary greatly due to the above mentioned aspects.

Chapter Eleven

Customs of Folk Art

1. General Introduction

(1) Definition

Folk art is the artistic works, as paintings, sculpture, basketry, and utensils, produced typically in cultural isolation by untrained often anonymous artists or by artisans of varying degrees of skill and marked by such attributes as highly decorative design, bright bold colors, flattened perspective, strong forms in simple arrangements, and immediacy of meaning. [1] In addition, due to its social function rather than political needs, it is an art of necessity of our daily life, production, rites, ceremonies, beliefs and taboos. Folk art sometimes features being primitive, since the untrained artists simply work instinctively with the basic knowledge known to average people.

Other terms that can be used interchangeably with "folk art" are popular art, traditional art, primitive art, etc.

(2) Features

In a sense, folk art reflects cultural identity like ethnic, tribal, religious, occupational, geographical, age-basedor gender-based elements by revealing common group values and aesthetics through a variety of practical and decorative materials, such as cloth, wood, paper, clay, metal etc. Furthermore, folk artists usually acquire skills and techniques through

---

[1] http: //dictionary. reference. com/browse/folk + art

apprenticeships in informal community backgrounds.

Generally, folk art possesses three elementary features:

Firstly, it is the art of the people. With the creators being the large number of ordinary people, it intends to meet the needs of their daily practical requirements such as food, clothing, shelter and transportation as well as those of their social life of festivals and ceremonies, beliefs and taboos.

Secondly, its cultural implication represents the philosophy of the community, their aesthetics, their life attitude and their psychological traits.

Thirdly, it is extremely marked with the distinct characteristics of individual nationality and geography, which is primarily produced with common tools and underdeveloped raw materials, and which was basically characterized by regional rural economy.

(3) Classifications

Folk art has two major elements: cultural tradition and individual innovation. The former is conservative, representing the common group ethnics; while the latter expresses a unique feature. Be it a painting, a sculpture, a carving or an object with decorative patterns, all folk-art works are appealing to the average people.

①Painting

Folk art painting is by no means the portraits hung on the wall in common people's home. In Europe, it is particularly known as votive offering, appeared in churches and chapels and in America pictures and local scenes executed in oil, pastel, or watercolor. More often than not, the drawings of folk art are incorporated into other objects. For example, the clock faces can be decorated with local landscapes. Another feature of given folk art is that the "picture" is displayed not only in paper but also executed in materials such as fern, cork, shells, or embroidery, other typical materials being silk, linen, or cotton fabric.

②Sculpture

Different form of sculpture can be applied to various objects, such as wood, stone, even Papier-mâché.

Wood sculpture is definitely one of the most significant folk arts, which is normally sacral, with the themes being associated with Catholic churches. Folk sculptors produced thousands of sculptures which were placed onto crosses and into chapels. Meanwhile, there also themes of secular works concerning work, life, holidays, folklore, mythology and ethnography etc.

Stone sculptures traditions are generally not as developed as wood sculptures. It is mainly presented in exhibition halls and those outdoors are mainly of commemorative nature. According to many views, stone sculptures are closely related to wood sculptures.

③The Folk Print

The wood block was the natural material for folk prints creation. Normally it is simply cut and sometimes crudely colored or stenciled to serve the purpose of expressing popular subjects. Besides, small prints of various saints were considerably produced in Europe, with Comic themes being prevailing as well. The 19th century trade cards, or notices for a shop or service are sometimes regarded as folk art, but in fact, it is difficult to separate the print of truly folk character from the field of popular or commercial printing.

④Other Arts

In the folkart field, there are other forms such as pottery, textiles, costume, and furniture, providing the most frequent opportunities for artistic creation and aesthetic appreciation.

Any attempt to make the analysis of folk art according to established categories fails to take into account a significant part of the art. Many typical folk works which are not subject to complicated aesthetic treatment have turned into the focus as a specific field of study due to its originality, say molds, decorated eggs, powder horns, trade signs, scarecrows, and figureheads, etc. There are also folk objects categorized functionally: for instance, the woven harness of donkeys representing animal gear; carved and painted ox yokes and sheep collars, brass-studded and tasseled headpieces, and ornaments with protective powers. Other kinds of folk art include decorated vehicles such as the caravans of Roma, circus wagons, boats with symbolic motifs, toys and miniatures.

2. Chinese Folk Art

(1) Folk Art of Han Nationality

Back to history of primitive society, folk art was created by the Chinese people besides the invention of tools, shelter and other elementary instruments indispensable in daily life. The emergence of social classes results in the distinction of private professional artist from folk art, generating two cultural heritages in China. The former was the folk art, or communal art of the people dating back to prehistoric times.

Throughout history, the development of folk art is rather stable, which can reflect the communal ideology; the national emotional and psychological features. In addition, traditional folk art will keep on growing and expanding with the passage of time.

①Bronze Vessels

Being the alloy of copper, stannum and plumbum, bronze soon led Chinese ancestors entered into the bronze era ever since its invention 5,000 years ago, which was particularly widely used as musical instruments in sacrificial temples, as weapons of war and other vessels in court life.

Decorative patterns were delicate and diverse, with popular patterns being the beast faces and dragons and phoenix. Gradually Bronze vessels turned to more complicated with increasing decoration such as inserted jade, turquoise, iron or copper.

In the Spring and Autumn Period and the Warring States Period, bronze was used to produce weapons such as knives and swords, among which the famous one is Goujian Sword, still sharp and shiny when unearthed. Till the Han Dynasty, the significance of bronze vessels was gradually replaced by those of jade, pottery, and iron. Afterwards, bronze was widely used for mirrors production.

②Chinese cloisonné (*Jing Tai Lan*)

Cloisonné is a special art form that dated back to the Yuan Dynasty in Beijing. In the Ming Dynasty, the coloring process was greatly improved with the creation of bright blue which was quite attractive according to Chinese aesthetics. Thanks to the processing breakthrough, the technique was applied to more daily articles and gained popularity among common citizens rather than being the favors of the imperial families.

The Qing Dynasty witnessed the artistic peak of cloisonné, with colors being more delicate and filigrees being more flexible. The types of cloisonné also extended from original sacrificial wares to more various scopes such as snuff bottles, folding screens, incense burners, tables, chairs, chopsticks, and bowls.

Generally speaking, cloisonné manufacture is the combination of bronze making and porcelain ware, coupled with the technique of traditional painting and sculpture. Today, Cloisonné art has been exported to various countries and is welcomed globally.

③Chinese Jade Carving

With a long history of more than four thousand years, Chinese jade carving is the perfect exemplification of Chinese civilization which was primarily produced for worship and burial rituals. Once being the luxury properties of the rich, only people of the high social ranks could afford to be buried with jade articles, as shown by the excavated funeral objects of the people in the Western Han Dynasty.

Representing morality and grace, jade has found its influence in all walks of life, with the most common carving patterns being peach which stands for longevity; mandarin duck which means love; fish which represents affluence; double phoenixes which embodies prosperity; and bamboo reflects integrity etc. A beautifully carved jade can be treated as an invaluable treasure that is even more precious than a vast land, with the most famous being "*Heshi Bi*", a very priceless stone that even became the trigger of war between the Qin State and Zhao State in the ancient times.

④Chinese Embroidery

The oldest recorded embroidered work in China originated from the Shang Dynasty. Like most other ancient artifacts, embroidery used to be affordable exclusively by aristocrats. With the passage of time, embroidered products entered the lives of average people.

The Han Dynasty witnessed a great progress in embroidery technically and artistically with the patterns being various such as sun, moon, mountains, dragons, phoenix, flower, grass and auspicious Chinese characters. It was historically recorded that all females in the capital of Qi, today's Linzi in Shandong province were capable of embroidering. The art was particularly favored by the royal families and embroidery was the common decoration of their homes, from mattresses and beddings to daily clothes even burial items, the genuine embroideries unearthed in *Mawangdui* Han Tomb being the best proof.

With Buddhism flourishing in China during the Wei, Jin, Sui and Tang Dynasties, embroidery was normally exploited in the exhibition of honor for Buddha statues. Besides, the subjects of Chinese painting all were treated as themes of embroidery. The religious aspect of embroidery was reinforced in the *Yuan* Dynasty when the nation held the belief of Lamaism. Therefore, embroidery was considerably applied in Buddha statues, sutras and prayer flags, with one typical product being kept in Potala Palace.

The Song Dynasty witnessed a zenith of embroidery progress and reputed workers sprang up. Even intellects favor this art, which was then evolved into two categories: art for life use and art for art's sake.

The embroidery in the Qing Dynasty took in new ingredients from Japanese embroidery and even Western art with new materials such as gilded cobber and silvery threads emerged.

Roughly speaking, there are four major traditional styles: *Su*, *Shu*, *Xiang*, *and Yue*, each representing four typical regional featured embroideries.

⑤Chinese Paper-Cut

Being a characteristic art of Chinese handicrafts, paper-cut can be traced back to the sixth century when females used to apply golden foil cuttings onto their temples and males employed them in holy rituals. Gradually, the paper cuts turned to decorations of the gates and windows during important festivals.

With simple tools of scissors and red paper, the craftsmen can create patterns most commonly found in the daily life. The pictures are particularly vivid, and the expressions of the figures are clearly portrayed. Unlike other art forms, the scenes are three-dimensional, requiring the craftsmen to visualize the patterns in advance by exerting their imagination.

Common paper cutting patterns are not difficult to produce, but the art is hard to master till perfection. Any wiggling will result in imprecision or even ruin the whole image.

Chinese are traditionally willing to express their benevolent wishes through paper cuttings. For instance, a big red paper character " Xi " or happiness is a necessary symbol to be pasted on the newlywed's door. On the birthday party of a senior, the character " Shou " is a must to signify longevity which will definitely add delight to the whole celebration. Another characteristic pattern of chubby children holding fish symbolizes wealth and abundance in the coming year.

⑥Chinese Porcelain

Porcelain, or fine china, has been one of the earliest artworks introduced to the west via Silk Road with its delicacy and refinement. Firstly produced in the Shang Dynasty, porcelain gradually gain popularity among people, especially the middle and upper classes, with various forms like bowls, tea sets, vases, incense burners as well as musical instruments etc.

In the Han Dynasty, porcelain began to be introduced westward. During the Tang Dynasty, a large amount of porcelain wares were replaced by the ones made of gold, silver, jade and other materials. With the passage of time, *Ru*, *Ding*, *Ge*, *Jun* and the official kilns were the representative types. Official kilns prefer simple decorative patterns; Ru kiln in Hebei Province supplemented treasured agate into glaze. Jun and Ding kilns existed in Henan Province. And porcelain of Jun kiln was made solely for the royal families.

Entering the Ming and Qing Dynasty, the blue and white porcelain, namely *Qinghua Ci*, was the stylish artistic wares which were mostly used for feudal art.

After 4, 000 years development, it is still a brilliant art appealing to folks from home and abroad.

⑦Chinese Pottery

Originated to the Neolithic Age of approximately 8, 000 years ago, pottery was probably the oldest artwork of humanity. Mixing clay and water before holding its shape, the ancient people employed the technique in various vessels and tools production to improve their life quality. Gradually, they became major wares in people's daily life such as cooking, storing and containing cuisine as dishes.

During the Shang Dynasty, bronze vessels grew into the symbol of social status. From the Warring States Period to the Han Dynasty, the pottery crafts thrived. Besides daily life pieces creation, ceramic beasts and warriors were produced and buried with the aristocrats, the Terra Cotta Warriors that were excavated in Xi' an being the finest representatives of burial artworks at that time.

Another example of crafted pottery is the tricolor glazed pottery of the Tang Dynasty, with the most popular colors being yellow, brown and green.

During the Song Dynasty, people found purple clay teapots more attractive than those of other materials due to its mild color, condensed structure, high intensity and fine particles. In the Ming and Qing Dynasties, individuals favoring drinking tea believe containers such as the purple clay pot would help to make the tea smelled balmier so as to retain the original quality. With these teapots transferring heat slower and being more endurable of heat, the teapot would not fade but become more lustrous.

⑧Chinese New Year Pictures (*Nianhua*)

Nianhua, or a new year picture, is a form of Chinese colored woodblock print, which was primarily the decoration for Chinese New Year Holiday.

The earliest record of *Nianhua* can be found in *Zhanguo Ce*, Strategies of the Warring States Period. In the Western and Eastern Han Dynasties, the images of various gods, "the door-gods" were stuck on the door for the purpose of scaring off evil spirits, particularly during the Spring Festival.

Nianhua was mostly the images of deities and spirits, but after the Tang Dynasty, the works expanded to more realistic pictures, and xylographic *nianhua* of religious themes emerged in the Ming Dynasty, becoming the household items of common people. And in the Qing Dynasty, large number of workshops existed for *Nianhua* production.

Nianhua can be roughly divided into the southern school and the northern school. The most typical *Nianhua* of the southern school were those from *Taohuawu* of Suzhou and *Foshan* of Guangdong, which were both originated in the Ming Dynasty and reached the summit in the Qing Dynasty. The representatives of the north are those from *Yangliuqing* of Tianjin and *Weifang* of Shandong. The themes of the former were chiefly images from traditional operas, chubby and healthy babies, coupled with fairy of New-Year celebrations. The subjects of the latter mainly centered around fairy tales, legends, and auspicious designs. The styles of the two were also distinct, the former featured a rich colored and refined composition while the latter is characterized by simplicity, vigorous lines and bright colors[1].

(2) Folk Art of Chinese Ethnic Minorities

①Tibetan Nationality

● Tangka

Tangka, a scroll painting on silk, owns both distinctive ethnic and religious features, with its origin traced back to as early as the 7th century, when King *Songtsan Gambo* united Tibet. Under his reign, he ordered the construction of Potala Palace and a great number of people were drafted to paint murals as decoration, immensely contributing to Tibet's art of paint-

---

① http: //www. travelchinaguide. com/intro/arts/

Figure 11 – 1   Tangka

ing. The Catalogue of *Jokhang* Monastery written by the Fifth Dalai Lama revealed that *Songtsan Gambo* used the blood from his nose to paint a portrait of the White *Lham*, which was later hidden in the abdomen of the statue. It is viewed as the earliest version of a *tangka* painting.

Tangkas are easily made, hung and stored, which contribute to its application in the spread of Buddhism in Tibet, making it one of the most significant folk art forms.

In the Ming and Qing dynasties, the art of *tangka* reached a new level, with the number sharply increasing and different schools appearing. Generally, the *tangkas* of Eastern Tibet are remarkable for the skillful reflection of man's inner world through fine brushwork while the *tangkas* of Western Tibet are similar to *gongbi painting*, traditional Chinese realistic painting featuring close attention to detail with the employment of bright colors[1].

• Butter Sculpture

Butter sculpture is another typical Tibetan Buddhist artistic treasure with over 400 years history, primarily made from butter and other mineral pig-

---

① http: //zt. tibet. cn/english/zt/xz_ arts/. . %5Cxz_ arts/200402004520171559. htm

Figure 11 – 2   Butter Sculpture

ments, with its size ranging from several centimeters to several meters. Tibetan monks used to employ butter from yak milk in the production
of elaborate images, and the subjects can be various, such as deities,
flowers, animals and Buddhist motifs during the annual Butter Lantern Festival. Conventionally presented as offerings, butter sculptures are exhibited
on monastery altars and family shrines. During the Great Prayer Festival, a
butter   sculpture   competition   will   be   held   before   the   Jokhang
Temple. Meanwhile, the butter sculptures in Ta'er Monastery enjoy the greatest reputation in the Tibetan world, which possesses a butter sculpture museum for the collection of fine butter sculptures.

The origin of butter sculpture associated with the Tibetan tradition of
presenting Buddha their possessions from their domestic animals. Nomadic
tribes treasured the first butter from the female yak immensely, offering it
to Buddhist monasteries, and lamas created it into exquisite colored sculptures. A tradition passed on for hundreds of years till today, groups of Tibetan monks work for months to make the sculpture ready before the 15th
of January, the occasion to celebrate Tibetan New Year. On that day, people pray in monasteries, and at night, they go to Lhasa's Barkhor Street to
appreciate the great exhibition of various artistic butter sculptures.

But in fact, the crafts are extremely hard to make due to a number of
reasons. Because of the butter's low melting point, monk craftsmen normally

have to work on their productions on the coldest days of the year in the freezing monasteries rooms, dipping their hands into the icy water. Despite the harsh working environment, the devout craftsmen are committed to the art production in the belief that their work results in a positive collective karma which brings them peace and harmony. It can take more than a month for half a dozen lamas to make a massive traditional sculpture, therefore, it is undeniable that the arduous process of the artistic creation has led to a great shortage of skillful lama artists[1].

- Tibetan Knives

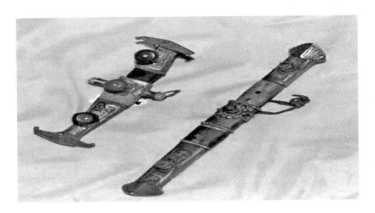

Figure 11 – 3   Tibetan Knives

The Tibetan knife can serve both for the functions of self-defense and decoration, with the male's being sharp and the female's being delicate.

The common material for the Tibetan knife is ox horn, ox bone or wood, with the upscale hilt being twined by silver and copper wire. The sheath is more exquisite, including simple wooden or leather sheath, ordinary brass or cupronickel sheath, and even silver or golden sheath, on which refined fowls, beasts, flowers, grass and other patterns are designed. Sometimes, the sheath is embedded with colorful gemstones and stones.

---

① http: //www. travelchinaguide. com/cityguides/tibet/butter-sculpture. htm

In specification, the Tibetan knives are normally classified as long knife, dagger and pen knife, with each being one meter at most, being about 40cm and being a dozen of centimeters long respectively. As to shape, they own distinctive local features like pasturing type, Kangba type and Tsang type etc. ①

②Uygur

• Xinjiang Rugs and Carpets

The Xinjiang Carpet, or Orient Carpet, is a conventional folk artwork of China, which is classified as Cover Carpet, Tapestry, Cushion Carpet and Kneeling Carpet etc.

The history of the Xinjiang carpet can be traced back to as early as the late West Han Dynasty, proved by the excavated remains of the Loulan Ancient Tomb.

Meanwhile, The Xinjiang Carpet is a living proof of the cultural exchange along the Silk Road since home and foreign merchants traveled there to transport Xinjiang carpets to the West while they brought ancient Persia carpets back to Xinjiang long before.

With phenomenal folk color and pattern, the Xinjiang Carpet features multilayer frame and geometrical image. Made of superb wools of Hetian sheep, the rug is tough, flexible, and thick with great luster and endurance.

Certain amounts of Xinjiang carpets were exported to European and American countries during the 16th century to the 19th century which were treasured and exhibited in museums like London Victoria Museum of England, Arabia Museum and Frankfort Manual Art Museum of Germany②.

• Atlas Silk

Atlas, a silk fabric, is remarkable for its various and splendid colors such as viridis, sapphire, indigo, yellow, peach, orange, gold, mauve etc. In addition, the patterns are well-knit to represent the vigor of na-

---

① http://www.tibetadvisor.com/culture/tibetan-knife.html

② http://traditions.cultural-china.com/en/16Traditions459.html

ture. Atlas silk is soft and flexible, used by the local for both costuming and interior adornment. Hotan, the birthplace of the silk, is one of the most significant parts of the Silk Route, with people creating silk fabrics for centuries. And the silk from Hotan is labeled as the "Khan Atlas" or "King's Silk".

Therefore, Uyghur atlas possesses an important position in Uyghur dress and ornament, representing the civilization of Xinjiang ethnic groups through its unique dying technique and cultural connotation. Atlas silk is one of the favorite dress materials of Xinjiang ethnic women, particularly Uyghur women.

Silk manufacturing remains an elementary regional industry, with silk being handmade in accordance with the ancient tradition.

Firstly, loosen the fragile threads in a basin of hot water before spinning them together onto reels. Once the silk has been extracted, it is tied and dyed. To make the multi-colored patterns, the silk needs to be dyed one color at a time. When the threads are placed into patterns, it is loaded onto the machines to complete the weaving[1].

③Miao Nationality

● Silver Ornaments

The elaborate silver adornment is viewed as the symbol of the Miao nationality, who is chiefly distributed in Guizhou and Hunan province, and the fascinating craft has been dominated the Miao culture for over 400 years.

It is anciently customary for Miao women to adorn themselves with silver jewelry during important occasions such as festivals, celebrations, especially the brides' weddings. The 15 - kiligram full set of jewelry consists of a silver crown, horns, earrings, chest plague, clothing ornaments, waistband, bracelets, hairpins, chains and bonnet ornaments, which is believed to be capable of scaring off evil spirits and bringing beauty and wealth to

---

① http：//www. retrospectivetraveller. co. uk/2011/03/china-archive/khan-atlas-king-silk-uyghur-hotan-xinjiang. html

Figure 11 – 4　Atlas Silk

the wearers, with the butterfly being a major image.

The Miao silver is commonly 40 to 60 percent pure, the rest elements being white copper and nickel. In the past, because the silver resources are not sufficient in the area, the Miao people used to melt all the silver coins they earned in the production of beautiful ornaments for the women in town. In 1950, the government initiated particular started silver allocation for the Miao communities, a method helped to regulate the silver purity.

Fusing the resources together, Miao silversmiths smelted and cut the compound silver into small flakes and threads. Then, the silver is carved, chiseled and welded into delicate forms of adornments. In certain villages, all Miao males are required to master the skill of silver making and the craft is passed on from generation to generation. The craftsmanship ranges from basics like common bracelets and necklace to elaborately made master-pieces.

Miao ornaments are different in shapes and patterns: rectangular or semicircular silver chest bands cover the chest and abdomen; silver hanging decorations are in the shape of butterflies, birds, fish and coins, with chains and pendants arranged in four to five layers; Silver rings are in the shape of lions, tigers, phoenixes, dragons and butterflies. Most of all, butterfly shaped bells are added to the bottom of women's gowns and wristbands, sounding melodically when they walk.

- Batik

Batik, or wax printing, is one of the three oldest traditional dyed and multi-colored textile handcrafts in China, the other two being bandhnu and hollow-out printing. With unique styles, rich patterns and eye-catching colors, batik is commonly used in clothing and other ornaments.

The technique of wax printing is widely spread among the Miao, Buyi, Yao and some other nationalities, with the origin derived from a story. A pretty Miao girl is not content with the monotonous color and style of her dress. One day, she slept in a bed of flowers when she dreamt a flower fairy who brought her to a flower garden with all flowers in full blossom. Then she woke up, finding that the bees had left spots of honey and beeswax on her dress. To cover the traces of wax, she had no choice but to put the dress into a bucket to dye it before rinsing the floating color with boiling water. With all these done, she surprisingly found that beautiful white flowers appeared on the dark blue dress. Therefore, she got the skills of wax printing and taught other villagers.

But actually, China's dyeing handcrafts progressed even as early as Western Zhou Dynasty during which period there were special officers to be responsible for silk production and dyeing according to historical records. Batik, wax printing, originated in the Qin and Han Dynasties and gained popularity in the Sui and Tang Dynasties and turned out to be one of the essential aspects of Chinese civilization.

The drawing tool is not a brush, but a knife made of two or several pieces of the same shape thin copper sheets, with one end tied on a wooden handle. Plus, the knife edge is always ajar to dip in and store wax. To draw various lines, the copper knives are of different types like half-round-shape, triangle-shape and axe-shape etc. The first step of wax-printing is to clean and bleach the cloth before drying it under sunlight. Then patterns are drawn on the cloth with beewax and the special knife. Following that, the cloth is to be put into a dye vat for nearly a week. The final step is to wash the cloth in boiling water. After the removal of wax, the blue and white pattern will be clearly seen[1].

• Miao Embroidery

Miao embroidery, namely, is an embroidery skill primarily developed by and handed down among Miao folks, which is popular in Leishan County, Guiyang City and Jianhe County of Guizhou Province with varying forms and styles.

Leishan County is one of the main settlements of Miao nationality, located in Southeast Guizhou, with Miao folks accounting for over eighty percent of the total population. Leishan Miao costumes feature elaborate embroidery and dazzling silver ornaments, which can be roughly divided into four categories of long skirts, medium-length skirts, short skirts and extra-short skirts.

Leishan Miao embroidery skills are various and typical, with the major ones being double-stitch locking embroidery, crepe embroidery, braid embroidery, sticking embroidery etc. despite that these skills can be found elsewhere as well. In addition, the combination of multi-dimensional shapes and pattern-in-pattern styles, coupled with the skills of analogy, metaphor, and symbols, etc. have been applied to reflect the aesthetics of the Miao.

The Huaxi Miao cross-stitch is another famous skill of the Miao embroidery in Guiyang City, Guizhou Province. Historical records reveal that the Jiuli clan, the ancestors of the Miao folks, firstly settled along the Yellow River. However, after being defeated in the battle against other tribes, they moved westward, with some branches entered current Guizhou Province. Among which, one branch called itself "Mou", also known as

---

① http://www.yeschinatour.com/chinese-culture/wax-printing/

"Huamiao", and it settled in today's Guiyang.

Initially using batik as their dress adornment, the Mou people created cross stitch on the shading of batik patterns which evolved into the unique style of Miao embroidery. Popular cross-stitch patterns comprise pig's footprint, calf's footprint, cow's head, snowflake, lotus flower, ear of rice, bronze drum, copper coin, sun, water reptile, swallow, pavilion, bridge, river and Miao King's imprinting, etc.

Huaxi Miao cross-stitch is normally used in the themes of ancestor commemoration, history record and love expression, together with the decorative nature. Because the Miao Nationality has no writing system, Huaxi Miao cross stitch just acts as a carrier of their history and legends. When making the cross-stitch work, Huaxi Miao women always follow the spirit of creation, and two identical works are rarely found, bestowing the craft with high aesthetics and originality. Therefore, the works of cross stitch are exhibited in a great number of museums both at home and abroad.

The unique cross-stitched Guanshou gown, made by cutting a hole for head in entire pieces of cloth, is so characteristic that it has been viewed as a symbol of the Miao Nationality. Besides, Huaxi Miao cross stitch is widely used in their daily life, during festival celebrations and spouse selection, weddings and funerals, as well as in religious ceremonies.

Miao Tin embroidery of Jianhe County has a history of approximately five to six hundred years, with navy blue cotton fabric as its base. The difference between Miao Tin embroidery and the embroideries of other ethnic groups is that the former uses tin wires rather than silk yarns to embroider on the cross-stitch patterns. The production process is in the following: First, threading the cotton yarns and cross stitching on the fabric before stitching the tin wires into the pattern; then, using black, red, blue and green silk yarns to shape flowers. The main pattern is as complicated as a maze, making the picture profound and mysterious. Silvery tin wires constitute a sharp contrast with the navy blue fabric, bright and dazzling. When accompanied with other silver jewelries, it is even more stunning.

However, with the development of modern society, the number of the

Miao nationality embroidery artisans is dramatically decreasing, and immediate measures should be taken to make sure that this ancient craft can be passed on to future generations[1].

3. Western Folk Art

(1) Europe
①Russia
• Russian Nesting Doll

The first Russian nesting doll, a set of wooden dolls of decreasing size placed one inside the other, was carved in 1890. Usually the exterior figure is a woman, dressed in a sarafan and a long traditional Russian peasant jumper. The figures inside can be of either gender while the smallest doll is always a baby, which cannot be taken apart. The images of the dolls vary from fairy tale characters to government leaders, with each being exquisitely made.

The dolls are produced from one block of wood to create the suitable model since each material has different trait of expansion and moisture. First, the innermost doll, which is made on a turning lathe, will determine the size and shape of the larger dolls. Then, the bottom and top halves of the next doll are made individually, with a ring on the bottom made to fit into an insert on the top part. The upper portion is put on the lower half, which tightens the ring to its upper fitting to ensure the halves will close securely. All the dolls finished, they are treated, painted, and coated before being nested inside one another[2].

• Wood Carving

Wood carving is a traditional Russian craft, with the ancient people believed that the wood serves as a connection between the sun and them. As a result, figurines of animals, birds and amulets passed from generation to

---

① http: //english. chinese. cn/chineseculture/article/2011 – 07/13/content_ 294736. htm

② http: //en. wikipedia. org/wiki/Matryoshka_ doll

Figure 11 – 5   Russian Nesting Doll

generation.

Besides, Wood carving is widely used in the wooden architecture, and it is also applied in the decoration of furniture, dishes and toys etc. Those craftsmen, the owner of the trees in Old Russia, possessed vast knowledge of art and a good taste of aesthetics, which enabled them to create impressive wood carvings.

Just as a fragment of a wooden column excavated in Novgorod artifacts can offer message for the historians to explore the way that people lived in 11th century A. D. , the monuments of wood architecture and household items reveal considerable information in the field of Russian folk art.

• Birch Bark Crafts

Birch bark is the thin upper layer of birch rind, and Birch bark handicrafts are traditional Russian popular craft.

Birch bark is widely used to make a food and drink container. tues. For instance, peasants use it to hold water or kvass, and the drink would stay cool even on a hot day. Besides, various boxes and baskets for keeping flour or honey, shepherd's horns, fishing net ropes etc. were made of birch bark too.

The origin of the birch bark processing technology can be traced back to the 18th century. Usually wicker birch bark handicrafts have no particular decorations, simply demonstrating natural material. But in certain regions they are decorated with colorful floral patterns, with the whole surface filled with smoothly curved thin stalks with leaves and branches. Elaborately carved birch bark "lace" is laid over a bright background which can be made of fabric, foil or paper so as to create an impressive decorative effect.

②the United Kingdom

● British Art Glass

British Isles is remarkable for glass making, which has developed under the influence of Venetians, Bohemians, and Belgians. Typically shaped as classic cylinders and trumpet, the vases feature romantic depictions of flowers and rural scenes with a range of colors from common tangerine to rare pewter.

The Birmingham area was another early English glass center, home to Bacchus, which produced paperweights with mushroom-like millefiori forms in the interiors. In nearby Stourbridge, Glass makers also produced paperweights, as well as Bohemian-looking vases with flared lips, hot-worked exteriors like ribbons and fruit, and colorful interior casings that ranged from bone white to fuchsia pink. Meanwhile, Stourbridge was also known for its carved and cameo glass.

To the north, in Perth, Scotland, a father-son team of Spanish glassblowers sowed the seeds for several firms: Monart (1924), Ysart Bros. (1947), Vasart (1956), and Strathearn (1965). Monart was the partnership between local John Moncrief and Salvador Ysart. The simple shapes of their vases and bowls were the perfect foils for the mottled abstractions and swirling designs Monart was known for. Ysart, Vasart, and Strathearn continued in this vein, expanding to include millefiori paperweights that are at once traditional and fresh, with rich coloration and lush interiors[1].

① http: //www. collectorsweekly. com/art-glass/british

• Scottish Tartan

One of the most important symbols of Scotland, the status of Tartan in folk art can never be understated.

Tartan, generally a piece of woven wool, has stripes of different colors, width, and depth, with the patterns being called "setts". For thousands of years, the Celts are known to have woven chequered or striped cloth, and a couple of ancient samples have been found across Europe and Scandinavia. It is generally believed that the introduction of this weaving form came to the West of Northern Britain with the Iron age Celtic Scots from Ireland in the 5th to 6th B. C.

One of the earliest tartans found in Scotland traced back to the 3rd century A. D. , where a small sample of woollen check called the Falkirk tartan was found as a stopper in an earthenware pot, a simple two-colored check which was identified as the undyed brown and white of the native Soay Sheep.

Another great boost to tartan attributed to Prince Albert who designed the now world famous Balmoral tartan. Today tartan still occupies a special place in the textile history and symbolizes the folk cultural identity of the whole Scottish nation.

③Germany, Austria and Switzerland

• Bauernmalerei

It is a certain kind of folk art associated with Germany, Austria and Switzerland, with the term coming from two words: "bauern" and "malerei" which means peasant and painting respectively which originated in the Bavarian and Austrian Alps and the Swiss Apenzell; therefore it is also usually referred to as "Bavarian Folk Art".

Despite the fact that it began as something simple, it has undergone several stages of development, resulting in the influences affecting the type of backgrounds painted on, the way the designs were arranged as well as colors used.

There were a number of regional variations as the art spread throughout Europe. Different craftsmen applied their best techniques to individualize their painted decoration.

The Tolzer Style is related with a town called Bad Tolz in Southern Germany. Tolzer Rose is the favorite of many folk artists, and the style is ideal for beginners.

The Rossler Style is painted mainly on schranks, beds and trunks by painters in a village neighboring Stuttgart with patterns such as flowers, animals, peasant scenes, fruit baskets, hearts and swirls. The painting is typically a combination of blues and greens as backgrounds coupled with characteristic red borders.

The Wismut Style is associated with "wismut", a metal mined in the Erz mountains of Germany. It is applied as background on small chests to resemble the silver chests of the wealthy after which flowers are painted on them.

The backgrounds of the Hessian Style are dark blue in which the flowers and borders are rather primitive.

The Franconian Style gets its name from Franconia, the northern region of Bavaria. The vases and flowers painted are not as delicate as those painted in lower Bavaria, with "Peasant marble" being the typical feature.

The Black Forest Style originates in the southwest corner of Germany, the place bordering Switzerland and France. The painting style resembles porcelain painting and white is used as highlight on flowers. Usually the background is painted in either off-white or almost black[1].

④France

● Quimper Pottery

Quimper Faience is a piece of fine grain earthenware decorated with an opaque, tin based glaze, produced in a factory near Quimper, in Brittany, France. Every product is completely handmade without the employment of decal or stencil and most of the patterns are painted on top of raw glaze. Produced by one artist from start to finish, each piece is highly individual and unique.

---

① http：//www. artezan. com/artezan/styles-n-techniques/traditional/bauernmalerei. html

Painting Quimper is definitely a true folk art which has been passed down for generation to generation. Since every pattern requires a combination of different strokes and brushes, the artists need to spend two to three years learning the quick flicks of the wrist, a painting technique known as "coup de pinceau". Commonly it takes 25 minutes to an hour for an experienced painter to decorate a plate, depending upon the intricacy of the pattern.

One of the most traditional patterns, Decor Henriot has existed continuously for over 100 years, and has been exported to America since the late 1800's. Over the years, thousands of molds and over 100 patterns have been produced by the artisans at the factory, with the patterns featuring roosters, the symbol of France, peasants who are in bright traditional costumes, birds and botanical scenes etc.

(2) North America

①America

The discovery of the American continent in the 15th century enables the European to gain insight into the culture of the North American Indians whose cultivation of agriculture was limited and semi-nomadic.

• Masks

Figure 11 – 6　Mask

Native Americans have along history of mask making and the exact meaning and significance of masks vary among different tribes which can be used for spiritual purposes, healing purposes or simply for entertainment and artistic expression. Primarily there are three kinds of Native American masks in terms of forms: The first is the basic single face mask. The second features moving parts. The third is a transformative mask which has several masks built together.

The materials for the mask are various, with the basic principle being indigenous. Wood was a popular material. In the Northwest, masks were carved from cedar wood. The Iroquois combined wood and cornhusks. The Navajo and Apache used leather and the Cherokee would use gourds. The Jemez made masks from baked clay. Some tribes used deer buckskin or pigskin, with the common decoration materials being feathers, horsehair, straw, cut glass, turquoise and bone pipe[①].

In terms of theme, the two major types are spirit masks and portrait masks. The former is to resemble animals which are spirits representing nature. It is believed in certain clans that each tribe descends from an animal and each animal stands for unique characteristics and particular philosophy.

The latter is made for Native Americans to narrate stories concerning certain characters which are recognizable to the audience. Performers wore masks to tell stories on special occasions such as dances, cultural dramas, traditional and religious ceremonies. Native American secret societies would also uses masks during their meetings, as would shamans. A number of Native Americans now make masks for sale to financially support their family and tribe. Other masks, such as the false faces, are not allowed to be sold or displayed. Some tribes are even requiring museums to remove those masks from their displays due to their religious connotation.

● Weavings

The weaving of Navajo Indian blankets and rugs is the most reputable native textile art in North America which was traditionally made in Mexico and the southwest United States: people kneel before a vertical wooden-frame loom, using a shuttle to weave colored threads together into large-

---

① http://www.ehow.com/info_ 8088190_ characteristics-native-american-masks.html

scale geometric patterns. At first, the blankets were made of hand-spun cotton thread which was later replaced by wool after the Spanish brought domestic sheep to the region.

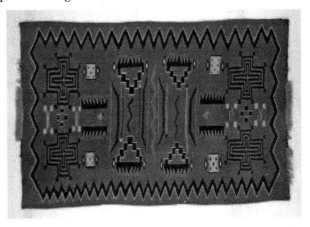

Figure 11 – 7   Weaving

Besides Navajo blankets and rugs, finger-weaving is also famous in the North America since ancient times, with finger-woven blankets, tapestries, and clothing still being made locally, among which the chilkat blankets of Tlingit people are one of the best representatives of finger-woven Indian blankets.

Another remarkable Native American textile art are Seminole sashes and patchwork. Star quilts, originated among the Sioux tribes, spread throughout the Great Plains. Actually, quilting was one of the Native American crafting techniques that developed from European traditions with ingredients of its own culture. For instance, star quilts are created by piecing a mosaic of cloth diamonds into the shape of the traditional eight-pointed morning star design of the Sioux. Before the appearance of star quilts, traditional Indian blankets were made from painted, quilled and beaded buffalo hide. Unfortunately, this craft largely died out after the extinction of wild buffalos, but some folk artists still make buffalo robes and blankets today from the hides of domestic animals[1].

②Canada

• Inuit Printmaking

Even though there is no particular word for art in the Inuktitut language, the Inuit does have art crafts such as decorated attires and carved articles since ancient times.

Compared with carvings, Inuit printmaking is more uncommon in that it hasn't substantial historical precedents, although it is related with carvings on bone or antler, women's facial tattoo marks, or inlay skin work on clothing. Generally speaking, carving materials such as stone, bone, antler, wood and ivory were available locally, but paper and drawing tools were unknown until introduced by early explorers and missionaries.

Figure 11 - 8　Inuit Printmaking

Even though print craft has a rather short history in the Arctic, with the techniques primarily being different from those in the south; it is undeniable that many Inuit have applied the art form to visually record their traditional life and the themes are generally related with the animals, birds and marine life of the Arctic; with other contents concerning legends,

①　http: //www. native-languages. org/rugs. htm

mythologies, and shamanistic practices etc.

• Inuit Sculptures

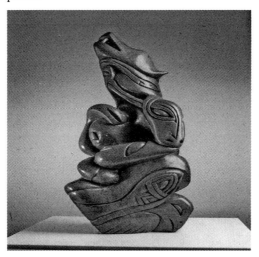

Figure 11 – 9   Inuit Sculpture

Basically, people use local material for the creation of folk art. Since there are no trees in the Arctic region from the sea along the coasts, wood would be impossible to be applied in Inuit sculpture and art, therefore, stones turn out to be the best choice. However, places with qualified stones are not always located near the established Inuit neighborhood, thus Inuit artists have to travel for several days to gather the materials by boat during the summer or by snowmobile during the winter. Collecting the stone from the land is tough labor with tools such as picks and drills since the stone cannot be simply exploded with dynamite which will ruin the stone. When substantial stones are extracted, the Inuit carvers would have them transported to their communities.

The most commonly used stone in Inuit sculpture are serpentine due to its hardness, with a variety of colors such as green, brown, black etc; other types of Arctic stone being marble, quartz, argillite, siltstone and dolomite.

Additionally, Inuit carvers prefer a primitive, unpolished appearance of the finish in some regions while a highly polished work is favored in other regions. Hence certain pieces of Inuit sculpture seem more shiny with the application of colored or clear shoe polish to improve the effect. Sometimes, beeswax is heated onto Inuit sculptures as an alternative finish. Other material used in Inuit sculptures are caribou antlers, ivory from marine mammals, and the bone of various animals[1].

4. Comparisons

The scope of art is too wide for us to compare the western and Chinese difference in limited room, thus one aspect is presented here to exemplify the major difference, namely, painting; particularly, landscape painting.

(1) Aesthetic Basis under Religious Influence

The aesthetic sources of the Chinese fine art are the philosophy of Chinese Buddhism, Taoist and Confucianism. Chinese landscape painting originally appeared in the Eastern Jin Dynasty, the prosperous period of the Taoism as well. The core concept of Taoism is mentalism, giving rise to the Chinese landscape painting's emphasis on manifestation. As the development of the other two religions, coupled with the fabulous landscapes, particularly the mountainous scenery, considerable drawings emerged in the Song Dynasty under the influence of both Buddhism and Taoism. In this case, painters always instill their individual emotions into the picture, instead of simply portraying the details of the object. As a result, white spaces and broad strokes are frequently seen in Chinese landscape paintings which are not unfinished spaces but an indispensable element of the painting to inspire the viewers' ingenuity. Normally, the Chinese does not paint his subject while observing it but produce the work with the imagination or at least the mem-

---

① http: //www. freespiritgallery. ca/materialsinuit. htm

orization of the object in the mind.

In the painting, painters usually imagine the scenes such as dragons, and human beings as symbolic objects, a reflection of Taoism thought that there exists harmony between human beings and the universe. To them, mountains are sacred since the Buddhists and Taoists built their first temples on the hillsides. In addition, the Chinese have long believed that the cosmic forces and the energy contribute to the endless renewal of the universe. If the mountain is regarded as the body of the cosmic being, then the rocks are its bones, the water is the blood, the trees and grasses are its hair, the clouds and mists are the vapor of its breath, which represent the very essence of life.

In contrast, western paintings are strongly influenced by Christianity faith. God is believed to create the world and beauty, with the painters always seeking to embody God's presence in the naturalistic environment. Therefore, the expression of the realistic natural scene is always regarded as contributions to the God, enabling people to be much closer to the God. Most of western painters normally attempt to produce ideal works to make viewers to be emotionally involved in the paintings.

(2) Composition

Chinese landscape painters always use strokes and lines as the major instrument to compose a painting, which are vigorous and expressive. As to the technique, a commonly adopted method is to consider all the parts as host and guests for the purpose of compositional balance.

The main part in a composition is definitely referred to as the "host," with all the rest being the "guests" as subordinates which are also essential to the whole picture just like the function of the leaves to a flower. For instance, in a Chinese landscape painting, the mountain is the host, whereas trees, a house, a person, would all be treated as the supplementary objects. In the process of composition, the first step is to decide what is the host and where to place it, then follows the arrangement of other parts to balance or to form sharp contrast to the major body.

Western landscape painting, however, aims at the perfect reflection of realistic scene. Therefore, painters usually honestly portray the object with the same color, appearance, light and shadow to enable the viewers to feel the real environment, with natural details being stressed in the composition of a picture.

In addition, random natural wildness is commonly highlighted in western landscape paintings. The painters know exactly how to handle color and light, patterns and textures, incorporating them into the wildest of settings. As to background, they are usually painted with loose and flexible brushstrokes to form disorganized shapes. Even if the same color is needed in both the foreground and the background, a neutral hue is in the background and a purer version in the foreground to create the depth.

(3) Colors

In Chinese landscape paintings, black and white are dominant colors. Rather than painting the details, Chinese painters always simplify the complicated landscape, only presenting an overall framework of landscape to viewers with ink and brush.

The ink, used in Chinese painting, is treated conventionally as " colors" in the exhibition of hues and shading when blended with different amount of water. What's more, the diffusion effect of *Xuan* paper allows the brush stroke to present numerous visuality which is utterly distinct from any other art medium. The mountains are painted in black and the rivers are depicted in white. In a word, Chinese landscape painting is characteristic of simple colors to leave more imagination for the observers.

In contrast, western landscape painting is a perfect exemplification of chromatic richness. In no other theme does such a range of hues come together. The color is originally various and the topics of western paintings are chiefly related with religion. Gradually, many painters began to aware that religious-themed subjects are not enough to reflect their perception to the world and they start to depict the natural scenery in daily life. As a painter, he should know the nature and be able to present the picture with the senses of color, light, sound and smell. Because of the strength of light and color, landscape painting is the best way to fully demonstrate hues. In a word, western painters favor vigorous colors to create impressive visual effect compared with Chinese landscape paintings.

(4) Perspective

The Chinese concept of perspective in landscape painting, generally speaking, is surrealistic, with the composition being two-dimensional. Therefore, most of Chinese landscape painters use flattened perspective, leaving viewers substantial room for reflection and imagination. Viewers can appreciate the work through their own perspective.

Unlike Chinese landscape painting, western painters often employ multi viewpoint to create a photographic environment. Based on their life experience, the work is created in the various perspectives, which can be inverted, augmented, diminished and partial or fragmented. The observer and painter are included in the picture as traveler, in the same way the painters would walk around a landscape. They are interconnected with sequences and layer on layer of key modulation. Likewise, the paintings have a subject with movement throughout and use visual inversions, augmentations or their equivalent based on physical feeling for the landscape.

Chapter Twelve

Customs of Entertainment

1. General Introduction

(1) Concepts

Folk entertainment is the general term for a diverse group of sports and games whose common element is their status as being "popular" or related to folk culture, including especially traditional, ethnic, or indigenous sports and games, but also new activities that are based on traditional practices. Noncompetitive games, mass gymnastics, spontaneous sports of the working classes, and games and sports associated with festivals all may be termed as "folk". Despite the origin of folk entertainment in the pre-industrial world, the idea of it is itself an invention of the industrial age. Folk entertainments are based on festivity and community, rather than disciplinary rules and production of results[1].

(2) Characteristics

The characteristics of folk entertainment are listed as the following:

①Recreational and Competitive

Recreation is the core of folk entertainment because various folk activities enable people to enjoy themselves. Meanwhile, folk sports are mostly competitive. There are many folk sports among the so-called Non-Olympic sports. The Olympic sport system also utilizes folk sports for the cultural

---

① http: //www. jugaje. com/en/textes/texte_ 5. php

framing of competitive events.

②Healthy and Diverse

The most important goal of folk sports is not to compete for a champion but to promote solidarity and to celebrate diversity and otherness. Different from the strict standardization of Olympic sport, folk sport pay more attention to both the variations among communities and the togetherness within groups. Rather than display sameness and hierarchy, they value distinction.

Meanwhile, on the margins of mainstream sport, sport for all movements use folk sports to advocate a healthy life. Large number of folk sports festivals were organized by the Trim & Fitness International Sport for All Association.

③Conventional and Festival

People can take the folk sports as the leisure activities in their daily life; besides, folk entertainments are based not on specified rules and rigid disciplines, but on festivals and meetings in an atmosphere of carnival, which is associated with different kinds of cultural activities such as music, singing, dancing, play, and outdoor activities.

④Regional and Social

Folk sports are related with various regional, ethnic, social, and national identities, in the opposition of uniform tendencies. In addition, they disapprove of a "folk" view from below to centralism and colonization from above.

⑤Instrumental and Educational

Despite the difference from the popular sports, folk sports in their past and modern versions are somehow inseparable with mainstream tendencies, which normally serve the function of practical use, such as sportive, educational, folkloristic or tourist aims.

Some people strive to incorporate folk sports into school education, exploiting them as a soft way of educational sport or as tools in the expression of regional identity in education. However, when act as educational instrument, the games tend to loosen their connection with people's life and self-organization.

(3) Origin

In the past, sports were the equivalence of pastimes, such as hunting, falconry, and fishing, basically among the upper classes and the nobility, who are in the opposite status with the "folk", or common people. At the same time, the civilians, both rural and urban, had their distinct culture of festivity and recreation, during which strength and agility games and competitions were integrated with dances, music, and rituals to celebrate the festivals. They were combined with religious events as well. In addition, sport games brought excitement as the supplements of the ordinary daily life, allowing physical contact even flirting between males and females, a reflection of the inner tensions within the folk.

Many pre-modern strength folk activities were reserved exclusively for men such as wrestling, stone lifting, tossing the caber, and finger drawing. In Scotland, the "stone of manhood" which was placed beside the house of a chieftain served as a test of strength for the young men to demonstrate their masculinity. Games of skill such as the bat and ball game played in the Valley of Aosta, in which a batter hits the ball as far as possible into a field where it is caught by the other team, were also attended by men only until the 1990s could women participate such activity.

Of course, there were folk competitions that were particularly arranged for women, women's foot-races or "smock races" being a typical local event in England and Scotland from the 17th to the 19th century. Generally speaking, the games were divided into the type for noble women and the type for women from the lower social ranks, say Gypsies and immigrant Irish women etc. However, the women's races disappeared and were excluded from modern women's track and field. Anyway, women's folk racing remains in Württemberg, Germany, among shepherdesses that dates to as early as the 15th century. As a modern folkloristic event, the participants maintained the tradition, trying to prevent the rivals from winning which gave rise to substantial stumbling and laughing, the typical characteristic of European folk culture.

Modern folk entertainment went through three main stages. The first stage was concerned with the Romantic revival in early nineteenth century. Before that, the word of "folk" had negative meaning of plebs, the vulgar people with low social status. Then, a new concept of Volk swept all over Europe when Johann Gottfried Herder (1774 - 1803), a literary and cultural critic, initiated the reevaluation of folk traditions, advocating the ideas of democracy, peoples' rights and the pursuit of national identities, as in German Turnen, the Slavic Sokol gymnastic movements and the Danish gymnastics, based on Swedish gymnastics, which were revived compared with English sport. In Ireland in the 1880s, folk hurling was promoted by the Gaelic Athletic Association as a means of liberation from the British governing. The Icelandic glima wrestling was regarded as "national sport".

The second stage of folk entertainment started at 1900, represented by "back to nature" movements labeled as "folk". Woodcraft Indians employed practices of turning to nature to promote peace among social community. Boy scouts also competed in this way but more militarily. In Germany, Naturfreunde movement began in the form of a workers' tourist movement, with participants building shelters for volkswalkers nationwide. Besides, Wandervogel, the German youth movement, carried out outdoor activities in small and self-administered children groups and the members walked, sang, folk-danced, matched in the green nature.

The third stage began in the 1970s in California, initially related to the "new movement culture". As a way of protesting against the war in Vietnam and hippie culture, the youth engaged in noncompetitive plays and games.

Meanwhile, considerable folk sports were organized in national and regional festivals as the result of a reviving interest in the preservation of conventional folk entertainments in the Europe, the representatives being the Flemish volkssport which were typically urban games organized by local clubs, Basque competitions of force and Breton folk games. In the 1980s, there followed the Danish traditional games movement concerning the folk gymnastic movement. Actually, the International Sport and Culture Association functioned as an umbrella organization to promote folk sports, popular gymnastics, and festival celebration in about fifty countries.

With the trend of globalization, some typical folk entertainment of the Third World countries spread to the western world as well. For instance, a traditional Afro-Brazilian sport named Capoeira gained popularity among the teenagers in cities like Amsterdam, Berlin and Paris. Pencak silat, the Indonesian martial art, turned to a Western sport. Tai chi and Wushu which was based on Chinese warrior training are now practiced worldwide, and even Japanese sumo wrestling are conducted in Western countries. Immigrant cultures contributed to the new movement forms like the bhangra dance of South Asians in Britain.

As a result, folk sports, on one hand, were transformed into western-characteristic sports in the forms of various tournaments. On the other hand, the penetration of "exotic" folk sports gives birth to new practices in the Western world as an alternative to western standard sport. At the same time, new games emerged, which can't find places in traditional sports. Bungee jump, for example, is regarded as one innovation which is based on a Melanesian folk ritual named "land diving".

Meanwhile, certain western entertainments have produced new folk practices in continents like Africa, Asia and America. Disco dance appeared in China as disike, which was particularly popular among female seniors. Trobriand cricket was practiced as a Melanesian folk festivity of dance, sport and carnival featuring gift exchange. Danish sport aid movement promoted the popularity of ngoma, an original local folk dance, in Tanzanian villages while Sukuma drumming was conducted among Danish youth. In Basque country, Catalonia and on the Canary Islands, folk sports practice contributed to the distinction of regional identity. Furthermore, the European Traditional Sport and Games Association was founded in 2001 for the development of regional folk sports. Even though new trends have appeared in the past few years in folk entertainment, it can be viewed as a new perspective to the future as well as a return to the past[1].

2. Chinese Folk Entertainment

(1) Folk Entertainment of Han Nationality

①Quyi

Quyi is a general term for approximately 400 speaking and singing art forms, deeply rooted in Chinese time-honored historical culture. Storytelling and comic performances, in particular, were popular among people, both nobility and civilians, in ancient times. Storytelling developed in the Tang Dynasty, with the main sources from Buddhist scriptures, and some were accompanied by folk songs. During the Song Dynasty, Quyi reached its peak due to the trade flourish and the urban growth.

Quyi is characteristic of simple, vivid and colloquial languages, with the performers striving to inspire the audiences' imaginations through their words and songs. Unlike drama or opera, Quyi normally has one or two performers who may act multiple roles. In addition, the contents of Quyi are comparatively shorter and earthlier than other art forms, with the artists taking up several tasks such as composition, edition and design of the works. The following are some of the most popular forms of Quyi.

● Pingshu

Pingshu, an art form of oral storytelling, is widely popular, particularly in Northern China. The performer normally wears a gown and stands behind a table, with a folded fan in one hand and a gavel in another, which is used to strike the table to ask for the quietness among the audience as well as to enhance the effect of the performance at the beginning or at the intervals. The language of Pingshu is Chinese Mandarin, which based on Beijing dialect. The contents of the storytelling are usually Chinese classics, such as The Romance of the Three Kingdoms and serialized novels, with the storytellers adding their own comments on the subjects and the characters. By ap-

---

① http://www. jugaje. com/en/textes/texte_ 5. php

preciating the performance, the audience not only is entertained, but also is educated and enlightened.

- Suzhou Pingtan

Suzhou Pingtan, a general term of Suzhou storytelling and ballad singing in Suzhou dialect, is prevailing as a folk art form in Jiangsu and Zhejiang Provinces as well as Shanghai. It can be performed in solo, duet or trio with the small three-stringed plucked instrument and Pipa utilized as accompaniment. Besides, the wooden clappers are employed to produce different kinds of tone and melody. After a substantial period of progress, Suzhou Pingtan boasts a great distinction of styles in singing and storytelling.

- Crosstalk

Crosstalk, or Xiangsheng, is regarded as one of the most influential forms of Quyi, which took the shape during Qing Dynasty under the reign of Xianfeng.

The first popular crosstalk folk artists were Zhang Sanlu and Zhu Shaowen, and the latter had the stage name of Qiong Bupa, namely fearing no poverty. His stage name derived from a poem inscribed on one of her personal belongings, a pair of bamboo clappers as a percussion instrument.

The poem reads like this, "Eating by begging from many houses and sleeping in ancient temples. Never do anything against the law, and don't be afraid of seeing the emperor." Zhu, who normally began with a ragged verse, something like a palindrome phrase, used to perform in Tianqiao area in Beijing and his performance features imitation of the street hawkers' cries and some ancient songs.

Since the late Qing Dynasty to the early years of the Republic of China, Crosstalk art has developed immensely both in content and in skills. Generally, there are three forms of Crosstalk. The earliest form is performed by one person namely Dankou Crosstalk with its contents being mostly jokes and funny stories. Later, Duikou Crosstalk appeared, which are performed by two people. The third form performed by three or more people is called Qunkou Crosstalk. It calls for one artist to say funny things, while others chime in and yet another makes them stray from the subject.

• Errenzhuan

Errenzhuan is a form of duet with over 200 – year history concerning storytelling, singing and dancing, originated in Liaoning, Jilin and Heilongjiang Provinces in Northeast China.

Errenzhuan features local flavor which is written in easy language, with the vocal music based on northeastern folk songs. The dancing originated from local farmers' dances to celebrate sowing and planting which also include the folk dance skills of waving fans or handkerchiefs[1].

②Folk Songs

Folk Song is a form of music for common people to express their emotions and feelings, reflecting their everyday life through years. Having been elaborated from generation to generation, Folk music is characteristic of simple language and vivid image with multiple genres and forms, such as labor songs, mountain songs, major aria, minor aria, and part singing etc.

Chinese folk music possesses a long history. In the primeval society, folk songs usually went with dancing. Guofeng, a part of the Book of Songs, consisted of the lyrics of folk songs in 15 different regions from the West Zhou Dynasty to Spring and Autumn. Most dynasties had their typical folk music: *Chuci* of the Chu Dynasty, *Yuefu* in the Han Dynasty, melodies in the Tang Dynasty, bagatelle in the Ming and Qing Dynasties, with other ballads from different areas in different dynasties. With the progress of the times, people recreated many new styles of folk songs by combining new words with old melodies or elaborating the old melodies. Meanwhile, as a large nation with multiple ethnic groups, China owns a massive reservoir of folk songs, an invaluable Chinese musical treasure.

Take the folk songs of Northern Shaanxi as an example, they are the product of labor people's spirits, thoughts and feelings. As the old saying goes, "A hungry man songs for the food and the labor man songs for his work", the song comes from the bottom of people's heart and is the second

---

① http: //www. topchinatravel. com/china-guide/quyi. htm

language of their life.

With rich contents, the folk songs have different forms such as labor songs, like rammers work chant and workers' song; *Shange*, with the representative being Xintianyou, also known as Shuntianyou, a kind of Shaanxi local melody; customs songs like alcohol songs and sacrifice songs etc.

To sum up, the Folk music features intense local color, vivid language, smooth melody and free rhythm to express the emotion and wish of the people in the loess plateau. The common themes of the songs are mainly love between boys and girls and also the opposition against the ruler before the liberation, with the well-known works being Arethusa flowers, going to the West Gate, driving the cattle etc. In addition, the folk song is created by the folk people who tend to express their emotions through parallel story-telling, such as the ten cups of wine, the twelve heroes, the five embroideries, and the eighteen fans etc.

③Folk Dances

Like other forms of primitive art, the origin of Chinese folk dances were normally rituals of superstitious beliefs practiced for a good harvest, or even for a good hunt because the earliest Chinese folk dances were performed by hunter-gatherers.

Though no written historical sources have been located, Chinese archeologists did find pottery shards dating to the 4th millenium B. C. , with dancers waving hunting weapons like spears. Likewise, the Cro-Magnon paintings on the cave walls of Lascaux in south-central France also are about cave dwellers' hunting dances who held the belief that they would gain power through the ritual performances.

Later on, the folk dances of the current ethnic minorities were already in shape during the Han Dynasty, as the product of a somewhat superstition that in making ritual sacrifices to the gods, people could gain a harvest like abundant nuts, berries and fishes etc.

Despite the fact that the descendants of these ancient hunters now have more stable agricultural forms, the ritual dances continue even if the ancient belief have been replaced by a modern concept that in sustaining the past traditions like the communal folk dance, one might therefore reinforce social bonds which benefit the perseverance of one's cultural identity.

The Dragon Dance and the Lion Dance, two of the main Chinese folk dances were originally performed among the Han Chinese before being spread to other Chinese ethnic minorities, with such dances usually performed during Chinese Lunar New Year Festival. What's more, one of the most refined Chinese folk dances, the Court Dance, or the Palace Dance, was firstly practiced by the royal court of Emperor Qin of the Qin Dynasty which influenced subsequent Chinese emperors even those of Mongol or Manchu background who continued the well-established custom of the Court Dance.

Originated from rice planting and farming, another typical collective folk dance is Yangge, a combination of folk songs, folk martial arts, acrobatics and traditional operas, with skillful manipulations of the silk handkerchiefs and diverse feet movements. There are basically two kinds of Yangge, namely stilted Yangge and ground Yangge.

Yangge is mainly popular in the countryside, being related with ancient eulogy songs in sacrifices to the Farm God. By the Qing Dynasty, it had spread across the country in somewhat different forms, and all of them demonstrate happiness.

The number of the dance performers is not limited, normally ranging from several to hundred. When dancing, the dancers are dressed up with a red silk waistband and a hat folded by colored papers. Female performers always carry a fan and most male performers beat a waist drum, other normal accompanying music instruments being suona, gong, drum and cha. Yangge is always performed during the first 15 days after the Chinese New Year. In some villages, the performers dance from family to family. In turn, the family offers some gifts to them and some also explode fireworks.

Currently, Yangge has extended to city parks, streets and squares, developing into a popular exercise for urban citizens.

④Folk Sports and Games

● Kicking Jianzi

According to historical documents and excavated relics, the origin of kicking Jianzi was in the Han Dynasty and it gained popularity in the Tang and Song Dynasties. Formal shuttlecock kicking matches arose in the Ming Dynasty, the form being the players kicking the shuttlecock over a net to gain scores. The Qing Dynasty witnessed the peak of the game, with both the shuttlecock producing and kicking techniques reaching unprecedented height.

Jianzi for standard competition typically has four feathers fixed into a rubber sole with several plastic discs, similar to washers. But more commonly, people play Jianzi just for fun by using all parts of the body, particularly feet except hands. The players kick the shuttlecock alternatively and those who keep it in the air for as long as possible are viewed as the most skillful.

Owing to its entertainment and flexibility, shuttlecock kicking is not only prevailing among the Chinese, but also gains increasing popularity globally. Currently, the game is widely practiced in many European and Asian countries.

• Flying Kites

The kite, known as "Zhiyuan" or paper glede in ancient China, was primarily considered an art form with unique artistic value.

Interestingly, the appearance of the kite was associated with the wars of the Spring and Autumn Period. According to historical records, Mo Zi, the renowned ideologist, once spent three years producing a wooden kite, but it unfortunately failed after one day's flight. Lu Ban, the master carpenter, also made some which could flew high to spy on the enemy situation.

The technology progressed further during the famous historical Chu-Han War in 203 – 202 B. C. The story went that Zhang Liang, the general of the Han troops, ordered his soldiers to fly kites in the thick fog around the opponents, with children sitting in the large kites fluting tunes of Chu. Hearing the melodies, the Chu soldiers missed their homes, scattering and giving up the war. Xiang Yu, the powerful leader of Chu troops, had no choice but to commit suicide. Another function of the kites during the war was to deliver urgent messages.

Tang Dynasty witnessed the prosperity of Chinese Kites and the entertainment thrived as the product of cultural and economic advance, with flying kites became the popular sports among people, both the royal families and the civilians. Particularly on tomb sweeping day, people not only worshipped their ancestors but also took the opportunity to tour to the countryside to enjoy pastoral life. Then flying kites became a typical pleasure of that day which was believed to be a healthy game on the occasion of outing.

The procedure of kite making can be simply described as three steps. Firstly, bamboo, the common material for the frame, is pared and bended into thin strips thanks to its tenacity, with the shapes being various such as a dragonfly, swallow, centipede or butterfly. Secondly, tough and thin paper with even and long fibers, sometimes even silk, is pasted onto the framework. Finally, the kites are decorated with colorful chiffon, ribbons and paintings.

Even though the basic producing procedure remains the same, styles of kite-making vary from region to region. Weifang, the city in Shandong Province, is known as the "World Kite Capital" who is well known for the elaborate kite craftsmanship. One centipede-shaped kite with a dragon's head won the first place in the International Kite Festival held in Italy with over 300 meters, or 984 feet long which is now exhibited in the Weifang Kite Museum. Now the kite flying festival will be held annually in Weifang, appealing greatly to the fans from the world.

In Beijing, swallow-shaped kites are quite common, with craftsmen refashioning them differently most of which are decorated with peonies, bats and other auspicious patterns to bring good fortune. Kites made in Nantong usually feature whistles and rings which resemble a flock of birds when flying in the sky. Tianjin is also reputable for large variety of kites which are in the shape of insects, goldfish, clouds and even a swallow linked with dozens of little swallows, with the size varying from hundreds of meters to the smallest no bigger than a regular envelope, all reflecting the elaborate skill of the craftsman①.

● Wushu

Chinese Kung Fu, also referred to as Martial Arts, Gongfu or Wushu, is a series of fighting styles which symbolize Chinese culture.

The Martial Arts originated in the Shang and Zhou Dynasties. During the following Qin and Han Dynasties, wrestling, swordplay and spear skills became well developed and were popular among civilians and troops. Following the Song Dynasty, various schools, boxing styles, movement sets and weapon skills sprang up.

Instead of aggression or violence, Kung Fu advocates virtue and peace which has been held as the common value by martial artists from generation to generation. Actually, Kung Fu keeps its original function of self-defense with a number of movement sets, boxing styles, weapon skills and some fighting stunts. What's more, it benefits body-building and fitness keeping.

The primary defensive and aggressive means included leaping, tumbling and kicking. Even though the martial artists knew how to fight with weapons like stones and wood, fighting with bare hands and fists became essential.

Over thousands of years' development, Kung Fu evolved into an immense system containing over 300 distinct boxing types. Therefore, the classification of Gongfu is rather complicated: some schools are divided by geographical locations, for example, the Southern Fist, Nanquan, prevails in southern China, and Shaolin School was named after Shaolin Temple in Henan Province. Some schools are identified by the creator and master, like the Chen Style Tai Chi and Yang Style Tai Chi. Some are named according to different training philosophy, such as the Internal Boxing Arts, Neijiaquan, stresses the manipulation of the inner breath and body circulation, and the External Boxing Arts, Waijiaquan, aims at the enhancement of muscles and the limbs②.

● Weiqi (The Game of Go)

---

① http://www.travelchinaguide.com/intro/arts/kites.htm

② http://www.bookmartialarts.com/news/kung-fu-a-chinese-martial-art

According to historical record, Weiqi, a strategic board game between two players respectively using black and white game pieces, was invented by the legendary Chinese emperor Yao and his successor Shun. With the history of over 3, 000 years, the game is considered the origin of all ancient chess games. Called "yi" in ancient China, the game reflects ancient Chinese philosophy of profoundness and flexibility.

Weiqi was already popular in the Spring and Autumn Period, with many folk sayings related with this game. For instance, "ju qi bu ding" means "holding a game piece but not sure what move to make", and it is used to describe political hesitation. Throughout history, considerable talented Weiqi players emerged and many emperors in ancient China were addicted to this game such as Cao Cao, Emperor Taizu of the Song dynasty and Zhu Yuanzhang.

The charm of the game lies in the plenty of choices to move the game pieces, and numerous strategic variations. The time for one game can be as short as 15 minutes or as long as a few days. Normally it takes one or two hours for the players to finish one round.

To sum up, Weiqi is a combination of science, art and competition which contributes to intelligence promotion, personality cultivation and flexible strategy acquisition.

• Xiangqi (Chinese Chess)

Xiangqi is a Chinese board game between two players. According to official documents, it was originated from military strategies in the Spring and Autumn and the Warring States Periods. The early-stage Xiangqi comprised six ivory chess pieces, a dice, and a square chess board. After a substantial period of progress, the modern form of Xiangqi appeared in the Northern Song Dynasty and became popular in the Southern Song Dynasty.

Dice has been eliminated from the modern Xiangqi, and the game is different in terms of pieces and board. The modern version has a total of 32 pieces in red and black, with one person having a half of that number of the same color.

The board is nine lines wide and ten lines long to form the square grids, with a total of 90 crossing points for the pieces to be placed and moved.

The area dividing the two opponents' battle fields is called "the river" and the area with two diagonal lines connecting opposite corners and intersecting at the center point is called "jiu gong", namely nine-grid pattern. In the game, the two players battle against each other on the board by deploying horses and chariots and organizing troops based on their command of the playing rules.

● Mah-jong

Mah-jong is a typical competitive brain game in China, with the pieces similar in appearance to the tiles used in dominoes but engraved with Chinese symbolic patterns and characters. Known as a "game of encirclement", mah-jong is also called by folks as an activity "move" or "lay" bricks, with its origins being an ancient Chinese strategist's attempt to simulate battle formations.

A full set of traditional mah-jong comprises 136 tiles, including 36 sticks (or bamboos, numbered 1 to 9, 4 of each number), 36 dots (or circles, numbered 1 to 9, 4 of each number), 36 characters of "ten thousand" (numbered 1 to , 4 of each number), 12 honors (4 red, 4 green, 4 white dragons), and 16 winds (4 east, 4 south, 4 west, 4 north winds). These do not include eight flowers, which are added in the midst of a mah-jong game. Besides, the number of the tiles may vary in some regional variations.

In most cases, each player begins by getting 13 tiles. Then, four players draw and discard tiles in turn until they complete a legal pattern using the 14th drawn tile to form four groups (melds) and a pair (head). General standard rules exist concerning the order to draw a piece or obtain it from another player, the use of simples (numbered tiles) and honors (winds and dragons) and the kinds of melds etc. Still, playing systems differ due to regional distinctions. Particularly, the scoring rule and the minimum hand pattern necessary to win vary from region to region.

The game was introduced to neighboring countries such as Japan then to the West during the 1920s, where it somewhat aroused people's interest to this day.

⑤Folk Performance

• Chinese Opera

Chinese opera is one of the three oldest dramatic art forms in the world, the other two being Greece tragic-comedy and Indian Sanskrit Opera. During the Tang Dynasty, the Emperor Taizong established an opera school named Liyuan, Pear Garden; that is why the performers of Chinese opera were regarded as "disciples of the pear garden". Since the Yuan Dynasty, it became a traditional art form which was favored by emperors and court officials. During the Qing Dynasty, it started to gain popularity among more people including common civilians, with performances being appreciated in tearooms, restaurants, and even on makeshift stages.

Evolved from folk songs, dances, antimasque, and distinctive dialectical music in particular, Chinese opera turned to the combination of music, art and literature as the unique stage performance. The opera also features the special melodies, accompanied by traditional musical instruments such as Erhu, gong, and lute. The beautifully written dialogues with high literary value even promoted the advance of literary styles, such as Zaju in the Yuan Dynasty. For Chinese, especially senior folks, listening to Chinese opera is a real enjoyment.

One of the highlights of Chinese opera is facial make-up which requires distinctive painting techniques that may find its origin from ancient religions and dance, with exaggerated designs painted on each performer's face to represent a character's personality, role, and fate. Normally, a red face symbolizes honesty and bravery; a black face embodies valor; yellow and white faces, disloyalty; and golden and silver faces, mystery. Lines also can be symbolic. For instance, a face can be painted with all white on his face or just around the nose. Generally speaking, the larger the white area painted, the more sinister the character is.

Among everything, the performers impress the audience by amazing acrobatics such as spraying fire out of their mouths or spurting while squatting to act as a dwarf.

Today, there are approximately 300 regional operas after the evolvement of over 800 years. Kun opera, originated around Jiangsu Province, is a representative ancient opera featuring gentleness and clearness which contribute to its status as World Oral and Intangible Heritages. Qinqiang opera from Shaanxi is remarkable for its loudness and wildness, and Yu opera, Yue opera, and Huangmei Opera are all very popular among folks. But all in all, Beijing Opera is definitely the best-known Chinese opera style which was developed through the combining features of these regional styles[①].

• Shadow Play

Shadow play, which appeared at the modern Shaanxi Province during the Western Han Dynasty some 2, 000 years ago, is regarded as the earliest ancestor of modern cinema and cartoon. It was reserved from the ancient times till today with its unique artistic value.

The characters, or silhouette made of hard paper, buffalo and donkey hide, are manipulated by performers who sing at the same time to tell the story behind the screen. Since the figure is projected on a white screen, this artistic effect is determined by multiple elements such as light, screen, music, singing and puppetry etc.

The appearance of shadow play is believed to be associated with Emperor Wu of Western Han Dynasty who was in deep sorrow because of the death of his beloved concubine. To relieve the emperor from the grief, one of his Minister made the concubine's shadow by cotton and silk. Later on, the shadow developed into a complete play during the Tang Dynasty, reaching the prime time during the Qing Dynasty in Hebei Province.

The shadow is normally made of clean cowhide or donkey skin with hair removed and colored by five pure watercolors of red, yellow, green, pale green and black. After chemical treatment, the shadow is endowed with transparent color on screen, bestowing the play a great charm. What's more, the shadows are exquisitely carved part by part, making it actually an art.

---

① http: //www. travelchinaguide. com/intro/arts/chinese-opera. htm

Generally speaking, every shadow is composed of 11 parts including head, two body parts, two legs, two upper arms and lower arms as well as two hands. Drawn by the performers through controlling bars and threads, the shadow can do various kinds of vivid movements. It is not an easy job to be a capable shadow play performer, since shadow play demands for high performing skills. Apart from manipulating three or four players at a time, performers should follow the tempo and musical accompany as well as do the part of dialogue and singing. Because of the progress of modern audio-visual media, shadow play can not be popular as it used to be. But as a high valuable cultural heritage in Chinese art field, it should be protected from going extinct.

● Acrobatics

Chinese Acrobatics is the performance that requires particular balance, agility and coordination, which can be found in many performing arts and sports such as circus, ballet and gymnastics, and many other athletic activities like Wushu and diving are highly associated with acrobatics as well. The universally recognized juggling in Chinese acrobatics are pagoda of bowls and wire walking etc, oral stunts being another different form.

With a long history of more than 2, 000 years, acrobatics can be traced to the Warring States Period with rudiments of acrobatics. By the time of Han Dynasty, the acrobatics art developed further and there arose stage performances with music accompaniment. Some of the representative activities were "pole climbing", "role walking", "fish turned into dragon", and "five tables", etc. Entering Tang Dynasty, the most flourishing period in ancient China, the number of acrobats was immensely on the increase and the performers' skills gained substantial improvement, the proof being the Dunhuang Mural Paintings in which images of acrobatic and circus performances were found.

Generally speaking, the ancient acrobatics derived from people's daily life and work. Labor tools such as tridents and wicker, coupled with life utilities like tables, chairs and bowl were commonly employed in performances. On important occasions of festivals, people often performed "flying trident", "balance on chair", "jar tricks" and "hoop diving" at the market places or in the street of town. "Lion dance" can be also viewed as a simplified form of Chinese acrobatics.

Characteristic style has been shaped during the long course of its development. For instance, it values the training of actors' waist, leg and head feats. The modern acrobatics, however, aims at creating impressive stage effect with the combination of harmonious musical accompaniment, props and lighting[1].

(2) Folk Entertainment of Chinese Ethnic Minorities

①Mongol Nationality

Mongolian wrestling, horse-racing and archery are the three most important manly skills for Chinese Mongolian ethnic group.

● Bokh (Mongolian Wrestling)

Bökh, Mongolian wrestling, is a conventional sport for Chinese Mongolian ethnic group living in grassland regions. Meaning "strength, solidarity and durability" in Mongolian, "Bökh" is an indispensable activity for important occasions particularly in sacrificial rituals and the Nadam Festival.

Bökh, an ancient sport, was originally regarded as a military sport mainly for strength, stamina and skills training. In the Yuan Dynasty, the game was greatly favored by the emperors, and during the important feasts, wrestlers were invited for the creation of entertainment atmosphere. Wrestling was also a significant activity for distinguishing the candidate rankings in imperial martial exams. Outstanding wrestlers were highly respected entitled with great honor.

Today, Bökh is still popular across Inner Mongolia Autonomous Region. But compared with past form, it is held in a rather simple and solemn manner. The number of wresters should be in even, ranging from several to thousand. When the match begins, wrestlers wave their strong arms, dancing into the competition terrain by imitation of the movements of lions, deer

---

① http://www.topchinatravel.com/china-guide/acrobatics.htm

and eagles etc.

As to the match rules, there's no time limit for the match and no weight limit for the participants. A wrestler loses when he touches the ground with any part above his knees. In general, this sport requires good coordination between waist and leg movements, and a wrestler is supposed to completely display both his strength and skills in the competition.

● Horse-Racing

In Inner Mongolia Autonomous Region, good horses and skillful horse-riders have always enjoyed high reputation since horse-racing has long been viewed as the favorite sports cherished by the herdsmen in this area.

The game is roughly divided as two types: namely, trotting-horse racing and galloping-horse racing. As to the former, it is a competition of stamina and steadiness. The horse, equipped with a full set of saddles and proper-sized horseshoes, is required to amble forward with different kinds of postures. For instance, it moves along using both legs on one side alternately with both on the other. The one gaining the highest score from the referees wins the competition.

The latter competes for speed and stamina, with the winner being the first to reach the destination. To ease the load of the horse, the galloping horses are generally not installed with saddle or simply with light saddle. Sporting splendid colorful costumes with flying red and green straps on their head, the teenage male riders will display their vigor and valiancy through the match. Compared with the trotting-horse race, the average 30 kilometer competition attracts more participants. Once the competition starts, the riders would spring onto the horse like a flash and bolt forward, leaving the audience gamboling and cheering for them.

According to the custom, the winning horses would be honored after the competition. Standing in sequence according to their performance, the horses are commended with a horse-praising poem chanted by some respectable seniors which is followed by splashing milk wine or fresh milk on the champion horse. Apart from the above mentioned two traditional horse-racing forms, new matches such as the steeplechase have also emerged, greatly enriching and vivifying this sports activity.

• Archery

Archery constitutes another Mongolian traditional sport. Legends had it that the great archer named Erekhe Mergen saved people from a drought by shooting down six suns. While few modern people are capable of shooting well on horseback, many just practice traditional archery on foot. Each year during the July traditional sports festival, the Nadam Festival, the participants compete at horse-racing, wrestling and archery.

Currently, the sport has three main divisions based on regional styles, namely Buryat style, Uryankhai style and Khalkha style respectively which shoot different targets from various distances, ranging from 35 to 75 meters. Buryat and Khalkha archery have many women competitors while Uryankhai archers are normally men. Another feature of the game is its special way which resembles singing as an indication of each competitor's scores.

Every bow, the instrument of the traditional game, is of different style in various size and draw-weight to suit men, women and children, which are made in traditional fashion by using wood, sheep's horn and sinew.

②Korean Nationality

• Tiaoban/The See-saw Jumping

The Korean nationality excels with sportsmanship, with the see-saw and swing being the favorite traditional folk sports among Koreans, females in particular.

The see-saw jumping is considered an athletic event which is popular in the Yanbian Korean Autonomous Prefecture, Jilin Province, as well as in other areas inhabited by Chinese citizens of the Korean nationality. Normally, the competition is held on traditional festivals such as the Lantern Festival, Dragon Boat Festival, and Mid-Autumn Festival etc.

A standard see-saw is about 6 – meter long, 40 – centimeter wide and 5 – centimeter thick, usually made of white ash, a kind of hard wood with flexibility. With a fulcrum, one person stands at each end of the see-saw, springing up in turn and using leverage to thrust the counterpart into the air. During the game, participants try to jump increasingly higher while even performing acrobatics in mid-air. An acrobat may jump into the air to land upright on the see-saw, stooping in the air with legs outstretched before landing on the see-saw with upright stand or throw her chest towards the sky, with arms outstretched and legs wide apart before landing. The players commit to the game with self-coordination and mutual cooperation, yelling in turn to encourage themselves.

See-saw competitions are different with various judging standard concerning height, creativity and skill. As to height, the participant who jumps the highest is the winner. Or in the match, the players employ instruments such as hoops and garlands while jumping to display their skills and the one who exhibit the most standard, difficult and graceful moves is the winner. Recently, the skills are taken into consideration in the height competition. Therefore, besides courage, the more proficient see-saw acrobat has to outdo a competitor in both creativity and skill. Needless to say, watching the see-saw competition is a great enjoyable and excitement to the spectators.

As a traditional folk exercise, the see-saw jumping is widely loved by ethnic Koreans who even hold the belief that "A girl who is not a good see-saw jumper may suffer hard labor when giving birth to a baby".

● Qiuqian/Swing

Enjoying a long history, swinging is another favorite event featuring aesthetics and amplitude among Chinese women of the Korean nationality.

A swing is typically hung on ropes from a horizontal branch, with a bell, drum or ribbon hung at a higher point in the amplitude of the swing. A player tries to swing until reaching the target to win the cheers and applause from the crowd. Wearing colorful dresses, the women swing back and forth, soaring like beautiful butterflies with the background of blue sky and green grass.

Apart from being a spectacular game, swinging competitions are held during certain festivals such as the Dragon Boat Festival and Korean women typically dress in festive costumes to participate in the contests. There are two types of matches, one being the height competition and the other being the endurance competition, in which a performer tries to kick as many times as possible a bell, drum or ribbon, and the most frequent kicker will be recognized as the champion.

Today, swinging is officially competed in the National Traditional Games of Ethnic Minorities of the People's Republic of China, occupying a special place in the arena of traditional Chinese ethnic sports[①].

③Tibetan Nationality

• Yak Racing

Yak racing is a traditional sport of the Tibetans which features danger and excitement, a game that reflects Tibetans' pursuit for happiness.

Living typically in the high and cold pastures, the yaks are able to walk on the steep and cliffy mountains or the snow slopes but they are not good at long speed running. In the race, the yaks might shoulder and fight each other due to their wildness; or they might leap and kick backwardly. Besides, joyful uncertainty can be added when some yaks are startled by the loud cheers from the spectators, and they might refuse to run and act as if they want to withdraw from the game.

Wangguo Festival, the traditional festival of the Tibetans, is usually a good occasion to have the yak race, which used to be held on 25, November but now is celebrated in middle summer before autumn harvest. Lhasa welcomes the experienced herdsmen with the bad-tempered yaks coming from different neighboring areas.

In the past half century, the game has developed considerably with the race being lengthened to 2, 000 meters. On the very day of the competition, both the herdsmen and the yaks are dressed up to take part in the annual yak racing. For the yak, it has red tassels on the head, colorful silk on the horns, gaily-colored ribbons on the ears and the fan-shaped Tibetan patterns on the tail, all symbolizing luck and fortune. The winning yak will be famous in the locals, enjoying special treatment from his master who will also be greatly honored by the local masses upon returning hometown.

---

① http://english. chinese. cn/chineseculture/article/2011 − 07/14/content_ 338138. htm

● Gesar Epic

In history, the status of Epic of King Gesar to Tibetans is what the Il-iad to the Greeks and the King Arthur to the medieval Europeans. This great works is deeply rooted in Tibetan folklore culture passing orally from generation to generation, with its written versions being traced back to 1716 when the Qing Emperor ordered to have it translated from Tibetan. The epic has been regarded as the Orient's Homeric Epic, the longest literary work in the world with over 120 volumes and 20 million words in more than 1 million verses.

The epic narrates the heroic achievements of Gesar, the fearless lord of the legendary kingdom of Ling, who waged war against the nearby King-dom. With Distinct Tibetan style, the epic was believed to be traced back to the time of the second Buddhism transmission to Tibet. Gesar is said to be able to subdue his formidable enemies, conquer monsters, help the poor, govern the strong, which benefits all the people.

Owing to the great efforts of generations of folk artists, the popularity and immortality of The Life of King Gesar was achieved, and their works is the exemplification of the great wisdom and spirits of the masses initia-tion. With intelligence and artistic talents, they have made substantial con-tributions to Tibetan cultural undertaking, which is worth to be remembered by people and the descendants.

Under the influence of the basic tenets of Buddhist reincarnation and the Lamaist Living Buddhas principle of the traditional Tibetan culture, the bards don't pass down their legacy from master to apprentice, or from father to son, believing that the performing skill lies in the inspiration of the gods, not by inheritance or acquisition. Therefore, the presence of the nar-rating artists is related with the reincarnation of a figure having mysterious connections with King Gesar.

In the hometown of Gesar, bards are invited to sing Gesar on impor-tant occasions such as weddings and birthday celebrations, and even the shorter pieces last for hours while longer versions persist several days, which requires superb memory of the narrator to recite the contents by chapters. Besides, local people find great enjoyment in telling stories about Gesar in their leisure time[1].

• Guozhuang Dance

Guozhuang means singing and dancing in a circle, homophonic with *Guozhuo* in Tibetan language. Originated from Tibetan campfire dances, the dance has become an indispensable part of life for the Tibetan ethnic group.

Guozhuang can be roughly divided as three kinds: Temple *Guozhuang*, Farm *Guozhuang* and Pastoral *Guozhuang*.

The Temple *Guozhuang* is performed with strong religious implications in temples or monasteries. It is also practiced for commemorating the Living Buddha, a way to express their gratitude for their expected bliss in their afterlife.

The Farm*Guozhuang* consists of singing, and quick singing and dancing, with the tempo being subdivided into slow, medium and quick. When the performance begins, males and females stand in circles respectively, singing in rotation while swaying and stamping their feet. The singing came to an end by a shout of "Ya!", followed by quickened steps which stop at an exuberant allegro.

The Pastoral *Guozhuang* is similar as farm *Guozhuang*, which differs in movement. In the former, the dancers leap while waving their hands in front of their chests and step forward before turning left or right, with their hands and feet moving in the same direction to achieve an impressive effect.

The Farm Guozhuang is popular in Qamdo, eastern Tibet, while the Pastoral Guozhuang is popular in the vast pasture land of Damxung, Heihe and Sog Xian.

In general, the dancing movements are agile and vigorous, particularly those of the males, resembling an eagle's wings-spreading, hopping and soaring. Moving in a circle, the dancers sway their hands frontward and

---

[1] https: //tibettalk. wordpress. com/2007/08/10/the-legendary-epic-of-king-gesar/

backward, keeping beats of their steps until late at night.

The folk performance values postures and expression of emotion. The verses for one song read: " Oh snow-capped mountains, make way for us. We fly with wings spread. Oh rivers, make way for us. We stride with huge steps", a reflection of Tibetans' bravery and boldness.

● Ache Lhamo

Ache Lhamo or Lhamo, Fairy in Tibetan, is the traditional Tibetan opera. Drupthok Thangthong Gyalpo, a monk in the 14th century, organized the first dramatic performance to raise fund to build bridges for the transportation improvement to facilitate pilgrimage. Through the development of several centuries, it gained popularity in the region and was held on various festive occasions such as Shoton, in which professional and amateur troupes are summoned to Lhasa to entertain the Dalai Lama and monks in Potala, Drepung or Norbulingka.

The traditional drama is a combination of dances, chants and songs, nourished by Buddhist preach and local history. A Tibetan opera performance normally follows certain procedures. Each performance starts with the stage purification and a blessing to the God. Then it follows a summary of the story in verse sung by a narrator before the performers' dancing and singing. The performance ends with a ritual of blessing.

Mask, "ba" in Tibetan, is the highlight of Lhamo which is developed from the masks worn by primitive mediumistic dancers and sorcerers at temples to drive away ghosts. The grand Tibetan opera performed to commemorate Songtsam Gambo, a hero once reigned over ancient Tibet, is said to be the earliest documentation of Tibetan opera masks, which chiefly features historical figures, mythological characters, immortals, ghosts and animals.

The masks differ in terms of the materials, such as wood sculpture, bronze image, paperboard, leather, cloth and so on. Usually on the forehead of the mask there is a motif of the Sun and Moon. The masks are generally classified into three categories based on their representative characters. The first is called "wenba", fishermen or hunters, which is viewed as the most important mask type in Tibetan opera. They come in white and blue colors. The former, the crude one popular in the early days of the Tibetan opera, is made of white fleece in simple structures. The latter is slightly bigger than the white one, which is usually exquisitely painted and decorated.

The second category is human masks, with different colors indicating different character features. Masks in this type are commonly in bright colors to form sharp contrast with one another. For instance, a red mask refers to the King; a green, the queen; a yellow, lamas and deities, etc. The third category is animal masks, such as goat, ox, horse and tiger etc, and each animal symbolizes a divine figure, normally used in lion dances and yak dances performed by Tibetan opera troupes in Ganzi, Sichuan Province.

In a sense, Tibetan opera mask is a reflection of the folk customs and religious beliefs, even living environment of Tibetans. With the progress of times, the ghost and god worshiping nature of the mask has faded, with emphasis being laid on its artistic and entertainment qualities. The masks, ultimately has evolved into the most phenomenal opera handicrafts in Tibetan culture①.

④Zhuang Nationality

• Throwing Embroidered Ball

Throwing embroidered ball is a traditional game of the Zhuangs in Guangxi Autonomous Region. But interestingly, the ball originally was a bronze weapon thrown in the wars and hunting. Later on, it was replaced by an embroidered bag for folks to throw in the entertainment. In the Song dynasty, it became a love symbol between the youth of the Zhuangs, which is now still prevailing in the areas of Guangxi province. During the traditional festivals like the Spring Festival, the Third Day of the Third Moon and the Mid-Autumn Festival etc. , the youth of the Zhuangs will attend the singing party and they are divided into two sides: males and females. Then they start to sing antiphonally, asking questions in the form of songs concerning various topics of agricultural problems to personal feelings. One side asks,

---

① http: //traditions. cultural-china. com/en/16Traditions323. html

and the other side answers. When the party progresses to the most exciting moment, the girls begin to swing the balls before throwing them to their favored boys, who are expected to catch the ball with quick reactions. If the boy also likes the girl, he can tie gifts to the ball and throw it back. The two continues to sing to express their feelings or date in pairs off the party.

In recent years, new competition rules have been carried out and it is turned into a traditional duel sport.

⑤Kazaks and Tajiks

• Sheep-snatching

Sheep-snatching is a traditional sport among Kazaks and Tajiks, held specifically on holidays or during festive gatherings. The sport is fiercely competitive, depending greatly on the riders' bravery and horsemanship.

There are basically three forms of the sport: team work, one-on-one and free snatching. For the first form, the participants are classified into a group of approximately ten people. Upon the order of the referee, the horse riders will run as fast as they can, but the faster and more skillful rider will catch the sheep and hold it under the stirrup tread or carry it on his back, running again to prevent others from chasing and snatching it. After repeated snatching for several rounds, the team that places the sheep to the designated place first will be the winner.

As to the second form, each team shall have a representative to snatch the sheep from each other, or a third person holds the sheep for the two riders to snatch upon his order. Any of the two who gets the sheep first is the winner. The last form is free snatching, in which all riders compete for the sheep together.

Then the winner, with trophy in arms, shall bolt out of the ground and cast the sheep by the yurt doorway, with his horse neighing and the audiences cheering, witnessing the end of the contest. The snatched sheep is believed to bring fortune to the household where it is placed. Finally, the people will cook the sheep for celebration and everyone can enjoy a bite.

⑥Miao Nationality

• Climbing a Ladder of Knives

Climbing a ladder of knives is the customary performance of the Miaos, a unique sport game held on the festival occasions or the important days to worship the ancestors or the gods.

Generally, the game is held three times annually: the first month of the lunar year, on the eighth day of the fourth month and the "autumn harvest". Every game has its special meaning. The game on the fifteenth of the first month intends to send off the old and welcome the new, praying for fortune and prosperity. The game on the eighth of the fourth month aims to worship the courageous heroes. The event held on the "autumn harvest festival" celebrates the harvest and expresses people's happiness. Before the game starts, people taking part in the rituals would pronounce the incantation around the wood post, doing the rituals led by the leader. Then, the man of the Miaos begins to climb the ladder of knives from the bottom step by step to the top to exhibit his unique skills and blows the horn to declare the success of the rituals.

3. Western Folk Entertainment

(1) Europe
①Spain
● Bull fighting

Bull fighting is regarded as the symbol of Spanish folk culture which can be traced back to 711 A. D. , with the first bullfight taking place to celebrate the crowning of King Alfonso VIII. Nowadays, it is said that the total sum of bullfight spectators in Spain reaches one million every year.

Primarily an aristocratic sport held on horseback, bull fighting was banned by King Felipe V, believing it to be a bad example for the public. However, average citizens picked it up and accepted it as a popular game. Since they could not afford horses, they changed the game by dodging the bulls on foot unarmed around 1724.

In a typical bullfight, firstly the bull is let into the ring. Then, the assistant fighter waves a bright yellow and magenta cape in front of the bull, prompting it to charge. The Matador, the chief bullfighter, watches what happens to observe the bull's qualities and mood before taking over the job.

Then a trumpet is sounded and several fighters called Picadores thrust spears into the bull for almost ten minutes to weaken the bull. Another trumpet is sounded and the Matador removes his black winged hat and dedicates the death of the bull to the crowd before beginning his faena.

The faena is the most exciting part of the fight for the matador to demonstrate his courage and wisdom, with the help of instrument like a muleta, a piece of thick crimson cloth draped over a short stick, which is held in front of the matador to make the bull charge and an espada, the killing sword.

Simply speaking, the bullfight is dance with death since one wrong move would result in the Matador's being impaled by the bull horns. But despite the danger, it is the Matador's responsibility to make the performance dramatic and enjoyable for the audience. The faena persists until the Matador has displayed his power over the animal. Once this is achieved the bull is on the edge of being killed.

The matador stands some ten feet from the bull, keeping arousing the bull's focus on the muleta. Then, the matador attacks, pushing the espada over the horns and deep between the shoulder blades. If the sword goes into the hilt, it is an estocada, mostly resulting in the bull dropping immediately to its knees and dying. But if the bull fails to die, the matador may take the descabello, a sword with a short cross piece at the end, to stab into the bull's neck to sever the spinal cord. Finally, the fight comes to an end.

After the fight, the audiences usually demand the matador be awarded the trophies, one or two ears from the bull, the tail or the hoof, by waving white handkerchiefs, which continues after the trophies have been presented, encouraging the matador to throw his booty into the crowds who in return hurl flowers to the heroic bull fighter[1].

● Flamenco

---

[1]   http: //www. spain-info. com/Culture/bullfighting. htm

Flamenco is a folk art emerged in Southern Spain over 200 years ago. As a combination of songs, dances and guitar mixed with improvised rhythms, it has wide themes ranging from stories, history to politics and romance, with the tragic lyrics and tone representing the hardships that the gypsies went through from whom it originated.

Flamenco primarily embraces three forms: Cante, the song, Baile, the dance, and Guitarra, guitar playing, the first being the core. In other words, the singers take important role with the guitar accompaniment. Entering modern society, flamenco has developed into a separate form of art, mixed with jazz, blues and pop music. Flamenco dance is characteristic of rhythm and complicated footwork, the upper body showing grace and posture.

Generally, there are two major styles in Flamenco: "jondo", a reflection of the outcry of oppressed people; and "chico", which presents happy, light and humorous atmosphere. Typically, flamenco intends to have the effect of "duende": demon or elf, a state of emotional involvement, profound group communication between musicians, dancers and audiences.

②Russia

● Russian Folk Dance

The number of Russian folk dances can hardly be counted. Even though having a great variety of names, all these various dances share some common features: they are movements with daring and special cheerfulness, a combination of modesty, simplicity with dignity.

Stage costume is an indispensable element of folk dance performance which was created on the basis of the folk dress but more comfortable to wear. The Russian folk dress is colorfully abundant in decorations and embroidery. Every local costume is unique in the cut of the sarafan, peasant pinafore dress, shape of the headdress, and specific ornament patterns. Girls used to spend several years in the preparation of festive clothes for themselves: beautify the sarafan and kokoshnik with ornaments and gems and embroider shirts and jackets. An elaborate costume is regarded as a piece of art with invaluable price inherited by daughters from their mothers.

Take an ancient dance, Russian round dance, for example, it can be performed by people of all ages: maidens and women, young men and old men. And it can be conducted in various places such as rivers, lakes, meadows, country churchyards, forests, cemeteries, gardens and yards etc. Some places were used for festive round dances while some are suitable for common round dances.

In terms of gender characters, women's dances reflect female features such as fluidity, softness, and stateliness whereas men's dances display courage, agility and wit.

● Chess

Chess in Russia, introduced from the Arabic East, can be traced back to over 1, 000 years ago to the Byliny, the ancient heroic poem period. In Russia, Chess is regarded as a noble profession favored by all classes, with many short stories and poetry written about the game.

Since the 1920s, Chess has also been viewed as a training field for Russian political life and talented youth are instructed by professional coaches to prepare them for the life of the elites in Russian society. Owing to state sponsorship, it has become a national sport in which Russia dominates the entire globe. Being the permanent treasure, chess is a reflection of Russian cultural supremacy.

③The United Kingdom

● Horse Racing and Betting

Britain modern horse racing finds its origin to Roman times, and in the 12th century, horse racing appeared on public holidays at Smithfield in London, and at Chester, records were made for Shrove Tuesday races.

During the reign of James I, horse racing firstly appeared under royal patronage, with a royal palace built near Newsmarket. The monarch's passion promoted the popularity of the game in Britain and public races were soon set up all over England. Many of the events were held at Bell Courses since the award for most races was usually a silver bell.

Meanwhile, the royal support results in the rapid development of race-horse breeding in England, with stallions mainly imported from Arab, the forefathers of the thoroughbred racehorses which compete in modern races.

Around the middle of the 18th century, horse racing became the first regulated sport in Britain. Gradually, the emphasis on stamina was taken place by racing younger horses over shorter distances. The late 18th century witnessed the establishment of the Classic races which are held till today.

In the 19th century, horse racing became an annual sport watched by millions of audiences due to the improved transportation and other technological innovations, and a remarkable increase appeared in the volume of horse racing betting.

In the 20th century, horse racing was one of the few sports that continued during both world wars. In 1961, betting away from racecourses was legalized, and the high street betting shop was born as a great contributor to the volume of betting turnover.

In the 1950s and 1960s, horse racing became a regularly televised sport. Even today, horse racing is one of the sports with most audiences, only secondary to football[1].

• English Country Dance

English country dance, a social folk dance originated in Renaissance England, was popular until the early 19th century in certain places of Europe, the American colonies and the United States. As the ancestor of several other folk dances such as contra and square dance, English country dance was revived in the early 20th century as the product of English folk revival, and is performed today chiefly in North America and Britain.

In a sense, English country dance share some features with other English folk dances, such as morris and sword dancing to embody a true "country" origin. Meanwhile, it somewhat resembles the courtly dances of Continental Europe, especially those of Renaissance Italy. Therefore, English country dance is generally viewed as the product of some synthesis of the above mentioned dance forms.

The typical choreography requires the interactions between partners and

---

[1] http://www.betref.co.uk/blog/58/amob17/history-of-british-horse-racing/

between couples in a set, commonly two or three, but sometimes four, who interact during a single progression. Simply speaking, English country dances are longways and progressive, with multiple sets of couples standing two long lines, along which couples dance from the beginning to the end to be alternated to new partners, conducting the series of steps repetitively. Or the dances can be finite and non-progressive, with a set forming an independent unit within which each couple retains their original positions.

By the early 19th century, new dance forms from the Continent, such as the quadrille and waltz, became increasingly popular in England and America. As a result, English country dance declined, and by 1830 it almost vanished from society ballrooms.

In the 1930s, the first new English country dances were composed. However, the publication of Maggot Pie in 1932, the first collection of modern English country dances, was controversial in the relative community. Only in the late 20th century did modern compositions gain full acceptance.

④France

● Tour de France

The Tour de France is an annual multiple-stage bicycle race primarily held in France, while also occasionally making passes through neighboring countries. The activity originally appealed not just for the sportive distance and its demands but to play to a wish for national unity, an urge to what Maurice Barrès called the France " of earth and deaths" or what Georges Vigarello called "the image of a France united by its earth. "

The race has been held annually since 1903 except for being stopped during the two World Wars. As the Tour gained prominence, the race was lengthened and its reach began to extend globally, with riders coming from all over the world.

The Tour is important for French citizens, with millions of spectators lining the route, and some even camped for a week just to get the best view. Crowds flank and cheer along the course with great enthusiasm, making it a truly national festival.

（2）North America

①America

● Baseball

Baseball is regarded by Americans as "the national pastime" which is played by many since childhood. Unlike football and basketball, baseball can be enjoyed by people of average height and weight.

Baseball originated before the American Civil War (1861 – 1865) as rounders, a humble game played on sandlots. Early players of the game transformed it to include skills and mental judgment that similar to the game of cricket in England. In particular, scoring and record-keeping make the game serious.

Baseball has had a great impact on popular culture, with dozens of English-language idioms derived from baseball. And the baseball cap has become an extremely fashion item.

Baseball has inspired many works of art and entertainment, including relative poems, movies, and various video games.

Baseball is also the source of new cultural forms. For instance, baseball cards were introduced in the late 19th century as trade cards. The 1930s witnessed the popularization of the modern style of baseball card, with a player photograph accompanied on the rear by statistics and biographical data①.

● Crossword Puzzles

Crossword puzzles are one of the world's most popular word games, which found the origination in England during the 19th century. In the United States, the puzzle developed into a serious adult pastime, with numerous folks addicted to the game.

Typically, the crossword features word squares, hidden words and connect-the-dots exercises. However, the first well-known crossword puzzle, created by Arthur Wynne for the eight-page comics section of the New York World was a sketch of a diamond-shaped grid without black squares.

---

① http：//en. wikipedia. org/wiki/Baseball

Crossword grids in most North American publications are characteristic of solid areas of white squares. Grids are supposed to be symmetrical. Therefore, the pattern will be the same when looked upside down.

Americans are truly fond of this entertainment, with crossword puzzles appeared considerably in print publications like newspapers and magazines as well as online.

• Talk Show

One of the American's greatest entertainments is enjoying TV programs, among which Talk Show is undoubtedly the typically favored activity. The first U. S. talk show was broadcasted on radio in 1921 in Springfield, Massachusetts. During the 1920s, the radio networks had as many as 21 talking programs, with the topics covering different areas such as public affairs, religion and housekeeping, which were immensely welcomed by audience to gain an insight into a more glamorous and exciting world.

Then gradually, the one-way discussions evolved into more interactive formats. For instance, people like to watch "man on the street" interviews, prompting many imitating programs.

The major reason for American folks to be enthusiastic about the talk show was that it required audience involvement, encouraging common people to participate by challenging the experts. Featuring the real-life spontaneity, folks even enjoy watching the embarrassing moments for the hosts under spotlight, and the sharp contrast between the impressive unknown amateur and the awkward famous celebrity.

②Canada

• Sports

Canadians are the people who are passionate about various sports. Due to the typical freezing weather of Canada, different kinds of ice sports are the most popular entertainment Canadians value, invented by Canadians or with the roots traced to Canada.

Ice hockey, simply referred to as "hockey", is Canada's most popular spectator sport, as well as the Canada's official national winter sport. Lacrosse, a sport with indigenous origins, is Canada's most traditional and official summer sport.

Football, or soccer, is the most played sport in Canada with all demographics, such as ethnic origin, ages and genders. Other popular team sports include curling, street hockey, cricket, rugby and softball. Popular individual sports include auto racing, boxing, karate, kickboxing, hunting, fishing, cycling, golf, ultimate frisbee, hiking, horse racing, ice skating, skiing, snowboarding, swimming, triathlon, water sports, and several forms of wrestling[1].

4. Comparisons

From the perspective of research, entertainments and sports is regarded as an essential part of culture, which can be analyzed in the following aspects:

(1) Philosophical Basis

Chinese traditional sports is rooted in the concept of harmony between nature and humanity, which can be typically reflected in notions such as Yin and Yang, ideas used to describe how apparently opposite or contrary forces are actually complementary, interconnected and interdependent in the natural world, and how they influence each other as they interrelate to one another. It is the central principle of different forms of Chinese martial arts and exercise, such as *baguazhang*, *taijiquan* (t'ai chi), and *qigong* (Chi Kung). What's more, in Taoist metaphysics, distinctions between good and bad, along with other dichotomous moral judgments, are perceptual, not real; so, the duality of yin and yang is an indivisible whole.

However, western entertainments and games are developed under the belief of external forces and analysis which focus on the struggle between human and nature. Western sports culture is originated from ancient Greece and Rome. It develops in the capitalist industrial revolution of market econo-

---

① https://prezi.com/1vgxppk25dgy/canada/

my which advocates the philosophy of competition and adventure, attaching great importance to fitness coupled with external and internal unification. Olympic sports culture is the product of western values such as respect, peace, friendship, unity and fair play, favoring man's comprehensive development as a product of the western industrial civilization.

(2) Medical Basis

To Chinese, the purpose of entertainments and sports is primarily *yangsheng*, nourishing life. Accordingly, there are various self-cultivation practices for personal health and longevity.

In the view of Chinese traditional medicine, a person's life is sustained by three principles, namely *jing*, *qi*, and *shen*. *Jing* is associated with reproductive energy. *Qi* is a complex concept referring to air and breath-the energy constituting everything in the universe. In the practice of *yangsheng* it retains these connotations while also stresses the energy that animates and sustains living things. *Shen* is both spiritual and mental vitality.

It is believed that every individual is born with *jing* and *qi*, both of which disperse with age. Longevity requires maintaining or restoring one's original allotment of *qi*. *Shen*, unlike *jing* and *qi*, is not allotted at birth but must be cultivated throughout life by involvement in different kinds of activities. As the three treasures dissipate or become out of balance, one's health declines. Physical exercises and meditative, medicinal, and dietary practices integrate body and mind, thus enhancing the circulation of *qi*, replenishing the three treasures, so as to extend and nourish life.

In contrast, the medicine basis of western entertainments and sports is the combination of aspects such as scientific experiment, anatomy, physiology and modern medicine. Meanwhile, with the rapid development of modern western material civilization, people are inclined to be tired of spiritual decadence of modern social life and need higher levels of physical and mental experience to alleviate the adverse effects brought by western high technology.

(3) Aesthetic Basis

Judging from perspective of aesthetics, we find that Chinese traditional sports value rhythm, connotation, harmony as well as abstract and implicit beauty while western sports admire the beauty of masculine strength, speed, external and physical beauty. Therefore, the pursuit of "faster, higher, stronger" leads people to pay attention to the features of endurance and flexibility.

In other word, Chinese entertainment culture is to pursue static beauty whereas the western traditional culture is a dynamic one which in turn determines the substantial differences of Chinese and western sports form and values. The former favors the cultivation of man's inner temperament, character and spirit of accomplishment, making the Chinese traditional sports values shows obvious personality tendency. But the latter stresses self-challenges and endless breakthroughs of new records and limits.

In sum, with the increasingly social development and more frequent international communication, the differences are bound to be insignificant with the two complementing each other to achieve common prosperity.

References

Books:

(1) 董晓萍，《全球化与民俗保护》，北京：高等教育出版社 2007 年版。

(2) 何其亮、张晔，《英释中国传统文化》，杭州：浙江大学出版社 2006 年版。

(3) 孟慧英，《西方民俗学史》，北京：中国社会科学出版社 2006 年版。

(4) 彭家海，《西方文化引论》，武汉：华中师范大学出版社 2009 年版。

(5) 汪德华，《中国与英美国家习俗文化比较》，杭州：浙江大学出版社 2011 年版。

(6) 张立玉，《英汉国俗语义差异性探究》，《中南民族大学学报》（社科版）2014 年第 5 期。

(7) 王娟，《民俗学概论》，北京：北京大学出版社 2011 年版。

(8) 张立玉，《中西语义学研究发展探究》，《湖北社会科学》2011 年第 2 期。

(9) 王祥云，《中西方传统文化比较》，郑州：河南人民出版社 2005 年版。

(10) 杨英杰，《中外民俗》，天津：南开大学出版社 2006 年版。

(11) 钟敬文，《民俗学概论》，上海：上海义艺出版社 1998 年版。

(12) Barbro Klein, "Folklore", in *International Encyclopedia of the Social and Behavioral Sciences*, Volume 8. New York：Elsevier, 2001.

(13) Ching Julia, *Chinese Religions*, New York：Orbis Books, 1993.

(14) Clarke Alison J, "Maternity and Materiality：Becoming a Mother in Consumer Culture", in Janelle S. Taylor, Linda L. Layne and Danielle F. Wozniak, eds. *Consuming Motherhood*, New Jersey：Rutgers Universi-

ty Press, 2004.

(15) Colin Blakemore and Shelia Jennett, "Funeral Practices: Cultural Variation", in *The Oxford Companion to the Body*, Oxford: Oxford University
Press, 2001.

(16) Crouch Mira and Lenore Manderson, *New Motherhood: Cultural and Personal Transitions in the 1980s*, New York: Gordon and Breach Science
Publishers, 1993.

(17) Davies D J, *Death, Ritual and Belief: The Rhetoric of Funeral Rites*,
London: Cassell, 1997.

(18) Dorothy Noyes, "Folklore", in Adam Kuper and Jessica Kuper, eds. *The
Social Science Encyclopedia*, 3rd edition, New York: Routledge, 2004.

(19) Ellis Clyde, "American Indian and Christianity", in *Oklahoma Historical
Society's Encyclopedia of Oklahoma History and Culture*, Retrieved 25
May 2013. http: //digital. library. okstate. edu/ encyclopedia.

(20) Eileen Fischer and Brenda Gainer, "Baby Showers: A Rite of Passage in
Transition", in *NA - Advances in Consumer Research*, Volume 20, 1993.

(21) Gelis Jacques, *History of Childbirth: Fertility, Pregnancy, and Birth in
Early Modern Europe*, trans. Rosemary Morris, Boston: Northeastern University Press, 1991.

(22) Johnston Sarah Illes, *Religions of the Ancient World: A Guide*, Cambridge: Harvard University of Press, 2004.

(23) Keightley David N, "Heritage of China. Early Civilizations", in Paul
S. Ropp, ed. *China: Reflections of How It Became Chinese*. San Francisco: University of California Press, 1990.

(24) Martha C. Sims and Martine Stephens, *Living Folklore: An Introduction
to the Study of People and their Traditions*, Logan: Utah State University
Press, 2005.

(25) Mitford J, *The American Way of Death Revisited*, London: Virago
Press, 1999.

(26) Musacchio Jacqueline Marie, *The Art and Ritual of Childbirth in Renaissance Italy*, New Haven: Yale University Press, 1999.

(27) Neusner Jacob, *World Religions in America: An Introduction*. Louisville:

Westminster John Knox Press, 2003.

(28) Paul Oliver, *Encyclopedia of Vernacular Architecture of the World*, Cambridge: Cambridge University Press, 1998

(29) Ronald W. Brunskil, *Traditional Buildings of Britain: An Introduction to Vernacular Architecture*, London: Victor Gollancz Ltd, 1981.

(30) Soothill W. E, *The Three Religions of China*, New York: Hyperion Press, 1923.

(31) Van Gennep Arnold, *The Rites of Passage*, Chicago: The University of Chicago Press, 1960.

(32) Yang C. K, "Chinese Thought and Institutions", in John K. Fairbank, ed. *The Functional Relationship Between Confucian Thought and Chinese Religion*, Chicago: The University of Chicago Press, 1957.

Online Resources:

(1) http://en. wikipedia. org/wiki/European_ folklore

(2) http://en. wikipedia. org/wiki/Folklore_ of_ the_ United_ States

(3) http://studyinchina. universiablogs. net/2013/08/23/what-are-the-features-of-traditional-chinese-staple-food/

(4) http://english. eastday. com/e/cy/u1a4035663. html

(5) http://english. eastday. com/e/cy/u1a4035705. html

(6) http://www. articles3k. com/article/318/12289/Regional_ Cuisine_ Of_ China_ Sichuan_ Style/

(7) http://www. chinaculture. org/gb/en_ chinaway/2003 - 09/24/content_ 29399. htm

(8) http://www. seeraa. com/china-culture/china-cuisine-culture. html

(9) http://www. chinahighlights. com/travelguide/chinese-food/southern-minority-food. htm

(10) http://en. wikipedia. org/wiki/Chinese_ Islamic_ cuisine

(11) http://en. wikipedia. org/wiki/Xinjiang_ cuisine

(12) http://english. visitbeijing. com. cn/play/culture/n214880745. shtml

(13) http://www. travelchinaguide. com/intro/cuisine_ drink/cuisine/medicine. htm

（14）http：//www. afternoontoremember. com/learn/etiquette

（15）http：//www. foodbycountry. com/Spain-to-Zimbabwe-Cumulative-Index/
United-States-Native-Americans. html

（16）http：//polaris. gseis. ucla. edu/yanglu/ECC ＿ CULTURE ＿ CLOTH-
ING. HTM

（17）http：//traditions. cultural-china. com/en/215Traditions9827. html

（18）http：//www1. chinaculture. org/library/2008 － 01/28/content
＿ 43933. htm

（19）http：//www. fashionencyclopedia. com/fashion＿ costume＿ culture/The-
Ancient-World-Greece/Greek-Clothing. html

（20）http：//www. vroma. org/～bmcmanus/clothing. html

（21）http：//www. fashionencyclopedia. com/fashion＿ costume＿ culture/Ear-
ly-Cultures-The-Byzantine-Empire/Clothing-of-the-Byzantine-Em-
pire. html

（22）http：//www. fashionencyclopedia. com/fashion＿ costume＿ culture/Ear-
ly-Cultures-Europe-in-the-Middle-Ages/Clothing-of-the-Middle-A-
ges. html

（23）http：//www. wisegeek. com/what-is-baroque-fashion. htm

（24）http：//www. vam. ac. uk/content/articles/i/introduction-to － 19th-cen-
tury-fashion/

（25）http：//www. nzs. com/new-zealand-articles/lifestyle/mens-fashion-cloth-
ing. html

（26）http：//www. randomhistory. com/1 － 50/003clothing. html

（27）http：//en. wikipedia. org/wiki/Vernacular＿ architecture

（28）http：//english. visitbeijing. com. cn/play/culture/n214960582. shtml

（29）http：//www. foreignercn. com/index. php？ option ＝ com＿ content&view
＝ article&id ＝ 5128：chinese-civilian-residence&catid ＝ 1：history-and-
culture&Itemid ＝ 114

（30）http：//www. chinaculture. org/gb/en＿ curiosity/2003 － 09/24/content
＿ 29639. htm

（31）http：//www1. chinaculture. org/library/2008 － 01/16/content＿ 38974.
htm

(32)　http：//traditions. cultural-china. com/en/124Traditions260. html

(33)　http：//traditions. cultural-china. com/en/124Traditions2097. html

(34)　http：//traditions. cultural-china. com/en/124Traditions111. html

(35)　http：//www. wisegeek. com/what-is-a-mediterranean-style-house. htm

(36)　http：//www. wisegeek. com/what-is-a-tuscan-style-house. htm

(37)　http：//www. aventerraestates. com/idea/modules/Topic/Topicitem. aspx? DocID = 483&PageID = 328

(38)　http：//www. google. co. jp/url? url = http：//www. dhow. co. uk/eva. pdf&rct = j&frm = 1&q = &esrc = s&sa = U&ei = woZdVeKFEeHtmQWWmoHgAg&ved = 0CBoQFjAB&usg = AFQjCNFPg8mRomukPXYZ-SdL1upS_ xT6Tg

(39)　http：//german. answers. com/architecture/architecture-of-traditional-german-homes

(40)　http：//www. womenintheancientworld. com/pregnancy% 20and% 20childbirth. htm

(41)　http：//traditionscustoms. com/lifestyle/strange-pregnancy-traditions

(42)　http：//listdose. com/top − 10 − rituals-performed-worldwide-newborn/

(43)　https：//www. listplanit. com/2011/07/list-of-birthday-traditions-from-around-the-world/

(44)　http：//www. wunrn. com/news/2006/04_ 09_ 06/041506_ china_ ancient. htm

(45)　http：//traditions. cultural-china. com/en/216Traditions9964. html

(46)　http：//traditions. cultural-china. com/en/216Traditions8972. html

(47)　http：//traditions. cultural-china. com/en/216Traditions8975. html

(48)　http：//www. chinaculture. org/gb/en _ focus/2005 − 10/27/content _ 75199. htm

(49)　http：//www. laroccacafe. com/#! Why-We-Eat-Cake-And-Blow-Out-Candles-On-Birthdays/c1ix4/0F15A3F1 − 8505 − 484B-B752 −4316298F1E22

(50)　http：//musiced. about. com/od/historyofmusic/a/happybirthday. htm

(51)　http：//www. kidsparties. com/TraditionsInDifferentCountries. htm

(52)　http：//en. wikipedia. org/wiki/Marriage

（53） http：//www. chinahighlights. com/travelguide/culture/ancient-chinese-marriage- customs. htm

（54） http：//en. wikipedia. org/wiki/Wedding_ customs_ by_ country

（55） http：//www. chinahighlights. com/travelguide/culture/ancient-chinese-marriage-customs. htm

（56） http：//www. chinaculture. org/chineseway/2011 – 08/31/content _ 422722. htm

（57） http：//traditions. cultural-china. com/en/115Traditions4116. html

（58） http：//en. wikipedia. org/wiki/Mosuo

（59） http：//traditions. cultural-china. com/en/115Traditions5080. html

（60） http：//www. limarriages. com/customs. html

（61） http：//zh. scribd. com/doc/202329521/R-E-Report

（62） http：//services. eveningnews24. co. uk/norfolk/weddings/Wedding-Guide/Traditions. aspx

（63） http：//bartonfuneral. com/funeral-basics/history-of-funerals/

（64） http：//en. wikipedia. org/wiki/Funeral#Ancient_ funeral_ rites

（65） http：//thefuneralsource. org/trad15. html

（66） http：//traditionscustoms. com/death-rites/european-death-rites

（67） http：//traditionscustoms. com/death-rites/native-american-death-rites

（68） http：//www. thecanadianencyclopedia. ca/en/article/funeral-practices/

（69） http：//www. travelchinaguide. com/essential/holidays/minority. htm

（70） http：//en. wikipedia. org/wiki/Ramadan

（71） http：//www. travelchinaguide. com/essential/holidays/minority. htm

（72） http：//www. travelchinaguide. com/intro/festival/minority. htm

（73） http：//www. gifts2015. com/valentines-day-celebration/

（74） https：//www. cbn. com/spirituallife/onlinediscipleship/easter/the_ tra-ditions_ of_ easter. aspx? option = print

（75） http：//www. halloweenhistory. org/

（76） http：//www. ibuzzle. com/articles/halloween-witches. html

（77） http：//en. wikipedia. org/wiki/Thanksgiving

（78） http：//www. theblaze. com/stories/2013/11/28/5 – thanksgiving-traditions-americans-love-a-brief-history-of-turkey-wishbones-football-and-more/

(79) http://www. allthingschristmas. com/traditions. html

(80) http://www. bootsnall. com/articles/12 – 03/best-festivals-and-events-in-europe. html

(81) http://www. okhistory. org

(82) http://www. religionfacts. com/chinese-religion/practices/ancestor-worship

(83) http://www. cultural-china. com/chinaWH/html/en/History140   bye 566. html

(84) http://www. nationsonline. org/oneworld/Chinese_ Customs/taoism. htm

(85) http://www. chinamonitor. com/pages/HistoryCulture. html

(86) http://en. wikipedia. org/wiki/Culture_ of_ Mongolia

(87) http://www. chinatravel. com/facts/tibetan-ethnic-minority. htm

(88) http://www. intochinatravel. com/etiquettes-and-taboos-in-tibet/

(89) http://www. chinatravel. com/facts/hui-ethnic-minority. htm

(90) http://www. chinatravel. com/facts/zhuang-ethnic-minority. htm

(91) http://www. everyculture. com/No-Sa/Russia. html

(92) http://kids. britannica. com/shakespeare/article – 44685

(93) http://trendwave. com/spirituality-and-religion/religion-in-germany ——internations. org

(94) http://about-france. com/religion. htm

(95) http://en. alzakera. com/2015/02/12/italian-culture-religions-of-italy/

(96) http://en. wikipedia. org/wiki/Native_ American_ religion

(97) http://thecanadianencyclopedia. ca/en/m/article/religion/

(98) http://en. wikipedia. org/wiki/Etiquette

(99) http://www. chinatravel. com/facts/tibetan-ethnic-minority. htm

(100) http://www. chinatravel. com/facts/hani-ethnic-minority. htm

(101) https://www. justlanded. com/english/France/Articles/Culture/Social-customs-in-France

(102) http://www. ediplomat. com/np/cultural_ etiquette/ce_ gb. htm

(103) http://www. ediplomat. com/np/cultural_ etiquette/ce_ it. htm

(104) http://www. ediplomat. com/np/cultural_ etiquette/ce_ ru. htm

（105）http：//www. ediplomat. com/np/cultural_ etiquette/ce_ us. htm

（106）http：//www. ediplomat. com/np/cultural_ etiquette/ce_ ca. htm

（107）http：//www. oxforddictionaries. com/definition/english/etiquette

（108）http：//dictionary. reference. com/browse/folk + art

（109）http：//www. travelchinaguide. com/intro/arts/

（110）http：//zt. tibet. cn/english/zt/xz_ arts/. . %5Cxz_ arts/ 200402004
520171559. htm

（111）http：//www. travelchinaguide. com/cityguides/tibet/butter-sculpture.
htm

（112）http：//www. tibetadvisor. com/culture/tibetan-knife. html

（113）http：//traditions. cultural-china. com/en/16Traditions459. html

（114）http：//www. retrospectivetraveller. co. uk/2011/03/china-archive/khan-
atlas-king-silk-uyghur-hotan-xinjiang. html

（115）http：//www. yeschinatour. com/chinese-culture/wax-printing/

（116）http：//english. chinese. cn/chineseculture/article/2011 – 07/13/con-
tent_ 294736. htm

（117）http：//en. wikipedia. org/wiki/Matryoshka_ doll

（118）http：//www. collectorsweekly. com/art-glass/british

（119）http：//www. artezan. com/artezan/styles-n-techniques/traditional/bau-
ernmalerei. html

（120）http：//www. ehow. com/info_ 8088190_ characteristics-native-ameri-
can-masks. html

（121）http：//www. native-languages. org/rugs. htm

（122）http：//www. freespiritgallery. ca/materialsinuit. htm

（123）http：//www. jugaje. com/en/textes/texte_ 5. php

（124）http：//www. topchinatravel. com/china-guide/quyi. htm

（125）http：//www. travelchinaguide. com/intro/arts/kites. htm

（126）http：//www. bookmartialarts. com/news/kung-fu-a-chinese-martial-art

（127）http：//www. travelchinaguide. com/intro/arts/chinese-opera. htm

（128）http：//www. topchinatravel. com/china-guide/acrobatics. htm

（129）http：//english. chinese. cn/chineseculture/article/2011 – 07/14/con-
tent_ 338138. htm

(130) https: //tibettalk. wordpress. com/2007/08/10/the-legendary-epic-of-king-gesar/

(131) http: //traditions. cultural-china. com/en/16Traditions323. html

(132) http: //www. spain-info. com/Culture/bullfighting. htm

(133) http: //www. betref. co. uk/blog/58/amob17/history-of-british-horse-racing/

(134) http: //en. wikipedia. org/wiki/Baseball

(135) https: //prezi. com/1vgxppk25dgy/canada/

Forward

Entering the twenty-first century, the world is developing into multi-polarization under the macro background of globalization. To learn from each other and to be stronger, each nation pays increasingly more attention to promote its own fine culture traditions; meanwhile to absorb other nation's advanced cultures.

The Chinese and western folklore are the two most glorious pearls in the human's civilization history. The former is an ethical culture mainly based on Confucianism, blended with the Buddhism and Taoism. The harmonious relationship between nature and the human being the fundamental spirit of Chinese traditional culture, the pursuit of truth, sincerity and beauty is expected to be realized. Advocating the spirits of being optimistic and ready to help, the Chinese folk culture is extensive and profound.

On the contrary, the traditional western folk culture is a developed worldly culture, deeply rooted in the soil of ancient Greek and Roman culture and dominated by Christian religion from the period of Renaissance, Reformation to the Enlightenment. Contract culture and the dualistic opposition of the human and the nature form the foundation of the traditional western culture, which focuses on expressing an upward and aggressive spirits in the battle of conquering the nature, showing the spirit of firmness and self-trust. In the premise of justice and law, it tries to get the interpersonal equality and esteem, presenting the typical religion consciousness and scientific spirits.

Culture is the footstone of the national spirit. This book aims to present the traditional Chinese and western ideological culture and art culture comparatively, helping the readers to preserve the Chinese cultural tradition and gain insight to the developed western culture to upgrade the overall cultivation of the whole nation.

On one hand, the knowledge concerned is immense and comprehensive. On the other hand, the relative English published works that we can obtain are somewhat limited. Therefore, when writing the book, we referred to some publications, coupled with considerable online resources attributed to unknown writers, which are all listed in the references. Despite that, mistakes are inevitable due to our knowledge limitation, and we would be delighted if readers are able to correct them for its future improvement.

Zhang liyu, Chen luoyu
May, 2015

Chinese Dynasties

Name	Dynasty Chinese	Dynasty Pinyin	Meaning	Ruling House or clan of houses	From	To	Term
Xia dynasty	夏	Xià	*Summer*	Sì （姒）	2070 BC	1600 BC	470 years
Shang dynasty	商	Shāng	*Toponym*	Zǐ （子）	1600 BC	1050 BC	571 years
Western Zhou dynasty	西周	Xī Zhōu	*Toponym*	Jī （姬）	1050 BC	770 BC	275 years
Eastern Zhou dynasty	东周	Dōng Zhōu	*Toponym*	Jī （姬）	770 BC	250 BC	514 years
Spring and Autumn period	春秋	Chūn Qiū	*As English*		770 BC	479 BC	295 years
Warring States period	战国	Zhàn Guó	*As English*		476 BC	221 BC	255 years
Qin dynasty	秦	Qín	*Toponym*	Yíng （嬴）	221 BC	206 BC	15 years
Western Han dynasty	西汉	Xī Hàn	*Toponym*	Liú （刘）	206 BC or 202 BC	9 AD or 23 – 25 AD	215 years
Xin dynasty	新	Xīn	*"New"*	Wáng （王）	9 AD	23 AD	14 years
Eastern Han dynasty	东汉	Dōng Hàn	*Toponym*	Liú （刘）	25 AD	220 AD	195 years

续表

Dynasty				Ruling House or clan of houses	From	To	Term
Name	Chinese	Pinyin	Meaning				
Three Kingdoms	三国	Sān Guó	As English	Cáo (曹) Liú (刘) Sūn (孙)	220 AD	265 AD or 280 AD	45 years
Western Jin dynasty	西晋	Xī Jìn	Ducal title	Sīmǎ (司马)	265 AD	317 AD	52 years
Eastern Jin dynasty	东晋	Dōng Jìn	Ducal title	Sīmǎ (司马)	317 AD	420 AD	103 years
Southern and Northern Dynasties	南北朝	Nán Běi Cháo	As English	various	386 AD or 420 AD	589 AD	169 years
Sui dynasty	隋	Suí	Ducal title (随 homophone)	Yáng (杨)	581 AD	618 AD	37 years
Tang dynasty	唐	Táng	Ducal title	Lǐ (李)	618 AD	907 AD	289 years
Five Dynasties and Ten Kingdoms	五代十国	Wǔ Dài Shí Guó	As English	various	907 AD	960 AD	53 years
Kingdom of Dali	大理国	Dà Lǐ Guó	Toponym	Duàn (段)	937 AD	1253 AD	316 years
Northern Song dynasty	北宋	Běi Sòng	Toponym	Zhào (赵)	960 AD	1127 AD	167 years
Southern Song dynasty	南宋	Nán Sòng	Toponym	Zhào (赵)	1127 AD	1279 AD	152 years
Liao dynasty	辽	Liáo	"Vast" or "Iron" (Khitanhomophone)	Yelü (耶律)	907 AD or 916 AD	1125 AD	209 years
Jin dynasty	金	Jīn	"Gold"	Wanggiyan (完颜)	1115 AD	1234 AD	119 years
Western Xia	西夏	Xī Xià	Toponym	Lǐ (李)	1038 AD	1227 AD	189 years
Yuan dynasty	元	Yuán	"Great" or "Primacy"	Borjigin (孛儿只斤)	1271 AD	1368 AD	97 years
Ming dynasty	明	Míng	"Bright"	Zhū (朱)	1368 AD	1644 AD	276 years
Qing dynasty	清	Qīng	"Pure"	Aisin Gioro (爱新觉罗)	1644 AD	1911 AD	267 years